THE REPATRIATE

THE REPATRIATE

LOVE, BASKETBALL, AND THE KGB

TOM MOORADIAN

Moreradiant Publishing
Seattle
2008

To my wife, Janice Marie, whose patience and understanding made this manuscript possible, and to my two lovely daughters, Jennifer Lynn and Bethany, who have patiently waited over the years to see in print what they have heard in part: their father's odyssey to Soviet Armenia and other places behind the Iron Curtain.

ACKNOWLEDGMENTS

When the three-book, one-volume, incomplete manuscript of *The Repatriate* had reached an incredible 1,013 pages, my wife, Janice Marie, shouted to me, "Stop! Enough! Not another word, not another page!"

And she pulled the plug to the computer.

It was, indeed, enough. I had spent more than five years of my life in solitary confinement, at scenic Hubbard Lake, Michigan, researching, writing, and rewriting the manuscript that represents but a speck of time in what became a life-and-death struggle to escape a cesspool I had plunged into when I agreed to join a group of Armenian Americans who had accepted Stalin's invitation to repatriate to Soviet Armenia.

Without my wife's encouragement and professional acumen as a teacher and a former newspaper woman, this book would have remained but a memory. I am grateful to her and to many others for their advice and expertise, guiding me across the unexpected pitfalls and over the numerous obstacles that lay in wait for a writer.

Second to my wife, I must acknowledge Alice Nigoghosian, who has become a friend and compatriot, and who acted as our consultant. She believed in the story from the first pages of the roughest draft, and she encouraged and supported this effort. It is with heartfelt thanks that I acknowledge her investment of interest, time, and energy.

I am especially grateful to Wendy Warren Keebler, whose invaluable knowledge and experience as an editor helped mold the raw, massive material into a true-to-life, readable story. Her insights made each word an organism that comes alive on the page. She taught me to respect the comma, the semicolon, and the period, reminding me that if a sentence is vague, then the reader is lost, and the book will suffer the indignity of the writer's carelessness.

I also want to give my heartfelt thanks to Mitch Kehetian, longtime manager of the *Macomb Daily,* and Roy Essoyan, Associated Press foreign correspondent assigned to Moscow during the mid-1950s, for reading the prepublished manuscript and offering valued suggestions that were incorporated into the text.

Many others deserve acknowledgment for their helpful considerations during the writing of this book. Those who quickly come to mind are former Soviet teammate Abraham Hamamdjian, Armenian French repatriate Jean Alexanian, and Massey and Paul Antaramian, as well as the Armenian American repatriates who were among the first group to travel to Soviet Armenia and Gerald E. Ottenbreit Jr. of the Armenian Research Center at the University of Michigan, Dearborn.

I also want to thank Jennifer Wapinski-Mooradian, Bethany Mooradian, Jonathan Cook, Lyn and Diva Williams, Sue Madro, Art and Judy Guren, and Bill Hoover for their input, patience, and assistance in a variety of areas.

PREFACE

This book is not in any way to be interpreted as a condemnation of the Armenian or Russian people, whom I learned to love and respect during my thirteen years among them. It also is not an attempt to justify my actions—what I did or did not do—in the course of my life behind the Iron Curtain from 1947 to 1960. Rather, this book is an account of my early life and conversations as I remember them and as best translated from the Russian and Armenian languages. This is the story of the adventure of my youth and my roller-coaster ride to manhood.

Any errors or mistakes during the reconstruction of the historic periods are the author's own. I was part of the story, not apart from it, and that may cause speculation about the objectivity of the text. I believe, as far as my memory and my research can tell, that the historic facts and dates herein are correct. This was my life—my love, my dreams, and my nightmares. With the limitation of space, there are obviously omissions, but I have not intentionally concealed anything. Fortunately, and I believe I can say miraculously, others have also survived the ordeal and remain as living testimony to this adventure.

Today, in an age when democracy is again under fire, I hope this story will serve as a warning to all those who take liberty and freedom for granted. Turn the page, open the door, and read how one mistake cost a young Armenian American his freedom, robbed him of his youth, and nearly ended his life.

Tom Mooradian
Southfield, Michigan
April 2008

Major Cities of the
Union of Soviet Socialist Republics
During the Cold War 1947 - 1960

CONTENTS

BOOK II

BOOK III

PROLOGUE

I was born an American. Raised an American. Will die an American. And I have always been an American in my spirit, my heart, and my soul. But I was not always an American citizen. In 1947, when I was nineteen years old, I became a Soviet.

I have been asked by friends and foes how it was possible that I, an American, could become a Soviet. Some ventured to ask whether I had denounced, even betrayed, my country. Their words would open, again and again, the wound in my heart. How could I explain to them something that I have tried, in vain, to explain to myself?

Youth has no explanation. The decisions of youth are usually a mishmash of meaningless attempts to justify that which is usually unjustifiable.

Nevertheless, as fate would have it, I found myself on the other side of the Iron Curtain during the height of the Cold War. I witnessed the rise and fall of Beria, Molotov, and Malenkov, and I was there when Khrushchev rose to power.

When I was told by the U.S. Consulate that they would not assist me in my efforts to return home unless I received an exit visa from the Soviets, having no recourse, I decided to exercise patience.

In the Soviet Union, I made my living as a teacher, a basketball coach, and a player. In the latter two capacities, I had the opportunity to see what no foreign correspondent, no Western journalist, no diplomat was permitted to see: the Soviet Union as the Soviets lived within it. Basketball became a passion for me. I knew how to play the game well. I was the first American-born ever to play basketball not only in Soviet Armenia but in the entire Soviet Union. I was soon accepted in an elite Soviet community that honors artists and athletes, and I became a regular fixture on the Soviet sports scene.

Although I lived as the Soviets did, I was never accepted by them as a Soviet. To them, I would always be an American, *Americanyets*. They knew that at the first opportunity afforded me to run—or fly like a seagull, as they put it—I would head back to my nest in America. Most relationships, therefore, were ephemeral.

No American will ever understand the rationale behind the campaign of terror that a Soviet citizen endured during the Stalin regime. Khrushchev put an end to Stalin, the cult of Stalin, and the insanity of Beria.

As a Soviet, you were required to carry a passport that allowed you to pass through life in servitude to the state, in order that some generation in the future would enjoy a utopian society. You were to sacrifice all of your todays so that someone would live heartily tomorrow. It just didn't make sense at the end.

I began my adventure not only to see but also to live the life of a Soviet in November 1947, when I went with 150 Armenian Americans who repatriated to the USSR. Our group was the first Armenians ever to leave the United States to establish residency in the Soviet Union. As one Armenian diplomat pointed out, "historically, Armenians have been fleeing Turkey and Asia Minor in fear for their lives. . . . Yours is the first group that is leaving American soil to return to our motherland. You are opening the trails for all of us to follow."

Immediately after World War II, the Soviet Union was in dire need of material goods and manpower to reconstruct its war-torn cities. Stalin opened the doors of the Soviet Union to members of all ethnic groups who wished to return and rebuild the "Motherland."

The Armenian Progressive League in the United States responded to the call from Moscow and began to launch a program to recruit repatriates. The APL hoped that thousands of Armenian Americans would respond, but there were only two caravans organized, consisting of approximately 300 people altogether.

In total, about 80,000 to 90,000 Armenians from around the world returned to Armenia, a Soviet republic in southwestern Asia, east of Turkey, reporting a population of about 3 million and an area of about 11,500 square miles. It is larger than the state of Vermont. Most of the Armenian Americans were resettled in Erevan, the republic's capital. Some were permitted to live with relatives in Leninakan, a stone's throw from the Turkish border, or Kirovakan, a rustic village with an agrarian population.

I found good with the bad during the years I spent roaming the streets of Erevan, Moscow, and Leningrad; in Kiev, Riga, and Kaunas; in Odessa and Tiflis and Baku—names on a map to most but real places with real people and real lifetime experiences for me. Playing basketball gave me the opportunity to see and touch the heart and soul of the Soviet Union as few Americans have done.

For journalists, I have read, the Soviet Union was an enigma. It was never one for me. If there was a puzzle, it was how Stalin had managed not only to fool his own people but to fool the leaders of the world for as long as he did. Stalin and his anointed members of the Politburo, the governing body of the Soviet Union, were master puppeteers, dangling entire republics on strings, making people sit, stand, leap, and shout on their masters' whims. As a human puppet, you learn quickly that if you don't want to be tossed into the fire, you had better move and dance when and how the puppet master pulls the strings. Yes, you can fool all of the people all of the time, as long as you have the power of life and death in your hands.

I learned to act like a Soviet, talk like a Soviet, and, of course, drink like a Soviet—but to make love to Soviet women like an American.

When the political chess game for my life in the Soviet Union reached its climax in the late months of the 1950s and the first months of 1960, I finally made the right moves to checkmate the Cheka. I was granted an exit visa to return home.

During my stay in the Soviet Union, nineteen-year-old U.S. Marine Lee Harvey Oswald had defected and requested Soviet citizenship. His request was rejected by Soviet officials, because the KGB believed Oswald was a loose cannon. He attempted suicide in his room at the Berlin Hotel in Moscow but was saved by a Western journalist who had had an appointment to interview him. She arrived in time to help pull Oswald from a bathtub where he was lying unconscious, his body soaked in his own blood. Oswald had reportedly slashed his wrists. He was rushed to a hospital and recovered. As a Soviet insider later commented to me, "You Americans don't even know how to kill yourselves."

The Soviets allowed Oswald to stay in the country and issued him a temporary permit renewable on a yearly basis. He took up residency in Minsk, where he courted and later married a Russian.

Although I did not meet Oswald while we both resided in the Soviet Union, our names do appear on the same page of notes prepared by members of the Assassination Records Review Board, which was created by Congress in 1992. Its charge was to collect all government records related to President John F. Kennedy's assassination in preparation to release them.

In the notes of the Review Board, Batch 13, Document 180-10110-10077 (© 1996, Joseph Backes), a question is asked by one of the investigators: "The Soviet government issued Lee Harvey Oswald a passport which described him as being without citizenship, and he was issued a Soviet visa on a temporary, year to year basis. Were these procedures customary at the time Oswald was in Russia?" The Commission then wanted to know of similar cases to Oswald's, and the State Department referred them to the following people and requested that they contact them.

"Tom Mooradian—Tom Mooradian was sent to Soviet Armenia in November 1947 by his American parents of Armenian background for the purpose of being educated in Soviet Armenia. He thereafter lived in Soviet Armenia and is believed to hold a Soviet passport. He became a national figure in Soviet Society as a basketball player and traveled extensively in this country. Only after many years (April 1960) was he able to get permission to leave the USSR. During the period in which he was trying to leave, he visited the American Embassy in Moscow a number of times. It was the Embassy's belief that his occupation enabled him to visit Moscow more frequently than other applicants for Soviet visas."

I know that Oswald and his Russian bride, Marina, returned home, and his name went down in infamy. I returned and went on to live in relative obscurity, grateful that I had somehow been able to repatriate to my homeland. The time finally came for me to face my demons and remember, with fondness, my thirteen years in the Soviet Union. Hence this book.

BOOK I

Chapter 1

THE INTERROGATION ROOM

The revolver was pointed at my head. The NKVD officer holding the weapon was seated directly across the table from me in a freshly whitewashed matchbox of a room. The paint had not covered the dark stains or the bumps on the walls. The room was below street level at the Ministry of Security Building on Nalbandian Street in Erevan, the capital of Soviet Armenia.

The interrogator said he was losing patience with me. He said I was not giving him the right answers. He shoved a sheet of brown paper and a pencil in front of me and ordered me to write, to confess.

"We know what your mission was in Moscow. We want to know who else is involved. We want it in your own words. You will write why you decided to go to Moscow, whom you planned to meet, and the names of all others who are with you in this plot. If you do not do this, I have no alternative but to carry out my orders." He tightened his grip on the weapon.

I knew that he was serious. Dead serious.

I repeated what I had told him and the two plainclothes Russian officers standing behind him earlier when they had arrested me at the airport. Using the little Russian I knew, I said that I did not know what they were talking about. I had planned to go to Moscow to celebrate May Day, the International Workers' Day, and to visit the heroic city of Moscow. I had no mission. No others were involved. There was no intent by me or any others to overthrow the Soviet government, I repeatedly told the interrogator.

The NKVD officer shook his head and said that I was a very foolish young American—soon to be a dead foolish young American. Then he turned to the plainclothes officers, one of whom had kicked me in the shins at the airport, and translated into Russian what I had said to him in English. The facial expressions on the two men standing behind him were indecipherable, but they did not appear impressed by my answers. The interrogator told me that I amused them. I did not see anything amusing. Standing a few feet behind the English-speaking interrogator, with their backs to the wall, the two thugs were motionless. They had stopped me from boarding the plane to Moscow from Erevan. I had been a fool to think I could go to Moscow without the secret police knowing about my plans. I had been dragged out of the airport, tossed into a truck by the one who had kicked me, and driven to the headquarters of the NKVD, which was the predecessor to the KGB.

I had strolled past these headquarters several times on the way to the Pioneers' Palace on Moskovski Prospect over the past year and a half and had heard rumors of what happened to those who were taken within the walls. My Russian and Armenian acquaintances had told me that once someone was taken inside, he or she was never seen again.

As the minutes turned into hours, fear took control of my senses, and I became convinced that I would not leave the building for a long time, if ever. Fear was alive within me, and I had never really known it before. My head ached. I was scared.

Why was it a crime for an American-born Soviet citizen, like myself, to want to go to the U.S. Embassy? I'd had no idea what I was getting into when I had agreed to carry a letter to the ambassador. I wondered if the others knew that I was not on the morning plane to Moscow. But how could they? There had been no one there to see me off. We had finalized our plans the evening before. Each of the family heads had signed the letter. Karibian was going to take the plane the next day and meet me in Red Square. I was convinced that the NKVD did not know our plans and wondered how I could get a message to Karibian. I knew that would be impossible now. I could only wait and hope for the best.

A cold sweat swept over my body. I felt hopeless. No one knew where I was. And even if they did, what could they do? Nothing.

With the exception of two chairs and a table and two portraits on the wall, it was a bare room. There were no windows, just one electrical cord strung from the ceiling providing a dim light. In the shadows, Stalin's and Beria's painted likenesses stared at us malevolently. The NKVD chief's thugs were filling their quotas. My small circle of friends had talked of Beria as the devil incarnate.

The man interrogating me was in his early thirties. His face did not look Russian; he didn't have the small, turned-up nose common to Russians. His light complexion, blond hair, and light blue eyes made me think that he was from the Baltic states, Latvian or Lithuanian or maybe even Byelorussian. He had little facial hair. He had been called in to interrogate me after I had convinced the plainclothes secret police that I didn't speak Russian and had only a limited knowledge of Armenian. I had sat there nervously waiting until they found someone who spoke English that I could understand.

One of the plainclothes officers had a very small head. His ears seemed pinned to his head as if he had trained as a boxer or a wrestler. His head didn't go with his broad shoulders and muscular physique. He said nothing and allowed his partner to do the talking. When I had refused to go with them at the airport, he had made threats and carried them out by kicking me in the shins. That had convinced me that I should do what he said, although I stood a foot taller than he. The other man was about my height, six feet. He had a pleasant smile and had made me feel comfortable at first. It was strange, I'd felt at the time, that neither man had searched me for weapons or incriminating evidence.

I understood the interrogator, and he understood me, but I did not understand Soviet law. I was exhausted and had no knowledge of inter-rogation methods. I didn't know what to expect or what law I had violated. I didn't know what time it was, and I'd had nothing to eat but some tea and black bread the morning I had planned to go to Moscow. I kept thinking that this all had to be a mistake. I could not fathom why they were detaining me, and I repeatedly asked them for an explana-tion. I got none, just more questions and threats. I wondered what they would do with me if I didn't tell them what they wanted to hear.

The English-speaking officer had an accent, more English than American. Although he had made threats, for some reason I did not take them seriously. They had nothing to gain by killing me if they wanted information. In fact, if they did kill me, when the news got back to America, it could hurt Soviet plans to recruit more Armenian American repatriates. The Soviets needed Americans for the wealth and the machines they would bring with them to the USSR. I was sure they were bluffing. They had to be bluffing. But I was not so sure about the musclemen. They looked as if they had killed before and would kill again. I tried not to think about what they might do to me. Braver men than I had confessed to acts they did not commit in hopes of striking a deal. I had read of the purges, the forced confessions, and the executions. I had not believed the stories, however, until now.

Although I had spent the last eighteen months of my life in the Soviet Union, I still felt as if the whole experience were a dream. I expected to wake up one morning and find myself at home in my own bed in Detroit, my mother calling me down to breakfast. But this was no dream; it had been a nightmare. Damn it, why hadn't I listened to my brothers, to my friends, and stayed in America?

I knew from the rumors on the streets that failure to extract a confession from a suspect was not an option for Soviet interrogators. Their superiors would not tolerate it.

"Why," the interrogator asked, "did you want to go to Moscow?" He repeated his words over and over. "We can be lenient to those who cooperate." He offered to inform his superiors that I was a misled youth whose mind was poisoned by the scum in my group, scum who had come to poison others, that I truly didn't understand the consequences of my acts. He said that if I did not reveal names, it would be out of his hands; there would be nothing he could do to help me.

"What do you mean by lenient?" I asked.

He suggested a few years in one of the Soviet Union's warmer-climate rehabilitation camps, maybe even a pardon for my acts. "You are young," he said. "Don't throw your life away for the scum who have betrayed you."

"No one has betrayed me!" I shouted at him. "There is no one else!"

He raised his eyebrows and his voice and stared into my face. "You are not only young, but you are also a fool."

He said they knew there were others. He revealed that the NKVD had watched me searching for food in the stores and knew that I had sold most of my personal belongings. They knew that I had little left.

I did not have the resources to finance the trip. "Who paid your plane fare? Who was going to pay your hotel bill? We know there are others."

"If you know, then why these questions?"

He closed his eyes for a moment. He pushed back his chair and stood up. As he walked around me, he said that killing came easily to them; the Nazis had taught them well. He exchanged a few words with the other two men. I found my mind drifting. I could not comprehend this world, not then, not ever. The man was following orders. If he was ordered to shoot and kill me, he would. Maybe I should have given them the names they wanted. If they knew what I had planned to do, they already knew about the others.

Rousing me from my thoughts, the interrogator turned to me and said that it was unfortunate that at my age I chose death over life. His tone sounded apologetic. He seemed almost sympathetic. He commended me for my courage, saying that he had met many others in similar situations who had gotten on their knees and written as fast as they could to save their own skins.

The NKVD officer didn't have to tell me that. Living among the Soviets as a Soviet citizen had made me aware of what could happen if I didn't confess. *Give them the names, damn you, Tom,* I told myself. *Don't you want to live?*

But to reveal the names of those who had planned and financed my ill-fated trip to Moscow would lead to a score of arrests. Not only individuals but also their families would be doomed. They had American-born wives and American-born children.

I had no one in Erevan, no family at all. My family was back in the United States. If I were to perish, I would go alone. Who would even know? If the others were arrested, who would take care of Jean and Irene and Alice? They, too, surely would be arrested. I could not betray them. It was far better that I go alone, wherever it would be, than take them with me.

The interrogator tried to explain the gravity of my situation. Did I realize that it was a capital offense for a Soviet citizen to contact a foreign embassy, let alone draw up a petition to present to a foreign power?

I informed him that I knew nothing of Soviet law.

He asked if I would continue what he called my "charade" when the others began their own form of questioning. Again, he asked about Moscow. Who had planned it? Who had given me the money? And why was I to be the messenger?

I refused to answer any of his questions. It was now only a matter of time. I felt sure that he would pull the trigger. I knew there was no escape.

I recalled my brother's final words as he bade me good-bye in New York on that November morning in 1947. I had turned to him on the gangplank and said, "Don't worry, I'll be back." He had replied, "Sure . . . sure you will. In a box."

If I were to go, I would not go as a coward. I had lived in fear for two years. It was that fear, fear of arrest and exile, that had convinced me, and the others, that we must act.

~ IT WAS only a few months before, in March 1949, that the Soviet secret police had conducted a massive sweep of anti-Soviet activists in every one of the fifteen republics, rounding up and indiscriminately arresting men, women, and children. Some of those earmarked to be arrested had not been at home, so neighbors had been arrested instead. The "counterrevolutionary conspirators," as the citizens were labeled, had been driven to train depots, shoved into cattle cars, and transported to internment camps beyond the Ural Mountains. It was such a thorough operation that even Nazi SS troopers would have been in awe of the expediency and efficiency of the combined Soviet secret police and military operation. Most who were forced into the slave camps had never been heard from again; those who remained behind had lived in fear, waiting for that midnight knock on the door, for when they, too, would be accused, dragged out of bed, and taken to the Soviet netherland.

For some reason, not one of the 151 Armenian Americans had been arrested. We'd considered ourselves lucky but realized that we were also living on borrowed time.

Four of us, including myself, had decided not to wait.

There would be many Westerners in Moscow on May Day, and we had determined that it would be the best time to go to Moscow and beg the American embassy to help us return to the United States. Several Armenians with spouses of Irish, Polish, and German descent who had been born in the United States had repatriated with our group. We all had signed a petition addressed to the U.S. ambassador, urging officials to intercede on our behalf so that those who wanted to return to America could do so.

Harry Karibian, whose wife was Polish, and I had been selected to be the messengers.

The NKVD apparently had discovered the plans.

~ AS I SAT in the interrogation room now, nauseated and feeling excruciating pain in my leg, I realized that my brother's prophecy was about to come true. Life was sweet but not when you stood in long lines to fight fragile old women every day to buy a kilo of bread that was soaked in water and plugged with pebbles to add weight so the seller could make a few extra rubles to pay *paparck* to his supervisor and protect his job.

The days had turned into weeks and the weeks into eighteen months of waiting for life to get better, as promised by the Party's Central Committee. Instead, life had become a living hell. Several bouts with diarrhea had sapped my strength and energy. There had been no drugs, no pills to stop or slow the illness, only tea and home remedies. Weeks and months on a diet of black bread, when I could purchase a loaf, and tea without sugar had taken a drastic toll on my body. I had been a solid 187 pounds, athletic, and in excellent health when I left America. At this point, I probably didn't weigh even 150 pounds. The suit I was wearing hung loosely on my frame. As far as I was concerned, the vultures could have the rest of me, for there really was nothing left.

Why doesn't he just pull the trigger? I asked myself. He would probably be doing me a favor.

Before I finished my thought, the door opened, and a distinguished-looking officer, in full dress uniform with every medal the Soviet Union awarded its military, burst into the room. His gray hair, square jaw, and excellent build indicated that he was in charge. I did not know his rank. He entered and slammed the door behind him. As tired as the men in the room were, all three immediately stood at attention, and there was a quick and fiery exchange in Russian among the four that I did not understand, having only a rudimentary knowledge of the two main languages spoken in the republic.

Abruptly, they stopped talking. As the senior officer turned, I noticed his owl nose, definitely Armenian. He addressed me, as customary in Russian, using my first name and my father's first name. "Tom Boghosovich?"

"Yes."

He scrutinized me coldly. "You are impudent, aren't you?" He ordered me to speak to him in Russian and stop pretending that I did not know the language. Using his hands, as Armenians do to make a point, he continued, "If you have enough knowledge of our language to seduce our young women, you know enough Russian. Then speak it. Do you understand?"

I nodded my head and answered in Russian, *"Ya vas panee my you."* The three others in the room did not utter a word. I carried on the rest of the discussion in Russian the best I could, looking to my interrogator-translator for certain words. He, however, had backed away. He did not want to intervene with his superior present.

There was a strange smile on the face of my new interrogator as he studied me. He offered to let me go free, go back to my apartment, and live my life as a Soviet citizen. I could forget what had happened, but I had to promise never again to try to contact the U.S. ambassador. He asked if I understood what he was saying.

"Da. Yes, I understand. Do you mean I can leave?" I asked with a sigh of relief.

He nodded his head, then tied the knot in the rope. I could go, but I had to give them, in writing, the names of those who had used me. He referred to them as those who knew better, those who exploited me, those who were traitors. He said they would be dealt with. He said he knew of the letter and its contents. All I had to do was give the names of the others, and then I could leave.

My first instinct was to surrender the names. *Tell them, damn it, and get your ass out of here.* But suddenly, I found myself laughing instead of confessing. It had to be a trick. This was all staged, wasn't it? It had to be, so that I would reveal the names of the others. No, I wouldn't tell them anything. If people were being shipped to Siberia and surviving, I would survive, too.

I told them to do what they pleased with me. They would not get the names from me, because there were no other names. No one had financed me. I had been going to Moscow to see the great parade, and I would write to Stalin and tell him that the Armenian security police would not let me join the heroic Russian people in the celebration of International Workers' Day. That was all I would write and say.

"Americans do not lie very well, but you have learned how in the short time you have been with us." Again, he ordered me to give up the names. If I would not confess my part in the plot, the operation was ended. He asked if I understood.

And again, I replied, *"Da. Ya vas panee my you."*

Once more, he asked who the others were.

"I do not know, sir, what you're talking about," I said in Russian. "I was going to Moscow to see the parade."

Without emotion, the officer said, "Then this operation has ended." He turned to the translator and said something I didn't understand. He exchanged words with the other two men in the room and left as suddenly as he had appeared.

When the door closed behind him, the mood of my abductors changed. There was a tense silence in the room, a feeling that the doors of a mausoleum had just been sealed. Time had apparently run out. But I did not care; I was too tired to care. I couldn't run. Where could I go? I was trapped in a country where I stood out like a Texas longhorn among sheep, in a prison within a prison. I still wanted to stall for time. I wanted to wake up from my nightmare. I wanted to live. It was difficult for me to believe that they could just kill me. Hoping to gain a few precious minutes, I heard myself ask my English-speaking interrogator if I was a Soviet citizen.

"Yes," he answered. "Why would you ask such a foolish question?"

I said that as a Soviet citizen, I had rights—a lawyer, a trial, a judge. I maintained that I did not know what crime I was being accused of, what laws I had broken. If I was a Soviet citizen, I demanded to be treated as any citizen would. I was not an American spy!

He nodded and acknowledged that he knew that. But, he explained with a strange smile, they could not allow me to go free, because then the people would say that the NKVD preyed on the innocent, and that would not be good.

He rubbed his eyes. He looked tired, very tired, himself. I wondered if he had a family, children. Then my mouth went dry, and I froze as he took out his weapon again and tightened his finger around the trigger.

"Your judge," he announced, nodding at the gun in his hands. "And the jury was just here. And the trial is over. You have been found guilty of being an enemy of the people. I am your executioner."

At the word "executioner," he pulled the trigger.

I heard a loud burst . . . then laughter as my body fell from the chair to the floor.

~ A BLINDING BRIGHT light traveled down a long tunnel toward me, then engulfed me and swept me into its midst. My body seemed to float toward the tunnel, which began to fill with water, warm water. As it reached my waist, I began to swim. I could hear voices ahead of me, around me, urging me to hurry, voices of close friends and relatives calling to me. "Tommy, hurry, we're waiting for you. You'll be all right." I began to swim faster, then desperately, to reach the end of the tunnel. Faces appeared: my father and my mother, my sister and brother. I saw George; he stretched out his hands to lift me from the murky water. He pulled me to safety. I looked at him; he was laughing, but at what? I turned to look at the water. It was a pool of blood. My blood. I turned to my brother, but he had disappeared. In the darkness of the tunnel, I heard his voice. "I told you . . . I told you . . . you'll come home in a box."

It was pitch black. There was silence, the silence of the dead.

I saw a bloodstained bed sheet over a body.

I pulled back the sheet. It was my own face that I saw.

Thank God, I told myself. *It was painless. It is over. Now I can go home.*

Chapter 2

IN THE BEGINNING

I stood by the window in my room on the second floor of our home on Crawford Street in southwest Detroit, my hand on the curtain, pulling it back ever so slightly so that I could get a glimpse at the street below. My brother George was packing our recently purchased red Oldsmobile with my two suitcases. After arranging the items in the trunk, he slammed the door so hard that the noise echoed like a gunshot down the street. He turned, lifted his eyes to the window, caught a glimpse of me, and shook his head. I knew I was the object of his anger and frustration. We had never argued until recent weeks. I idolized him.

I could hear him as he climbed the seven steps to the front door, opened it, and slammed it so that the window rattled. Mother and my sister Rose were in the living room, and I could hear an angry exchange of words among the three, though I could not make out what they were saying.

It was a sun-filled, cloudless autumn morning in October 1947. George was driving my mother and me to New York City.

The Second World War had ended eighteen months before, and the men and women of the armed forces who served America were slowly returning home. Both of my brothers—Robert, the oldest, and George, three years older than I—had been honorably discharged from the U.S. Navy. Robert had returned to his wife and their son. George was at Wayne State University studying under the GI Bill. Although I had shared the upstairs room with one or the other of my brothers during the years leading up to the war, after Pearl Harbor, the room had been all mine. Robert had joined first; George followed shortly in his footsteps. They had hoped that I would join the Navy, too.

I'd been too young to serve my country during the war. But, like most young men of my generation, I had ached to be in the service. I had kept up with the battles by religiously reading about them in the three Detroit daily newspapers—the *Times,* the *News,* and the *Free Press*—and by listening to the radio. Television had not yet appeared in the living rooms of most American homes, although some sets were on display in store windows.

I had turned nineteen that July and attended Lawrence Institute of Technology, with the goal of becoming a mechanical engineer, but I dropped out after a month or so, deciding instead to travel to the Soviet Union with a group of Armenian American repatriates. My decision had split the family; my father approved, but the rest of the family did not.

For several weeks, family, friends, and high school classmates had been converging on our two-story wood-frame home to say their good-byes to me. Many hoped to persuade me to stay. I had graduated magna cum laude from Southwestern High School and had a firm knowledge of mathematics, but chemistry was where I had excelled. In addition, I was considered one of the finest high-school basketball players in the state by the Detroit daily newspapers. Yet none of that enticed me to remain in Detroit.

I stood at the window of my room for the last time in silence. I had not slept well during the recent weeks, but my decision to join the group repatriating to the Soviet Union was irreversible. I had admitted only to myself that I had second thoughts.

Mother, fixing sandwiches in the kitchen for the trip, gave her daughter last-minute instructions. Rose, two years my junior, was still in high school. She held back her tears well.

There was an eerie silence in the house, closer to mourning than celebration. Mother did not want me to go, but she would have lost any argument with her husband. She had told me, "If we part, there are no assurances we will ever come together again," and she had hoped that I might change my mind. She knew better, of course; once I made up my mind, I didn't change it. I was stubborn, very stubborn, like my father, she said. My confidence, my exuberance, my smiles, and my words of encouragement that I would return safely had not changed the gloom in the house during the final days and hours before my departure.

No words could convince Mother that I could take care of myself.

I knew my father, and, above all, I trusted my father. The others were not as close to him as I was. Our closeness had evolved during the war years, when I drove him to union meetings, helped organize the workers, and raised funds for the Communist Party. I was there beside him at all times.

I had been warned about the dangers, even about the possibility of war between the two new superpowers, the United States and Russia, but I brushed them aside. I chose to disregard the criticism and hatred some had for Communists and the Soviets.

I had driven George to the train station when he went into the Navy, and he had promised me he would not get killed in the war. He would drive me to New York, show me the big city, and walk me to the ship. Mother would tag along, I believed, to ensure that there would be no more fighting between us; fighting was rare among the Mooradians.

I looked around the familiar place: a table with an old oil lamp on it, where I had spent countless hours doing my homework while looking out the window and dreaming of far-off lands, a cushioned chair, and a four-shelf bookcase crammed with books as well as my basketball trophies. The room was where I retreated to shut out the rest of the world. It had been mine; no trespassers were allowed. All of my clothes and sundries had been packed into the two suitcases that George had carried to the car. I had $117 in my wallet, and I believed that I would be able to survive on that until I reached the Soviet Union. Once there, I would register for college, and, if I was turned down, I would work until I had developed enough language skills to reapply. The Soviets had guaranteed work for the repatriates.

~ MY FATHER had said his good-byes the night before and had left for work early in the morning. He had always been disdainful of those who put their emotions on display in public. He possessed the strength and will of a coal miner called upon to help pull a trapped worker out of the debris of a cave-in. He was more at ease with dirty-faced, oil-stained-overall-wearing workers than around those who wore double-breasted suits, white shirts, and neckties. Father was a mystery to his three other children but never to me.

Father also believed in the Bolsheviks and the Soviet Union at a time when Winston Churchill was warning the world of an Iron Curtain descending across the European continent and of Stalin's "indefinite expansion" designs. He was not a man of violence, but his fists would clench. He had little tolerance for the opponents of socialism and communism, for he believed that it was the Soviet Union that had defeated the Nazis, and it was the Bolsheviks who had come to Armenia's assistance when the rest of the world turned its back on the small Christian nation, allowing the Turks to slaughter more than 2 million of his countrymen. Father taught me that if you were indifferent to protecting the rights of the common man, you were a traitor to "the cause."

It embarrassed my brothers that Father was so zealous, but I had always been proud of it. He also believed that time was running out on capitalism. A new day had arrived, ushering in the dawn of the working class. Like millions, he had lost everything he owned in the Great Depression—three coffee shops on Solvay Street in southwest Detroit that catered to Armenian expatriates. He, along with millions of others in the United States, was saved when FDR persuaded Congress to allocate $3 billion to finance the nationwide public-works program outlined in the president's National Industrial Recovery Bill. The NIRB helped put food on dinner tables for millions of the unemployed in the country. Like many Americans who became angry when the stock market crashed in 1929, Boghos Mooradian vented his anger by joining the labor movement and the Communist Party and pulling people off the streets and into the ranks of union organization.

"Each generation has its challenge; ours is to fight for jobs," he would tell me and anyone else who would listen. He was a member of the NAACP when it was unpopular to belong to the civil-rights group. Some local leaders of such groups would meet in a room at our house on Solvay and later in a room on Crawford, where we had moved just before Pearl Harbor.

A labor writer, Billy Allan, noted in Father's obituary: "Paul Mooradian, foundry worker from Kelsey Hayes on Detroit's West Side, was one of my early mentors. He was a power of a union rank-and-filer. Always on the line, always with the workers, answering their questions and making contributions about why workers must stand together and fight for whats [sic] coming to them. . . . You read these days about certain figures whose names don't need mentioning, the capitalist scribblers do it often enough, about who led the sit-down at Kelsey Hayes, who was inside sitting in. . . . Well the plain truth is that it was workers like Paul, long before the sit-down took place, that worked quietly, underground to sign up workers into the United Auto Workers (UAW). They were the historic figures to be remembered, without them some folks just passed through the old plant on McGraw would never have their names in union history books as leaders if it had not been for Paul. . . . He walked so many picket lines one could not count them all. He never wanted credit or his name mentioned. . . . And one of the lasting remembrances about this great man was his struggle for Black and white unity in the union and amongst the people of the communities. . . . He thought and correctly so that Paul Robeson was one of the great human beings, artists that he had ever met. . . . And Paul was a tough, but a gentle man with his fellow workers, he never walked but in one direction—for his class, of which he was an outstanding example, a revolutionary worker."

When I had told my father of my decision to join the repatriation group, he was not surprised. With a stern expression on his face, he said, "From head to toe, you are an American, but you have the heart of an Armenian. I hope it isn't broken in the old country."

"The only way I will find out is if I go."

"Then go," he had said in a soft, sad voice. He did not want to lose me, but if he had to, what better place than the Soviet Union?

I was intrigued by the opportunity to travel and attend college in the Soviet Union. My friends and relatives felt that I was a fool. Maybe I was. I had graduated from high school and had been accepted to a college where I could pursue my favorite subjects: mathematics, physics, and chemistry. I was engaged to my high school sweetheart, and we planned to marry as soon as I graduated. I wanted for nothing and had everything. My body and my mind were trained to compete. Thanks to basketball, my future seemed secure. Why, then, was I leaving the world I knew for the unknown?

~ MOTHER AND ROSE were waiting, in silence, in the living room.

I approached my sister, gave her a hug, kissed her. She told me she loved me and to take care of myself. I told her I loved her, too, and that I'd be back. I promised I would be back.

She gave me one last hug.

Mother took off her apron, handed it to Rose, and looked for her purse. There were regrets but no tears on that hardened face. She grabbed her coat.

It was time.

We walked to the car, and I slipped into the front passenger seat. George took the wheel. My mother got into the backseat, and George turned the key. I took a last look at my sister standing on the porch, a handkerchief in her hand, weeping and waving good-bye.

"Take care of yourself. And write, please write!" she shouted.

"I will." Those would be my last words to her for more than a decade.

George shifted into gear and pressed his foot on the gas pedal, and the eight-cylinder engine responded. We were on our way.

Chapter 3

AN UNEXPECTED DETOUR

George did most of the driving. When he got tired, I took over. I loved to drive and had done it during the war years for my parents, who did not want to learn how to operate a car. But for the long journey to New York City—there were no superhighways in the late 1940s—George was older and more experienced, according to Mother, and she preferred that he drive.

I sat in the passenger seat next to George, barely speaking. We had argued so much over my decision during the past few weeks that there seemed nothing further to say. I did not want to return to the subject of repatriation, for it would only disturb Mother.

As we drove, an America unfolded before me that I had never seen before. We passed a tapestry of colorful towns, rustic villages, and farms. Farmers waved, and we responded with smiles. If a car broke down, the next driver coming along was sure to stop and offer assistance. This was the America I was raised in; this was the America I was leaving.

At each rest stop on the way, with each apple pie à la mode and every glass of milk, I wondered why I was giving it up, why I was willing, even eager, to trade my relatively easy life for something nebulous, undefined. On the roads between the tree-topped hills of southern Michigan and the mountain country of Pennsylvania, my doubts began to increase, but I quickly brushed them to the back of my mind. I reminisced about the string of events that had led up to my decision to go to Armenia. I recalled what one of my mother's friends had told me. Completely taken aback, she had exclaimed, "But Tommy, there are no bananas in Armenia," implying that there was little or no food.

My grandmother, "Nana" to all her grandchildren, was shocked to hear that I was going to the old country, the country she had fled after the Turks burned down her village, killed members of her family, and sent those who survived on death marches and into exile. Usually supportive, or silent if she did not agree during family controversies, she could not contain her anger about my repatriation: "Your father is a fool. And you, it seems, are not much better." I had stood there, studying her, her white hair pulled back from her face, a face etched with the deep lines of pain of the past, and that black dress. She must have had more than one dress, but they were all black. Then, after chastising me, she had motioned me toward her. I went obediently. The bear hug was next, then a deep, moaning sigh. "But if you don't change your mind, and I know you will not, for you are your father's son, remember, I will not die until you return home to these arms." I had promised her that I would come back to her.

The vehicle sped from the flat landscape and farmlands of Michigan and Ohio and wound its way into and around the autumn hills of Pennsylvania. It was beautiful country. I took in each mile of it in awe.

I had seen so little of the United States before this trip. I had never been to the west or east coasts. I had lived in Michigan all of my life, and except for a few train trips from Windsor to St. Catherines, Ontario, to help my great-uncle harvest crops, I had never been out of Michigan.

After several hours of driving, George tired and asked me to take over. I was only too glad to change places. I was getting bored just sitting and thinking. Mother joined me up front, and George stretched out in the rear seat for some rest.

~ THE SUN had set, and nightfall followed.

The night plays tricks on drivers, especially on strange and desolate country roads. The darkness provided a blackboard for my thoughts, and my imagination conjured up images that questioned my decision. My mind was on the past and not on the road.

A light rain began to fall. I put on the windshield wipers and turned on the radio.

Mother sat silently but remained alert to our surroundings. She had said all she was going to about my plan. Hers had not been an easy life. The Turks had murdered her father, her mother, and three siblings. The stories came from Uncle Garabed in Canada and were never uttered by my mother. After she had settled in the United States and started her own family, she learned that a sister and a brother had also survived the massacres. She would not talk about the experience. "To recall the horrible is to relive it," she would tell me. "Why would anyone want to relive a nightmare?" I had learned to hate the Turks.

Uncle Garabed told me that a Kurd family had taken my mother to a Presbyterian orphanage, where she spent some years. Nana picked her to become the bride of her second-oldest son. Mother left Marseilles with Nana, planning to marry a man she had only seen in a photograph. Once in Kitchener, Ontario, however, instead of marrying the intended groom, she had run off with Boghos, the oldest of Nana's sons, because, she said, he looked as if he could provide for her. "And besides," she would tell her children, "Boghos was better-looking." She had married at the age of fifteen. My father was eleven years older.

~ SOMEWHERE in the foothills of Pennsylvania, the rain intensified and was followed by sleet. The windshield and the roads quickly iced. I felt confident, but Mother quietly suggested that we find a hotel or a cabin.

I told her not to worry; I had driven in worse weather. No sooner had the words escaped my mouth than a deer dashed across the highway, followed immediately by another. I reacted quickly, missed both animals, but hit a patch of ice, and the car spun into a skid. I managed to correct the wheel, but the car hit the shoulder and came to rest in a ditch.

George was tossed against the front seats, and Mother lunged forward, her head barely missing the windshield. I looked at her first, and although she was dazed, she said she was all right. George was not hurt, either. With expletives he normally would not use in Mother's presence, he commented on my driving skills and the fact that I could have killed all three of us. I said nothing.

Turning to George, Mother said, "No, he could only have killed you; I died a long time ago."

George and I got out of the car. A bent front-end passenger-side fender and my pride appeared to be the only damage. George ordered me behind the wheel to see if we could rock the car out of the ditch. After several unsuccessful attempts, we stopped trying. We were stuck in the mud for the evening. We got back into the car and stayed there. It was too cold to try to walk for help or look for shelter, so Mother got out some sandwiches. When she packed a lunch, it was more like a seven-course meal.

At daybreak, George and I managed to free the vehicle, and we were on the road again, with George driving. Before we reached New York, Mother insisted that we stop at a hotel and get some sleep.

Later, in our rooms, Mother came to me and urged me to reconsider going to Armenia. She said that the accident was a sign, an ill omen. She looked directly into my eyes and begged me.

There could be no other choice, I said. I did not want to disgrace Father or our family name. There would be no turning back.

"God only knows how I raised someone as stubborn as you."

"I am your son."

"Yes, you are."

It was strange to hear Mother speak of God, for, although she allowed her children to go to church, she herself would never attend services. I had overheard her tell her friends that if there were a God, he would have stopped the killings.

~ THERE WAS no better place to be in the world after the war than New York City. It was alive with people and entertainment, and George seemed to know every bar, tavern, movie house, dining room, and whorehouse in the city. He took me everywhere, except for the whorehouses, in hopes, I believe, of showing me what I would miss. I was only nineteen, and the age of majority was twenty-one. That would not stop him. The two things George loved, I learned, were booze and women, and not necessarily in that order.

In the bars, my youthfulness and air of innocence drew women to our table, but after I said a few words and displayed my ignorance of life, the gals quickly turned to George. His obvious experience—or was it his thicker wallet?—made him more appealing. George found my inexperience around women humorous. He bought drinks, pushed a glass over to me, and told me to try it, saying it wouldn't kill me. But I pushed the glass back and smiled and reminded him that whatever happened, I would not return to Detroit with him. It just wouldn't work. It was he who got drunk, and it was I who drove us back to the hotel, where Mother was waiting to chastise us for making her worry.

Those two days in New York City would linger forever in my memories.

On November 1, 1947, the day of my scheduled departure, George drove to the dock and parked the car in a lot near the wharf. We were in clear sight of the *Rossia*, a magnificent 18,000-ton former German ship that the Soviets had seized as part of the $12 billion they had demanded from Germany in war reparations. The *Rossia* was scheduled to leave New York Harbor and, after stops at Marseilles, Naples, Port Said, Haifa, and Batumi, return to its home base in Odessa.

George got out and went to the passenger side of the car to survey the damage again. He told me that every time he looked at the crumpled front fender, it would remind him of me. I told him to fix it and forget me. No sooner were the words spoken than I began to apologize.

"I hope I never again hear you say you are sorry for anything," my mother said.

I had said enough.

My brother opened the trunk and removed my suitcases. I tried to take my luggage, but he held on to it. It would probably be the last thing he ever did for me, he said. We began walking toward the ship, with Mother a few steps behind us.

Crowds were gathering on the dock, and I was getting a bit nervous. I had never been on an ocean liner. As we approached the ship, my brother began shaking his head, frowning, and murmuring softly, "Son of a bitch, son of a bitch. Do you see that?"

"What now?" I asked. "What the hell are you mumbling?"

He pointed to the red flag on the ship. The gold hammer and sickle stood out clearly in the morning sunlight. "It's a damn Soviet flag. I never thought I would ever live to see one of those f—." He stopped short of using the word when he remembered that Mother was right behind us. "Flags in our harbor."

He handed me my suitcases, dug into his shirt pocket, pulled out a cigarette, and lit it.

I did not say a word but walked a step or two ahead, trying to disassociate myself from him. I never would have believed that my brother could hate so much, be so prejudiced. The Navy had taught him to smoke and drink, to fire weapons and kill, why not also to hate? But why the Soviets? They were our allies, our friends in World War II!

In what appeared to be his last-ditch effort to change my mind, he reminded me that I was dividing the family and going over to the enemy.

He's looking for a fight, to make a scene, maybe even get us arrested, I thought, *right here, in front of all of these people.* I would not fight back. My brother accused me of being self-centered, arrogant, thoughtless, and brainless for what would happen to the family once I was working for the enemy. Through clenched teeth, he repeated that I had broken the family into pieces. He said that everyone would know that his brother was a goddamned Communist. He didn't think I understood what that meant, but he said it anyway. As for me, I thought he was the one who didn't understand.

We continued to walk toward the throng gathering to board the ship.

Although I felt the need to respond, I didn't. I was glad we had reached the gangplank.

But George wouldn't give up. He offered to take me to the nearest recruiter. He would reenlist with me. He begged me not to leave the family, not to betray my country.

I finally turned and stood toe-to-toe with him, ready to fight. Mother saw it coming and stood her distance.

"OK, George. You win. I won't go." He didn't flinch. He knew I was lying. He waited for my next words. "You go in my place." I challenged him to walk up there and say he was me.

"You are nuts!"

"Am I?"

I presented my final argument. This was the first but not the only caravan going back; there would be others. The next caravan could include Father and Mother and possibly Rose. Father had come to America not with the idea of staying but with thoughts of returning home to Armenia one day. And he would take Mother with him for sure. We all suspected that he had plans someday to go.

"How would you stop our father from going to Soviet Armenia, George?"

George looked shell-shocked. My mother's face froze. She knew that what I had said could become a reality one day. Her eyes moistened.

"Don't be a fool, George. This way, I go. If all is what they say it is, then fine, let Mother and Father join me. And if not, believe me, you will hear from me. Even if I am in hell, you will hear from me."

We stood there staring at each other. There was nothing more to say. My next step would be on the gangplank, one foot on American soil, the other on a Soviet vessel. Men and women and children swept past us in waves to board the ship.

I turned and gave Mother a long hug and a kiss. We both knew that it would have to last us a while. I took out my handkerchief to dry her tears. She didn't say anything, just held me as long as she could.

Her final words to me were, "My son, whatever happens, do not blame your father."

I turned to George and told him that I would return.

"Sure you will. In a wooden box."

My body left American soil. A few more steps up the gangplank, and suddenly, my brother shouted for me to wait. I paused and turned nervously. *Now what?*

He raced up the plank, squeezing past some passengers, one a very young and attractive dark-haired girl. The girl looked at me. Then she took a long look at George and continued to board the ship.

I kidded him about noticing the pretty skirt and deciding to join me.

"I'm no fool. No woman in this world could entice me to go to Russia," he said as he slowly slipped his high school ring off his finger and put it in the palm of my right hand. The ring had brought him luck in the Navy, gotten him through some rough times, and he wanted me to have it for good luck. He hugged me. "I want it back."

I promised I would return it and told him to hustle his ass off the gangplank, or he could be arrested. With a smile, I reminded him that he was standing on Soviet property.

He turned and walked slowly down the gangplank to where Mother was waiting for him. I blew them a kiss.

As I walked up toward the deck, I felt my stomach churn. America was to my back, and I was strolling willingly toward the gateway to the Soviet Union.

Was the Iron Curtain a myth?

Chapter 4

GOOD-BYE, AMERICA

I turned to wave good-bye to my mother and brother, but as I looked down into the crowds, I saw only a wall of humanity waving flags and kerchiefs, throwing kisses to loved ones. Mother and George had disappeared into that gigantic wave of hands. I felt a sudden jolt, followed by the hum of the ship's engines.

The *Rossia* was tuning up for its long voyage across the Atlantic.

I continued to watch the faces of people coming up the platform in single file onto the deck. There were young couples with small children, middle-aged men and women, and the elderly, some of whom needed assistance to make it up the plank.

There were no bands playing, no speeches, no reporters or newspaper photographers.

Though few in number compared with the thousands who repatriated from Europe and the Middle East, Armenians of America had packed up their belongings and were returning to what they believed was their homeland. Hope and enthusiasm and optimism were on all of their faces. They believed in what they were doing, and nothing could destroy their dreams.

They had left the thunder of the hoofbeats in Anatolia, made it to the shores of America, rolled up their sleeves, worked hard, merged with mainstream America, and lived good lives. Some became noted writers, such as William Saroyan and Michael Arlen and Roger Tartarian, and others were industrialists, such as Alex Manoogian and Sarkes Tarzian and the Kazanjians, and Edward Mardigian, the brains behind the Maridian Corporation in Detroit.

Most countries welcomed the "starving Armenian," and Armenians quickly became known as the hardworking people they are. The world soon forgot them and what had happened in Turkey in those bloody years of the First World War. As Hitler proclaimed to his officers at Obersalzberg on the eve of the Nazi invasion of Poland on August 22, 1939, "Who today remembers the extermination of the Armenians?"

But the Armenians could not forget. The blood of their loved ones had been spilled in the hills and the plains of the Turkish hinterland. Many on the *Rossia* believed that if it had not been for Lenin and the Bolsheviks, the Turks would have completed their task of resolving the "Armenian question."

As I stood watching the last of the repatriates board, I thought that surely good would come from all of this. I thanked God that this group of Armenians was not fleeing tyranny, that America had opened its heart and arms to embrace them in a time of crisis.

There was no reason to think that the Soviets would not do otherwise. Armenian Americans, along with others across the world, had been invited by the Soviets. We brought gifts to the land of the Soviets that would help rebuild their war-torn country. In exchange, the Soviets promised work, housing, and education, all free of charge. It sounded too good to be true.

~ SOMEONE TAPPED me on the shoulder. He excused himself for disturbing me and asked if I was one of the repatriates or a visitor aboard ship.

I replied that I was a repatriate.

He directed me to a table to check in, where I would also be assigned a cabin.

I approached the table. Two of those seated there seemed out of place. They wore medals and ribbons, military-service ribbons, I believed, on the breast pockets of their English wool jackets. I wasn't accustomed to seeing such a display of medals on uniforms and jackets, except in movies. George had a few, including a sharpshooting medal. When I was growing up, I had seen Civil War and World War I veterans dazzle with the decorations on their military uniforms during Memorial day Parades. I had played drums during the parades to the gravesites of veterans in Woodmere Cemetery.

One of the shipboard officials, in his forties, his iron-gray hair in sharp contrast to his coal-black mustache, giving him an Edwardian appearance, cordially greeted me. He asked my name and the city I was from. I waited as he quickly checked the list in front of him. He glanced up and asked me to repeat my name. I did. This time, he slowly perused, using his finger to check each name. The others in the group continued their work, checking the passenger list and assigning cabins to those in line.

It was apparent that the official I was in front of was having difficulty finding my name. He asked me to repeat it several times before he gave up. He apologized and asked again.

"Can you spell your name for me?"

I did. Mooradian, Tom Mooradian, from Detroit, Michigan.

His head went up and down as if he understood, but he couldn't find my name. Was I with family? No. Registered under my Armenian name? No.

His litany of questions quickly drew the attention of the two men with the medals on their jackets. They zeroed in on me and give me a closer look, but they did not interrupt.

I confirmed that I was traveling alone. The official seemed surprised that someone as young as I was traveling alone. I repeated that I was a repatriate. He asked if my parents would be joining me on the next caravan. I said I wasn't certain. I stood there, confused at the confusion. If they didn't want me, there was still time to get off the ship and catch up with George.

Finally, the official announced that my documentation could have been misplaced. He told me to wait until they found someone who could help. He left the registration area, and I stood nervously at the table.

Shortly afterward, the official reappeared, accompanied by a frail old gentleman with a shawl draped across his shoulders. He introduced himself as Dr. Panoughni, the head of the Repatriation Committee. Whether the "Dr." was a medical or an honorary title I did not know. He looked directly at me, then said, as if it were a statement rather than a question, "You are Dzovinar and Boghos's son, are you not?"

I nodded, wondering how he knew the names of my parents.

"Yes. I'm Tommy Mooradian, from Detroit. I am one of the repatriates."

"I know," he said. And then he warmly embraced me. "We need more young people like you in this group. Unfortunately, the youth do not believe in our cause."

There was a wave of relaxing bodies around the table as soon as Dr. Panoughni identified me. To confirm my identity, he asked if I had any documents on me that would prove who I was. I told him that I thought they had received all the documents necessary from the Detroit committee. I explained that I did not have a passport, which raised some eyebrows, but I had my driver's license and asked if that would do.

"It will do."

I took out my wallet, slipped my out my license, and handed it to the doctor, who then gave it to one of the men. Then, on second thought, I said I also had my draft card and Social Security card and handed those to Dr. Panoughni.

He took the documents from me, glanced briefly at them, and handed them to the men at the table for their inspection. They didn't say a word but appeared satisfied that I was who I said I was.

Dr. Panoughni explained that when Mother and I had not shown up at the reception planned for the repatriates, some of the people from Detroit had informed him that they thought I had changed my mind.

After a short conference with the others at the table and a quick look at the passenger list, Dr. Panoughni directed the official to continue to process my papers and then ordered a member of the ship's crew to take my things to Cabin 4. He said that I would be traveling with a New Yorker about my age and a barber from Philadelphia, Mr. Simonian. If I had any questions, Dr. Panoughni was certain that he would be able to answer them. He invited me to join him for lunch and a chat once I was settled in, and I accepted.

Dr. Panoughni's manner and gentleness calmed my anxieties. I thanked him, picked up my luggage, and followed a crew member to the cabin. We went through a doorway and entered a maze of tunnels and doors. I banged my head on some of the lower-hanging pipes. The crew member—a Russian—laughed and said something I did not understand. It was the first time a Soviet had addressed me.

When we got to the cabin, he again said something in Russian. I nodded my head, not having any idea what he'd said, and he quickly disappeared down the corridor. At that moment, I remembered that I had not retrieved my driver's license or the other two documents. I was about to turn back, but I realized that I could get lost in the maze. I decided that since I would be seeing Dr. Panoughni later, I would collect my documents then.

I knocked on the cabin door. A voice from within shouted, "Come in!"

Chapter 5

MY FELLOW TRAVELERS

I opened the door and found a young man about my age struggling to store a suitcase under a bunk. His khakis and white T-shirt made me think he had served in the military. As he looked up from his kneeling position, I saw a friendly, deeply tanned face that quickly broke into a smile. He had dark hair and a pleasant face, and his body provided proof that he had done physical work most of his life. He swore as he noted the lack of space in the cabin. He stood up and moved a step or two to offer his hand. He introduced himself as Johnny Kadekian, from New York—via Cuba.

No New York accent, I thought as I introduced myself. *He must not have lived in New York for very long.*

He asked me if I wanted the upper or lower bunk. I said it didn't make any difference.

He explained graphically that if I peed in bed or if I got seasick, he would prefer that I sleep on the lower bunk; if I didn't, he'd like the lower.

I told him I had stopped peeing in bed years ago, but this was my first ship cruise.

"I'll sleep in the upper, if you don't mind." Johnny dug into his hip pocket, brought out a pack of Camels, and offered me one.

I told him I didn't smoke.

"Bet you don't drink, either," Johnny said.

"I don't."

"I hope you like women."

I smiled. "No reason not to."

"That's good."

He continued to arrange and rearrange his suitcases until he gave up in disgust.

"It's going to be pretty crowded in here with four of us," Johnny said, indicating the four bunks. (The fourth one would never be filled, actually.)

Had he met the other two?

"No."

He said that he had been raised in Cuba and loved the sea.

When I asked him if he had been in the service, he responded, "Hell, no." If he had been, he wouldn't be on this trip. I didn't understand the connection between service and repatriation and asked why not. He looked at me as if I were kidding. He told me he'd explain later, saying that it was going to be a long haul before we reached Russia. There would be plenty of time to talk.

He said his folks weren't with him, that his parents and younger brother would be in the second caravan. I told him my parents were back in Detroit and that I wasn't sure of their plans.

I tossed my suitcases onto the unoccupied bunk, opened one, and began to unpack as Johnny continued to question me. Had I knocked up some girl and decided to run? I told him I wasn't running from anyone or anything. I just wanted to see the Soviet Union for myself. I was interested in the free college tuition the Soviets offered. I was going to get a degree, then return home.

Johnny took out another cigarette. "You think you're returning to the States after studying in the Soviet Union?"

"Of course."

Before we could exchange another word, someone knocked on the door. In chorus, we shouted, "Come in!"

The man I saw standing in the doorway was about my height but three times my age. His most striking features were his John L. Lewis eyebrows—thick, unruly, and black, incongruent with his full head of graying hair. He stood erect as if seated on horseback. Deep brown eyes, accented with thick glasses, complemented his wrinkled but pleasant face. Before Johnny and I could introduce ourselves, he said his name was Haratoun Simonian. Haratoun, he said, was Harry in English, but he preferred his Armenian name. He looked at Johnny, then at me. Actually, he stared at me, which made me feel uncomfortable.

"You're Tommy, aren't you?" Before I had time to answer, he explained that he had visited Detroit on several occasions and stayed with my parents. I was too young to remember. He remembered seeing me in cloth diapers, crawling on the linoleum floor. Ignoring Johnny momentarily, he asked about my parents and their health, saying he knew that they would have loved to be on the first boat. He expected that they would join me next year. I said nothing to the contrary. He observed that I had given them more purpose to return to our homeland.

Johnny introduced himself, said his folks would be on the next boat. He was to get everything ready for them. They planned to bring a Jeep with them.

"It will help rebuild the country," Simonian said.

A sudden jolt caused the three of us to stumble. We were moving. We were on our way!

Johnny grabbed me by my arm and yelled, "Let's go!"

"Where?"

"Go with him, Tommy, and get a glimpse of the New York skyline and the Statue of Liberty," Simonian urged.

"Yeah!" Johnny shouted. "And we can check out the young broads, too!"

Chapter 6

AN IDYLLIC CROSSING

I never did see the Statue of Liberty or take a stroll in Central Park or a ride in the New York subway.

But what I did see, standing there at the rail side, was the incomparable, incredible New York City skyline with its mammoth skyscrapers as the *Rossia* slipped out of the harbor with the repatriates, a small cadre of Jewish youth, and a Chicago furniture dealer who was traveling alone to Naples.

I knew that I would be back someday.

The first two or three days out at sea were idyllic. For the first time in my life, I had no cares, no concerns, no one questioning my motives. I got up in the morning when I wanted. I had breakfast, dinner, and supper whenever I wanted. I strolled the decks alone. Greetings were cordial but superficial. Encounters were brief. Everything I needed I had. I answered to no one and was responsible to only one person: myself. I felt I was fully prepared to face any challenge that confronted me.

On every face I passed on deck, there was a smile. Their stomachs were filled. Life could not have been better that first week in November.

We were steaming toward the Straits of Gibraltar, the gateway to the Mediterranean. In the evenings, I felt so close to the heavens that I could reach out and pluck from the millions of stars a handful to put in my pocket. The beauty and the mystery of the universe stood before me. Ours was an unequaled and mesmerizing, harmonious planet. Why did nations have to go to war? Moonbeams bounced off the waves, casting shadows of those who had gone before. I now understood why men had been seduced by the seas.

Once my mind was settled, I had to take a serious look at my earthly possessions. The food and the passage were not concerns, as they were being paid for by the Armenian American community. I had two suitcases filled with clothing and also a larger trunk, which was crated and would be delivered to the address in Armenia where I would be staying.

I could expect warm summers and cold winters in the part of Armenia where I planned to reside. I felt confident that I could make it for a while. My parents had assured me that if I needed anything, they would send it to me.

There were some concerns over the cars, stoves, and refrigerators that were scheduled to be shipped at a later date. Crates of heavy machinery, purchased by the Armenian American community, to be donated to the Soviets, also were on the ship. Armenian Americans who supported the Soviets' annexation of Armenia gave generously to the cause. My father had helped raise funds for the equipment.

Despite my confidence, though, I did find myself wondering as I stood there under the stars whether I had made the right decision and what Johnny had meant when he said that if he had served in the U.S. armed forces, he would not have been on the ship. And I wished I had read carefully the several papers my father had put in front of me to sign in order for me to become eligible to join the repatriation group.

Chapter 7

THE BARBER OF PHILADELPHIA

I had been meditating, almost solemnly, for some time when a familiar voice broke into my thoughts.

"Prayer never hurts," I heard someone mutter behind me. I turned and found Mr. Simonian standing behind me. For a moment, I was speechless. I did not know how long he had been there. He apologized for startling me and offered to leave. I told him I was enjoying the sea and was "just thinking."

"Aren't we all?" He asked if I was having second thoughts about leaving America.

I admitted that I was.

"It's natural. When you get to Erevan, you'll be too busy to think."

"What is it going to be like when we do get there?" I asked.

His face lit up as he said, "It will be what you want it to be." He did not elaborate.

I asked if he was having second thoughts. He admitted that he was. He had had a successful business, and Philadelphia was a great place to live. He paused a moment, allowing me to digest his words. Then he added that he didn't think there was a single man or woman aboard the ship who didn't have doubts; they wouldn't be human otherwise. We were making history, opening doors so that others would follow. We, like the Jews, would someday have a nation, and people like Johnny and me would help build a solid foundation. Then he looked to the heavens and smiled, saying that only time—and God—would reveal how successful we were.

A devout Communist who believed in a supreme being?

He read my face. I would find, Mr. Simonian said, many Communists—especially among Armenian Communists—who still believed. "Look up there into the heavens and down into this ocean. There is harmony all around us. It is man, not God, who disrupts it. But it is far better, for now, not to express our religious beliefs." In time, he said, I would understand everything.

I thought he would leave to continue his walk, but he didn't. He asked if I felt ill, mentioning that there were two doctors in our group who could look at me.

I shook my head and said that I felt exceptionally well. "I love the sea. It seems the going-to-sea genes are in the family. George and—"

Simonian finished the sentence, "George and Popkin also served in the Navy."

It seemed so strange that Simonian knew so much about my family, even Robert's Armenian name.

Putting his hand around my shoulder, he repeated that he knew my parents well, and he knew I wouldn't want to disappoint them. He said that if there was anything he could do for me, I should not hesitate to ask. It was going to be tough for a while, but I would adjust. It was natural to be homesick, even after a few days at sea. He then turned and disappeared into the darkness.

~ THE FOLLOWING DAY, I remembered about my driver's license and draft card and decided to seek out Dr. Panoughni. I had been very reluctant to bother Dr. Panoughni, for he seemed to be very busy accommodating repatriates with families and those who had physical problems. I had neither, but I would need my papers to get off the ship in Marseilles.

Dr. Panoughni was enjoying the warm ocean breezes when I approached him on the second deck, where he had found solitude in a chair. He had on a wide-brimmed hat for protection from the sun, and a blanket covered his shoulders, although the weather had turned warmer, not colder, in mid-Atlantic. When I greeted him, he extended his arm and his hand to indicate that I should sit next to him. He smiled and asked if everything was all right. I replied that it was but that I was concerned about why my documents had not been returned to me.

He seemed surprised and had no answer. He reached into his jacket pocket, took out a gold cigarette case, and fumbled to retrieve a cigarette. He took one and extended the case to me, inviting me to take one. I shook my head. He seemed pleased and said that it was not healthy to smoke. He said he smoked from habit. Then he said that he didn't know where my documents were but would ask those who might try to locate them.

I thanked him and remembered that I also had not been issued my American passport. I told him I thought that we would need our passports when we debarked. Dr. Panoughni's hands began to shake, and he turned to look at me. We would receive our Soviet documents when we landed in Batumi and not before, he informed me. I said I thought he had misunderstood. I was talking about my American passport.

Dr. Panoughni stared, making me feel uncomfortable. He answered nervously, and he questioned whether I understood the conditions of repatriation. Did I not understand—or had my parents not explained—that the repatriates had to give up their American citizenship? I was now a Soviet citizen.

His words shocked me. I played them over and over in my mind. As they slowly caught hold, I was enraged. It couldn't be true. The blood boiled in my veins, and I mumbled something incoherent. I did not want my anger to be spewed onto this old man, but why hadn't my father explained all of this to me? Did my father know? It couldn't be true. I had promised that I would return, and return I would. Dr. Panoughni saw the frustration in my face. After taking a long puff on his cigarette, he said he was sorry, truly sorry, but there was nothing he could do. There was a long pause. I got up and left, not knowing what to say.

I heard Dr. Panoughni asking if I was all right. My answer remained within me. *No. No, damn it! I am not all right!*

I headed straight to my cabin and slammed the door behind me.

As I paced the room contemplating my next move, I remembered what Mr. Simonian had said to me. If I ever needed help—and I certainly needed it—I should seek him out.

Chapter 8

ARE WE LEMMINGS?

B efore I could find him, the barber of Philadelphia found me.

A short time after my talk with Dr. Panoughni, Mr. Simonian burst into the cabin. He was extremely upset, and his anger was reflected on his face. Dr. Panoughni had summoned him and told him of our discussion.

Mr. Simonian told me to sit down, saying that we needed to talk. I started to interrupt, but he held up his hand and asked me to hear him out first. He began by praising the work my father had done for the Party, how devoted he was to the cause. He mentioned how proud both my father and mother were of me. One the other hand, if I felt that my father had coerced me to join the group, or if I thought I was being railroaded, there was still time to correct it.

I laughed. I asked sarcastically if he was going to turn the ship around. None of us had that power, he acknowledged, but there was still an opportunity for me to leave the ship if I chose to, and he would help me get back home. Under those thick eyebrows were eyes of compassion. I believed in him. But I still remained skeptical. And I definitely did not want to give up my American citizenship.

He asked, "Why, in heaven's name, did you ever agree to repatriate?"

I told him that I was afraid my father would uproot the family. I reminded him of how strong-willed a man he was. Simonian nodded. I said that I had not been told that I would lose my citizenship.

We sat there, I like a lost puppy, he amazed at my naiveté and ignorance.

"I am not willing to give up my country for another." I said. I told him that I felt that if I left the ship, I would be betraying my father, but I also felt that I had been betrayed by my father.

Simonian reassured me that he understood. His promise to help was irrevocable. But, I thought, if I couldn't trust my father, how could I now trust Mr. Simonian? There wasn't much time left. The *Rossia* would be in Marseilles in two days. He had friends there who would be waiting for him. He asked if I had any money, and I told him how much I had.

"That is not enough. You'll need more."

I told him I would manage on very little, but he just laughed.

He said he would lend me enough money to hold me over until I could return to America. Once I was back, I was to send it to him with someone who was coming in the second caravan. I agreed.

"I have close friends in France who will treat you as they would treat a son. When we land, they will be waiting for me. They will get you back to America."

I reminded him that I didn't have a passport or any documents identifying me.

"They will get you back," he repeated.

It was settled, then. I would leave the ship at Marseilles.

Simonian did not need to tell me that it would be best if no one else aboard the ship knew about this conversation, not even our other cabin mate, Johnny. He turned away, opened the door, and left me to my thoughts.

Chapter 9

THE MARSEILLES OPTION

I slipped into my bunk. I needed time to think, but all I could do was toss and turn and mull over what I should do. If I had signed away my birthright but was not yet a Soviet citizen, and I had no documents to prove who I was, then who was I? An idiot! That was the conclusion all the evidence led to.

Should I risk going to the Soviet Union, forever losing my birthright? The Soviets could not hold me against my will. Could they? Should I place myself at Simonian's mercy, get off the ship at Marseilles, meet his friends, and hope they could manage my passage back? At the time, it seemed the logical course of action. But I wanted a way out without getting Simonian involved. I feared that there could be repercussions if someone discovered he was involved in my return home.

Sometime during the late evening, I heard Simonian and Johnny come into the cabin. They were whispering, and Johnny called my name, wondering if I was awake. I did not answer.

As they undressed and slipped into their bunks, I heard Johnny say to Simonian, "Anyone who sleeps all day has a problem."

Simonian whispered, "He'll be all right. He just needs to get his feet on land."

In the morning, my body ached. I had not slept. Simonian had been up and about several times during the night. At daybreak, he shook me and said, "Get up. Let's go to breakfast." Before I could accept, Johnny tossed back his covers and looked down at the top of Simonian's head, saying that he would be ready in a jiff. I could tell by Simonian's furtive glance at me that this was not in his plan. But I was too tired to think or say anything. We dressed and headed for the dining hall.

As we walked on deck, the fresh air and gentle breeze off the ocean brought me back to life. I wondered if it would be possible for me to return to America, to resume the life I once enjoyed. How would it affect my family? I was scared. And the more I thought about the mess I had created, the further I sank into the cesspool.

The ship's officers and some of the crew members were just finishing up their breakfast when the three of us walked in. We exchanged "Good mornings" in our languages, found a table, and sat down. I did not hear one English word uttered by the Soviet crew, though I suspected that some of them understood English. Like many Americans, I felt that everyone should speak English. It never entered my mind that others thought we should speak their languages.

With Johnny present, there would be no opportunity to discuss Marseilles with Simonian. That subject had to wait for another time, although we both realized there wasn't much time left. We were due to dock at the French port the next day. I did not know at the time that Simonian's plan was not complex.

Once we had selected our breakfasts from the buffet and sat down to eat, I asked Simonian why there were passengers other than Armenian American repatriates booked on the *Rossia*, since it had appeared that the ship had been designated specifically to carry repatriates. Even though I couldn't single them out, I knew there was a group of six or seven young Jews and the American businessman.

Simonian explained that it was cheaper to travel on the Soviet ship than on any other ship. If there had been more repatriates, there would have been no others aboard. The first caravan hadn't attracted the numbers that the committee had anticipated. Nearly two months ago, the *Rossia* had transported more than a thousand French Armenians to Batumi.

"And what about the Chicago businessman?" I asked.

"He's definitely from the FBI," Johnny said.

My eyes popped. "FBI?"

"Sure," said Johnny. "What better way to get information about a Soviet ship and its crew than assigning an agent to a ship loaded with Communists?"

I looked at Simonian, and he smiled at me. "Johnny's right, Tommy. But he'll get off in Naples, and that will be the last we'll see of him."

I thought perhaps I should approach the man, strike up a conversation with him, and see if he could help me get back. But Simonian zeroed in on what was on my mind and said, "Once we get to France, everything will be all right. Right, Tommy?"

I nodded, turned to Johnny, and asked if he had had to denounce his American citizenship to join the repatriation group. There was a knowing smile on Simonian's face.

"No," was Johnny's reply.

"And why not?"

"I was born in Cuba. I am considered a Cuban national."

Others began to come into the dining hall. I noticed a very attractive young lady accompanied by a tall, good-looking man. I could not take my eyes off her. I asked Johnny if he knew who she was. He turned his head, spotted the woman, and immediately announced, "She's Jewish. Forget it. She is getting off at Haifa."

Simonian quickly pointed out that he didn't think I was interested in young ladies, reminding me that I had someone waiting for me back home. I changed the subject and asked Simonian about his plans for when he got to Erevan. He said that he was going to open a barbershop and would install six modern barber chairs. Johnny asked where the chairs were. Simonian replied that he hoped they were in the cargo hold.

"So, Tommy and I get free haircuts, don't we?"

Without hesitation, Simonian replied, "Of course, of course. In fact, you kids look as if you need one now!"

Johnny caught the eye of a young, attractive brunette who had been looking at us and excused himself. He went over and briefly talked to her, returned to the table, and apologized. He had to leave, he said, needed a stroll around the deck. He returned to the girl, and the two of them left.

"She's Armenian," Simonian said. "And has a sister. Do you want me to introduce you to her?"

I shook my head. I said I preferred "talking about tomorrow."

"Are you sure you want to . . .?"

Not allowing Mr. Simonian to finish his sentence, I said, "Yes."

Simonian's face turned pale. He placed his hands on mine, and I could feel a nervous twitch in them. "Then, God willing, it will be." He slowly raised himself from the table and left the dining hall.

Chapter 10

THE JEWISH CONTINGENT

A mid the clatter of dishes, children crying, and parents scolding them, I sat alone at the table, dreaming about home. I thought about sending a postcard to my parents to tell them of my plans, so that they wouldn't be shocked when I showed up on the doorstep. But upon reflection, I canceled the idea. It would be wiser to wait until I got through the political channels, out of France, and back to the United States before notifying them.

There was not a single reason, as far as I could see, for U.S. officials not to restore my citizenship. I would tell them I had made a youthful mistake and ask for forgiveness.

In fact, I surmised that the United States would be elated to have me back and would expedite my application on the basis that I chose America over the Soviet Union.

Oh, how naive a nineteen-year-old can be!

As for the Armenian American community? I really didn't know. Or care.

I was an American. That right could not be taken away from me by one foolish and youthful act. Simonian had warned me that if I came out against the repatriation program or the Soviet Union, there would be groups in America that would come down very hard on me and my family. He reminded me of Leon Trotsky's fate and the Armenian archbishop's assassination. He warned me not to get involved in the ideological war between our divided peoples. It would be best for all concerned that I return to the classroom and pursue my career. "Forget politics for a while," was the way he put it. And that was what I planned to do.

The breakfast crowd was beginning to leave, and I stood there in my surreal world of "what ifs."

The Jewish group sitting behind me was exuberantly chatting, laughing, and joking. I could hear, but I could not understand them, for they kept switching from English to French to German. The one who accompanied the only female in the group even spoke Russian, which I found fascinating. How could people speak so many different languages so fluently? It made me feel uneasy and uncomfortable. I turned to get a better look at the group, and my eyes fell on the raven-haired beauty, whose dark almond eyes greeted mine with a *Mona Lisa* smile. I turned away as blood rushed to my face.

I sat motionless, my back to the group. But I could not dismiss her from my mind. Did I dare turn to look at her again? I continued to sit there, hoping that their conversation would turn to English.

Boisterous, even argumentative at times, those at the adjoining table seemed to be having fun.

The tall, muscular young man in his early thirties, with striking blond hair, blue eyes, and a square jaw—I thought he looked German—got up from his seat and strolled around to several tables, apparently looking for something. As I felt him near me, I turned and looked up.

"We don't have a salt shaker at our table. Can we borrow this?" he asked, pointing to the shaker on my table.

"Be my guest," I replied, handing the container to him.

He thanked me, paused, and offered his hand, introducing himself as David. I gave him my name, and we exchanged pleasantries. He asked if I was Armenian and if I was with the repatriation group. When I answered yes, he looked at me strangely and invited me to join his group. At first, I hesitated, but I couldn't resist the lure of meeting the girl at the table.

As he introduced me to the others, I discovered that the only name I heard was Kiva. She, along with her male companions, stood up to shake my hand. My legs immediately weakened. I barely heard David saying, ". . . Armenians and Jews have a lot in common." He could have said he was the president of the United States, and I would not have heard a word. My eyes could not leave Kiva, and she kept staring at me.

David spoke English impeccably. I quickly concluded that he had been educated in the United States, but I would later learn that I was wrong. His blue shirt matched his eyes, and the top three buttons were open, revealing a very hirsute chest. The shirtsleeves had been rolled up to the elbows, and his hands were huge, his arms muscular. Judging by his overall demeanor, I decided that if I were ever in a fight, I would want him on my side. I would never want to cross him or be the object of his anger.

Everyone in the group spoke English, some better than the others. They did not speak in any other language while I was at their table. The wide range of topics we discussed included the United Nations resolution on the partition of Palestine and war and peace in the Middle East. I believed I had a thorough understanding of politics and history, but it was nothing compared with that of those seated at that table. I had little of value to offer to the discussion. My eyes would circle the group but would always stop at Kiva. She was slim and tall, about five feet, eight inches. She wore khaki pants and a short-sleeved khaki shirt, and she seemed to have a strong body. Her accent immediately gave her away as a New Yorker.

David told them that I was with the group headed for Armenia.

"Armenia? Soviet Armenia?" asked Kiva.

"Yes," I replied. "Soviet Armenia. I don't know of any other Armenia." I tossed the remark out as a joke, but it fell on deaf ears.

She asked if I was Armenian.

"My father and mother are," I said, sarcastically for some reason. "Why, don't I look Armenian?"

"Not really," Kiva said. "I have a lot of Armenian friends in New York, and they have much darker complexions."

One in the group interrupted her and asked me what I would do once I arrived in the Soviet Union.

I told him that I planned to study for a year and then return to the States. I don't know why I gave that answer, since my plans had now changed. But it kept the dialogue flowing.

David asked if I was joking.

"No," I replied. "Why do you think I'm joking?"

He said that he didn't think the Soviets had an open-door policy, and he was positive that they didn't have a revolving-door policy. In fact, they weren't allowing any of their citizens to leave the country. It surprised him that they were allowing our group in.

I found myself defending the Soviets. "They were on our side during the war. Didn't they beat the shit out of Hitler while everyone was appeasing him?"

David paused to consider his answer. He retreated instead and said, "You're absolutely right."

The Soviet Union was taken off the table, and Haifa moved to the top of the discussion.

"Why are you going to Haifa?" I asked.

"Some of us have relatives and friends there," said someone in the group. They all laughed. It seemed to be an inside joke.

Then, becoming quite serious, David asked if I had heard about the *Exodus*.

"Only what the Bible tells me," I replied.

Kiva burst out laughing. I looked at her and smiled. She reciprocated.

"If you two don't stop flirting," David threatened, "you'll have to go to your rooms." Again, David asked, "Have you ever heard of the ship *Exodus?*"

I said I hadn't.

He told me the story. Three months had passed since the *Exodus* roamed the seas with its forbidden cargo. Originally an American vessel, it was purchased by the Jewish underground and fitted to carry about 150 passengers. When it neared the port of Haifa, it was seized by the British in international waters off the coast of Palestine. There were more than 4,500 displaced Jews on that ship, David said. Many were old men and women and children, all in dire need of food and shelter. They were refused refuge in Haifa and sent back to France on three other ships. In returning the entire group, the British meant to tell all of Europe that emigrants to Palestine were unwelcome. They refused to debark in France, and the French authorities would not force them, so the ships were sent to a British-occupied German port, where the passengers were housed in displaced-persons camps, virtually homeless. These were people who had suffered under the Nazis and managed to survive the gas chambers and the concentration camps, and the British had sent them away. David said there were those who were willing to give up their lives to make sure that there would never again be another *Exodus*.

I looked at David, his face rigid, his hands in fists, his eyes ablaze. I didn't know what to say. He quickly came out of his trance but the silence surrounded him as his face softened. I could not understand at this time of my life the passion these people had to help others. I only thought of my own problems.

Kiva and David exchanged glances. I wondered if they were lovers.

I got up from the table, thanked them for inviting me, and left.

Outside the dining hall, I was surprised to find Kiva a few steps behind me. She apologized for David's behavior. I told her that it was nothing to worry about; in fact, I had learned a lot.

"This weather has been gorgeous, hasn't it?" I said, turning to a noncontroversial topic.

"It is very beautiful. Have you ever seen anything more beautiful?"

"Sure I have! She's standing right next to me."

With a smile, she calmly explained that comments like that would get me into trouble. She reminded me that I was going to Armenia and she was getting off the ship in Haifa. She declared that there was no way she was going to set herself up for a relationship that could not go anywhere. "Do you understand?"

Of course, I did.

My curiosity about David had been aroused. I asked her if she was in love with him.

"In love? With whom?"

"David."

There was a long pause before her answer made it clear that I didn't have a chance with her. "Yes, I am. I love him more than anyone or anything else in this world."

So, where would we go from there? Nowhere, that's where.

She revealed that if there was anything that David hated more than the Nazis, it was the Communists.

I replied, "There is just too much hate in this world."

Kiva agreed. Her next question caught me off guard. "We'll be in Marseilles tomorrow. If you're going ashore, do you want company?"

I didn't know how to respond. A few seconds ago, she had said that David was the love of her life.

"I'd love to," I said, "but I have made other arrangements."

"I understand," she said. "Maybe some other time."

I don't know what I would have said or done if I hadn't planned to leave the ship with Mr. Simonian. We both smiled and said our good-byes.

As I turned and took a few steps away from her, I thought I heard her whisper, "And you didn't even kiss me good-bye, did you? You definitely aren't Armenian!" But perhaps it was the wind.

Chapter 11

MARSEILLES ON THE HORIZON

The dots on the French coastline slowly came together, and as they connected, a bustling waterfront emerged. The *Rossia* headed toward port. Chimneys, then buildings, villas and chateaus, and hilltop trees appeared on the horizon. Miniature figures carried their loads in one continuous line, marching up, then down the hills, in and out of dark tunnels. Soon they became people, busy longshoremen working on the docks and high above on cranes, like birds seated in nests. Crowds on the wharves and rooftops were shouting, their voices carrying over the water but garbled as they reached the ship. Small crafts soon surrounded the *Rossia,* and those aboard the big ship exchanged greetings with them. The French coast guard approached the small crafts and ordered them to return to shore.

As the *Rossia* neared the port, we could see an unusual number of uniformed police on the docks. They appeared to be holding back the throngs. I could only speculate that they were the French Armenians waiting for the ship to dock.

I was ready, waiting for Mr. Simonian to join me and take me ashore. I was going home. My mind was made up. I was human; I had made a mistake. Thanks to Mr. Simonian, I could correct it.

The Armenian community of Marseilles had, indeed, come out to greet the Americans en route to Soviet Armenia. Literally thousands had mobbed the docks and the shoreline. It was awe-inspiring for those aboard the ship.

The ship's engines stopped, my heart with them. What next?

In the distance, a band played the "Marseillaise." As the last words were sung, the band began to play the Armenian national anthem. The cheers from the shore were deafening.

There was commotion aboard the *Rossia*. Where were the tugs to guide us? I knew nothing of maritime rules and regulation.

I waited and waited. Maybe Simonian was in the cabin. I raced down the flight of stairs to see. He was not in the room. Where was he? Was he playing games? Why had he given me five hundred dollars in cash if he was playing games?

The doorknob turned, the door swung open, and Mr. Simonian entered and stood before me, his face contorted in pain.

"What's wrong?" I asked.

"Nothing!" he said as he slammed the door.

"I don't believe you. Something is wrong!"

"Unpack," he fired back. "Unpack. We're not going anywhere. We can't get off the ship!"

I stood paralyzed. Had he just told me to unpack? I didn't understand. All passengers were going ashore. Why couldn't we?

"Put your things away before Johnny gets here and tells you," Simonian ordered.

"Tells me what?"

"There's a national strike, and the longshoremen are not moving a thing." He waved to me to sit down on my bunk. Slowly, he explained that because of labor turmoil in France, there would be no ships docking or leaving Marseilles. And nobody knew when the strike would end.

Now I understood. I had taken part in many strikes at Kelsey Hayes Wheels Company, where my father worked.

But there had to be a way to get off the ship. There was, but Mr. Simonian said he was too old to swim. And without him, there would be no way for me to contact his friends. I was not going home; I was going to the Soviet Union.

Because there were no American or English newspapers aboard the ship, neither of us could have known that the newly elected French premier, Schuman, had refused to discuss antistrike laws with France's labor unions, so, with the help of the Communists, the longshoremen had retaliated by getting cooperation from labor leaders and unions for a nationwide strike. France had also expelled nineteen Soviet citizens for alleged spying.

I stared at Mr. Simonian.

"God," he said after a long silence, "has other plans for you, my son."

Deep within me, I knew he was right. I had sensed that there was a greater force controlling my fate, and for the first time in my life, I felt that I was not the master of my destiny.

Chapter 12

LOST SOULS MEET

The relationship at first was more didactic than romantic. In the wake of the unforeseeable events in the port of Marseilles, I sank into a deep depression. I became like a hermit.

I did not need Kiva in my life. But she was there, everywhere. And without David. I just couldn't get her out of my mind. She fascinated me, intrigued me. Why on earth should I have even been thinking about that girl, any girl, with the baggage I carried? Besides, seriously, did I think I stood a chance with her?

Kiva was two or three years older than I. Somewhere I learned that she had been born and raised in Germany. This surprised me, because she did not have any trace of a German accent in her English. This probably was because her primary education had been in New York. Her father was an art dealer, and her mother was devoted to music, so she had a cosmopolitan upbringing, traveling around Europe before the war.

On the other hand, I, a provincial Detroiter, had carved out my life on the dirty, sooty streets of Detroit. I spent a lifetime in the Delray Presbyterian Church gym learning how to play basketball. During the war, when the older kids were all drafted, I filled the void on Ford Motor Company's truck-production line, picking up wheel drums and bolting them onto the axles.

Kiva was sunlight and moonbeams and waves dashing against rocks. She read Robert Burns, Browning, Wordsworth, Shelley, Keats, and Byron and hummed operatic arias. I was all about sweat socks, jocks, locker rooms, comic books, Studs Lonigan, and listening to big-band music. I was raised in the alleys of Detroit, scrounging for toys, she in the museums and opera houses of Europe and New York. I loved classical music but did not understand it; she knew the operas by heart.

I was a dreamer, she a realist. She could look straight into your eyes and know what you were thinking. I blinked quickly, not wanting people to read me, to know me. I knew my eyes provided a window to my heart and soul, and I would never allow anyone to enter. I would raise my voice to make a point. Her words, like a quiet mountain stream meandering softly down a hill, formed a bridge of understanding.

We did have some things in common, such as a love for Edgar Allen Poe. We looked a bit alike, we both acted and laughed spontaneously, and we both sulked if we did not get what we wanted. Some mistook us for brother and sister.

She had nothing, I believed, in common with David.

I wanted to be near her always; his absence spoke for itself.

She knew in her heart that our story would not have a Cinderella ending.

Chapter 13

SOMETHING IN COMMON

The first touch is the alpha and the omega of a relationship.

For Kiva and me, the embrace that united us forever—she used the word "reunited"—happened somewhere in the Mediterranean on a breezy, star-glittering November evening. We were standing on the upper deck at the rail of the *Rossia* as the Soviet vessel plowed its way toward the Bay of Naples.

There, standing alone and looking out to sea, silhouetted against a full moon, in a white dress and a silk scarf, with a gentle ocean breeze brushing against her face, was Kiva. Oh, how I envied the gentle breeze that repeatedly embraced her. I felt tremors throughout my body as I watched her. She stood there, her hands on the railing, gazing out into the darkness. I felt guilty for invading her privacy. She looked so serene, almost surreal. And sad. What ghosts haunted this beautiful vision? What did she see surfing on the moonbeams of the sea?

We stood apart, two young and solitary people from different worlds, wondering why fate had put us on this ship together. I wanted to reach out and touch her, hold her in my arms, and forget tomorrow with her.

"A penny for your thoughts."

She turned, looked at me, and smiled. "So, the hermit has finally decided to join civilization. Now, that is something."

My face flushed, but I felt it would have been foolish to try to explain my absence. Instead, I observed, "It's a beautiful night, isn't it?" And I continued, "Where's David?" I regretted the words as soon as they slipped out of my mouth.

"With the others," she announced. "Always with the others." Responding to my initial comment, she said, "I miss New York . . . and I'll take that penny now."

"OK. But I don't have a penny."

"I didn't think you did."

She invited me to join her at the rail, and I eagerly accepted. We stood looking into the darkness for a while. She questioned me about my absence, and I was terribly flattered that she had noticed. I told her I had apparently had a touch of seasickness.

"You're homesick, too, aren't you?"

I admitted that I was.

"I'm not sure I know what I am doing on this ship, either. If it weren't for David, I would be back in New York."

I told her I understood.

She turned to face me. "No, you don't!"

I wanted her to explain, but I didn't want to spoil the evening. I did not pursue the subject. "If it's any consolation, I really don't know why I'm on this ship . . . why I'm repatriating."

She shook her head. "No, you aren't . . ."

"Aren't what?" I asked, puzzled by her taunt. "On this ship?"

Kiva grinned. "To repatriate is to return to the country of one's birth or citizenship."

"You win again," I conceded.

"Women always do."

We laughed.

Just then, a breeze caught her scarf and lifted it. I snatched it in midair and saved it from a watery grave. But as I caught the wayward scarf, my lips grazed her face. I apologized as I handed her the piece of silk.

"Damn it," she said. "Didn't those girls back in Detroit ever teach you how to kiss? That was not a kiss." Tossing the scarf around my neck, she pulled my face toward hers and pressed her lips to mine as she whispered, "Thank you. My mother gave me that scarf a long time ago."

One kiss was not enough, yet a second would spell disaster for both of us.

I knew about David. Kiva wanted to know about the girl I had left behind.

"She's pretty, isn't she?"

I nodded. I explained that when I had introduced her to my folks, my mother immediately knew she was an *odar,* and, though she said nothing, she made it clear she did not want another *odar* in our family. Robert had married an Italian against her wishes just before we went to war.

"What's an *odar?*" Kiva asked.

"Anyone not Armenian," I replied.

"How did your mother know that she was an *odar?*"

Blond hair, blue eyes, and every inch of her body and mind were *odar,* I explained.

I shouldn't worry about the girl I had left behind, Kiva contended. If she were that beautiful, she assured me, I would be getting a "Dear John" letter before I reached the Soviet Union.

I maintained that she would wait.

"You are a dreamer." Looking out across the sea and pointing to the red-tinted clouds in the far distance, Kiva said, "That's Vesuvius over there. I guess you'll be going ashore with your friend."

Though I had not made any plans, some were beginning to form.

I didn't want to dissuade her and was caught without an acceptable response.

"Do you want company? I do speak Italian," she said with an air of apprehension.

"Kiva, I don't care how many languages you speak. If they allow us to go ashore, I'd love to see Naples with you. But honestly . . ." I wanted to tell her that if I got off the boat, I wouldn't be coming back. I didn't. I finally admitted, "I don't know what my plans are."

"That's strike two." She laughed.

Chapter 14

DAVID'S WARNING

I struggled with my emotions. I felt embarrassed that I had turned down an invitation from Kiva for the second time, but if the repatriates were permitted to leave the ship—and with the farce in Marseilles fresh in my mind, I wasn't certain we would be—I wasn't coming back. They would have to handcuff me, drag me, and beat me to get me back

But the touch of Kiva's lips had released feelings I had subdued for months. The tense, stressful, emotional process of repatriation had driven a wedge between me and my high school girlfriend, as well as between me and my family and my friends. Why add further complications now?

Her voice haunted me, taunted me. She was often in the company of David, but when by chance we passed each other anywhere, even with him there beside her, she would turn, smile, and blow me a kiss.

Whether I wanted to admit it or not, I was hooked.

In the ship's dining hall, I sat so that I could see her. I knew it was foolish and childish, but what did love do but make children of us? I knew I should abandon the dream, but I was smitten. "Obsessed" might be a better way of putting it. I tried to act my age, but how did one act at nineteen, or any age, when love entered the equation?

I had made one grave error. Was I about to follow with another? How many mistakes did one make on the road to adulthood? Did we ever grow up?

If it was wrong to be with Kiva, why did I suddenly feel alive? There was no rational answer, and even if one had surfaced, I would have dismissed it.

I could not offer her anything but heartbreak.

"Things would have been different," I said one day on deck, somewhat apologetically, "if we had met back in America."

"I am sure of that," Kiva said sadly. "But we didn't. We're here on this ship, you going to Armenia, I to Haifa." She placed her index finger on my nose and traced it downward until her fingertip rested on my lips. She observed that I did not have the traditional hawkish nose that most New York Armenians she knew had.

With her finger lingering near my lips, I acted as if to bite it but instead reached for her hand and kissed her fingertips and was about to kiss her lips when I turned and saw David standing a few feet away.

He was enraged. He spoke directly to Kiva, avoiding eye contact with me.

"I wondered where you were. It's late." He paused for a moment and looked angrily at me. "Stay away from her."

I wanted to respond, but Kiva intervened. "We were sharing some memories."

"There are Armenians aboard. Let him share memories with his own people."

Kiva and I said our good nights, and as she took hold of David's arm, she turned to me and said she had had a wonderful evening.

As they strolled away, David raised his voice, chastising Kiva. Then he stopped and turned to warn me, "Keep away from her, if you know what's good for you."

As they turned the corner, Kiva glanced over her shoulder and blew me a kiss.

And I thought I had problems.

Chapter 15

CONSIDERING MY OPTIONS

I t was shortly after midnight when I returned to my cabin. I opened the door quietly, figuring that Mr. Simonian and Johnny were asleep. Johnny was, but Simonian wasn't. He was in bed reading by the light of a small lamp. When I entered, he put his book down, looked over his bifocals, and asked how I was doing.

I said I was fine.

He said, "She's pretty, very pretty."

His remark caught me by surprise. I decided to play it dumb and asked, "Who?"

He identified the young lady and smiled. He commented that he thought we made a handsome couple. I thanked him but said I didn't think we were a couple; we had just been sharing some thoughts. I didn't know what else to say.

Johnny, who had been sleeping with his face to the wall, turned and asked, "What the hell is going on?" Without waiting for an answer, he rolled around and went back to sleep.

Mr. Simonian and I remained silent for a few more seconds. Then he sat up and moved to the side of his bed. He put his book down on the table next to the bunk, grabbed his robe, and motioned for me to step out of the cabin. Though I was tired and wanting to sleep, I obliged, because I secretly hoped that he would help me.

We left the cabin and walked to the rail. The bright lights of Naples could be seen. Mr. Simonian's manner was pleasant, but there was concern on his face.

He asked if I would be leaving the ship in the morning. I said I would if we docked and were permitted to leave.

"And will you return to the ship?"

I told him that my plan was to find a way to get home. I added that I had enjoyed meeting him and appreciated his help.

He thanked me for being honest with him. He said he understood. But he couldn't assist me in any way, for he feared for my safety and wanted me to rethink things. I told him I was not seeking his help.

He said that if I stayed in Italy after the *Rossia* sailed, I would be considered an illegal alien. I had no passport or visa, and, in fact, I was not a citizen of any country. Without documents to prove who I was, the road home would be a long one. He implored me to reconsider.

"I don't care. I don't belong here. I am going home," I repeated.

Simonian slowly nodded his head as if he agreed. It was not wrong to want to go home, but everything was wrong with the way I wanted to do it, he argued. There would be no problem, he explained, if I found a sympathetic and understanding American embassy official. On the other hand, everything in Europe, especially in Italy, had been turned upside down by the war. People were struggling to survive. And whenever there was no food, people turned to illegal means to obtain what they needed.

"I can take care of myself," I assured him.

"I'm sure you can."

He sounded sarcastic to me, although he might not have meant to be, and I fired back, "If I had a passport, this would never have happened."

Simonian took a deep breath. "But you don't. None of us does. Understand, please understand, you are no longer considered an American citizen. Is that clear?"

It wasn't. There was no reason for me to believe that my nineteen years as an American didn't count for anything. There was only one thing for me to do, and that was to get in touch with an embassy official.

Chapter 16

ANOTHER CHANCE FOR FREEDOM

I spent another sleepless night. I got up at daybreak, and, after shaving and showering, I tossed on a pair of blue jeans, a T-shirt, and gym shoes, for the all-American look. Before I put my wallet into my hip pocket, I checked to make sure that the money was there. It was. I figured I had enough funds to last until I made contact with the American consulate. I wasn't thinking what would happen if the consulate turned a deaf ear to my plea or what I would use to purchase a ticket to get back home. Mr. Simonian had lent me money before, but I had returned it. I didn't want to ask for another loan, although I was sure he would have obliged.

I also decided against packing a suitcase. Lugging a suitcase to the gangplank would cause suspicion. And if Simonian were right, strolling around Naples with a suitcase would have lured undesirables.

I was extremely confident that after the people at the consulate heard my story, they would put me on the first plane to the States. I did not have the vaguest idea how the U.S. foreign service worked.

There was something in my life, though, that seemed to keep the demons away. I knew I had a guardian angel. I had had close calls before. Once, at the age of ten, when I crawled under the boxcar of a freight train, I had barely made it to the other side as the train started up. And one summer, my cousin, a high school diving star, and I went to Stony Creek to swim. He climbed and dove from a cliff into a rock-filled lake, making a perfect splash. I, who didn't know what it took to guide a body down from the cliff, followed him and barely missed the pointed edge of a rock. And when the same cousin and some friends and I walked a railroad bridge just before the train crossed, I knew that my guardian angel was there as I leaped to safety in the murky Detroit River and fought the strong current to shore, catching a glimpse of the train rushing overhead.

I knew now, as I walked down the *Rossia*'s gangplank and onto Italian soil, that I would not be coming back to the ship. I was going home.

~ IT WAS mid-November, and I could not have asked for better weather. There was a cloudless blue sky, a radiant sun, and a castle standing on top of a nearby cliff. Poets sang about the beauty of this land; its history embraced me as I took my first steps onto shore.

It was picture-postcard perfect. My fears and concerns dissipated in one deep sigh.

But it didn't take long to see that all was not as it appeared.

The boats in the harbor and the men and machines loading and unloading crates concealed the fact that Naples was a city hiding some deep social and economic wounds that had not yet healed.

Fascism had been born there, and its father, Benito Mussolini, had promised his countrymen a better life. An unholy alliance with Hitler assured the Italians of only grief and a one-way ticket to Dante's Inferno.

Naples was a tormented city in 1947. Its social decay, in the aftermath of the earth's most destructive war, had Romans looking to the East, not the West, for answers. They were on the verge of entering another suicidal pact, this time with a madman who had most of Europe in his clutches.

And I was seeking refuge there. Only the cunning and the ruthless would survive on these streets in the months ahead. Did I really want to join them?

For the moment, though, I felt like a caged bird that suddenly finds the cage door open. Fly away, fly away . . . but where was the nest?

Chapter 17

THE STREETS OF NAPLES

There were no phone books, no signs, and no roadways that pointed to the American embassy in Naples on that beautiful day.

"Mister, mister," in chorus they shouted. "You have chewing gum, no?"

"No, I have no chewing gum. Go away."

"Mister, mister, you American, no?"

"Yes, I am an American."

"You have American cigarettes, no?"

"No, I have no cigarettes. I don't smoke. Go away."

"Mister, mister, you want buy watch? Five dollars. Cheap. Very cheap. No?"

"I have watch. No need watch. *Merci.*"

The urchins lower their price. "Three dollars."

I shook my head no, and their disappointed dirty faces continued to beg.

What next?

"Mister, mister, come, come, I take you to girls. Beautiful girls, no?" said the eldest of the group.

"Go away," I said, and suddenly, surprisingly, they did. As fast as they had appeared, they disappeared behind me. I thought they had spotted a police officer, but that was not the case. They scampered in the direction of a group of repatriates who had just reached the street. *Good*, I said to myself. *They have spotted a bigger hunk of cheese.*

I began my trek toward the taller buildings that hovered over the dock's warehouses. There were no buses or cabs in the port area. I thought it strange that a major city like Naples, the third-largest city in Italy, did not have a transportation system. After all, two years had passed since the "unconditional surrender."

As I continued my walk on the potholed streets, I spotted groups of old men in strange hats, in rags, gathered at corners. Their language was more Germanic than Italian. As I strolled by, they turned and watched me. The one word they uttered that I understood was "Am-e-can." It was painful for me to look at them. They appeared hungry but did not ask for a handout. I had nothing to offer them, nor could I help them.

I continued on, turned a corner, and came across three old women, dressed completely in black, reminding me of what my grandmother wore. They were selling flowers and other items. They greeted me with smiles and pointed to the flowers. I raised my hand and showed my palm. "No, no, thank you," I said with a smile, shaking my head.

I felt helpless and wished I knew Italian, wished Kiva had been at my side. I realized that I would have to use body language to make myself understood the rest of the way.

One flower vendor, an elderly, hunched-over woman, refused to accept my excuses. I tried to explain that I didn't have any money to spend on flowers, that I needed every penny I had, and that I knew no one to give a flower to. She persisted, I resisted, and then she plucked one of the red roses from a bunch. Her eyes sparkling and her hand trembling, she presented it to me. Then she kissed me on my cheek.

I accepted the token of kindness and thanked her. I was an American, and I figured this was her way of showing appreciation to the America armed forces that had liberated her country.

I had nowhere else to put the rose, so I put it in the fold of my wallet.

As I walked, taking in the three-story apartment buildings and the churches that I passed, I wondered if I would ever find the embassy. I kept looking for a building that had an American flag on it, but none appeared.

I sat down in a park on a bench to contemplate what I should do.

"Buongiorno," said a round-faced, middle-aged, bespectacled gentleman, whose massive black hair with its streaks of white left the impression that he was a piano teacher.

I was startled that someone had spoken to me and did not immediately answer. Before I could explain that I didn't speak Italian, he had identified me as an American tourist.

"You're an American, aren't you?" he said in perfect English, again catching me off guard.

"Yes," I replied, and asked if he was an American, too.

"No, I'm Italian. But I lived in America many, many years ago." He asked if I was lost and needed any help. I told him I wasn't lost, but I hoped he could direct me to the American embassy.

With a smile that shattered any suspicion about his motive, the man told me that the United States had not reestablished its consulate in Naples and that to his knowledge, the nearest U.S. embassy was in Rome.

I did not want to hear that. I explained that I had just gotten off a ship and was visiting Naples, but I wanted to check in with embassy officials.

The gentleman rubbed his forehead with his hand, thought a moment, and said that I would have to go to Rome. It was an hour or two by train, he told me, and suggested that I not take the bus, even though it would be cheaper. They were very unreliable, and you never knew if you would make it. There were still bandits in the mountains.

I nodded and thanked him for the information. I got up and had begun to walk out of the park when he shouted to me, "Son, take your wallet out of your hip pocket. The pickpockets are the best in Italy!"

I thanked him again.

The news about the embassy threw a monkey wrench into my immediate plans, but I was determined. I needed to find the train station. It was getting hot, and I was beginning to sweat. I was also getting hungry, but I didn't dare spend any money on food until I knew what it would cost to get to Rome. I continued toward the piazza, and with each step, I found the load on my shoulders getting heavier. I needed divine intervention. But Rome apparently was not in the business of hearing the prayers of Neapolitans, since the Communists were winning the people over by the thousands. Why should my prayers be answered?

It was midday and hot, and I was sweating and hungry.

As I strolled past many fountains adorned by statues of angels, I realized that if there was any time I needed guidance, it was then. I passed store windows that reminded me of Hudson's in downtown Detroit and stopped to look. I wasn't happy with the reflection I saw.

Shit! What a mess I'm in.

I looked up and prayed for help. *Damn it, I need some help down here. Get off your cloud, will you?* I stared into the window. "You're . . . you're fired!" I shouted in anger at my image, and I thought, *You deserve this crap.*

A soft voice murmured behind me, "I'm unemployed at the present time. I could use a job."

I turned and looked at the angelic figure behind me. It was Kiva. In one swoop, I picked her up and brought her lips to mine. The anger, the hurt, and the fear were replaced with ecstasy.

"Does this mean I'm hired?"

Chapter 18

AN ANGEL APPEARS

I poured my guts out to Kiva. I told her I needed to find the embassy, that there was none in Naples and Rome was my best bet. I wanted to go home. I took a deep breath and waited for her to say something.

She laughed. "So, she is that beautiful." And with a smile, she said, "Let's find the train station."

It was shortly after noon when Kiva and I began our walk hand-in-hand through the narrow streets of war-scarred Naples. She wore a white sleeveless cotton dress, which draped loosely over her lithe body, cinching in at the waist. Small blue, six-pointed-star buttons, beginning at the deep V neckline, extended the full length of the front of the dress, ending at mid-calf. The dress must have been chosen carefully for the hot weather. Kiva's mere physical presence would have stirred the imagination of any man, no matter what she wore. She was one of those rare women who are alluring and provocative not because of what they wear or the jewelry they display but for their demeanor. She was sensual, knew it, but did not flaunt it.

As we strolled, our bodies at times inadvertently brushing, I felt myself blushing, wondering what she really thought of me. Did she think I was as weak as I appeared? I also dreamed of what it would be like to make love with her. But the image of lovemaking quickly dissipated in a wave of reality checks. I needed her help, not her body. There would be no tomorrow for us.

I was extremely jealous of David. I could not understand why he wasn't with her.

My concern now had to be my resources. Remembering the advice of the man in the park, I touched my hip pocket to confirm that my wallet was still there. I was embarrassed that Kiva noticed the movement.

"Do you have enough money to get to Rome?" she asked.

I told her I didn't know and checked the amount I had in my wallet.

"They aren't rubles, are they?" She laughed.

"No, of course not. They're American dollars."

"Good. Rubles are worthless."

I told her I didn't have much money.

The Soviet Union, she said, was the only country in the world whose money was not only worthless but where money was not an asset. I wondered how she knew so much about the Soviets, but since I was not going to the Soviet Union anyway, I didn't care. She continued calmly, emphasizing each word, stressing that my road back to the United States was not going to be an easy one. She told me this not to discourage me but rather to prepare me for the obstacles that might appear before me. She repeated almost verbatim what Mr. Simonian had told me the night before. If I were stopped and questioned by Italian police and could not present them with documents, I would probably be detained and considered an illegal alien.

Kiva looked at me, her dark eyes serious as she said, "Do not talk to strangers while you're on the train. And don't be surprised if the embassy officials turn their backs on you."

I looked at her, surprised. "Why the hell not? They're there to help, aren't they?"

"No, they aren't. They are there to protect their own asses. Not yours. Because you don't have an American passport and were en route to the Soviet Union, you're too controversial. In fact, you had joined the enemy's camp. They could order you to stand in the back of the line until they investigate your claims. And that, my dear, handsome ex-American, may take years."

Fuck. Fuck. Fuck. No, I didn't say those expletives aloud. I muttered them to myself.

As we walked along, she continued to attract the eyes of passersby. She did not avoid eye contact with strangers on the streets, as many women do, but would greet those who glanced with a pleasant, innocent smile, using the appropriate Italian words. Kiva spoke Italian flawlessly, I surmised. She even paused and talked with the men I had seen earlier, dressed in the long coats and strange hats. Each had his hair in a single braid. She appeared saddened by these short chats but would not reveal to me their content.

To my inquiry, she simply answered, "Someday life will be good for them, but today is not that day." I didn't understand, and Kiva knew it. I would eventually piece the puzzle together.

Women, the few on the streets, looked long and enviously at her. She was charming as well as charismatic. I told her they were being very rude staring at her the way they did. She smiled at me and said that they were really looking at me. She said they were wondering what this young, handsome American was doing on their streets with this ugly Italian. They wanted to know where this American had come from and why he was walking so nonchalantly on their street. Then, with a twinkle, she warned, "Beware, Italian women can be very seductive."

I accepted her humor with laughter and paused before I countered, telling her that if they were glancing at me, it was because next to me they saw the most beautiful woman in the world.

"Now I am sure you have Jewish blood in you," she said with a smile.

I automatically told her I did not.

"Prove it," she fired back.

I blushed.

She turned and gently kissed me on my lips. "Maybe you should come to Haifa with us."

"Thanks for the invitation. But I think I'd better restore my American citizenship before I go anywhere else."

We laughed together. It was such a relief to have someone like her at my side. She said that we were made from the same mold. In the same breath, she said that we had better hurry to the train depot.

We strolled past ruins of medieval churches whose towers had collapsed from the bombings. Debris was strewn nearby, and workers were busy trying to restore the edifices. Scars of the war remained everywhere. So this was what was left when the armies left, I thought. What man took centuries to build was destroyed in a flash. God forbid we would have another war.

Despite the scorching heat of the afternoon, workers laughed, joked, and played as they attempted to put back what their ancestors had accomplished.

We entered a section of the city where the streets were lined with little shops of all kinds, filled with everything one would find in American stores, with patrons rushing in and out with handbags made of cloth, filled with an assortment of items. There were no queues, but it seemed that people were haggling, arguing, shouting in the marketplace. I was surprised; Kiva wasn't.

"In every society, there will be people with wealth. What one loses the other will win."

The streets became tree-lined boulevards, with colorful cafés where men sat and drank their coffee, read their newspapers, and glanced up from time to time to catch a glimpse of whoever or whatever passed by. Men of all ages played the game. Kiva remarked that Italians were great for singing, sitting, sex, and talking politics. I thought that an interesting observation but wondered when and if they worked and where the women were.

"Either making babies, pregnant, or looking for a man who could pay the bills." She smiled as she said it. She reminded me that there was no divorce in Italy; the pope wouldn't allow that. No official divorce, anyway. Italians, like the French, kept mistresses.

The word "mistress" confused me, and I asked for clarification.

My question was greeted with spontaneous laughter. People at the tables of a nearby café, who had not been watching us, looked our way. Shaking her head in disbelief at my ignorance of life, Kiva explained. A mistress was a sex object, to be used, supported, and then tossed for another as soon as she became too demanding or too costly or wanted the man to divorce his wife for her.

She painted an unpleasant portrait of men, I told her.

"Don't all men have secrets? Two faces?"

I said I couldn't speak for all men but that I didn't.

"Take a look at them," she said, pointing to the café crowd. "They would give anything to get into bed with me." She addressed a table of unsuspecting Italians, catching the lecherous old men off guard. "Good afternoon. I am not for sale today." She laughed. The men sat there with their mouths open, speechless.

After she translated what she had said, I was embarrassed. "How far is that train station?" I asked.

"Just around the corner," she replied.

When we reached the station, she told me to wait outside. She said it would be best for her to purchase the ticket.

"Two, please," I suggested.

"Only one."

Kiva warned me not to talk or even look at strangers until she got back. I handed her my wallet. Shortly afterward, she returned with a ticket to Rome and my change. Passage was booked for the following day because the train had already departed at seven that morning.

She asked if I wanted to see the city and visit the castle on top of the hill. I was more than happy to have her accompany me.

The asphalt street yielded to a cobblestone path, which led into a wooded area and up a steep gravel incline. Looking above the treetops, I could see the medieval castle—the one I had seen from the bay—

majestically seated on the clifftop. We paused briefly, and I wondered if we could make it to the top.

The afternoon heat was unbearable. The sun had roasted our faces and arms. Kiva asked if I was game. If she was, I surely was.

We began our ascent, following pebbles to a sandy path into the darkness of the forest, whose branches acted as an umbrella with their gigantic outstretched limbs. They blocked the sun's rays from penetrating, creating an eerie, darkened path. It was silent in the tunnel, but I felt, as Dorothy did, that there were strange creatures on the yellow brick road.

We found the tunnel inhabited by men, women, and children of all ages, all undernourished, their bodies draped with rags. The discards of Italian society. No, said Kiva, those with courage who had survived the Nazi concentration camps in Italy. They hid and waited for their day in the sun. Cardboard, charred boards, and debris from shattered buildings made up their housing stock. Meals were cooked on bonfires. Surely, the police knew these masses existed, yet they had not been helped or provided accommodations. Nor had they been dispersed.

Why had Kiva led me here?

"These are illegal aliens," she said pointedly. She did not say another word until we emerged on the other side of the tunnel.

We paused to catch our breath, and even though the air was hot, it was refreshing. We proceeded to the castle, looked up at its huge walls and turrets and down into the moat. The view was breathtaking. We walked to the ledge and stood there above the Bay of Naples. There I thought nature was at its best, earth and the universe before me. If only I could find such harmony within myself. Was this what Kiva had wanted me to see? In the distance stood the awesome Mount Vesuvius, the sleeping giant volcano, the playground of the gods, nemesis of Pompeii and Hercules, timeless witness of earth's permanence and man's insanity and cruelty. Was it mocking or pitying me today?

From my vantage point, at that moment in time, nature's panorama offered me an unforgettable glimpse of what the Romans saw: a vast and inviting sea before them, challenging them to look beyond, yet unconquerable and untamable. Only the gods knew what the future would hold for these people, for all of mankind.

"Kiva, everything here is so beautiful, so peaceful."

"It is, isn't it?" She looked down to the bay and, without looking at me, as if reciting before a class or a crowd, began a story. Her father had brought her to this cliff as a child before Europe entered its madness. He was on a business trip, purchasing antiques and art. She wanted to see it again and share it with someone, someone like me. She said that I was so much like him, so innocent and naive.

"Like your father?" I asked.

She did not answer but broke the melancholy mood by saying that we would share our time, at least until the next beautiful girl caught my eye.

"Not fair," I said.

She conceded that nothing was fair after the first breath of life, that death had its own claim on all of us.

"The hell it does!" I exclaimed. "Not on me!" I was serious.

She laughed, saying, "Now, that's much better. You will be a survivor." How I wished I had been a part of her life back in New York or she a part of mine in Detroit.

We discussed which presented more of a challenge to man, the mountain or the sea, climbing to the top or staying afloat. "Both are part of life," she said.

Before we began our descent, she maneuvered me to a spot on the cliff. I moved as she asked without a question. She stood at my side and told me to close my eyes. I did. As I stood waiting for her next command, I asked her if she was going to push me over the edge. It would be the perfect murder; they would never find my body down there.

I had seen too many Hollywood movies, she said. Besides, she had other plans for my body. I was intrigued. Then Kiva told me that Lord Byron's mistress had had the great poet do as she had just ordered me to do. Byron had stood there, Kiva alleged, as I had, eyes closed, and when he opened his eyes, he got a surprise that lasted a lifetime.

"And what was that?" I asked.

She said that Byron had also wondered if his mistress wasn't going to give him that extra shove over the cliff because he had not divorced his wife. I told Kiva I thought she had read too many Agatha Christie novels. She told me to open my eyes.

"And what do you see?"

"The most beautiful woman in the world."

That, she said, was the right answer and what Lord Byron had told his mistress. Kiva lifted her lips to mine and kissed me in a way that I would never forget.

Below, in the bay, sailboats and small craft skirted swiftly over the blue and turquoise waters of the glassy sea, a sea that seemed to reach as far as the ends of the earth. On the horizon, the sun was lingering to greet the stars and the moon, and dusk was swiftly arriving. Pint-sized tugboats sounded off belligerently, releasing steam and black clouds into the sky as if to prove their superiority over the silent giants they had in tow. The subservient larger ships, with little resistance, acquiesced, for they had no recourse but to follow their leaders into safe harbor. Seagulls, riding the currents of soft, warm breezes, tailgated the ships, seeking handouts, the impatient ones skimming the waves until their eyes caught a glimpse of the dinner special and dove to retrieve their meal. Then, just as quickly, they soared to the skies. I envied their freedom. We could see long stretches of sandy beaches, their sands now starlike, sparkling, inviting the casual swimmer. The warm breeze and the sea called to us, as they had to the Romans in bygone times, to come and play and escape from the heat of life, to refresh the body and the soul there in the warm waters of the Mediterranean. The beaches were barren now, for the inhabitants knew it was November, and only the seagulls played.

"How peaceful," I said, breaking the solemn moment of our thoughts.

"Very."

"Peace like in our times," I said with a smile, and was surprised at her reply.

"There will never be peace in any time. I told you, you are like my father," she continued, "and like David. You men are all dreamers!"

I was surprised to hear her mention her father and David together, and I wondered about the connection.

For a second, she hesitated before she said that David believed there would be a State of Israel one day. And when that happened, the Jews of the world would gather in the Promised Land, and the scriptures would be fulfilled.

"And your father, does he believe that, too?"

"No. He's dead." Her eyes did not show one bit of remorse, and I wondered why. She did not miss a beat. "What dreamers! Even if the United Nations was scheduled to vote in a few weeks on the Palestine Partition Resolution, if the Jewish state became a reality, would the millions of Arabs who surround the Jews welcome them with open arms? There will be no peace, and both sides will draw in others, for war is inevitable." Kiva's body was shaking and trembling all over. Suddenly, she moved closer to the cliff's edge and shouted to the world, "Dreamers! Dreamers of the world, wake up! The only things you have to lose are your heads if you don't!"

I couldn't and didn't try to reason with her. I just wanted to know everything I could about her and said so.

"Why?" She laughed. "Soon you'll be a paragraph on a page of my life. I don't even think I will make it onto one of your pages."

I asked if she was hungry. She said she was famished. I suggested we find a restaurant, and she said that was probably the most sensible thing I had said all afternoon and the best offer she had had all day.

Chapter 19

THE LAST SUPPER

On one of the ridges overlooking the bay, we found a restaurant. A dark-haired gentleman with a bounce in his gait greeted Kiva and me with a smile. He led us into the dining room, but when Kiva saw the terrace, she asked if we could sit outside. The waiter warned us that it was very hot on the veranda, but Kiva didn't care.

With the waiter in the lead, we strolled through the dining area. It was immaculate, with oak floors and statues of Roman gods and the Caesars dominating in several niches. Although employees moved gingerly about and there was a symphony of Italian voices coming from the kitchen, the silence in the restaurant made it feel more like a museum or a library. Elaborate canvases in gilded frames depicted restless seas, fierce winds, and tossing sailboats struggling to make the bay. Vesuvius dominated one large canvas that Kiva paused to admire. Royal red tablecloths and napkins, polished silverware, and gold-rimmed dinnerware placed flawlessly on the tables quickly reminded me that I might not have enough money to pay the bill. I prayed that I did. It would be too embarrassing otherwise.

From the terrace, we could look straight down at the sea and watch the toylike freighters and steamers enter and leave the harbor. I was mesmerized by the magnificent view. I wondered where these people got their money, then remembered what Kiva told me, that even in the worst of times there are those who can make it the best of times.

The proprietor approached our table, and I thought he might ask us to leave because I was improperly dressed. My T-shirt, blue jeans, and gym shoes were definitely out of place. But he greeted us with a bow and a smile and asked me if I was an American. I said I was.

After he left, Kiva said, "That's good."

"What's good?" I asked.

"You have learned to lie."

When the waiter returned and presented us with menus, I glanced not at what food was available but at the cost of the items. I was stymied. The prices were listed in lira, and I had no concept of exchange rates.

I asked Kiva to order for both of us. She selected red wine and pasta. I admitted that I had never had wine. She laughed and said it was on her family's dining table every night. I asked her to ask the maitre d' if they accepted American dollars.

"They'll take anything except—"

"Except Russian rubles," I finished her sentence for her.

She smiled.

We sat across from each other at a table for two, overlooking the Mediterranean, and what else, except the restoration of my America passport, could I have asked for?

A waiter brought us the wine list, and his face lit up as he chatted briefly with Kiva. He was certain that she had been raised in northern Italy, probably Florence. He said she spoke Italian better than the Italians. I heard the names of cities, Dresden and New York.

Raised in Dresden, and she spoke Italian! What other secrets did Kiva hide behind that gorgeous smile?

When we were alone, she explained that Italians, like the French and the Spanish, but not the Germans or the Baltic peoples, were very gregarious and eager to exchange tidbits with strangers. They wanted to know everything; Americans wanted to know how much you had in the bank.

"And Russians?" I asked.

Russians, she said, were very suspicious of foreigners. The czars, Peter the Great being the exception, didn't want anything to do with Western Europe. They had dropped an iron curtain across their land long before Stalin came into power. Stalin had studied history and exploited it and his serfs well. "But why should you care," she said sarcastically. "After all, you will be in Rome dining with the pope very soon."

The waiter arrived with the wine, opened the bottle, and poured some into my glass. He looked at me as I waited for him to pour Kiva's glass. I became nervous, for I did not know what I was supposed to do. Kiva rescued me. She told me to take a sip, turn the wine in my mouth, drink it, and then tell the waiter it was excellent.

I wondered what to do if I didn't like the wine. What should I say then? Reading my mind, she added that even if it wasn't, I should say it was excellent.

"Excellent," I said to the waiter after tasting the wine. Then he poured wine into Kiva's glass, turned, and filled mine. She raised her glass and said we should drink to my quick and safe return home.

I thanked her and quietly added, "And to the most wonderful girl in the universe."

We toasted everyone and everything. I was surprised at how smoothly the wine went down, bottle after bottle.

"Was she pregnant?" Kiva asked.

"Who?"

"The girl you left behind."

"No, she was *not* pregnant."

"Good. Only a cad would do that."

"Do what?"

"Abandon a girl when she needs him most."

After the second, or was it the third, glass of wine, I hardly knew where I was. I decided to ask her how many broken hearts she had left behind on the wharves in New York.

She said, "Only one."

"Whose?"

"My own. I loved New York."

I had enough wine in me to ask her about her past. Germany, Dresden, and a New York accent? How and when had this all come about?

Kiva laughed and asked, "Do you really want to know?"

"Yes, Kiva, I really want to know. I am fascinated by you, and you know that."

She said that her father had been a very prosperous art dealer, as was his father before him. The family name went back centuries in the city noted for its culture. She remembered her father as being quite debonair, gallant. He had been respected by everyone, and he had believed in everyone. He was tall and had dark hair and long eyelashes—handsome. I reminded her so much of him in many ways. She said she would never forget him.

She paused and took another sip of wine. She said the wine was good, but she wasn't surprised, for Italian wines were the best. Her conversation skipped from one topic to another, like a bird flitting from one tree branch to another. Instead of Germany and her father, she switched unexpectedly to killing.

She looked at me seriously and asked, "Have you ever killed another human being?"

I was amazed. "Kiva," I whispered, "I couldn't even kill a fly."

She smiled. "David told me you couldn't kill."

"David? How did he get into this?"

Kiva's face lit up. "David has killed. And he would kill again. And again." She explained that he had killed Nazis during the war.

She said that the day in the ship's dining hall when David had strolled over and asked for the salt, he was really on an exploratory mission. Some in the group had believed that I was going to the Soviet Union to be a spy, and David wanted to get a closer look at me.

He believed that eyes told a lot about a person, that the eyes were windows to a man's character.

I told her that I didn't know anything about David or the group, but

I didn't think that killing was a solution. Negotiation, face-to-face, across tables, words would lead to solutions, not more wars.

"Yes, Tommy, peace in our time."

Of her life in New York, Kiva said that she'd hated it at first. Everything was strange. Americans were cold, especially to those who had accents. Her heart was back in Dresden, with her father and mother and elder brother and everything she loved. In America, she lost herself in her books, at movies and plays and Broadway musicals, and, with her brother, she took swimming lessons. She got so good that she swam on the club team. But there was always a cloud over her that prevented happiness from penetrating. No matter how much or how hard she wrestled with her past, she found herself living there.

The appearance of stars and a full moon awakened us to the reality that it was getting late. There were more couples in the restaurant now, and it appeared that a young American man with his beautiful dark-haired companion were slowly becoming the center of attention. Were we drunk? At least two couples questioned me in Italian, and I had to defer to Kiva, who satisfied them. She told them that yes, I was an American, and my ship was leaving in the morning.

Someone nearby looked over at us and said something that made Kiva laugh. I demanded the translation.

"He wanted to know if we are newlyweds."

"What did you tell him?"

"I told him we are on our honeymoon."

"You're joking," I said. Another look at Kiva, and I knew she wasn't joking.

"Why should I spoil the fun?" she said, and leaned over to give me a passionate kiss to seal her argument. The crowd applauded.

I waved to the waiter and asked for the check. He came to the table, and I took out the money to pay. The waiter shook his head. Again, I turned to Kiva for an explanation. She talked to the waiter, and after a rapid exchange in Italian, I noticed a surprised look on her face.

I asked what the problem was. Was the bill exorbitant?

Kiva explained that our dinner was a wedding gift, compliments of the owner. I felt guilty, but I accepted the generous gesture with a smile.

After we were outside, I asked Kiva what she and the waiter had talked about. She said he had wished us happiness in our life together. I asked if he'd said anything else. Casually, Kiva remarked that he had suggested that since we were such a beautiful couple, we would make many beautiful children. My response was an embarrassed silence.

Chapter 20

TICKET TO ROME

T he sun had baked us.
        Beads of sweat had formed on my forehead and meandered down my face, my neck, and my body, thoroughly soaking my clothing. My T-shirt was glued to my back and chest. The blue jeans had not stood up to the heat, either.

I did not have time to think about appearances, for I realized that I was soon to lose Kiva.

Everything would be better soon, I tried to reassure myself. Through Kiva, I was learning about the world of passports, visas, illegal aliens, and displaced persons. Although I had heard of concentration camps and the skeletonlike human beings who survived Hitler's slave camps, until now, I had seen only the images in newsreels, in Lowell Thomas's "Time Marches On!"

Castles and seas and beautiful landscapes and stories about great poets told by a beautiful young woman had opened a new world for me, which unfortunately would become only a memory. I tried not to think about it. I tried to convince myself that soon I would be knocking on the U.S. Embassy door.

Kiva was silent while we walked. She, too, had also paid a price for her afternoon in the sun. Her dress was drenched with perspiration. Occasionally, she would pull it away from her body, and I would notice the nipples of her breasts. I would secretively glance her way, then quickly look away. She didn't seem to mind and even smiled. The exposed parts of her body—her arms and face, even parts of her legs— were baked red by the sun. Her nose was completely sunburned.

As we passed a store window, she stopped, grabbed my hand, hauled me to the display window, and said, "Look!" I did not recognize the creatures in the reflection. They must have been aliens from the red planet. My face was scorched. We would each pay for our foolishness the next day, but there would be no next day for us.

It was not an easy walk. Each step brought us closer to being farther apart. Our next good-bye would be our final good-bye. We knew it and did not want to talk about it. We began to chatter about everything but our parting.

We stopped, and I turned and looked at her. "Kiva, buy another ticket. Come with me. Come with me to Rome!"

"You're crazy." She pulled out the reality card and tossed it into my face. "Good," she said. "Let's go together. And we'll make love all the way to Rome. What then? What do we eat, and where do we stay the day after tomorrow? How will you support me while we wait for my visa, your passport? Or did I suddenly forget that I don't have a passport? And if, God forbid, the Italian authorities arrest you—and me—then what? My dear and handsome dreamer, dream on. Isn't that what got you here in the first place?"

I tried to think of something to say. I couldn't.

"I have a better idea."

"What?" I said, hoping for a solution.

"Let's go swimming."

"Now who's crazy?" I took a second look at her. "You're serious."

"Yes."

"Kiva," I said with some doubt in my tone, "I don't have a bathing suit."

"Neither do I. Who needs a bathing suit to swim?"

Chapter 21

A NEAPOLITAN NIGHT

We twisted and turned down narrow streets and through dark alleys. I hadn't questioned whether Kiva knew where she was going; she obviously did. No matter where you were in Naples, you were only a short distance from the sea, and soon I could hear the rhythm of the waves and the shrieking calls of the gulls. We came out of a wooded area onto a sandy beach. A few hundred yards before us was the Mediterranean.

The flora in this remote area of the bay provided a haven for wildlife and young lovers. Birds squawked as Kiva and I disturbed their nightly rituals. We were as startled as they were, but they seemed to accept us.

We reached a deserted area of the beach.

I looked out at the magnificence of the sea. I had not noticed that Kiva had kicked off her shoes and her white dress had slipped from her body. She was naked. Stark naked.

"Take a good look," she whispered. "It's going to have to last you a lifetime." She put her arms around me, kissed my neck, and whispered into my ears, "I was a child, and he was a child, in this kingdom by the sea; but we loved with a love that was more than love."

She kissed me, then bolted from my arms and dashed toward the sea. I watched, entranced, as this raven flew across the warm sands. She reached the shoreline, turned, and said, "Are you coming in?" With that, she raced into the waves, dove into one of the whitecaps, and disappeared. For a second or two, all I did was stand there spellbound. I could see Kiva's arms cutting through the water, and I could hear her shouting. "The water is great! I love it . . . I love it!"

Then, suddenly, complete silence.

I stood looking, searching for her. When she didn't appear, I raced to the shoreline. I waited, but all I felt were the waves silently brushing against my feet. I shouted her name, pleaded with her not to play games. Still no response. I peeled off my jeans and T-shirt and dashed into the sea, looking for a trace of her, wondering if she had hit her head on a rock. The water reached my neck. Panic was setting in. There were no signs of her. Something grabbed my ankles. In seconds, I was flipped into the water. I gasped for air and suddenly found myself entwined with Kiva. I mumbled something about how she'd had me there for a moment.

"But dear," she whispered in my ear, "I haven't had you yet."

Her breasts pressed against my chest as we kissed. When our lips parted, she asked in a whisper if I had ever made love in the sea. I said no. I hungered for her. When she drew me inside her and held me close, we moved to the rhythm of the sea. We became part of each other and part of the sea. I longed to tell her how much I loved her, I ached to find the words, but she put a finger to my lips. "Hush," she said, moaning. "Do not say one word. Do not spoil it."

I would not have done that for anything in this world.

We struggled, hand-in-hand, to the shore. I reached down, picked up her dress, and handed it to her. Then I got my jeans and shoes. After we had walked a few feet in silence, she tossed her dress down onto the sand and sat on it. She pulled me to her.

"Make love to me," she whispered, "and never stop."

Under the star-filled sky, we were tired, warm, and aching for each other. She told me that from this night forward, every time I saw a body of water, I should think of her. I promised I would. She then gently put her head on my shoulder. "There will be others, but think of me. Please, remember me."

If I had been more attentive, I would have noticed the tears in her eyes. I would have heard the whisper in the wind, the tragic tale of Annabel Lee, "that the wind came out of the cloud by night, chilling and killing my Annabel Lee."

I never forgot you, Kiva. I never forgot that night.

Chapter 22

RETURN TO SHIP

K iva and I were a mess. Her dress was dripping wet from the sea, and grains of sand were embedded in her hair, glowing and sparkling. I was a living sandman, with jeans and T-shirt and body that needed to be washed down and washed out from head to toe.

Kiva suggested that we go back to the ship and shower and dress. I couldn't go on the train the way I looked. She didn't think His Eminence would grant me an audience, looking as I did.

I didn't want to return to the *Rossia,* but I knew I had to. In spite of the moon and the stars, it was a very dark night. We made our way through the streets, occasionally marked with shadowy figures. When we reached the shipyard, we kissed. And kissed again. She reminded me that I had until midnight to get off the ship, then the ship's crew would draw up the gangplank. I told her I would see her in Haifa. She told me I was full of shit.

She turned and disappeared into the darkness.

I was certain that I would never see her again.

I raced up the *Rossia's* gangplank and to my cabin. I was showering when I heard Johnny come into the room. Mr. Simonian followed shortly afterward. When I emerged from the shower, both of my cabin mates looked at me strangely. At first, I thought the sand had not washed off, but then, as I looked into the mirror, I saw what they saw: I was sunburned. Johnny said that my face was redder than a Washington apple.

But there was a mysterious look on Simonian's face that I could not trace. He did not say anything but only smiled, and that said everything. Under his suspicious eyes, I began taking out a white shirt, a blue sports jacket, and a pair of gray gabardine slacks.

"It's quite late, isn't it? To be dressing up?" Mr. Simonian commented.

"Mother used to say that if I was down and out, a good shower and fine clothes would perk me up."

"It is truly an old Armenian saying," Simonian said, nodding his head.

I told Simonian that I needed some fresh air.

"I would think you had enough in Naples."

I wasn't in the mood to argue with him. As I dressed, I felt Simonian's eyes following my every move. He looked at me as if he were a boxer eyeing his opponent right after the bell had rung. Johnny preferred the verbal bout, and he separated us.

"You really look sharp in that jacket. If she has a friend, I can get ready in ten minutes. Make that five!"

I told Johnny there was no friend. I wanted to stroll the deck.

"Good hunting, then."

My watch told me that it was almost half past ten, so I had little time to lose. I needed to get back to the city and the station.

When Simonian insisted again that it was quite late, I said with a huge grin on my face that I was getting off the ship, taking a cab to the train depot, and going to Rome to meet with embassy officials in order to go home.

"You're kidding," said Johnny. He suddenly burst into laughter and said I wouldn't dare.

Simonian was not laughing. He looked at me as if he were a mongoose sizing up a cobra. "Are you sure you don't want to talk this over with someone who has been down your path?"

I looked directly at him, studying his face and each line etched into it, each hair on his bushy eyebrows, which were standing out like porcupine quills.

"No, Mr. Simonian," I said with a deep sigh. "There is nothing else to talk about."

I felt guilty because he had been so helpful and so kind to me.

I walked to the door, turned the doorknob, and left the cabin.

Chapter 23

IN SEARCH OF KIVA

Thunder and lightning greeted me on the ship's deck. The sea was restless. A storm, the first of the journey, was about to break, and I needed to get to the station in a hurry. Although it had not yet hit with its entire might, it was gathering strength and energy in the distance. Eardrum-piercing thunder heralded its approach. I had always loved the storms that came off the lakes in Michigan, and I wasn't afraid of one that would come out of the Mediterranean. I welcomed it.

But I needed to see Kiva for one last time. To thank her. To give her my address and telephone number in Detroit.

I cursed fate for having brought us together and then separated us in one breath. My heart pounded faster as I thought of her. Time was not on my side. When I reached the gangplank, the wind quit, and the rain came straight down. I found shelter in an alcove, which gave me a clear view of the walkway. I watched as several rain-drenched passengers struggled up the gangplank. I could barely make out their faces, but I overheard one of them say that he was happy to get aboard before the full force of the storm hit.

"This ship may not leave harbor tomorrow," I heard another voice say.

I stood there waiting and struggling with myself. If only I could see Kiva one more time.

"Tommy, you're not going to go through with this," said a familiar voice in the darkness.

I turned to see a rain-soaked Mr. Simonian in his robe looking right in my face.

"And why not?" I asked.

"Because tomorrow morning, you'll either be dead or in the hands of the authorities."

"Bullshit. I will be in Rome. Just leave, leave me alone, please."

He shook his head and repeated his message so passionately that I felt he was begging me to stay.

I told him that I did not understand him. A few days before, he had been willing to help me. Now, suddenly, adamantly, he stood against it. "Damn it, Mr. Simonian, whose side are you on?"

"Son, I will always be on your side." He took off his steel-rimmed spectacles, wiped off the raindrops with a handkerchief, and replaced them on his face. "In Marseilles, I have friends who fought side-by-side with me in the Spanish Civil War. I would do anything for them, and they for me. You would be guaranteed a safe journey home if I presented you to them. There are no such guarantees here in Italy. You would be a lamb among wolves."

He seized my shoulders, grasping them with both hands. I could feel the power in his fingers. He repeated softly but forcefully, "Don't do this."

"I'm going home."

He finally seemed to give up. He turned and left me.

"God, where are you, Kiva!" I moaned.

"Well, if you turn around, I'm right next to you."

I was shocked. I didn't believe it. She was there.

"What was that all about?"

"Let's get out of the rain, and I will tell you."

It was eleven o'clock. We had one hour. She led me down a flight of stairs into a maze of corridors. She walked a step or two in front of me because of the narrow hallway. She whispered, without turning to see my face, that she thought I would have been off the ship by then. The storm rocked the boat and us as we made our way to her cabin. She turned and asked, "He didn't want you to get off the ship, did he?"

I didn't know what to say. We reached her room. She opened the door, and we walked into the darkness.

I asked where the lights were. She said we didn't need them. I started to say something but forgot what I wanted to say. I forgot everything as she told me to lock the door. I did. I removed her raincoat and kissed her. We moved toward her bed, but it was too small to accommodate us. I grabbed the mattress and tossed it off its frame. Then I knelt down and pulled her to me. We were in our own cocoon. We clung to each other. We wanted the world to go away and leave us be. We laughed and cried. But they were tears of joy that we could spend another hour together.

Exhausted, we fell asleep in each other's arms.

Chapter 24

NAKED AWAKENING

The early rays of the morning sun penetrated the cabin's lone port-hole and caught Kiva's sleeping face. I watched as she slowly opened her eyes, rubbed them, and turned to kiss me. She suddenly pushed my body from hers. The smile on that beautiful face faded abruptly.

Her first no was soft. The second was louder, and the third reached eardrum-shattering decibels.

Neither of us had heard the ship's engines start or the tugboats guiding the ship away from the dock and through the harbor. The *Rossia* was en route to Port Said.

The reality had struck Kiva first. She sat up, not believing what her senses told her had happened, and it was her moans of disbelief, repeated over and over, that convinced me that something was definitely wrong.

"We're out at sea!" she shouted in my face. "I'm sorry, Tommy, I am so sorry!"

The rueful awakening had belatedly sunk into my senses. She told me to listen. I did. I heard the ship's engines groaning. I heard the waves brushing against the hull of the ship and reached to kiss her as the rising sun hit my eyes. Sun at night . . . impossible! Before our lips met, she gently shoved me back, and I finally understood. We were at sea. I was not at the train station. Or off the ship.

The pleasure of the evening became the pain of the morning.

I stood up, naked, and ran to the porthole, hoping that the overwhelming evidence was a figment of my imagination, that the real *Rossia* was still docked in Naples, that it was night, and that I could get off the ship. But from the porthole, I could see the Italian coastline slowly fading in the distance. The ship was heading south, and I was still aboard.

I—we, in our bliss—had overslept.

I heard footsteps coming down the hallway, echoing loudly in the corridor as they neared. Whoever it was stopped in front of Kiva's door. There came a soft knock, followed by a man's voice asking Kiva if she was up.

Kiva clamped my mouth shut with one hand and with the other put a finger to her lips for silence. She answered that she had just stepped out of the shower and was getting dressed.

"Can I come in?" was the next question.

"No, David, I'm dressing."

He asked if she was all right. Tightening her hand on my mouth to ensure that I wouldn't say a word, she responded that she was and that she would join the group in a few minutes. He asked again if he could come in. She responded again, but this time nervously, that she still wasn't dressed. I watched as the door handle slowly turned. I was glad I had locked it. I was certain he would have entered if I hadn't.

"I'll see you at breakfast, then?" he asked.

"Yes, yes, at breakfast."

His footsteps moved away from the door.

Kiva took a long, deep sigh as she released her hand from my mouth. She kissed me. "Tommy," she said, "maybe you didn't realize this, but David is my brother."

There was a long silence.

We dressed and left the cabin together. She headed to the dining hall for breakfast, and I went to my cabin. Johnny was still asleep and did not move a muscle, but Simonian sat up in his bunk when he heard me open the door. His eyes lit up, and those bushy eyebrows seemed to dance when he saw me.

"My dear boy," he said. "You don't know how happy I am that you took my advice."

Chapter 25

A HEARTY BREAKFAST

W hile I was in the shower, Simonian dressed and left the cabin, I assumed for breakfast. Many thoughts raced through my mind. I filed them under "To be dealt with later." I was tired and drained and wanted to sleep, but instead I decided on breakfast, hoping to see Kiva there. As I dressed, Johnny awoke. I told him that Mr. Simonian had already left and that I was on my way to breakfast. He said he'd join us as soon as he could get ready.

I was back at square one and resigned to the belief that there was a stronger force at work that wanted me to go to the Soviet Union. I wasn't angry now, for who else could I get angry at but myself?

The storm was behind us, but the heat, even that early in the morning, stuck. The *Rossia* was on a southerly course, heading for the northern tip of Egypt, to Port Said.

I found it difficult to believe, but it had been only two weeks since I had left Detroit.

As I entered the crowded dining hall, I felt I had entered another world. People looked—no, stared—at me. And I stared right back. In fact, I flirted with some of the young Armenian girls, who giggled and made room for me to sit at their table. I thanked them but declined their invitation, saying that others were waiting for me.

Simonian spotted me holding a tray and beckoned me over to his table. At first, I hesitated to join him, for I was embarrassed about our discussion the night before, but I found myself walking toward his table. As I squeezed between the chairs, my eyes continued to search for Kiva. I did not see her.

I sat down to scrambled eggs, bacon, sausage links, potatoes, pancakes, a variety of fresh fruits, jams, and two desserts. Simonian's eyes popped when he saw what was on my tray and how I was devouring the food.

"You're lucky," Simonian said.

I lifted my head from the tray and waited for one of his fatherly lectures.

"Why?" I asked.

"If you had been surrounded by *odars,* not Armenians, the *odars* would point their fingers at you and say, 'Now, there is the perfect example of a starving Armenian.'"

I laughed, and Simonian smiled.

"You know, this is the first time I have heard you laugh since you boarded this ship. Do it more often."

I thanked him for being a friend.

As I continued to eat, a dark thought crossed my mind: What if I had not returned to the ship? What would Simonian have done, and how would the repatriation officials have handled the mystery of the missing repatriate? I would never know.

Tables began to empty, and diners left. Eventually, there was a clear view of the dining hall, and I saw Kiva on the opposite side, sitting next to David. She looked concerned and nervous. Our eyes met, and I immediately saw the hurt in them. David turned quickly around to see what had distracted his sister. Our eyes clashed. He looked back at her, then returned his focus to me. There was no smile on his face.

David knew. It was written in red, sunburned onto Kiva's and my skin. David turned back to discuss something with his group.

I soon realized that Simonian also knew. He, too, read the writing in scarlet on our faces.

Simonian said amiably, "It's too bad she isn't Armenian, and it's too bad she's going to Haifa."

It would have been foolish of me to plead innocence. I said nothing.

I heard a voice behind me confirming Simonian's observation. I turned to see Johnny standing there with a full plate. I moved over so he could sit with us.

Simonian continued to talk about the *odars* across the room.

"That is one brave young woman," he said.

He certainly had my attention. He explained that in a few days, the United Nations would split Palestine, granting the Jews part of Palestinian land to create the State of Israel. The Soviet Union and America would not oppose the partition, but the Arab nations would. And war was imminent. Simonian said that Jews from all over the world were flocking to Palestine to fight. "It is not a place where you would want to be today," he said.

Chapter 26

A BROTHER'S CONCERN

The *Rossia* had two stops—Port Said and Haifa—before heading home to the Soviet Union.

It was David, not Kiva, who was waiting for me on the upper deck of the ship the night before the *Rossia* reached Haifa. He was pleasant and welcomed me with a smile. He invited me to have a bottle of beer with him, and I, eager to have a one-on-one talk, agreed.

I told him that I would like to join his group, if he could get me off at Haifa.

He did not laugh. He looked me seriously in the eyes and asked, "Can you shoot a weapon?"

"No," I replied.

"Would you hesitate to kill someone who threatened your or Kiva's life?"

I did not answer immediately. I said I had to think about it.

As I thought, he ordered another round of beers.

Then I told him honestly that I didn't think I could kill.

"The first one is always the toughest. After that, it becomes natural."

David sized up the situation and was unmistakably more realistic than I. Like a chess master who has studied not only his opponent's first move but also the series of possibilities, he checked each of mine. David told me he respected me and thought I was brave to go behind the Iron Curtain. Kiva didn't belong there. I could not support her, nor could I protect her.

We drank our beers. He ordered another round.

To say I understood him would be exaggerating. Our conversation remained friendly and without confrontation. There were long silences, but I must admit that we made short work of the beer that seemed to keep arriving at our table whenever we had finished the last one.

"I must be a fool," I said, "to have wanted to go to the Soviet Union."

David smiled and agreed.

"And I love Kiva," I said.

"Of course you do," David said.

"And I want to marry Kiva."

"Of course you do," he said.

Everything was blank after that.

Chapter 27

THE MORNING AFTER

The last thing I remembered was sitting with David in the dining hall and talking about Kiva and laughing, loudly and boisterously, and David agreeing with everything I said. He was a pleasant guy, after all, I thought. I didn't remember going back to my cabin; I didn't remember saying good-bye to Kiva or being in her cabin, yet that was where I opened my eyes.

I tried to get up to look around, but I couldn't move. I lay motionless on her bunk. The ship's engines sounded like bombs going off in my head. Every time I tried to move, my head seemed to go one way, my body the other. Neither cooperated. *Get up,* I told myself over and over. *Go out on deck. Things will be clearer.* I didn't know how many hours had passed before I finally managed to get my shoeless feet to the floor. I looked around. There was nothing. No luggage. Nothing on the dresser . . . nothing except an envelope with my name on it. I stuffed it into one of my pockets. I looked in the mirror; I did not recognize myself. So, that was what a hangover looked like.

I looked for my shoes, found them, and struggled to put them on. My mouth was dry, as if it was stuffed with cotton. I wanted a drink of water. I needed a cold shower. I made it to the basin, turned on the faucet, and splashed cold water on my face. It helped but not much. I struggled to get the cabin door opened. The spiral stairway leading to the first deck seemed to move and sway as I approached it. Nothing seemed right. The sun, the shoreline, the sea were not where I knew they should be. I thought we were going the wrong way. I looked out the porthole in hopes of seeing Haifa. It was not there.

"Where the hell have you been?" Johnny shouted once I had finally crawled up the spiral staircase to the deck. He and Simonian had searched every corner of the ship looking for me. They even thought I might have fallen overboard. Or jumped ship.

I did not hear a word Johnny was saying, but I had never appreciated seeing him more than I did at that moment.

"Where are we?" I finally asked.

"Approaching the coast of Turkey."

I asked what had happened to Haifa. Johnny didn't answer. He said I looked sick. I asked again when we would reach Haifa. He asked me what kind of drugs I was on. His eyes searched mine for clues.

He finally said, "We left Haifa hours ago."

I told him I was sick.

"You look like hell."

I rushed to the rail and spilled my guts into the sea. Johnny was right there behind me. He thought I was going to leap overboard. I collapsed onto the deck. He summoned another repatriate, and the two carried me to our cabin.

Later, Johnny told me that the British had had a couple of cruisers accompanying the *Rossia* into Palestinian waters. The *Rossia* was not allowed to dock there. British naval officers had come aboard to inspect the ship and had left without any incident.

I asked about Kiva and her companions.

Johnny said he hadn't seen them get off the ship. But they must have left, because they weren't there now.

Kiva was gone.

～ THE NEXT DAY, as I was strolling alone on deck, I remembered the envelope. I went back to my cabin, found it in my suit jacket, and opened it. It was from Kiva.

"Darling, David is right—damn him. He is always right. This is not your war. You will be all right, and we will meet again, believe me. Have hope, and don't allow those Russian women to spoil you.

"I love you, and I will never forget you, no matter what happens."

I felt angry, angry with myself because I was not the man I thought

I was, angry that I had not even been able to make a proper farewell to her. I read Kiva's closing words.

"We shared a moment in time together that I know we will never forget. I leave you because there is greater work to be done for those who need help. I don't know how or when, but I know we shall meet again. We will be together, I promise. Until then, here is something from Shakespeare that I want you to keep close to your heart and read each time you think you are losing hope: 'No sooner met but they looked; no sooner looked but they loved; no sooner loved but they sighed; no sooner sighed but they asked one another the reason.'

"Every time I look upon another man's face, I will see yours.

"Good-bye—for now. Kiva."

BOOK II

Chapter 1

GHOSTS OF MY ANCESTORS

A nervous but silent restlessness came over the repatriates as the *Rossia* steamed toward the Dardanelles, a forty-four-mile gateway into the Bosporus and the Sea of Marmara. The narrow strait serves as the West's southernmost door into the Black Sea and the Soviet Union. The watery passage also separates the European continent from Asia Minor.

Turkey cast its dark shadow on the *Rossia*.

Crowlike chatter whirled down the corridors of the ship and broke the silence of the dawn. When the banter reached my ears, I immediately decoded it. Although I did not understand it, I recognized it as Turkish, a language spoken by my grandmother, my mother, and my father.

On rare occasions, my mother and father, both born in eastern Turkey, would retreat from their children to discuss serious domestic issues. Usually, those chats took place behind closed doors and were conducted in Turkish. None of us knew what they were discussing, but the closed door would send a message that something was wrong. We never interrupted them.

Although Robert and George knew some Armenian and Rose and I only a word or two, none of us could speak Turkish. Later, I would discover that some of the words my mother and father used in their Armenian conversations were actually Turkish.

I also suspect that my mother knew more English than she would lead her children to believe, for she always seemed to know what we were up to and into. When it came time for her to take the tests to become a naturalized U.S. citizen, she had not needed additional tutoring—she breezed right through. Not so with my father. He eventually passed and became a naturalized American citizen, but only after Rose and I sat down with him and drilled him on the exam questions.

Now Simonian was on the second deck, standing rigidly at the starboard rails, both hands clenched to the railing, his face pale and his eyes watery, staring blankly into an early-morning fog that was slowly vaporizing.

A spectacular panoramic portrait of the Turkish coastline unfolded. Streaks of golden orange penetrated the darkness and soon flushed the purples of the night into the sea. The great Blue Mosque, Saint Sophia of Istanbul, dominated the skyline. Istanbul, known through the centuries as Constantinople, was the broken heart of the once great Byzantine and Ottoman Empires.

I asked Simonian if there was anything wrong. His face softened as he replied, "Wrong? Well, no. Why would you think so?"

"You look so distraught."

There was no response.

"Can I help or do anything for you?" I pleaded.

"You can. But we will discuss that later." I detected trouble in his calm manner. Then he tried to hide his swollen eyes and pain behind a mask. I knew the mask well. It was a mask of death.

I had seen it on my mother's face. She occasionally would sit in the living room on the couch, looking out the bay window, staring into space, her right hand softly caressing a scar on her left wrist, rocking back and forth in deep thought. I would ask, "Mother, what's wrong?" Interrupted, she would turn and look at her youngest son. I would see her rosy-cheeked, beautiful face, as white as porcelain and as if she had seen ghosts. She had. They would give her no peace. The hazel eyes could not hide the tears. I would stand there wondering, what horrific pictures were trapped in her mind, what ghosts of her past continued to haunt her, cheat her of enjoying her life? She would never tell me or any of her other children.

My question would be ignored with a simple "It is nothing." She would regain her poise. "It is nothing of importance." After a sigh, she would get up from the chair, walk over, and hug me. "I was dreaming of how it would have been if it hadn't all happened."

"If what hadn't happened, Mother?"

"If there had been peace, but then . . ." She would pause. "Then I would not have had you and my beautiful family, would I?" She would hug me again and kiss my forehead. "It was my *jagadakeer,* my kismet."

How many Armenian mothers and fathers could not escape their pasts, as my mother could not? What terrifying events had occurred so long ago in that land that my mother and millions like her, Simonian and millions like him, would not talk about? How cruel a force was unleashed on those shores in that insane year of 1915 that survivors could not forget but refused to talk about it?

"Would you," Simonian now asked me, "talk about something that was so painful, so horrible in your life, to your wife and children?"

I was oblivious to their suffering, for I was not one of them, yet I was part of the story. I bit my lip.

"One day, you, too, will know the story. I know this," Simonian said. "Within you is the heart and the compassion of an Armenian. Someday soon, you will understand why you are on this ship"— Simonian pointed to the coastline—"and not over there, on that land in your father's village of Keghi."

The *Rossia*'s engines abruptly stopped, almost popping Simonian's steel-rimmed spectacles off his face. A small craft had tied up, and a Turkish crew was about to board the *Rossia.*

"What the hell is that? Did we hit an iceberg?"

Simonian chuckled. "No icebergs in these waters. Nothing serious. We're stopping to pick up a Turkish captain. He'll take us through the straits to the Black Sea."

I heard outraged voices as the Armenians saw the Turkish boat and crew. They could not fathom having Turks aboard a ship whose passengers were among the victims, some of them parents who had had to abandon their children during the genocide.

The fuse to the keg of dynamite was lit.

"What's going on?" I asked Simonian.

"These are their waters, and it will be their crew that will take us through to the Black Sea. Simple as that." He took my arm and warned, "Do not get involved if any foolishness occurs."

Chapter 2

TURKS ABOARD THE *ROSSIA*

O ne by one, the Turkish crew boarded the *Rossia*. They were greeted cordially by the ship's captain and his officers. With Simonian at my side, I watched a small group of repatriates appear. The mood was black.

Simonian's voice could be heard over the crowd. "The Turks are to be treated as guests." His words were not heeded. The Turks disappeared with the captain. Some of the men in the crowd also disappeared but soon returned.

"There will be no incident on this ship. We are a civilized people," Simonian asserted.

He was wrong.

"Fuck them!" someone shouted in Armenian—words I would soon know in several different languages.

I looked and saw Johnny standing in the crowd. Simonian summoned him over and ordered him not to participate.

The *Rossia* steamed through the Dardanelles and reached the Black Sea. The Turks prepared to leave the ship. They waited for the small craft to convey them to shore.

The *Rossia*'s engines began to churn so that we could slowly continue on our southeasterly course to the port of Batumi.

As the Turks waited, one of the repatriates said something in Turkish. I asked Simonian to translate. He refused. I knew they were Turkish expletives. The air around us seemed sucked into a vacuum, and there was a sudden explosion as hundreds of loaves of bread were fired by the mob at their targets, the Turkish officers. The Soviets dared to intervene. I waited for the Turkish response. They did nothing.

The lines were drawn. But neither side violated them. They stood there and stared at one another. One by one, the Turks left the ship. As the last one was about to leave, a loaf struck him in the back. He turned, picked it up, and looked at the crowd. Then he tossed it onto the deck, and it rolled toward the crowd. He uttered something, turned, and left the ship.

I asked Simonian to translate. "It is nothing," he said. "There is no need to translate." I asked another of the elders and was told in a whisper that the Turk had suggested that we save the bread, for where we were going, there was none.

There was laughter in the crowd, and someone proclaimed that the Ukraine alone could produce more wheat than all of Europe. It was the bread basket of Europe. And the Ukraine was a part of the Soviet Union.

I asked Simonian if that were true, and he answered that it was. I was satisfied.

The *Rossia* was approaching Batumi. There I—all of us—would know the truth.

Chapter 3

A NEW RULE BOOK

S imonian cautioned me, "The Soviets do not play your game the way you want them to; they make their own rules as they go along."

Simonian and I found a secluded place to discuss our pending arrival in the Soviet Union. Reflecting on the debacle at Dunkirk and Kutuzov's evasive actions against Napoleon, Simonian told me that it was not cowardly to retreat and regroup to fight for what you believed in another day. He continued calmly that my world was about to change drastically—as if that hadn't happened the day I stepped aboard the ship.

"If things had been different in France, by now, you probably would have been back in Detroit. But events out of our hands stopped our plan."

"What are you telling me, Mr. Simonian? I'm hungry. I want to get something to eat."

"Simply that as soon as you step on Soviet soil, you must stop talking about going back, stop talking about America. You are a Soviet citizen and must live by their laws." His face turned grim. He looked me in the eye, looked into my soul, and said, "There is freedom in the USSR, but it is not the kind of freedom you or Johnny or the rest of the American-born are accustomed to."

A frown crossed my face. "I am an American. You want me to change that overnight?"

"No. But events shall change you. And I hope you never learn what I mean." His voice was very firm when he continued, "Listen to me, before your world is shattered to pieces and I am no longer around to help you put your life back together."

I had heard enough. I told him I was going to breakfast. He rose and grasped one of my shoulders. I was surprised at the strength of his grip.

There was an unmistakable look of concern, more of pity than anything else. Shaking his head, Simonian warned me again, "When you get ashore, no more talk of going back. Forget America and the U.S. Embassy. I beg you to heed my advice, for your sake . . . for your mother's and your father's sake. Step back and learn from your experiences, and you will live to . . ."

"To do what?"

"To fight for what you believe is right."

I didn't respond.

He reminded me about breakfast. But I wasn't hungry anymore.

Chapter 4

BATUMI, PORT OF NO RETURN

T he debarkation at Batumi in the last week of November was a
sobering moment in my life and in the life of every Armenian
American repatriate. It was our first glimpse of Soviet humanity, of
Soviet life stripped naked of all of its propaganda and lies. Indisputable
proof was evident on the weary, tired, famished faces of the army of
paupers who stood eagerly waiting on the dock before us.

America was behind us. The Soviets had us. We bowed at the sacred
altar of communism as we stood face-to-face with Soviet gods—Stalin,
Lenin, Engels, and Marx—whose mammoth portraits decorated the
front wall of the warehouse that would become the living quarters for
the 151 repatriates for six days.

More than fifteen hundred Armenians from France had walked down
the *Rossia*'s gangplank just a few months before and had left their
marks and debris. Food would be scarce. There was no running water
in the building, and the outhouses reflected neglect.

I heard the cries of the seagulls. They mocked me. I envied them
their freedom.

I remained a passive observer of what was drummed into us as a
great historic event. The bridge had been crossed. On November 21,
1947, His Holiness Kevork VI, Catholicos of All Armenians, had said,
"The souls of all those who have come home as repatriates are filled
with warm feelings of gratitude . . . and I, their aged Catholicos, fer-
vently pray that all Armenians suffering abroad will soon be able to
return home and enjoy happiness in their fatherland."

A lifetime of waiting had ended.

As the repatriates left the ship, most were greeted by long-lost loved
ones. The embraces were heart-wrenching. Years of separation were
over, and every human emotion was released as people cheered, cried,
fainted, came together.

From the crowded dock, people continued to shout out the names of
villages in Turkey, of loved ones, of relatives and friends, waiting

eagerly, nervously, for responses. And if someone they sought was discovered in our group, screams were followed with "God has answered our prayers," a statement that could cost them their freedom if uttered in public back in Erevan.

Immediately after the Soviet Union's national anthem, Armenian and Russian folk music filled the air.

My eyes continued to roam the crowds. What if some distant relative of mine had survived the genocide and was in the crowd? I dismissed the thought as impossible. Mother would have cautioned me.

I would be among the last of the repatriates to leave the ship. For a brief moment, I considered stowing away, thinking that maybe the ship would be returning to the United States to pick up the second caravan. But then I reached the gangplank and watched one of the older repatriates. As soon as his feet touched the ground, he fell to his knees and kissed the soil.

"Thank God, I am home!" he shouted as tears streamed down his cheeks.

I had come too far to turn back. Someone behind me whispered something. I turned and saw Mrs. Karibian, her two small children at her side. There was a strange look on her face.

"Where's Harry?" I asked.

"He's down there somewhere trying to find us living space."

"Can I help with anything?"

"Not really."

We began our descent together as the chaos below continued. Mrs. Karibian whispered, "These people frighten me, Tommy. They look like they're starving."

I nodded with complete understanding.

And then my feet were solidly planted on Soviet soil.

I turned to get my last glimpse of the *Rossia*. All I could see was a vision of Kiva standing at the rail, blowing me a kiss.

Chapter 5

HE WHO LAUGHS LAST

A *xhbar! Axhbar! Paree kaloust!"*
An unshaven, uncouth stranger who apparently hadn't bathed for years had locked me in a bear hug, heartily kissing me on both cheeks, shouting as he tightened his grip on me. "Brother! Brother! Welcome home!" he would repeat over and over as my face was rubbed against his sandpaper stubble.

I broke his hold and stood bewildered before him. "I don't speak Armenian." The words were useless. He lunged at me again, and I eluded his grasp. It felt unnatural, even bizarre, for a person of my own sex to kiss me, even on the cheeks. It would take years, many years, for me to get accustomed to Middle Eastern culture, especially a man kissing me or a woman presenting me with flowers.

Movie cameras were everywhere, focusing in on me, then sweeping past to others. The Soviets were busy shooting historic footage to be shown in the United States so that others would get caught in the web. (A year later, my parents would write to me that they had seen a film depicting the Armenian Americans getting off at Batumi, and the narrator had focused on a young lad—me—who had left his parents back in America to help rebuild the fatherland.)

I slowly worked my way through the throngs and headed for the warehouse. I passed several men who were conspicuous by their suits, black or navy blue, not an American cut, uniquely Russian, I thought. They were wearing white shirts, with their collar buttons opened. None sported a tie. They wore crudely manufactured shoes, made of felt, as did most of the local population. As these men in black mingled among the masses, a wave of silence came over the local group. People seemed to step aside or avoid them completely when possible, as if they were carrying a deadly virus.

The band surrendered the stage, and the speeches began. Praise for Stalin and Lenin was never-ending. Each time their names were mentioned, there was a collective cry of "Hurrah!" from the audience, accompanied by "Long live our father!" The speeches went on for hours, with their emphasis on the inevitability of the triumph of communism over capitalism. There was not even a perfunctory acknowledgment of the role the Allies had played in the defeat of Hitler or the help the United States had provided to the Soviet Union to turn the tide.

I saw Simonian nearby and moved to avoid him. I did not want any more to do with him.

The sun was sinking fast, but the political oratory and propaganda continued to flow into the late evening hours. We were tired, and most of us were hungry, but what we received was tea, cheese, and bread—black, containing sawdust. Some repatriates dug into their luggage and came out with canned goods and sugar. The scarcity of food in Batumi was attributed to Georgia's war effort—or the lack of it. Stalin, it was believed, was punishing the Georgians because they didn't give one hundred percent in the fight against the Nazis.

A makeshift dormitory was set up, and cots were everywhere. We stood in line and were issued sheets, mattresses, and pillows but no pillowcases. Individuals were assigned to areas according to marital status. Families stayed together, and bachelors were assigned beds in one of the corners.

For our first breakfast, we were served tea, cheese, rice, sausages, and black bread. We ate heartily. There was no milk, no butter, no fresh fruit, and no vegetables. Before the week ended, most families looked shell-shocked.

Repatriates were invited to exchange their dollars for rubles. I quickly got in line, and the money exchangers were glad to take my dollars. I received five rubles and forty kopeks to a dollar, the official exchange at the time, and I was elated. For my one hundred dollars, I got more than two hundred fifty rubles. I felt rich—that is, until I visited the local market, where I discovered that one orange, not a dozen of them, would cost me fifty rubles.

I came to regret not having paid more attention in my economics classes. The law of supply and demand was meaningless in a planned society that didn't produce enough food for its population. The peasants would have given me anything I wanted if I had literally taken off my shoes and bartered them for food.

When I shared my shopping experience with a group of other repatriates, they said they too were shocked at what they had found, or had not found, in the market. Then one of them broke out in nervous laughter.

"Maybe," he said with a deep sigh, "we should have heeded that Turk's advice back on the boat and kept the bread."

Chapter 6

PROPAGANDA VERSUS REALITY

In the warehouse, I heard the other repatriates say over and over that when we reached Erevan, life would be better. The words were there to reassure themselves, their families, and their friends. We seemed to have fallen into the Soviet quagmire.

I saw women dressed in white smocks, their hair pulled straight back and tied in tight buns, identified as nurses who were there to provide care for the elderly. The stale black bread and cheese that the repatriates did not eat but left as garbage was swept off the tables by these nurses, who hid it under their smocks to take home to their families. It was heartbreaking to see. But when one was hungry, as my mother used to remind us around the table, especially during those jobless days of the Great Depression, "one will even eat a dog's tail."

The first time I needed to use a bathroom, I asked one of the repatriates where it was. His terse answer: "Follow your nose." I did and soon came upon the makeshift outhouse. The stench nauseated me. I did not want to but was forced by nature to open the door. When I saw the human filth piled knee-high above the hole, I quickly retreated.

Back at the warehouse, I sought out Johnny, who quickly registered my look of disgust.

"I see you found it!"

"Yes. But I can't believe it."

"Wait until dark," he suggested. "Go near the shoreline. There's nobody there."

"Wait? I can't!"

"Then pee and shit in your pants," he said.

I never did use the outhouse in Batumi the entire time we were there. I held it in as long as possible. Thank goodness, I couldn't eat the food. I decided that once we were aboard the train, I would take up residency in the restroom.

As if the stench opening our nostrils to the reality of Soviet life were not enough, community life in the warehouse took a psychological toll on the repatriates. I did not see a smile or hear a positive comment during the entire week.

During the day, we scrounged around for something to eat and discussed the latest rumors.

At nightfall, when we returned to the barracks, our thoughts became the most disheartening. As soon as the lights were out, I heard the whispers in the dark begin, followed by the tears.

Sleep came hard.

Women cried themselves to sleep after tucking their children in. Most knew that a dreadful mistake had been made, but it was not the time to dwell on it.

I cannot say how many times I heard the elderly women—the *nanas*—of our caravan wail, "*Vi, vi, e chou egant!* Oh, oh, why did we come!" Their cries remain deep in my heart to this day.

Chapter 7

MY NEW WORLD

I was living in a world of body and sign language. I had to point to objects or use my hands or facial expressions, sometimes both, to make my needs and my feelings known. It was frustrating, for often I couldn't make myself understood, and this caused much confusion in my life.

To survive, I knew I needed to learn the language.

I was surprised at how quickly words, especially Armenian words, were being added to my vocabulary. I could not bring those words together to form a sentence, but soon I would be able to.

I certainly could identify with the suffering of those who had been swept from their homes and their country during war and dropped into a foreign country. I remembered the influx of Jewish, Hungarian, and Polish immigrants who wound up in our southwest Detroit neighborhood not speaking English. Now, for me, the tables were turned.

There was another hurdle I had to overcome: What was a kilo? I had to learn the metric system. Inches, feet, yards, miles, and pounds didn't mean a thing to people who talked in grams and kilograms, centimeters and kilometers. My new world was the Old World way of doing business. And if I didn't learn, it would prove costly. A dollar may have been worth five rubles and forty kopeks, but how many rubles bought a kilo of bread?

One day as I mused on this, someone jolted my arm with a handshake and, in a pleasant voice, said, *"Paree kaloust."*

I turned to look at the clean-shaven gentleman dressed in a brown jacket and dark pants. His hair was pitch black. He could not have been more than thirty. He introduced himself as a journalist. He was on the staff of *Sovietakan Hyestan*, a daily published in the city of Erevan.

He was interested in writing a feature story about the youth of America, and Simonian had told him I had repatriated without family.

One of the older repatriates was translating for him, but he was quickly replaced by Johnny, who saw my body language asking for help.

The journalist identified himself as Emile. He took out a pencil and paper. I told him that I was not interested in the interview, that I had too many other things on my mind. Johnny translated, but the journalist refused to take no for an answer. He took out a pack of Russian cigarettes and offered one to Johnny and me. Johnny accepted; I refused.

"These," Emile said, pointing to the cigarettes, "no good. American *poperoszy* very good."

I wondered how he knew about American cigarettes and left it to Johnny to ask him. He had served in the military and had managed to finagle a pack or two from American soldiers.

"Are your parents going to come to the fatherland with the next group?" Emile asked. That was the question everybody who met me asked.

I told Johnny to tell him I didn't know. When he scribbled what I thought were more words than I had said into his pad, I became suspicious. I suggested that Johnny ask the man for some sort of identification.

Johnny was suspicious, too, suggesting that Emile might be profiling some of us for some other agency. He asked the reporter if he had any credentials. Emile stuck his hand into an inside pocket and pulled out something. Johnny looked at the document and said, "He seems legit."

I was surprised and impressed that Johnny could read the document.

Emile resumed the interview, repeating a question I had not answered: Why had I, an American-born Armenian, joined the repatriation group and left my parents behind? Johnny sensed that the politically explosive question would land me in trouble, and he quickly answered, "His parents will join him. They, too, are loyal to our cause." I proceeded, with Johnny's translating help, to answer a litany of questions about my life in America.

Johnny asked when the story would be published.

"As soon as I get back to Erevan," Emile replied.

"And when will we be leaving this place?" I asked.

"Soon. Very soon," Emile said with certainty. "I will be on the train with you."

"Thank God," I said. "This is a hellhole if there ever was one."

Emile responded with a smile, "No. Thank the Communist Party."

I wondered if something had been lost in the translation.

~ NO ONE was prepared for life in a warehouse in Batumi.

Stench was everywhere. From head to toe, the body yearned for a bath. Sponge baths were impossible, and swimming in the sea was prohibited.

The men had not changed their clothes or shaved, for there was only drinking water; and the women, so meticulously dressed aboard ship, did not bother with makeup. Some did not seem to care what they wore. Their main concerns were to feed their families and keep them healthy.

It had been only a month since we had left the United States. It had been only seven days since we had landed on Soviet soil.

We were destroyed. The bubble had burst much sooner than anyone had expected. We lay on our cots reading, and when we tired of that, we stared at the bare ceilings and at the walls. We avoided the one with the portraits of Lenin and Stalin and Marx. Under socialism, we were all equals. The Soviets were preparing us for the day when we would look like them. Some of us already did.

I sympathized with what the heads of families must be thinking. How could they explain the situation they found themselves in—how could they justify their move? They had decided to repatriate. Their children had been yanked from their schools, moved away from their friends, their culture, everything, and for what? Now they had their wives and children to answer to, and it must have been difficult to try to justify. I pitied them. I was glad to be alone there without family.

Disenchantment, disappointment, disbelief, and depression hit us all in one package. Those among the repatriates who had heard horror stories from their loved ones who lived in the Soviet Union had not dared to reveal them. They had been told to seal their lips.

We would soon find out what awaited us in Erevan.

Those who had survived the Turkish massacres knew suffering. The tragedy was that they would know it again.

Chapter 8

THE TRAIN TO TIFLIS

From a subtropical climate and the blue skies of the Mediterranean, our train would leave the coastline and head east, following the shadow of the Caucasus Mountains, the great divide between Asia Minor and southern Russia. We would pause at the ancient city of Tiflis, the capital of Soviet Georgia.

From Tiflis, the train would turn southwest and scale precipitous terrain, climbing snowcapped mountain ranges that rose more than

1,000 meters above sea level before reaching the highlands of the ancient lands of Armenia, the Socialist Republic of Armenia.

The western centerpiece of the horseshoe plateau is the two-headed Mount Ararat, where God gave his children a second chance. Noah and his sons—Shem, Ham, and Japheth—according to the scriptures, descended from the mountain and built the city of Erevan, whose name means "Come, come, welcome."

There could not have been a more hostile environment to start life anew for Noah and his family. The region, though the hills are tree-topped, has volcanic-rock-laden ridges and soil. The river Araks, the western border between Armenia and Turkey, is at Ararat's feet.

Sandwiched between the biblical mount where the Ark settled after the forty-day deluge and the capital city sits the Etchmiadzin, the holy see of the Catholicos, the spiritual leader of millions of Armenians and the administrative head of the Armenian Orthodox Church. The Etchmiadzin stood as the silent witness of the rise and fall of the great empires—Byzantine, Persian, Arab, Seijuk, Mongol, Ottoman, and Romanov.

In A.D. 301, Armenia became the first nation to declare Christianity as its state religion. It was this acceptance of Christianity, as preached to them by Saint Bartholomew, and their passion for protecting their religion that inspired the Armenians to fight the great armies of the Seljuks, the Turks, and the Ottoman Empire.

~ WE RUSHED to get a glimpse of the train that was to take us to our final destination. We would have joined a mule train to leave the stench of Batumi. Our train was not a Pullman, but it was a train with an engine. One member of our group said he believed that it had transported the last Russian czar, Nicholas II, and his family into exile in 1918. Another offered that perhaps it was the freight car the Germans had used to smuggle Lenin out of Switzerland in 1917, fomenting the Bolshevik Revolution.

There would be no other passengers, just the repatriates and military personnel to protect us and our belongings. We were told we must not take any photos en route; Soviet law forbade it, since we would be traveling near international borders. Cameras would be seized, and photographers could be arrested.

The so-called passenger cars were divided into several open compartments, with no sliding doors to close them off. There would be no
privacy, no assigned seats, only wooden benches to sit on. One side of
a compartment was divided into two sections with three layers of
wooden shelves, each about six feet long. The bottom two shelves
could be utilized as beds. The third tier was for storing luggage. On the
other side were two seats facing each other with a table between which
could be used for cards, chess, backgammon, or eating.

Repatriates were issued stained mattresses, white sheets, and wool
blankets. There were no pillowcases. There was no restaurant aboard
the train. Each passenger, before boarding, had received a lunch bag
with sausage, cheese, two or three hard-boiled eggs, bread, and jam. A
samovar supplied hot water for tea, but there was no sugar.

Compared with repatriates from other parts of the world, some of
whom made the journey in what Americans would call cattle and pig
cars, we were expected to be grateful to Stalin for these "first-class
accommodations," but as one repatriate pointed out, it wasn't out of
the kindness or the generosity of the Soviet government. The Armenian
American repatriates were traveling "first class" because we were bear-
ing gifts of machinery and consumer goods valued at more than a million dollars. I was told that in 1946 alone, Armenian Americans raised
more than $1.5 million for repatriation efforts.

Although I was among the last to get off the *Rossia*, I was probably
the first to board the train. I needed to stake out the lavatory.

Chapter 9

THE ODD COUPLE

O h, there you are," said Simonian, standing in the corridor with
two other men whom I had seen but not talked to on the ship.
"I have been looking for you. I want you to meet a couple of your
father's old friends."

"Friends?" I asked with a cherubic smile. I had been avoiding

Simonian and hoped that Batumi would be the last I would see of him. "I didn't know my father had any friends in this caravan."

"Oh, yes," said Simonian as he introduced Momigon and Sabu to me. The men had lived in Detroit during the Depression and frequented my father's coffeehouse. Both men were well into their sixties—very old, I thought.

Sabu looked the older of the two. He wore the thickest glasses I had seen, like Peter Lorre's in the movies. Sabu even dangled his cigarette the way Lorre did. His jacket was stained with who knows what and nearly two times larger than his skeletonlike frame. His false teeth moved and clicked, rattled and rolled when he opened his mouth to say something. Momigon stood a foot taller, about five-foot-seven, and carried a protruding paunch. The belt around his belly had been tightened a notch recently. His round face, rosy cheeks, and full head of white hair gave him a respectable appearance. Both men wore a week's whiskers. Sabu allowed Momigon to do most of the talking. I speculated that he didn't want to lose his teeth.

Momigon immediately began telling stories of his and my father's misadventures in the days before and after the Great Depression.

"So you're Tatos, Boghos's son. Did your father ever tell you we tried to make booze in the bathtub during Prohibition and almost burned down your house on Solvay? Or the time the Fort and Green cops were closing in on Sabu because they wanted him for questioning in a series of cat burglaries in Delray?"

I blinked but didn't say a word.

"Sabu and I owe your father a lot. Where is he?" Before I could answer, Momigon continued, "Did he ever tell you how he got me and Sabu across the Canadian border into Detroit from Windsor and found us jobs? Your parents put us up for a couple of months. Poor Dzovinar—what your mother had to go through. She's an angel."

Momigon talked nonstop until Simonian announced, "We're nearing Tiflis. We'll be able to get out and stretch our legs. And pick up some fresh fruit and vegetables." As he had done throughout the journey, Simonian cautioned me to stay close to the platform area, "because you never know when the train will pull out."

Momigon laughed and told him, "Haratoun, if he is Boghos's son, he can take care of himself—and you, too!"

I looked at Simonian, and he looked at me. Our faces broke into smiles. "I am sure he can," Simonian said.

Chapter 10

A STARVING ARMENIAN

My eyes were glued to the window, and my spirits lifted as fruit and palm trees, rivers and rolling hills passed swiftly by. The valleys looked so fertile that I thought surely there would be something to purchase at the depots. I did not remember when I had eaten my last decent meal. The lunch package from the warehouse was insufferably smelly. And although I was extremely hungry, I would have preferred the dog's tail to what was in that lunch. I suffered silently, for I knew that most of the other repatriates were in the same state.

As the train reached what appeared to be the outskirts of the city that had been the capital of Georgia for centuries, it suddenly stopped. The wheels reversed themselves, and the passenger cars were driven to a sidetrack for no explained reason. There the train sat. One, two, three frustrating hours passed, and the engines just huffed and puffed and snickered at us. Some got off the train to look down the track. Nothing like a depot was in sight. I was ready to get out and walk the rest of the way, but I did not know what I would find ahead. Then, as mysteriously as it had stopped, the train started up and, at a snail's pace, moved toward the city.

The Armenian Americans had arrived at Tiflis. As far as my eyes could see, the platform was jammed with people. The omnipresent portraits of the Soviet gods were there to greet us, displayed on the depot's red-brick wall. Some among the crowd were dressed fashionably, but many wore their shabby uniforms or long brown or grayish military coats. The women and children looked healthier than those we had encountered back in Batumi. Most were pushing, shouting, shoving, and moving toward the train; some even attempted to board the cars.

Many were Armenians residing in Tiflis. They sought information of long-lost loved ones, of relatives and friends who were in America. This scene would be repeated in Kirovakan, Leninakan, and Erevan.

But these Armenian Georgians were the best fed and the best dressed. It was no secret that many of the Armenians who fled Turkey eventually settled in Tiflis, and when the Bolshevik Revolution spread to the Caucasus, some managed to slip across the border to Iran or Iraq.

Those who followed the rail tracks to Georgia preferred to stay in the warm climate and till the fertile soil, growing the grapes they and the Georgians were noted for. To backtrack to Erevan, where they would have to live in constant fear of the invading Turkish armies, would have been disastrous. They knew that their death warrants had been signed by the Young Turks and forwarded to the Turkish war minister, Enver Pasha, who ordered his military chiefs to carry out the executions. All Armenians in the Ottoman Empire more than five years of age must be taken out of town and destroyed.

It was soon apparent that the local police could not control the crowds. Many people boarded the train, rushing from car to car shouting the names of lost relatives or friends or cities where they had resided in Turkey, in hopes of finding someone from the same village who had survived the killings and had news or information. I sat frozen in my seat as they rushed by, and I did not get out of the coach. The guards assigned to patrol the coach did nothing to stop them.

The men in black suits carefully studied the incoming passengers, took mental notes on them, but did not try to detain them.

When a stranger shouted something at me, I would look up, lift my shoulders and hands, and say, *"Hyerenen jem has gonum.* I don't understand Armenian." I had learned the expression in the warehouse. I sat there, uncomfortable and numb to what was going on around me. I wanted to get up, stretch my legs, go to the platform and look for food. But I didn't think I could make it back through the unruly crowd to the train. Besides, there was no assurance that my suitcases would be there when I returned.

Finally, long blasts came from the train's whistle. There were Georgians on the train when it pulled out. They hustled to the door, and I could see them jumping off and landing on their feet as the train picked up speed. I could not believe how athletic these people were.

Shortly afterward, Simonian came to my seat. There was a delicious aroma of roasted lamb coming from the newspaper he held in his hand. He opened the paper and handed me a sandwich of roasted lamb, tomatoes, onions, and peppers, wrapped in lavash bread.

"*Kabob!*" I shouted.

"I knew you would be hungry." He smiled.

I seized the savory gift and devoured it. After the last bite, I remembered to thank him.

Chapter 11

INTO THE SHADOWS

A s the train approached Alaverdi, the first notable hamlet within the borders of Soviet Armenia, the Mediterranean summer deserted us, and winter was quickly felt in the unheated train car. I pulled one of my suitcases off the top shelf, found a sweater, and put it on. I glanced out the window. Snow had blanketed the landscape.

The green and fertile fields of Georgia were at our backs, replaced by jagged peaks cloaked in white, like ghosts silently witnessing the man-made serpent disappearing at their feet.

Each turn unveiled a new galaxy of rocks and ridges, cut to form by nature over the centuries. Deep gashes revealed valleys and rivers. There was no flatland. Suddenly, the train lights dimmed. Soot in black clouds engulfed the coach. Women screamed, and children cried; everyone choked and struggled for air. The train had entered a mile-long tunnel carved into one of the mountains. The ancient train windows would not budge; they were fastened shut.

When we reached the other side of the mountain, everyone gasped for air.

The train stopped at Alaverdi to pick up escorts, Red Army border guards who were to ensure our "safety" and discourage enterprising bandits who also knew that the Americans were aboard. Everyone from

America was wealthy, according to the local people. In comparison with the populace there, it was true.

The train was heated, just barely. Those around me lit up cigarettes to keep warm, and I welcomed the additional heat.

The engines tugged, struggling to carry their load higher and higher. The train climbed more than 6,000 feet above sea level before it reached the flatlands, and I chuckled as I remembered the trials and tribulations of "The Little Engine That Could" from the children's book I'd read as a little boy. At times, I didn't think the train would make it; its wheels spun and moaned but appeared to stay in place.

Night came early in that part of the world. I expected to see village lights but did not. It was a bare and cold and hostile land, apparently abandoned. I wondered how much blood had been spilled for it.

I had felt the aching pangs of homesickness before, when I was away at camp in the summers, but this ache didn't want to leave me. Everything seemed so meaningless when thoughts of home surfaced.

I walked to the lavatory. The hole made me want to vomit. But when one must, one must.

No food. No restaurant. I swore if I ever got home again, I would never take another trip out of the United States.

I returned to my seat and watched as frost painted an icy portrait on the windowpane. My mind flipped back pages to my other life. As a child of nine or ten, I had broken my leg and was forced to stay home from school. I kept pace with my classmates by reading and doing my lessons on a divan by the window. Bored at times, I would put my lips up to the window and blow my warm breath against the icy pane, watching as my breath created strange forms and shapes. I would press a penny to the window and engrave Abe Lincoln's portrait. It was something to do until Simon arrived with a creamsicle in hand. He was the ice-cream vendor. A leprechaun of a man, Simon would knock on the front door. Mother would open it, greet him with a smile, and, before ushering him into the living room, ask if he was hungry or would like some tea. Tea was always "fine" for my gnome. With his swaying gait, he would approach me and ask, "How are you, today, Tommy?" I would say, "Fine." Simon would take a seat next to me as he handed me my treat. He was a survivor of the genocide. He, too, talked of the "old country." And I listened to his incredible stories of survival.

"Someday, someday, Tommy," he would tell me, "I'm going to go back and kick those Turks in their asses."

"Can I go with you, Simon? Can we go together to the old country?"

"I would like that," Simon would say. "I would like that very much."

Then my mother would bring in the tea. And there would be no further talk of going back, because my mother would not tolerate that kind of talk.

In the frost-painted train window, I could almost see Simon's wrinkled face. My dear gnome was shaking his finger at me. "Tommy, we were supposed to go back together."

Thank God, Simon, you are not with me.

The train made stops in Kirovakan and Leninakan, and crowds were waiting on the platforms again. It was a repeat of Batumi and Tiflis. All of Armenia seemed to want to see the faces of America. Sometimes the train was moved to a sidetrack, and we would wait impatiently, maybe for hours, for it to start up. During those occasions, the well-informed barber of Philadelphia would turn schoolmaster and regale Johnny and me and the other tired and weary repatriates with brief tales and histories of the region. I did not skip the lectures, for what else was there to do?

And what did the barber of Philadelphia preach? That Kirovakan was named for the popular first secretary of the Communist Party of Leningrad, whose murder in 1934 triggered mass arrests, expulsions from the Communist Party, purges, and the deportation of many "enemies of the people" to, where else, Siberia. That the purges cleansed the USSR of Nazi sympathizers and would-be Bolshevik "revisionists," which was why the Soviets did not have the Quislings, Lavals, or Fifth Columns that Hitler had counted on to bring his enemies to their knees. That Leninakan was named in honor of Vladimir Ilyich Lenin, the architect of the Bolshevik Revolution. It was also the city purportedly built and named Anee by Noah, a name that stood until the Russian czar, Alexander I, invaded the Caucasus in the early 1800s, and it was changed to Alexandropol. Weatherwise, the city was the Siberia of

Armenia, for temperatures could plummet to thirty or forty degrees below zero.

Simonian added that when Noah descended from Mount Ararat, he brought with him the roots of the first grapevines that would produce the grapes that become the world-renowned Armenian cognacs and wines. Did we know that a piece of the gopher wood that Noah had used to build the Ark was kept secured in a glass case at the Holy Etchmiadzin?

And at one time, Simonian told us, the Armenian Empire stretched from the Caspian Sea to the Black Sea.

Johnny proved to be a better student than I, for I usually dozed off listening to Simonian's lectures. He never chastised me for it.

~ AT DAYBREAK on the first day of the last month in 1947, Simonian shook me violently out of a restless sleep and ordered me to look out the window. His usually soft voice thundered as he shouted and shook me.

"The Ararat! The Ararat! Get up! Get up! We have arrived!"

Chapter 12

ARARAT, NOAH, AND ME

Night had not completely lifted its shroud as I brushed my hand against the pane to clear the moisture from it. The frost had dissipated, and I was pleasantly surprised to find that the coach was warmer and there was no snow on the ground.

Through the window, I could make out a silhouette of something mammoth, the likes of which I had never seen. It took on an awesome form, two-headed. One of the summits was concealed by clouds, the other ice capped and draped in a white poncho that ended at its belly.

The train was coasting on a plateau, traveling parallel to this phenomenon. When dawn finally broke, it was still there. I had never seen a mountain so awe-inspiring. As far as one could see, soaring to the heavens, towering nearly 17,000 feet, was the mount that saints, poets, and writers had sung about throughout history. Within its heart was a secret that no man had been able to uncover. The secret was more important to the Christian world than all the gold hidden beneath the surface of the earth.

Noah's Ark.

"If the Ark were found, who would ever again deny the existence of God?" Simonian whispered to me. "There upon that mountain is where God gave man a second chance. Tommy, we all deserve a second chance."

I could not even turn to comment. My eyes could not leave the magnificent panorama standing silently before me. The window provided a frame for me to remember that spectacular view forever.

A bright sun made its appearance. It would be a sunny, warm December 1 as the train picked up speed and raced parallel to Ararat before turning eastward toward the capital.

I jumped off the makeshift bunk and stood facing Simonian.

"Better get your things together," he said. "Don't forget anything. That's Erevan over there."

Chapter 13

EREVAN WELCOMES AMERICANS

Everybody who was anybody, excluding the top Communist Party officials of the Soviet Armenian Republic, was at the train station to greet the tired and haggard members of the first caravan of Armenian American repatriates.

The speeches were many. The embraces were long and emotional. And the tears were never ending.

Like it or not, Tom Mooradian was in Erevan, the capital of Soviet Armenia, and he had better get accustomed to it.

The political banners proclaimed: *"Hyrenik! Hyrenik! Havitjan! Fatherland! Fatherland! Forever!"* The words were plastered on the walls of the station, with the portraits of Soviet leaders, their faces austere, looking down upon the *norkaloghs*—a name attached to the new arrivals. The sounds of the Armenian highlands, from the ancient Armenian instruments—*duduk, kamancha,* and *d'hol*—filled the festive air.

The repatriates had arrived safe and sound.

Missing from the gathered masses, I was told later, was the inner circle of the local Communist oligarchy. The Party had sent its expendable sycophants to represent it at the podium. Those at the higher levels dared not attend, for fear that they would incur the wrath of Moscow.

And there would be no extemporaneous speeches that morning. Those assigned to address the repatriates would use dialogue memorized from the Party Book. Any deviation could have been fatal.

The NKVD was busy. The secret police was certain that in our ranks were those who were former Dashnaks. The men in black, the inexplicable dress code of the secret police, were everywhere. Their task was to search out the "political undesirables" and compile a detailed dossier of everyone associated with them, to be used to expurgate the tainted or anyone who manifested signs of "cosmopolitanism."

The Trotskyites and the Dashnaks may have seen the "true light" and converted to communism in their later years, returning to the Soviet Union, but they were made to pay for their past transgressions. Many were arrested and sent to labor camps.

Unknowingly, although I had been warned by Kiva and David, I stood out to the NKVD. Like sharks, they circled me, attempted to question me, smiled as they discovered I did not know their language. My blood would eventually spill on the basement floors at Nalbandian. I was young, educated, well mannered, the perfect seed planted by the FBI, or so they apparently thought. They had determined that I had been placed in the caravan by the "filthy capitalist pigs" to help promote and spread the evils of capitalism among the innocent and dedicated youth of communism.

But on that memorable morning, I felt no fear, for I did not know then what a *kulak* or a Trotskyite or a cosmopolitan was. I did not realize at the time that my name would rise to the top of the NKVD's list as a possible "sleeper." I was, in fact, as were many of the other repatriates, living on borrowed time.

If only my high school history classes had included a lesson about Lenin and the Bolshevik Revolution. It had been eighteen years since Lenin, on his deathbed, inked his final message to the Soviet people. In his will, Lenin warned that his comrade from Georgia, Iosif Vissarionovich Dzhugashvili, also known as Stalin, was not only not fit to rule the land of the Soviets but also was not to be trusted. Lenin preferred Trotsky. Stalin made sure that Trotsky would not succeed the founder. He ordered Trotsky's execution, carried out by an assassin with an ice pick in Mexico City.

Was it a wonder that the top echelon of the Party would not be there to greet us at the station with open arms? They stayed away, as if the Armenian American repatriates carried an infectious fatal disease.

My concern as I got off the train was not about speeches or politics or secret police. Greater than those, my concerns were where I would put my head down to sleep and where my next meal was coming from.

Chapter 14

A MARRIAGE OFFER

After the last of the speeches and the last of the songs, the repatriates were ushered into the depot's restaurant for their last breakfast together. I could have eaten a dog's tail—that's how hungry I was.

It would be my last free meal at the expense of the state.

But before I went into the station, I rushed to a drinking fountain and began to drink as if I never expected to see water again. The water was cold and refreshing, and I drank so much that my stomach grumbled after I stopped. Simonian may have been wrong about a lot of things, but he had been right on target when he said that the mountain water in Erevan was the best he had ever tasted. I could not stop drinking. I thought that maybe one could survive on water alone.

Refreshed and rejuvenated, I returned to the line and waited to be seated. The waitresses, their dark hair in chignons or concealed in white cloths, were wearing dark ankle-length dresses covered by white aprons, and they pranced silently around the tables. We had scrambled eggs, something called cutlet, which looked like hamburger, plus black bread, tea, and mineral water. I waited patiently, yielding to families with children to be seated first. However, hunger pains soon overcame me, and I surveyed the large room, hoping to spot an empty chair. I pressed forward alone. As I passed one of many tables set up for six and occupied, I heard a familiar voice. It was Mrs. Karibian inviting me to join them.

As I slipped into the empty seat, I glanced around to see what they were serving. Everything looked delicious, but it could have been that I was just famished.

"I'm Harry Karibian," offered the gentleman who extended his hand as he stood up. "You have met my wife, Jean, and these are our children, Michael and Christine."

Christine smiled, but Michael, who I learned was three years older than his sister, did not. There was a frown on his face. The children and their mother—*odars*—did not know Armenian.

I nodded, sat down, and had started to introduce myself when Harry said, "We know who you are, Tommy. We're also from Detroit. It was too bad we didn't have time on the boat to talk; you seemed rather busy."

I apologized. He pointed out that his wife was an *odar.* Her blond hair and blue eyes made that obvious. "She's Polish American," Karibian offered.

"I do know a few words in Armenian, and *odar* is one of them," Jean Karibian said as she broke into a smile. She was a short, plump woman in a cotton dress with a yellow sunflower print. Before her husband could say another word, Jean announced, "Many of his Armenian friends say I am more Armenian than he is."

Her children had inherited their mother's blond hair and blue eyes, though Michael's hair could be described as sandy. Michael, tall and lanky, not at all like his father, was about thirteen. He was bashful, but his sister, ten-year-old Christine, was quite the opposite. Outspoken and reminded repeatedly by her father not to "interrupt," she was a Shirley Temple lookalike. She wore a white dress with frills in the hemline and sported a Mickey Mouse wristwatch. Her questions camouflaged her age. She fired a fusillade of them and would not have stopped if she had not been reminded to do so by her mother.

"Where is your beautiful wife?" Christine innocently but mischievously inquired. This comment warranted a stern admonishment from both parents.

Not prepared for the question, I blushed. "My wife? I am not married, Christine."

"But that pretty lady on the boat? Isn't she . . .?"

Mrs. Karibian was now upset with her daughter. "Now, Christine," she said in a controlled but raised voice. "One more comment . . ."

"That's all right, Mrs. Karibian," I told her, before turning to Christine and explaining, "The beautiful lady got off at Haifa. She is a dear friend I met on the boat."

"Oh!" exclaimed Christine. She took a deep breath, looked carefully at each of her parents, and announced, "Good! Then I shall marry you when I grow up."

I smiled and replied, "Good, then we are officially engaged as of today."

The Karibians shook their heads at their unpredictable daughter.

Our table was served, and we ate slowly, admitting that the food wasn't bad. Mr. Karibian asked if I knew where I had been assigned housing.

I told him I didn't know. "I'm hoping to go to school and stay in one of the dorms."

"Sounds good, but you're going to have to stay somewhere until then. Best see what they have, then make a decision."

I agreed.

Although the adults ate, the children only picked at their food. Mrs. Karibian did not push the issue, softly remarking, "Remember, we may not eat for a while, until we are settled into our new home." The warning appeared to encourage Michael to take more of the food on his plate but not Christine. I hesitated to ask what had motivated the Karibians to bring two so typically American children to Armenia, but then I realized that it would have been foolish, for what was a typical American teenager like myself doing there?

Out of nowhere, Simonian appeared, waving papers in one hand and moving repatriates out of the way with the other. As he reached our table, he was nearly out of breath. He greeted the Karibians cordially, then turned to me and asked, "Have you finished eating?"

"No," I said, with a *Please, Mr. Simonian, would you get out of my life?* look.

"Then finish up. I've got your papers for the apartment. You and Johnny and I will be together."

I was more than slightly resentful. Simonian had no right to take it upon himself to get me accommodations. I said nothing. I did not want to embarrass him in front of the Karibians. I would have to tolerate my self-appointed surrogate father for a little longer. On the other hand, I realized that at least I would have a place to sleep until I could make other arrangements.

I stood up and bid farewell to the Karibians.

Simonian turned to Mr. Karibian. "By the way, Harry, I saw your name on the list. You're in the same building."

The Karibians thanked him for the information. Christine, who had also heard, broke into a big smile. "Mother, does that mean Tommy will be with us?"

"It appears so, Christine."

"Good! We'll have a lot of fun!"

We all burst out laughing, but that would be the last time we would share a laugh together.

Chapter 15

VIEWS FROM THE TRUCK

We gathered our bags and carried them to one of the antique GM trucks waiting to transport the repatriates to their new homes. The vehicles were gifts of the Lend Lease Program, transferred to the Soviet Union by American taxpayers to fight the war against Hitler.

Johnny and I carried our luggage to the designated area and waited for Simonian. When the driver finally appeared, he instructed us in a friendly but loud and animated manner, using his eyes and arms to make a point, to place the suitcases in the stake-sided bed of the truck. He smiled when Johnny spoke to him in Armenian and told him that there was a third passenger. The driver replied, *"Lav, lav.* Good, good. I can't move automobile. Need documents.*"*

The dialogue terminated when Simonian appeared, talked briefly to the driver, and presented him with the papers he'd been issued.

Simonian was late, he had told us, because he had wanted to check the status of his crates, which contained his barbershop equipment, including the chairs. His gear would arrive at a later date with the other heavier equipment, such as the trucks and the cars that the repatriates had brought with them. Apparently, several repatriates had purchased new vehicles with the purpose of using them in Armenia. These were personal and not gifts to government officials.

Simonian asked the driver to wait for the Karibian family, but the driver brushed him off, arguing that there were other trucks available. Simonian turned to Johnny and me and told us to get onto the back of the truck. He explained that we would be traveling through the center of the city, past the marketplace. He said the driver was willing to stop at the market to pick up some things if we wanted to. But Simonian suggested, and we concurred, that we should go straight to the apartments and get settled.

Although it was December, the weather was mild, even warm. We were about 6,000 feet above sea level, and although Johnny and I had no problems with the altitude, Simonian was already breathing heavily.

From the train station, we would head to the part of the city called Yeroth Mas, or Section 3, which was being developed and settled by the new arrivals from France and Greece. There were still pockets of *teghatsis* living in the area. We were about thirty miles from the Turkish border.

Divided by the mountain, the Armenians had served two masters: the czars of Russia and the sultans of the Ottoman Empire. When the Great War of 1914 broke out, Armenians found themselves crossing swords with their own brothers and cousins across the river. Those on the other side of the mountain had fought for the Turks; those on the Erevan side wore the military uniforms of Imperial Russia. Turkey aligned itself with the Axis Powers in October 1914 and branded all

Armenians as traitors, even though many Turkish Armenians fought and gave their lives for Turkey against Russia and the Western Alliance.

I did not want to think about what I would do if Soviet Russia and the United States went to war.

Johnny and I leaped onto the back of the truck, turned, and extended our hands to help Simonian up. He refused our hands. "If I cannot do it myself, I don't belong here." His face turned crimson as he lifted himself aboard.

The three of us and our luggage filled most of the vehicle. Johnny and I stood in the front of the truck bed, holding on to the cab. Simonian sat with his back against the cab. The driver ordered us to sit down. I told Simonian to tell him that I preferred to stand because I wanted to see the city. The driver explained to Simonian that a young French repatriate had fallen from one of the trucks and broken his neck. I sat down.

The driver, his dark beard partially hiding a pockmarked face, wore an oil-stained brown military tunic, cinched with a wide black belt, its shirttails reaching far below his hips. The unkempt and soiled condition of the uniform convinced me that, as with the many others I had seen in Batumi and on the train journey, it was probably the only clothing he owned. He puffed constantly on an elongated cigarette, which he had rolled himself, as he waited for us to get settled.

Johnny offered him an American cigarette, and the driver grabbed it up while thanking him profusely. After he had put it to his mouth, lit it, and smoked a few puffs, he hugged Johnny as if he were a long-lost son, saying in Russian, *"Harashol, ochen harashol."*

Simonian translated: The driver was pleased with the smoke and thanked him for it.

The driver got into the truck and turned the ignition. The engine coughed, groaned, and moaned, then died. The driver got out, lifted the hood, tinkered with the engine a few minutes, got back in, and turned the ignition again. It did not start. Johnny got down and helped the driver tinker with the engine. This time, the motor hummed.

The driver hugged Johnny again and said, *"Axhbar, motor lav gee des.* My brother, you know the motor car very well." I, too, was impressed. I knew little about engines. Robert and George were the mechanics in the Mooradian family. Johnny explained that he had trained to be an electrician. "In Cuba, I had to learn a lot of skills."

We slowly pulled onto a two-lane street that had streetcar rails down the center. I was impressed to see that at least one of the conveniences of the twentieth century had arrived in this part of the Soviet Union.

As we drove away from the station, I could see other repatriates rushing to get their luggage and belongings, people scrambling with suitcases, moving toward other vehicles in the lot. I wondered how many would be housed in the apartment building we were assigned to.

Shortly after the driver pulled away from the station, Johnny and I decided to stand up and get a view of the surroundings. Simonian remained seated.

The truck passed buildings that appeared out of place in architecture and design, for they were multistory rather than the mud huts the train had passed on its way into the depot. The truck drove onto Lenin's Square, the heart of the city, where there was a concentration of government buildings, the post office, the museum, and a five-story building that housed the Central Committee of the Communist Party of Soviet Armenia and other various ministries, including the Ministry of Culture, Education, and Foreign Relations. The ornate windows and doors decorating these dazzled us. The façades of the buildings had a pink, almost scarlet glow as the sun struck them.

Although conversation was difficult on the noisy truck, I attempted to relay what I saw to Simonian. Simonian seemed pleased and impressed by my report. He explained that the rock of the building was tufa, abundantly available on the Armenian plateau, a soft, porous, malleable volcanic rock that artisans shaped without much effort.

There had been nothing there, Simonian said, when he had visited the city back in the thirties.

As our vehicle inched onto narrower streets, we saw construction workers busy digging, moving dirt to the side of the road. The grandeur of the majestic buildings quickly disappeared from my mind as I saw the conditions for those charged with building them. There were no cranes, no machines, no chisels, no hammers in the hands of the construction workers. Their hands and feet were wrapped in rags. There were no thick leather shoes to protect their feet, no eyewear to provide protection from the chipped stones and rocks. There were no mortar or cement mixers, no drills or hydraulic hammers cutting away at the rock. Human beings, hunched over the boulders, pounded with prehistoric tools to shape the rock. Women, their skin mercilessly burned by the sun, in rags, worked side-by-side with the men. They, too, picked up the rocks, placed them on makeshift wooden boards or wheelbarrows, and carried the heavy loads up precariously unstable wooden planks leading to the skeleton of a building. Their prematurely wrinkled faces belied their ages but reflected the gloom and sorrow of their toil. There was an endless line of human beings—human ants—struggling to reach the top of the hill, moving at a snail's pace, with armed uniform soldiers looking on.

Humans were the Soviets' beasts of burden. I wanted to convey this picture to Simonian, but something within ordered me to remain silent. Johnny and I exchanged glances and did not comment on what we saw. Any dream of a good life in this country died when that portrait of labor was imprinted on my mind. I was there as an eyewitness, not, I hoped, to become a victim.

"And you want to bring your parents into this?" I said to Johnny.

"What did you say, Tommy?" Simonian asked.

"Nothing," Johnny and I answered simultaneously.

We turned onto a wide four-lane street with a long and difficult name to pronounce: Ordzhonikidze. We were headed straight in the direction of Mount Ararat, which meant that we were now going west. The ice-capped mountain loomed even larger as we traveled toward it. We passed the open market, a rotunda that housed the circus, several factories, and a medical clinic, but just before we came to a gated green patch of parkland along the Hrazdan River, something caught my eye. Along a stretch where the sidewalk disappeared into nowhere lay the ruins of an ancient mosque. The minaret had vanished, but the crumbled foundation still supported the mosaic dome. It was a relic of the Persian and Ottoman rule in the region that had accepted Jesus Christ as its savior. The state was unsuccessfully attempting to stamp out all religions. It was an exquisite edifice in its time, with its blue ceramic-tiled dome attesting to its past glory. In the days to come, I would explore and honor its existence.

The road had become rough and dusty. We passed another cadre of ill-fed and ill-clothed workers laying streetcar tracks. They were

Romanian and Bulgarian and German prisoners of war who had yet to be repatriated, I would later learn. Red Army soldiers, well armed, stood and watched these shattered men.

At an intersection, we headed north, hitting pothole after pothole, one so significant that it launched Johnny and me into orbit. We landed hard on the bed of the truck.

"He warned you," Simonian said, smiling when he realized that we were safe.

Not too long after that, the driver pulled between two buildings onto a barren and sandy courtyard and stopped the vehicle. There were several people lingering about, and they turned their attention to us. At the sound of the motor and the ensuing commotion, women appeared at curtainless windows of a three-story building. Some ventured out onto balconies, and I overheard one of them say, "The Americans have arrived."

Chapter 16

OUR NEW HOME

Ours was the first of several trucks to arrive in the courtyard with American repatriates and their belongings. The apartment complex manager led us up three flights of stairs into an apartment whose walls had yet to be painted. There was electricity but no light bulbs, and there was no running water.

"This is not acceptable," said Mr. Simonian, raising his voice for the first time since I had known him.

The manager, recently repatriated from Lyon, France, bit into his cigarette, straightened his beret, and looked into Simonian's eyes. "It is this or nothing. Come and see how my people are packed like sardines. I am sorry, but this is it."

The third-floor apartment contained one room that the three of us would have to share as a bedroom, an alcove that would be a communal kitchen, and a hallway where we could leave our crates.

The plaster on the walls had not yet dried. The windows were not squared in their frames, which allowed the wind to flow through the cracks. There was no central heat.

"No!" Simonian shouted at the top of his lungs. "We are three adults, and we also have much luggage. Most of our things would have to remain in the yard. Do you understand this? One of us would have to stay up all night guarding our belongings! Do you understand?"

"*Oui, monsieur!* I know. We have also assigned guards. We have lived this way since we arrived six months ago. There is little I can do. I have my orders, too. There are others coming, as you know. Not even He can help." His eyes turned to the heavens.

After Johnny translated, I whispered, "Are you ready to go back now?" He jabbed his elbows into my ribs.

The manager continued, "There are two families with many children sharing one room across the courtyard. My countrymen are also angry. Very angry. But there is no housing available. It is either that you accept what I say, or you sleep under the stars . . . and it can become very cold at night."

Accepting the reality of cold, Johnny asked where we could get a stove and wood. The manager replied that the French had started a furniture-building artel and that we could take as much of the sawdust as we wanted to burn. A stove, cots, and mattresses would be provided.

"I guess there is nothing we can do, boys." Simonian said that he would talk to some people he knew who may have risen in the Party ranks and might be able to help. Until then, we had better decide how to cope.

The manager used a few English words in hopes of pacifying us. "I am not villain here. I have two grown children, wife, and my mother living in one room. Not an easy life after France."

There was nothing more to say.

I looked around the room that was to be my temporary home. There were doors leading onto a balcony that overlooked a courtyard. Another balcony from the larger room faced west, giving a magnificent view of the Ararat. In the kitchen area, there was also a balcony that overlooked the courtyard.

The floorboards were uneven. The planks had an inch or two

between them, and in spots you could actually see through to the apartment below. It was obvious that we, and those who would occupy the rooms below us and adjacent to us, would not have any privacy.

"Only certain times of the day will you have electricity," the manager told us. "And then you don't know when it will come on."

"Where are the bulbs?" Johnny asked.

The manager said that they would be issued. To leave them in empty sockets would invite thieves. "You understand, yes? We French survived the Nazi occupation. This is nothing compared with what we had to go through." Then, after a pause, he said, "For you Americans, we have been authorized to issue bed frame, mattress, sheets, pillow, and blanket. If you follow me, I will give them to you. You must sign for them."

"And where can we pee?" Johnny quickly asked.

"Behind our building is a latrine. You are welcome to use it until your group digs its own."

"And drinking water?" I asked in Armenian, using my hands to explain my question.

"In the courtyard is a spring we have tapped into. Most of us carry the water to our apartments; some even wash there, and our women wash clothing there. The water is pure and good."

Simonian said something to him in Armenian, and the manager replied in Turkish. It was obvious that he didn't want Johnny and me to understand, but Johnny did. His folks had also taught him Turkish.

Later, I would ask him what had transpired.

"He told Simonian that he was truly sorry he couldn't be of more assistance. The Americans helped him and his family during the war and gave them food and shelter. He said, 'We have all fallen into a pile of shit.' Some of the Armenians from France have already been arrested for complaining. Some have even tried to escape across the border to Iran."

There was a commotion in the courtyard, and I moved toward the balcony, taking a step out to get a glimpse of what was going on. Simonian shouted at me, "Don't take another step!"

I froze, looking back at him, and asked, "What's wrong?"

"That balcony may crumble under your weight," he explained.

I moved back quickly. "We'll see how sturdy it is some other time."

I decided to go downstairs to see who else would be living in the building.

"Wait up," Johnny called. "I'll go with you. I want to see the expressions on their faces when they find out what their new apartments really look like."

As I turned to leave the room, I got a glimpse of Simonian. His was not a happy face. He had owned his own home, had owned property and a car. The same was true of others, some of whom had even been considered wealthy. They had willingly given up their world and gone back in time to when there was no running water, no electricity, no gas or heat. The women would have to wash clothes in a cistern in the courtyard and travel into the city to the *vanya* to bathe. Those would not be their greatest hardships. Most would lose their husbands as they attempted to take their families back home, one way or another. Their youth spent, they would find it difficult to brave the draconian Soviet life.

Chapter 17

OUR NEW NEIGHBORS

W as there anything Americans coveted more than financial security and privacy? Armenian Americans quickly found their privacy violated in this new world. Voices carried to other rooms, other apartments, and we learned to speak in whispers.

The struggle came within us, not shared, for each had sacrificed in his own way.

With only one exception—the apartment complex manager—the three-story building's occupants were Armenian Americans. Only five of us, however, were American-born.

In the room adjacent to ours were two elderly gentlemen, one a Turkish-speaking Armenian and the other a Russian-born Armenian who had left Erevan during the Bolshevik takeover. They had hoped to find family but did not. They would be buried with little ceremony in

Tokhmakhquel within a year. I would get to know the cemetery well over the next few months, for young bodies were needed to carry the wooden coffins.

A family of three from Nice, France, would move into that one-room apartment when it became available.

Garo Kachuni, a forty-something divorced New Yorker who had opinions on just about everything, had married one of the nurses he met in Batumi. The newlyweds occupied a room on the third floor, next to two longtime New York City residents, the meek Edward Papazian and his irascible wife, Alice. A childless couple occupied the other room on the floor. Among their prized possessions were two American cars, one a brand-new station wagon.

The Karibians lived on the second floor, immediately below us. They would have to put up with Sabu and Momigon, the two bachelors, as neighbors. Soft-spoken Joseph Sourian and his equally quiet Irish wife, Irene, shared a room in the apartment across from the Karibians. The complex manager, his wife, and their two children occupied the other room in that apartment. They had moved out of the French buildings because, he said, he was sick of listening to all of the complaints from his compatriots. Johnny's theory was that he was ordered to move into our building by his NKVD bosses to file reports on our activities.

Many of the Armenian Americans were given rooms in a building about three miles from ours. It was an elongated rectangular facility, resembling a military barracks, behind an elementary school named Toumanian. The accommodations were no better than ours: no water, no heat, outdoor plumbing. I would sometimes meet one or two of them at the state-sanctioned black market, where we would sell personal belongings.

Most families in the caravan had brought electrical appliances, including refrigerators and stoves, and tools, but unfortunately, there was no gas or electricity to operate them. Electricity would be turned on and off at the whim of who knows who. The appliances were eventually sold to the city dwellers who did have electricity, at times, to use them. Those who did not exchange their dollars in Batumi also fared well in Erevan. Later, to my chagrin, I learned that the *teghatsis* would scoop up the dollars at forty rubles to one. They preferred hundred-dollar bills because they could be concealed more easily than the smaller denominations. I kept what I had, because I knew I was going back someday.

As the weeks passed, Johnny and I kept busy assisting the older repatriates. Large crates with belongings arrived daily in the courtyard. We would help the owners dismantle them and use the wood as firewood.

One evening, I asked Johnny, "You're going to get a message to your folks, aren't you? We have fallen into this shit, but they don't have to."

I couldn't believe his answer: "What for? They wanted this, didn't they?" Then he mellowed. "Even if I could write, do you think I can stop them? Would they understand this crap?"

Rough paste was used to reseal letters from abroad, so by now, we knew our mail was being opened and destroyed if the contents did not please the censors. In the first weeks and months, I could not write home. I didn't know what to write.

Most evenings, we lit our room by candlelight, thanks to Simonian's resourcefulness. Although he was busy setting up his barbershop, he still watched over Johnny and me during the winter of 1948.

Simonian would ask, "Do you kids care for some beans and bread?" And before Johnny or I could answer, he had dished out the food onto paper plates and placed it before us. I don't think I ever scooped up anything from a plate and sent it down into my stomach as fast as the meals Simonian provided for us during those winter months.

Somehow, we also found a place to lie down and sleep, and we kept ourselves warm under a ton of clothing and coats. We believed that the good Lord had sent us that mild winter.

But it seemed that just before I closed my eyes each night, I would hear sobbing from the room below. It was Mrs. Karibian. Her tears would pierce my heart, for they made me think of what my mother must have been going through at that same time.

Chapter 18

FOR BREAD ALONE

P andemonium usually accompanied the bright, warm daybreak. The noise in the courtyard always was nerve-wracking. A truck loaded with bread would spark the commotion, which sometimes turned physical, especially if the bread vendor didn't have enough stock to distribute to the masses.

At first, the bread was specifically designated for the French repatriates. The *teghatsis,* who worked at cooperatives, would receive their allotments at their worksites. But there were always speculators who used their muscle to reach the trucks and purchase their kilos for resale elsewhere at a higher price.

The battle line, especially between the French and the *teghatsis,* had been drawn. And I soon learned that some would fight, even die, for bread.

On one particular morning, I looked around the room. Johnny was nowhere to be found. He wasn't between the crates or the suitcases. Then I peered into one of the corners where Simonian had staked out an area. He was covered with sweaters and a coat, apparently sleeping.

I got up slowly from the floor and walked over to the window to see what the commotion was in the courtyard. As I opened the door and took one step onto the balcony, the movement apparently awakened Simonian, who immediately shouted a warning: "Step back."

I did.

"That balcony will collapse with your weight on it," he reminded me, as usual.

I took a step back and stood near the window. Simonian joined me. He pointed to the building across the courtyard and asked, "What do you think were on those ledges over there?" I looked and saw where concrete once supported structures, but now only steel beams protruded. "Let's wait until spring and take a closer look," Simonian suggested.

By then, the *teghatsis* and the French repatriates were shoving and pushing one another. I was surprised to see Johnny in the middle of the melee. The truck driver was in the bed of the truck and was exchanging loaves for rubles. From the third-floor window, I could see that he was running out of bread. Old women, dressed in their multicolored rags, their heads covered with black shawls, and young women, holding infants, some with rubles clutched in their hands, struggled, fought, jumped up and down, leaped onto one another's shoulders, hands outstretched to exchange their rubles for the bread, shouting, *"Hahcecz!"*

Johnny was making sure that the young and the old would get their bread that day by taking their money, reaching over to the vendor, exchanging the rubles for the bread, and handing the bread back to those who could not reach the vendor.

I asked Simonian how far the Ukraine was from Armenia. He smiled. "You're learning fast, aren't you?"

"But why are they standing in line, Mr. Simonian? That's a mob down there."

"Because they know if they don't get any bread, their children will go hungry."

"There are women and children down there, being trampled on, and for what? A loaf of bread?" Then I lost it. "You lied on the ship, to me and the rest of us, didn't you? You knew that people here were starving, didn't you?"

"No, I did not lie. There is bread, plenty of it. But in this country, you must work to earn your share. If you do not work, you do not eat. It's a simple Soviet truism."

"You mean simple Soviet shit, don't you?"

"Listen, listen to me . . ."

"I have, all these weeks."

"Then listen again. When you work, there will be bread provided to you at the worksite. If you don't work, you will not eat. The state doesn't feed parasites."

"And if I don't work?

"There will be no bread, and as soon as you sell all of your belongings, you will starve. Go find work, and quit feeling sorry for yourself." Simonian turned and retreated to his cubbyhole to dress to go to his barbershop.

I stood at the window and continued to stare, watching as one trampled another to reach the vendor. I wanted to step out onto the balcony and shout down to the crowd that this wasn't the way civilized people acted, but who cared what a *norkalogh,* a new arrival in their country, had to say? After all, I had heard *teghatsis* tell other repatriates, "If it was so good over there, why are you here?"

Before he left, Simonian turned to me and said, "You can't change these people, but they will change you."

The door burst open, and Johnny entered with a huge grin on his face. He was chewing on a hunk of bread he had broken off a loaf he was carrying under his left arm. He looked at me first and then at Simonian.

"Hey, haven't you guys ever heard of Darwin?"

Chapter 19

DESCENT INTO DEPRESSION

It may have been the warmest winter in memory, as the *teghatsis* would note, but the twelve months of 1948 would be the time I descended into the nadir of my life in the Soviet Union.

The university turned down my application for enrollment. I lacked language skills and was told I needed to learn to write and read before reapplying. Johnny, with his electrical and mechanical skills, wound up working in a factory and eagerly awaited news of the second caravan. Mr. Simonian made daily trips into the city to meet with officials. He finally did receive approval to set up his barbershop on the four-lane Field Marshal Ivan Bagramian Boulevard, in one of the more prestigious sections of the city. He donated all of his barbershop equipment and the hydraulic barber chairs to the state and also agreed to accept students in modern barbering techniques. Johnny and I helped install the chairs, the first of their kind in the Caucasus, and Simonian thanked us by cutting our hair for free.

I interviewed unsuccessfully at several factories. It seemed to me that the managers didn't want someone with whom they couldn't communicate. I later discovered that most factory managers feared having an American on their payroll.

All I had were the rubles I received from selling personal clothing and items, and I lived on bread and Erevan's most tasteful water. I had too much pride to ask anyone for any kind of assistance. I soon became a victim of diarrhea and dysentery, diseases I thought I could subdue by myself. With roommates gone early in the morning, I suffered alone. My two roommates probably suspected something was ailing me because of my frequent evening trips to the latrine, but they were too busy reestablishing their own lives to pay much attention to me, and they also attributed my unbroken silence to homesickness. That, too, compounded my depression.

I was not the only repatriate having problems. Patience and broken promises had forced many to the breaking point. I could hear Mr. and Mrs. Karibian arguing. "Why did we come here?" It usually ended with her in tears. The Papazians were more vocal and made no secret that they would give up everything to go back. Alice, at times, would step out onto her balcony and shout obscenities at the "filthy, uncouth *teghatsis.*" While the Sourians, though discreet, could not hide behind the masks they wore every day, they left their room to venture out to buy bread in the courtyard.

Most of the repatriates in our apartment unit—with the exceptions of Simonian and Johnny—did not work. Some did not want to work after inspecting the sites and the health hazards they posed. They, like myself, survived in those early days and months by selling what they had brought with them. Unlike the others, I did not have much to sell.

Shortly after our arrival, the Soviet government passed a currency reform that further deepened our misery and distrust for the system. All Soviet citizens were required to exchange their old rubles for new currency at an exchange rate of ten old rubles for one new ruble. Consumers would be able to purchase more with the new ruble, the newspapers stated, and the currency reform would also invalidate the counterfeit rubles with which the Nazis had flooded the USSR during the invasion. The official rate of exchange between the dollar and the ruble was revised at four to one. Those Armenian Americans who had not exchanged their dollars in Batumi laughed, for the going rate on the streets of Erevan leaped to almost fifty to one, because the *teghatsis* knew the reform was just the beginning. They were right. During the next decade, there would be two more devaluations of the ruble.

Rubles were meant to be spent, not saved for a rainy day. Those who stashed away sums of money were subject to a visit from the NKVD when they exchanged their old currency for the new. How, they would have to explain, had they gotten all of that money, except by speculation and exploitation of the working class?

The government-sanctioned black market, where sellers of Western-manufactured goods paid a small fee to sell anything they possessed, became a popular place of exchange between the locals *(teghatsis)* and the new arrivals *(norkaloghs)*. This backfired on the Soviets, for it also provided the *teghatsis* with their first real glimpse of what a worker in a capitalistic society could amass if he worked. It was a lesson that the *teghatsis* would not soon forget. Every Sunday, there were long lines and huge crowds atop the hill at *sev shuka,* exchanging Western goods for Soviet rubles. The first seeds sown grew roots of discontent that would find their way to every corner of the USSR.

Soviets already knew—and the newcomers learned from experience—that you couldn't bank on Soviet banks. If capitalism was so evil, how did these *norkaloghs* have so much?

My shirts went for more than 400 rubles each, nearly the average unskilled worker's monthly pay. A pair of woman's nylon stockings sold for more than 1,200 rubles. Unfortunately, I didn't have any, and I did not want to write home to ask for nylons because I did not know what my family would think—if the letter even got through. The dollar could be exchanged for forty to fifty rubles.

I had the rubles to buy my daily bread, but there wasn't much more on the shelves, though the war had ended nearly two years before our arrival. Items stocked on the shelves of the stores during the winter months included rows and rows of bottled wines and cognacs, cigarettes, bottled jam made of roses, and sometimes cheese, smoked fish, canned stuffed cabbage, green peas, tomatoes, and grape, apple, plum, and tomato juices. But whenever they were available, they were swept up quickly by those who knew they would be there. To be a store clerk was a prestigious position. They had the inside information. Unless you knew a store clerk or learned from the grapevine that a store was about to receive goods, you were out of luck. I seemed to be always out of luck.

Was it not from the Bible that I had learned that man could not live on bread alone? I was living proof that this biblical saying was definitely wrong.

In one of those bread lines in the city, I suddenly realized that somewhere or somehow, I had picked up enough Armenian words to create sentences, to speak and understand when spoken to. It was a great moment and a discovery that I would never forget. How beautiful it was to be able to communicate in words with those around me. While I was waiting in the line, an elderly woman, with a pleasant smile on her face, asked me if there were bread lines in America. I answered her honestly, saying that during my lifetime, I had not seen one, but from books and movies, I had knowledge that there had been bad times.

"You are one of the newcomers, are you not?" she said, detecting the accent of a *norkalogh*.

"Yes," I replied, fully understanding the complete question.

"From where?"

"Detroit."

She had heard of the city. "It must have been very bad for you and your family over there."

I said it wasn't.

"No? Then why did you leave?"

"I wanted an Armenian education."

She nodded understandingly. "Are your parents Armenian?" she asked.

I told her they were.

"Are they also happy to be here?"

I said that both of my parents were back in America.

She looked at me strangely. "No Armenian mother would allow her son to come here. Shameful. Disgraceful. I am sure she is not Armenian." And with that, the old woman moved out of her place in line, walked a few steps away, then turned and said, "May God forgive her."

I didn't know whether to laugh or to cry.

Most evenings during that first winter, when most of us didn't have wood to burn, we gathered around the bonfires we built in the middle of the courtyard from the boards of emptied crates. We would discuss the day and the latest rumors before returning to our cold and dreary rooms. Parked at the front of our housing unit were the two vehicles that the Papazians had brought with them. Mr. Papazian usually had to stand guard to protect them from thieves who were eager to steal parts. They also were on display for the local inhabitants. The *teghatsis* could not believe that an American worker could buy one vehicle, let alone purchase two, without being a capitalist. The New York couple regretted bringing them over, because Ed could not find the gasoline to operate them. That was the least of his worries. Owning two cars branded him as wealthy in a socialist country where everyone was supposed to be equal in poverty. And night after night, some part—first the windshield wipers, then the hubcaps—disappeared. Ed had to sleep in one of the cars to stop the thieves.

The French repatriates were our ties with the Western world. They had shortwave radio sets tuned to the BBC and could get the Voice of America in English and in French. There was a natural camaraderie between the residents of both houses. They would join us around the bonfire and share their war and repatriation experiences with us, as wine bottle after wine bottle made the rounds. Whether it was our common history or our common misery, we trusted them explicitly and respected them. The Armenians of France, too, had climbed the mountain and slid down the other side hoping to get away from European wars. Instead, they discovered that they were deep in "excrement." For some, a few weeks of Soviet life were enough to convince them that they should try to get back to France. A few made quick and hasty plans to leave. One picked up his bike, headed for the Iranian border, and was never heard from again. There were others, but no one knew what had happened to them—that is, until the end of the Cold War.

In the year I had left the United States, Winston Churchill had warned the free world during a speech in Fulton, Missouri, that "an Iron Curtain has descended upon the Continent." Those around the bonfire may not have heard Churchill's timely warning. I know I didn't. And if we had, would we have heeded it? It would get worse, not better.

Instead of an age of peace and reconstruction, 1948 marshaled in an age of a war unlike any known to civilization. At Yalta, Stalin had been given the key to enslave Eastern Europe by FDR and Churchill. The

Soviet dictator began to consolidate his gains and had been preparing to block all egress from East to West Berlin when the Western nations began their long and costly counteroffensive.

The Berlin blockade was on; it would become the first major test of the Cold War. There would be many confrontations on land, on the sea, and in the air before the Iron Curtain collapsed.

Each day, the Armenian American repatriates came back from the city with a bit of information that was more gossip than news. Each day, our hope grew dimmer that the two superpowers would sit down and iron out a sustainable peace agreement. It would never happen during most of the repatriates' lifetimes.

Because of their radios, the French knew that the two sides were as far apart as the North and South Poles. They shared information freely and bravely with us around the bonfire.

No breathing space in their apartments, long lines for bread, the lack of basic food, heat, water, and adequate plumbing all led to expletives about the system but no formal action. Fear still controlled your mind when the odds were immeasurably stacked against you. The Soviet state stank, but we were still outside the prison walls.

And somehow, whatever had been said was neatly exchanged between informers and their handlers for the twenty pieces of silver. Information had been assembled in our dossiers, to be used against us. I could not believe that any of the Armenian Americans in our building would serve as informers. The *teghatsis* did not trust the *norkaloghs,* and the *norkaloghs* did not trust the *teghatsis.* That was the bottom line, so where could the NKVD possibly get anything on any of us? The sum total of my knowledge of informers and their operations came from the silver screen, from Hollywood movies. Informers looked like Peter Lorre in *Casablanca.* They were not real people; they were makebelieve people. Or so I believed. The French knew better. They had survived the Nazi occupation. But they trusted the Americans and would offer help in any way they could.

I listened and tried to make sense of all that I heard. It was difficult for a nineteen-year-old to understand those who were twice, even three times his age. One evening, as we gathered around the bonfire in the courtyard, after several bottles of French wine had circled the fire more times than I could count, Karibian pulled me aside and whispered, "Tommy, how would you like to go home, back to America?"

I heard what he had said, but I wasn't sure what he meant. I asked him to repeat what he had asked me. He did. Then he explained, "Some of us are gathering at our place tomorrow night. We have something we'd like to discuss. If you're still interested in returning, you are invited to attend."

I told him that I would be there.

Chapter 20

A PLAN EMERGES

There were five of us—Karibian, Sourian, Papazian, Kachuni, and myself—at the meeting. I was the last to arrive. The other four were seated on crates. Mrs. Karibian was serving tea when I knocked and was invited into the room. As soon as she saw me, Christine shouted, "Tommy!" and ran to give me a hug. I lifted her chin and gave her a kiss on the cheek. There were dark circles under those pretty blue eyes, and she had lost weight. I looked at Mrs. Karibian; though you could see the hurt in her eyes, she forced a smile. Jean asked me if I wanted tea, and I said I did. She found a cup, poured tea, and handed it to me. Then she gathered up her two children—Michael had been in the bedroom—and said she thought she would pay Irene a visit. "Good luck," she said, looking at her husband, then moved toward the door. Before Jean left, she turned and reminded him, "Harry, please keep your voice down, no matter what happens."

Harry Karibian didn't waste any time in getting to the point. "I know we're all sick of everything we have seen—I know my family is—and I don't think there is anyone here who doesn't want to go back."

Before he had finished his sentence, Garo Kachuni looked at his host strangely, then around the room. "I don't think I want to hear any more. I'm married to a *teghatsi.*" Garo got up, walked to the door, and closed it without a good-bye.

Sourian's face turned sickly, and Harry looked frustrated. It was Eddy Papazian who told Harry, "I told you Garo wouldn't go for it."

Go for what? I thought.

I glanced around the room, waiting to find out and wondering what was going on. The men in the room were twice my age, and in the eyes of youth, elders are supposedly wiser and more experienced. As I patiently waited for someone to say something, anything, I wondered why I had been included in the group.

The soft-spoken Sourian broke the silence. "What do you think he'll do?"

"Nothing," replied Karibian.

"I'm not too sure of that."

"He won't do anything," Papazian reassured Sourian. "When he opened the door and walked in here, he made himself part of this group. The NKVD won't believe he's innocent, because if he rats on us, I'll tell them he came up with the plan."

The discussion made me extremely nervous. I felt the knot in my stomach turn a couple of times, and at that point, I still did not know what they were talking about. To relieve the stress that was building within me, I needed to say something, anything. "Where's Johnny?" I asked, not caring where he really was.

"We didn't invite him. His parents will soon be here."

So there will be a second caravan, I thought. Nobody had attempted to stop them. With Garo quickly removing himself from the room, would I ever know what was in the minds of these men?

I didn't wait for an explanation and asked Karibian why I was there.

He explained, "We need someone to go to Moscow and contact the embassy, to plead, yes, even beg, if necessary, to help us get our families back to United States. If they don't want the men, that's OK, but let them at least assist our wives and children, those born in the United States, to go back." Although he thought he was speaking in a whisper, his voice could have been heard throughout all of the units. "We just can't go on like this."

"Why not just write a letter to Moscow?" Sourian asked. I was sure the question had been debated before but was being thrown out for me.

"Too dangerous," Papazian said. "You know the NKVD's censors read our mail, and I'm sure they would read anything written to the embassy from here. How many times have we heard the French say that their letters are opened and some of them don't even reach them? No, someone has to deliver the letter personally to make sure they get it."

Sourian had his doubts and expressed them. But he was willing to listen to the plan and take it back to his wife to see if she agreed to it.

"All right, Harry, just what do you propose we do?" he asked after a long silence.

Karibian's proposal was a simple one: that the group draft a petition to the U.S. ambassador and ask for his help. If the United States could not assist, we would implore the ambassador to intercede on our behalf and at least present our petition to the United Nations.

"If our letter is made public, we are doomed. The Soviets will come back at us," Sourian warned.

"We are doomed anyway," Karibian said. "Just take a look at what we have become. Take a look at what is left."

All were silent. We were desperate men, doing desperate things in desperate times.

Karibian continued, "Do you think the USSR wants to incur the wrath of the United Nations? And what will happen after the rest of the Armenians around the world who are planning to do what we did hear of it? I think the Soviets will allow us to leave because they can turn around and say, 'See, we are a free country. You don't like it here, then leave.'"

Sourian wasn't convinced. "I'm not so sure the Soviets give a damn about worldwide opinion. Look at all of the negative articles we read about what the Dashnaks were saying, and look where we are. If you believe, you believe—and if you don't, you don't."

"Then you're out?" Harry asked.

Sourian didn't answer.

Papazian nodded, and I thought he, too, was in agreement with what Sourian had just said.

No one asked my opinion, probably because they had heard that I had been ready to jump ship on Day 1. I sat there waiting to discover what role they wanted me to play.

Karibian summed it all up. "If we do nothing, we are all doomed. Every Sunday, all of us go to the *sev shuka* and sell what we have worked for all these years. There will come a day, and that will be sooner than we think, when we have sold everything. Then what? Each day, the *teghatsis* look more like us, and we look more like them. I do not have to ask what Irene or Alice tells you each night, because my wife says the same thing. There has not been a night since we arrived in Erevan that my wife hasn't cried herself to sleep. Hell, there's no privacy at all. We can't even put our heads down on one pillow together. Our children are but a few feet away."

Karibian need not have said another word. We all knew he was right.

Eddy turned to me and asked, "Well, Tommy, what do you think about all this?"

I took a deep breath, and what came out of my mouth was, "I have nothing to lose. I have no family here. Nothing to keep me here. Thank God. And I am selling everything. I'm already scraping the bottom of the trunk."

"Then you're with us?"

"Of course."

I told them that if there was even a slight chance of getting back home, I wanted to try. I had not known these men as well as I did Johnny and Simonian, but I trusted them. After all, they had come over on the same boat.

Now it was up to Joe Sourian to decide whether the group would move forward as a team.

"I guess . . . I guess, for my wife's sake, hell, I don't care what happens to me," Sourian slowly said. "I'm just worried that if something did happen to me, what would happen to Irene? I am all she has."

Papazian also was worried not about himself but about his wife. "It's no secret, Alice and I would give everything we have—both those cars—to anyone who could get us out of here. If we don't get out soon, you know they'll come for Alice. She can't keep that big mouth of hers shut, no matter how much I warn her. She alone keeps those fools on Nalbandian Street busy."

The plan would move forward, but I still had some unanswered questions. What wasn't clear to me was who would deliver the petition to the embassy and when. I presumed Harry and Joe, who had American-born wives, would be the logical candidates to make the trip to Moscow. I presumed wrong.

"Tommy," Karibian said, "you are the most presentable, the youngest, and you have a college education." I'd only attended one semester. "You and I will take the letter."

Sourian and Papazian both nodded their heads.

I started to explain the embarrassing facts of my recent illness, that I was having diarrhea and nothing was helping me, that my illness had sapped my strength. But wouldn't that be interpreted as cowardliness? A nineteen-year-old could never admit he was a coward. I said instead, "Harry, I don't have funds to go anywhere. But I will write up the petition and be the first to sign it."

Papazian looked at me. "You don't have to worry about money. You'll have more than you need. I will make sure of that."

His answer satisfied me. Secretly, I was elated about the prospects of going to Moscow. I wanted to go home, and I was not going to fail this time. On the other hand, I was nervous.

Simonian may have warned me that the Soviets didn't play the game according to American rules, but I was cocky enough to believe that I would make up the rules as I went along.

I was wrong. It almost cost me my life.

Chapter 21

DRAFTING THE PETITION

During the next few days, and always after Johnny and Simonian left for work, I labored diligently on the text we were to present at the embassy. I thought it would be a simple task. It wasn't. I could not, on paper, justify what I, and the others, had done. We had, after all, given up our country. There was too much emotion involved, too much at stake. How does one justify such a blatant wrong? And usually, intelligence flies out the window when emotion intervenes. How had I ever reached that point? I sat there struggling to write something rational, but all I could think of was how I had screwed up my life. I should have been completing my first year of college, going out on dates, enjoying my family. Instead, I was asking the country of my birth to forgive me for betraying it.

I sat in that one room filled with crates, which I shared with two other adult men, petrified. I could not think of anything to put down on paper. I saw myself sleeping on the floor, with no source of heat or water, getting up in the middle of cold winter nights to pee in a bottle or trek hundreds of yards to a latrine that reeked so strongly that I wanted to puke.

Draft after draft, written on precious white paper that would soon be irreplaceable, was torn to shreds, then stuffed into one of my jackets, to be tossed later into the bonfire, ensuring that other eyes could not see the frustration and the contents of the letter. I was running out of paper and patience. Neither I nor any of the others knew the name of the U.S. ambassador to Moscow. I didn't know how to address him. I wondered if I should date the letter. I wrote and rewrote. I needed to be clear and honest, for there were others to consider. I knew that I—we—had to succeed.

Finally, I decided that the text of the letter should be simple and direct. When we met with the U.S. ambassador, Harry and I could explain in detail.

The text read as follows:

"My dear Mr. Ambassador,

"We beg the Ambassador of the United States of America to use his powers, his office, to assist several members of the Armenian American repatriation community who arrived in the republic of Soviet Armenia, USSR, on the First of December, 1947, and are presently residing in Erevan, the capital of the Republic of Soviet Armenia, to return home to the land of our birth, that is, the United States. As adults, we have made our mistakes, but we do not believe our children should suffer the consequences of our foolish actions. There are several naturalized American citizens who also implore the Ambassador to help them to return home. Our belief is that 'once an American, always an American' is a truism that cannot be altered or changed by a signature. Moreover, we will not be a burden upon American society, for most of us have loved ones—mothers, fathers, brothers, and sisters—still residing in the United States. We would be returning home to them and attempting to pick up the pieces of our lives.

"For whatever assistance, Mr. Ambassador, you can render us, we would be greatly appreciative and humble to you and the country we all love so dearly.

"We realize that our problems, created by our own actions, should not be yours. Or the United States'. But our children, born American, raised American, belong in the land of their birth, America.

"We implore you, we beg you, take us back home."

I signed the petition first, followed by Karibian, Papazian, and Sourian.

There was no turning back.

"You kept it brief, to the point. And there is no criticism of the Soviets. Excellent, " said Sourian after reading the letter. "Let us pray that the ambassador can help us, for if he can't, and this falls into the wrong hands, God have mercy on all of us."

Two copies in my handwriting were made. One I kept, the other Karibian took. He would accompany me to Moscow. We debated when to execute our plan.

"As fast as we can purchase tickets, we should go," said Karibian in a determined voice.

I felt as Karibian did. The sooner we got to Moscow and made our pitch, the sooner we would go home. When I returned to the United States, I would tell those who asked why I came back that I simply couldn't adjust to Soviet Armenian culture.

There was a dispute over when we should execute our plan. Sourian emphatically wanted us to wait. "We need to, we must, wait for an appropriate time."

"And when do you think there would be an appropriate time to do this?" asked Papazian, who had raised his voice to a level that caused Karibian to plead, "Keep it down, Eddy. We don't want the others to hear."

"Someone may learn what we're up to if we wait," Papazian insisted.

Karibian and I agreed with him.

"It is too dangerous," Sourian replied. "There are not too many foreigners in Moscow these days. Tommy and Harry will stand out on the streets. Stalin loves to show off his military might during the holidays and invite everybody to Moscow. Pick one of the major holidays, May 1 or November 7, when hundreds of foreign diplomats, Communists, fellow travelers, and foreign correspondents are on the streets. That's when we should go. You may even bump into one or two correspondents and tell them our story. The two of you won't stand out on May Day; everybody will be drunk. You will on any other day. You'll be too conspicuous. Maybe you can even persuade one or two Americans to take the letter to the ambassador. Let's not take any unnecessary risks. I'm sorry. We should wait."

None of us could punch a hole in Sourian's argument. It was mid-March, and it would give us some time, about seven weeks, to prepare for the May 1 trip. Karibian and I would finalize our plans. The less the other two knew, the better.

Harry and I decided that we would travel by plane, on separate flights and on different days. I would leave first. Once I reached my destination, I would check into a hotel, get to know the city and where the embassy was located. Then we would meet after the May Day parade in the vicinity of Lenin's Tomb. The mausoleum was located on Red Square. If I had not made contact with the embassy by then, when Karibian arrived, we would telephone for an appointment. Then we'd jump into a cab, drive to the embassy, and present the letter and our case to the officials.

It seemed like such a simple plan.

Chapter 22

DREAMS AND NIGHTMARES

I had nothing but time on my hands.

Papazian made rubles available to me. He also offered me the use of one of his cars, and to demonstrate my driving skills, I drove the Papazians and a few of the French repatriates to the circus. But when

Simonian heard what I had done, he pointed out that if I had struck a pedestrian and, God forbid, fatally or even slightly injured him, even though it was not my fault, it would be an automatic life sentence in Siberia, I decided that I didn't need to drive in the USSR. The drive to the circus was the first and last time I would operate a vehicle in the Soviet Union.

I walked everywhere. I usually skipped the trams, because they were filled beyond capacity. Passengers hung on to windows, then jumped off the moving streetcars as they neared their destinations.

The girls I encountered in stores and on the streets wore drab dresses and little, if any, makeup. The opposite sex did not appeal to me at this time. Besides, most of them looked, but many were not, much older than I. The high elevation and the sun had scorched their skin.

There were several my age in the French apartment building across the courtyard. They were pleasant to look at but unapproachable, it seemed, because their overprotective mothers stood constant vigil. Besides, Kiva was right; I would always compare.

I missed Kiva. I wondered where she was and what she was doing. I hoped that I would see her again, but the news from Palestine wasn't good, either. The Jews were still fighting for a homeland. War in that region of the world was imminent.

Johnny was staying out later each evening. Simonian told me that Johnny had met a nurse in Batumi and was thinking marriage.

"Would they move in with us?" I asked Simonian with a smirk on my face when I heard the news.

"I am certain they have made other arrangements."

Late one full-moon evening, as I stood at the window to the balcony overlooking the courtyard, enjoying the serenity of the night and the silvery summit of Ararat, I saw something move in the dark shadows of the arched entrance to the French apartments. At first, I thought my eyes were deceiving me, but they were not. A slender figure dressed in an ankle-length black gown moved gracefully onto the moonlight-bathed stage, first as an apparition and then definable as a young woman. She moved ever so slowly toward the water fountain. My eyes followed every movement. Intrigued, I had an urge to dress and go down to the cistern on a pretense of washing. I was mesmerized and found that I couldn't move from the window for fear that whatever was down there would vanish. I concluded from her dress and her veil, held with her right hand to cover her face, that she was a Moslem, but none seemed to live in our area. My mind was vulnerable to tricks, I realized, but what I saw was real. I was sure it was not a dream. As she bent to fill the jug, an uncontrollable mass of black hair fell across her forehead, and she was forced to remove her hand from securing the veil. As she brushed the hair aside, her dark eyes and natural red lips offered a portrait of a young lady of breathtaking beauty, like the ethereal beauty of Wordsworth's "phantom of delight." She disappeared as quickly as she had appeared.

It had to be Kiva . . . it had to be a dream.

When I related my experience to Simonian, he looked at me with a smile. "What you're describing is someone who appears to be a Moslem, but there are no Moslems, only the French across the way. True, our older women do dress in black, especially if they are widowed, but they do not hide their faces. They are Christians. I don't think you're going to find anyone like that in the French buildings. Chalk it up as a dream. And besides, if there is anyone like that, Johnny surely would have seen her long before now."

Johnny smiled at me. "My friend, what you need is a woman."

Chapter 23

THE WAITING GAME

M y entire life at that time was consumed with preparing for my trip to Moscow. The rest of the world passed me by. I stayed in and around the apartment most of the day, and, because we had minimal, if any, electricity, I was well asleep before my roommates returned home. It was peculiar that I could become exhausted sitting around a room, looking at crates, and having little, if anything, to do.

"Get out; go for walks," Johnny suggested one evening after he had returned from work. "Or one day, I will open this door and find your body on the floor."

"I'm not at that point."

"Not yet, but . . . ." Johnny sighed, deeply concerned for my welfare. He tried to lift my spirits by suggesting that we go out on a double date. "My girlfriend can fix you up with one of her friends. She knows a lot of women who want to date repatriates. How about it?"

"Johnny," I started, struggling to find words that would not offend him. "Look at me. Take a good look. Am I really ready to meet one of your girlfriend's friends?"

He stared and saw only the frame of the man who had boarded the ship in New York. I had lost some twenty pounds. My clothes didn't fit, and my hair, though not down to my shoulders, was nearing them. I did not shave regularly, for I found it to be a chore. I had to go down into the courtyard to the spring and use cold water, while women washed clothes and diapers. I looked like the Neanderthal man.

"Please, Johnny, forget it. Leave me alone."

He did.

I regretted that I could not confide in him. I had but one mission—to get back home—and I didn't want to get involved with anyone. I didn't want to forget the life I had left or attempt to share my life with someone who could never understand or identify with that life. If I married, as Johnny apparently was planning to do, I would live in the past; she would be living in the present, hoping to build a future together.

I dared not share my thoughts with Johnny or Mr. Simonian. I did take Johnny's advice about long walks. They were therapeutic. I would walk to a nearby park and sit in the grass along the Hrazdan River. I made several trips back to the mosque to explore but was ordered out of the ruins because they were archaeological dig sites.

The city of Erevan was growing, thanks to the repatriates, but there was little entertainment unless you drank. There were only a few drinking spots, and they were filled with cigarette smoke and drunken Soviet military from the border villages.

Those who had signed the petition had decided that it would be best to avoid visits to one another's apartments, so as not to raise suspicion. Anything we had to say would be said around the bonfire when the French and the other Americans retired for the evening. Garo, of course, knew something was brewing, but I was certain that he was not privy to the details. As Papazian indicated, Garo would be implicated as a conspirator if our plan were revealed. It never once crossed my mind that we could fail.

I continued my charade, pretending that I was slowly adjusting to my new life. To ensure that Simonian believed I had accepted my fate, I sent several postcards home. I wrote that I was well and healthy and learning Armenian. I suggested to Mother and Father that they encourage Uncle Avak and Auntie Vartouhie (who were actually deceased) to repatriate. "Our homeland needs more workers like them. They will fit right in with the rest of us who are dying to see them," I wrote. Childish, maybe, but fortunately, my parents and my sister understood the coded message.

Walks helped to ease the tension, and walking around, but not with people, lifted my spirits. I never seemed to be hungry, although I always found myself in one line or another, more out of curiosity than anything else, to see what the store had to sell. How ironic it seemed that others, like myself, had the rubles to buy, yet there were no food or consumer products to purchase. The Soviets apparently had also shelved one of the fundamental law of economics—and of life—that of supply and demand. People who worked in America, who earned wages, had many choices.

On one of those occasions when I strolled the city streets, I found myself on Abovian Street, glancing at a marquee that said "Kino." I had no idea what I was getting into; the word was not yet a part of my Russian vocabulary. I paid three rubles to be admitted, strolled down a darkened hallway, and seated myself in an even darker chamber before a large white screen. It was a movie house. As my eyes adjusted to the darkness, I discovered that there were two, at most three, other patrons. *Teghatsis.* The seats were of wood and had no cushions. I waited for the movie to begin. I do not recall the name of the first Russian movie I saw, but strangely, I found it amusing to sit through a movie that I knew nothing about, in a foreign language with no subtitles. As the movie began, I thought that it would be an excellent way to learn the language.

The plot was predictable: Boy meets girl, or girl meets boy, on the local *kolkhoz,* or collective farm. There is conflict. One of them (it alternates) struggles to meet his (or her) state-mandated production quota, set by the far-from-farm Moskovian bureaucrats. The young lad is about to be ousted in disgrace from the collective for not meeting his quota. But upon encouragement from the fairer sex—and a few holdings of hands later (no kisses allowed, please)—the worker, his morale boosted, proves that he is up to the task. The two, of course, fall in love and continue feverishly to harvest the corn or wheat or barley. They meet, even surpass, their production quotas. The *kolkhoz* director is pleased, the members of the collective farm are overjoyed, and they all live happily ever after.

The end? No. There is more. In a socialistic society, the viewer must get his or her three rubles' worth. So, one golden autumn day, after the harvest is completed and the numbers are in, the director, with a huge smile on his face, rushes to the couple and, waving a document high above his head and flashing a smile with his gold tooth showing, announces to the couple and all assembled farm workers that the two young workers have been honored by the first secretary of the Communist Party as "Heroes of the Soviet Union" and will be going to Moscow to meet him and receive their bright five-point gold medals for their achievements. They are married, of course, before they leave, with all of the hoopla of a Russian wedding. The movie ends with the smiling newlyweds riding into the sunset on a tractor, as a portrait of Stalin, superimposed on the Red Banner of the Soviet flag, slowly rises on the horizon.

Two, or could it have been three, moviegoers would stand up and shout at the top of their lungs, *"Salva Stalinu, nasha otez!* Glory to Stalin, our father!" After several such movies with little variation in the plot, I decided that I would learn my Russian elsewhere.

All through March and until mid-April, I could not tell one day from another. But I knew that I could not avoid Mr. Simonian any further. I desperately needed a haircut. I could not recall my last one.

When I entered his plush (by Soviet standards) barbershop, the barber from Philadelphia laughed. "I wondered when you would pay me a professional visit."

"I'm here."

Simonian's eyes gleamed with delight. "And you sure need to be!"

There were no other patrons or students in the shop. I questioned him about that. Simonian explained as he invited me to sit in one of the chairs, placing a lily-white barber's sheet over my chest and tying the back strings. He said that his students felt threatened by the hydraulic chairs, couldn't operate them, and thought they would seek another profession.

"They'll be back," Simonian said with a chuckle in his voice. "The Ministry will order them back." Then he gently took hold of my hair and glanced at the fuzz on my face. After appraising both, he said, "You really need a haircut and a shave, don't you?"

"That's why I'm here."

"Let's see what we can do."

I asked him why he didn't seem to have many patrons.

"Oh, this place hasn't caught on yet. It's new, and anything new seems to come under close scrutiny."

He got out his scissors and comb and got down to work. I was his captive for the next forty-five minutes. And there was so much catching up to do, much to my chagrin.

"Who is this special woman I am making you handsome for?"

"Haven't found her yet," I said.

"The love bug hasn't bitten you? It will. It will. You'll see."

"If you say so . . ."

"What have you been doing with yourself, then? I get home late, you're asleep, and I leave before you're up. How do you fill your time?"

"The movies."

"Good, very good. Have you seen any you like?"

I wanted to tell him the truth, but I didn't. "It's a learning experience."

"Good, very good."

When he swung the chair around, I was facing the boulevard, and the unshaven *teghatsis* had stopped in front of the shop and were peering in to see the show. Their faces formed strange grimaces as they pressed them against the display window to get a better look inside the shop.

"What are they looking at?" I asked Simonian, puzzled at the attention.

"At you . . . and me and the way I cut hair. They haven't seen a revolving chair like the one you're sitting on. You know, there are no merry-go-rounds, so they are in awe when the chair and you turn."

"You're kidding me, aren't you?"

"No, watch." Simonian twirled the chair, and the eyes in the window seemed to pop. "It's very new to them."

He finished my haircut and put his foot on the hydraulic pedal, and the chair and I slowly moved from horizontal to vertical. Simonian got a hot towel and swirled it around on my face to soften my beard, and I could hear gasps from outside the window. Perhaps they thought Simonian was about to suffocate me.

After he lifted the towel from my face, he got out the razor and sharpened the blade on the leather strap hanging from the chair. There was more gnashing of teeth from outside. I supposed they thought that Simonian was going to cut my throat and that was why he had sharpened the razor blade. I expected the *militzia* to burst through the door at any minute and arrest the barber from Philadelphia. As he prepared to make his first sweep of whiskers with his razor blade, he asked, "Have you been to the opera house?"

"No," I replied. I had moved my mouth to answer, and his blade nipped my chin.

The first drops of blood.

Simonian quickly apologized, grabbed a towel, and put it on the wound as I mumbled, "It's all right," over his apologies. The sight of blood, I thought, would have driven the fans away; instead, a few of the braver ones in the crowd ventured inside the shop and took seats to watch the bloody massacre.

Simonian greeted them with a smile as I tried to explain that I had never seen an opera or a ballet, except in the movies. I hated ballet. "I prefer the movies," I said, as I took my hand from underneath the sheet and attempted to feel the cut.

He moved my hand away. "Like most Americans, you prefer movies to culture."

"I like the movies back home," I said. "Don't see any sense in ballet. I can't see any sense in adult men and women tiptoeing across a stage, waving their hands up and down, asking us to understand why they are doing it. And doing it to music."

Simonian burst into laughter, and tears began to roll down his cheeks. He turned the chair around so that I would be facing him and managed to say, "The opera house is only a block or two from here. Why not stroll down there? Take in a performance or two, and maybe that will change your opinion." Then, as if it were an order, he said that I must go to the little park, where I would find a lot of young people. "It's a popular place. Go and meet kids your age."

"Maybe I'll do that."

Simonian brushed the hairs off the sheet, pulled the cloth away, and whirled me around so that I could get a good look at his work in the mirror. "You actually look human," he said with a smile. "Ah, if only I were young again." He paused and then, as if it were a command, ordered, "Go to the opera. There you will find the intelligentsia, the intellectuals of our society. White hair and wrinkles will come soon enough. Don't waste your life in that room."

I thanked him for the advice and attempted to pay him for the haircut, but Simonian reminded me that Johnny and I had lifelong free haircuts in exchange for the help we had given him installing the chairs. He refused to take my money, and I felt embarrassed as he pressed it back into the palm of my hand. I thanked him again and slowly walked to the door, with Simonian a step or two behind me, acknowledging the crowd with a smile.

He raised his voice, and I knew that he was not addressing me when he said, "See, your haircut took many years off you. I can make anyone look like you." Suddenly, two of the spectators rushed to the barber seat and tried to sit down. "One at a time," he told his new patrons.

As I reached the door, I looked out at the five-story, city-block-long building that was directly across from Simonian's shop and asked, "Can't we get an apartment over there?"

Simonian looked in the direction I had pointed to and replied, "I don't think so. The high echelons of our government and their families live there." Then, as if in a warning for me not to go around asking questions about the occupants, he added, "There are also a few top NKVD officers and their families."

"Very solidly built structure," I said nonchalantly. "Didn't know we had anything like that except those few I saw near the depot."

"If you're impressed by that building, then when you leave, look down the street at the hilltop, behind those massive iron gates, and you'll find the home of the first secretary of Armenia."

"Nothing like where we live, is it? Guess I have to join the Party," I quipped.

"They won't accept you. You're carrying too much American luggage."

I wanted to see the first secretary's home, introduce myself, and discuss the inequities in the distribution of food and housing. The working class just wasn't getting its share of just about anything. Instead, like a magnet, I was being drawn the other way, in the opposite direction, down the mulberry-tree-lined Bagramian Boulevard toward the opera house.

Chapter 24

AN ENCHANTED AFTERNOON

It was a sunny, warm, but windy afternoon. The March winds whistled between the branches of majestic trees, which unselfishly shared what little space they had with newly planted mulberry saplings along the boulevard. The mulberry tree is to Armenia what the apple tree is to Michigan. They were everywhere. When the fruit ripened, the *teghatsis* would stop, pick, and eat the gray or deep-red fruits as if they contained the secret to everlasting life. It was not rare to see an old woman or two under a mulberry tree, gathering the fruit in their aprons or picking the fallen berries off the sun-scorched sidewalk, later to dry them on sheets spread atop their mud huts. The *toot,* as the fruit is called in Armenian, would be sprinkled with their scrambled eggs, if they were fortunate enough to find eggs at the market. It was good for the digestive tract, they told me, or whatever else might ail me.

Although spring was in the air and winter had never clearly identified itself during the months of January and February, the buds already were awakening, but the plants and flowers had yet to arise from their short winter slumber.

On this quiet boulevard almost devoid of vehicular traffic, there were no restaurants, no boutiques, only a series of bread and wine stores. The boulevard, named for the field marshal whose bravery had helped turn back the Nazis at the gates of Leningrad, was one of the city's showcases.

The opera house was a short distance from Simonian's shop. As I neared a fenced-off area, I could see it soaring above the chestnut-tree branches, the gray rotunda of a stone structure. I crossed Bagramian and headed toward it. Ornate fences almost seven feet high and made of wrought iron separated the sidewalk from the park area. I walked along the fence line, spotting benches within, occupied by young and old, men and women, some in military uniform, others in civilian clothing. At the corner, just before the entrance, a muscular woman, her hair drawn tightly back, with a white apron over a cotton coat and a dark skirt that ended near the middle of her felt boots, was selling fruit juices. She acknowledged my existence by moving her hands, inviting me to buy a glass of her "lemonade." I smiled at her but rejected the offer, because she had only one or two water glasses to use as containers to serve the public; the Soviets had not yet discovered paper cups.

I walked into the park, where an oasis of flowerbeds, shrub-lined lanes, and clusters of trees awaited me. Most benches were already occupied. Simonian was right. It was a place where one could retreat.

Each face I passed had a story written on it. I wished I could have sat there and compiled them. I nodded to return the nods as I strolled by. A young stranger in suit, white shirt, and necktie was an anomaly among these people.

In the park were several paths, some cobblestone, that led to a central statue, enclosed by a small wrought-iron fence and a flowerbed. As I reached the statue, I thought at first that it was an image of Lenin. But it was not. It paid tribute to the nineteenth-century founder of the opera house and its first director, the noted Armenian composer Shahumian. As I strolled in the park, I came upon young lovers holding hands. They looked up and smiled. How I envied them. But there were no embraces, not in public, because it was *ne'culturney* (not cultural). Just touch her. Tell her in the language she will understand, "I love you." Who knew what tomorrow would bring?

Others sat stoically with their copies of *Pravda* or *Soviet Hyestan*, reading the Party's version of the daily news, pausing to glance at the time traveler. They had seen many changes and had survived them. But they had taken time to look at the one from across the sea—was he a messenger from the future?

People bent over chessboards stopped whispering with each move, while others, as I strolled by, whispered, *"Americanetz,"* and then returned to the game.

With the exception of a small billboard announcing the evening's opera program, there was nothing political. Strange. No portrait of Lenin or Stalin; even the omnipresent loudspeaker that broadcast directly from Moscow was absent. This was a haven where one could contemplate and think and not worry that "Big Brother" was watching. Arguing politics, a way of life for most Armenians, seemed forbidden in that oasis.

There were men in military uniform but not the kind who reported to their superiors. They were brave and decorated Red Army soldiers who wore not only their medals of valor but also the scars of the battles they had fought—a lost leg or arm, a severely burned face. They, too, sat and contemplated the next battle. No one seemed to care about the past ones or what they had accomplished for mankind. Empty vodka bottles in their pockets or next to the benches told the stories of where they were right now. They were the forgotten heroes. Time had forgotten them, and in time, we forgot them. These men had come back from battlefields believing that a nation and its leaders would be grateful, but words of a better life to come were meaningless when current needs were not being met. There was no fight left in them, just empty bottles in their pockets and empty promises in their hearts.

I found an empty bench and sat down. Had it been only a year ago that I had been in high school, looking forward to graduation, looking forward to changing the world?

I heard laughter, giggling, and gooselike chatter in the distance. The unintelligible noise moved slowly but erratically toward where I was seated. It abruptly stopped a few yards from the bench. There stood five young women, equally attractive, as if cut from one mold. As we all exchanged glances and smiles, it was they, not I, who spoke. In a chorus, they asked, *"Norkalogh?"* Of course, a newcomer, they all agreed. But from where?

"From Egypt?" said the first swan.

"No."

"From France?" said the second swan.

"No."

"From Greece?" said the third swan.

Then the one with the long Armenian eyelashes, the fairest of them all, said, "Hush. Can you not see? He is an American!" She turned to me and begged confirmation.

I was too embarrassed to reply. She insisted that I answer. My face reflected my embarrassment.

"He is blushing," said the first swan.

"How cute," said the second.

I replied in my best Russian, *"Da, ya Americanetz."*

The swans giggled—all except the young lady who had recognized my clothing. In order not to compound my ignorance of their language, I refrained from saying anything else. They looked at me, and I looked at them.

Then, as they prepared to leave, the one who had guessed where I was from asked, "You attend the opera tonight . . . it is ballet?"

If she was brave enough to practice her English on me, surely I could reciprocate. *"Nyet."* I shook my head to make sure she understood. She looked disappointed. I had not stood up, for manners were not on my mind when this lovely group of young ladies first approached me. She turned and said something to her friends, who burst out laughing. I would have asked what the joke was, but I couldn't put the words into a sentence.

"Seechaz," she replied, and then, almost in a whisper, said to me, "Come to opera tonight. It is ballet. Tchaikovsky, *Swan Lake*. I . . ." She paused and pointed to the others. "We will dance."

I wanted to say, *"Nyet,"* but she had cast her spell over me. The word would not come out. Instead, I nodded to indicate that I would be there.

"Harashol. Good."

"Pietrome, seechaz!" the young ladies shouted to their friend. "Come now, let's go. We cannot be late."

For one long moment, she did not respond. She stared at me and I at her. Then she joined the others, but as she moved away, she reminded me again about the ballet.

I shouted to her, "What's your name?" in Russian.

She shouted back, "Tatiana! What's yours?"

"Tommy."

She nodded and smiled. "Tommy . . . and Tatiana."

The curtain came down on the first act.

As I strolled out of the park, I shook my head several times and asked myself why I had agreed to attend the performance. But all I could see was the budding of flowers reminding me that the first of May was only a few weeks away.

Tatiana had cast a spell that I did not have the power to break.

Chapter 25

AT THE OPERA HOUSE

I was in the audience when the plush red curtains, embroidered and emblazoned with the golden hammer and sickle of the Soviet flag, parted at eight o'clock in the evening on Tchaikovsky's magical, enchanting ballet *Swan Lake*.

The stage, the scenery, the music, and the dancing all left me breathless. Whether it was the Tchaikovsky or my being awestruck at a live stage performance, I could not say. I was completely ignorant of the arts, for most of my youth had been spent in gymnasium after gymnasium, learning the art of basketball.

My eyes were pinned to the stage, trying and hoping to pick out Tatiana. Unfortunately, I could make little distinction between the ballerinas. The women and the men on the stage had perfect physiques. Like Siegfried, I, too, soon became confused. Tatiana could not be the golden-haired Odette, though her body and its grace and eloquence surely would have qualified her as the queen of the swans.

If I had not been so intent on what was occurring onstage, attempting to single out Tatiana, I would have realized that there were others who kept focusing their attention not on the stage but on me.

At the first intermission, I slipped out of my back-row seat, left the auditorium, and joined the hundreds of others in the lobby. I felt conspicuous even there, for my suit, white shirt, and necktie didn't seem to fit in with the crowd. Many of the men were in military uniforms, the women in black skirts and white blouses. Even there, at the center of culture, ballet enthusiasts wore their working-class shrouds and masks. The men not in uniform were without ties, and their shirts, blue or brown, were not buttoned at the neck. I was sure that some were wearing the same clothing they had worn to their offices or worksites that day. Only those in military uniforms, with every campaign ribbon and medal imaginable, looked distinguished. The women with the officers also were more attractive, more fashionably dressed, and they smiled more. This was not a Metropolitan Opera of New York crowd, like those I had seen in movies—no furs, no jewels, no red lipstick or makeup. There was little, if any, evidence of wealth.

I retreated to one of the niches in the lobby, observing the noisy, cigarette-in-hand crowds strolling up and down the lobby. It amused me to watch the men and women flirting as they passed one another. One human trait that the Soviets could not regulate or dictate, I quickly concluded, was the natural attraction of men for women and vice versa. Men eyed women, even those who were with other men. Women instinctively responded, either with a faintly concealed smile of approval or a most stern expression of rejection. But there was no aggressiveness, no wanton or vulgar gestures exchanged, no brash moves.

I joined the crowd and began the circular trek. I could not help but notice the appraising, even vicious looks I caught during my stroll. I did not understand the attention. I decided to stop and glance at the opera's upcoming program: Bizet's *Carmen,* Gounod's *Faust,* Mozart's *Don Giovanni,* Mussorgsky's *Boris Godunov,* Verdi's *Aida,* and Puccini's *Madame Butterfly.* As I perused the schedule, I sighed, shook my head, and muttered, probably a bit too loudly, "How sad it is that only the music of the past can drown out the woes of the present."

A soft voice conveyed me back to the present. "What is sad, *maya Americanyets?*"

I turned and discovered Tatiana. She was standing there smiling at me, and after the initial surprise, I wondered why she wasn't backstage. Her face was flushed, and she was wearing a jogging suit, blue with white stripes from the shoulders to the sleeves, which seemed so out of place in the plush lobby with its red carpeting, gold-rimmed mirrored green walls, and stucco ceilings. Her eyes had a sparkle to them, but a closer look revealed dark shadows under them, evidence of stress and sleepless nights.

"I was just talking to myself, and I guess a bit too loudly," I replied, after the surprise faded, momentarily forgetting that she might not understand me.

She asked in a teasing manner what I had said to myself.

"Nothing, nothing really . . . except how great you were onstage." It was a lie, for I had not been able to pick her out onstage. Unfortunately, she knew it. The compliment I had hoped would impress her didn't work.

"Do all Americans lie?" she asked.

"I don't understand."

"I was not onstage. I could not perform tonight," she replied. Then she pointed to her right ankle. "I hurt it in rehearsal. I will not perform for five or six weeks."

"You mean you twisted your ankle?"

"Yes . . . twisted."

I felt bad for her. "There will be other times . . ."

"Yes, I know, but I wanted so much to perform tonight."

I looked around for somewhere to sit, but nothing was available. I was tempted to ask her if she would like me to call a cab and take her home, but before I could, she asked me if I wouldn't mind having company for the final act. I told her I would be delighted.

As the orchestra tuned up, Tatiana turned, her eyes studying me, and her hands reached for my tie. She slowly loosened it and took it off, then tucked it into one of my suitcoat pockets. I was completely puzzled. But I had noticed earlier that no one in the auditorium was wearing a tie.

"Cravat, n'leza. Bourgeois . . . cosmopolitanism."

I understood that the tie was unacceptable, but the rest of her statement confused me.

"You must teach me Russian," I told her, "and I will teach you English."

She agreed. I was about to guide her to where I had been seated, but she decided that it was too far from the stage. Since there was no assigned seating, she took my hand and led me to the middle of the auditorium. I was nervous as other patrons turned to look at us. We slipped into our seats, our shoulders briefly brushing. We looked at each other. I was amazed that such an innocent touch had aroused such strong feelings in me. It seemed like eons since I had touched a woman. Only the parting of the curtains and Tchaikovsky saved me from my memories.

As the enchanter Rotbart wove a web of deception around Siegfried, whose unwavering love for Odette broke the enchanter's spell, Odette shed her wings and was personified. It was a beautiful finale to a wonderful ballet. When the curtains were drawn and the performers took their bows, as people screamed and tossed flowers onto the stage, I could barely hear Tatiana ask, "Did you like it?"

"Yes, yes, very much. They were excellent, the music and the dancing. Everything."

"Do you want to go backstage?" she asked.

I was stunned at the invitation. It terrified me. Although I was tempted to accept, I declined.

Tatiana's eyes laughed as she sensed my fear. Then, gently, she lifted my hand to her face and said, "They, too, are real. Just like me. Just like you."

"I know, but that is like a dream. And I don't want to wake up."

She nodded.

"When war was here, I thought it, too, was dream—a nightmare. We lived in Moscow. Moscow is so big. Mother and I came to Tiflis, then Erevan."

"And your father?"

"He went to the front. He was military."

"Did he come home?"

"Yes, Father came home. Two brothers did not. They died at Kursk."

"I'm sorry."

As we stood there motionless, I realized how much taller I was and how frail she looked. I wondered about the others who danced with her, if they were as frail and as diminutive as she.

I asked if I could take her home. She hesitated before she replied,

"I must go with my friends. They are waiting for me. I must be with them."

I was disappointed, but I didn't feel rejected; after all, this was only our second meeting. As she moved a few steps toward the stage, I inquired, "Will I see you again?"

"Only if you want to."

"Where?"

"In the park. I must still attend my training."

"Even though you have an injury?"

"Yes. It is mandatory. No excuses to skip rehearsals; one can be dismissed."

"Seems pretty harsh, doesn't it?"

"If you want to dance like Ulanova, Semenova, and Plisetskaya, then you have to train hard."

I guessed they were names of ballet stars.

I was about to wave good-bye when Tatiana reminded me, "Please, Tommy, don't wear cravat."

"I won't. I promise."

Tatiana disappeared into the crowd.

Chapter 26

NECKTIES AND COSMOPOLITANISM

W hat is this crap called cosmopolitanism?" I asked Simonian the next morning as he placed the tea and the cups on one of his large crates, which we used as a table.

"Ah, I see," Simonian said with a grin as he poured the tea, offered me two pieces of hard candy, and took a seat across from me on the other crate. "You have finally started reading the newspapers. That is good. Very good."

Simonian was having fun in his own peculiar way at my expense, for he knew I did not yet know how to read Armenian. There were no

English-language newspapers or magazines that I knew of at the time in Soviet Armenia.

I looked at him and said I was serious. "Someone accused me of it, and I just wanted to know what I was guilty of."

"Oh? Accused you? That *is* serious. Who was she? Is she as attractive as that girl on the boat?" He leaned over the table to study my face for my reaction.

"How do you know it was a she?"

Simonian chuckled. "You are sitting here, aren't you?"

I asked him to get to the point.

"These days, cosmopolitanism is a pretty serious offense, and if it was leveled by an official, he would have to be someone with authority. I doubt we would be discussing the topic if someone of authority, like the NKVD, had accused you. Now, tell me what this is all about."

I did not answer immediately; I wondered if I should. But in the end, I decided it would be best to find out what Tatiana had meant. I told him I had been at the ballet.

"And who is she?"

I said that a young dancer had happened to chat with me and had mentioned the word *cosmopolitanism* and had said that I should remove my tie. I watched as a smile crossed his face.

"You went to the opera house? You had a date. She must be a great looker for you to tell me all of this."

"No, it really wasn't a date. I just met someone in the park after I got the haircut."

"And who was this someone?"

"I really don't know her."

"Someone you don't know accuses you of cosmopolitanism, and you don't know who she is? Tommy, this doesn't make any sense at all. I think I will need more information."

So I told him everything that had happened since leaving the barbershop—the walk in the park, the discussion with Tatiana, attending the performance. "If you can't explain cosmopolitanism, I will have to find someone who can."

"Calm down, calm down, and I will try to sort this all out. First, this person, whoever she is, must be attracted to you." I was going to disagree, but I allowed him to proceed with his explanation without interruption. "She wants to protect you. How old is she?"

"About my age, I think." He was waiting for me to give him more information about the girl, but I didn't. I didn't have any. I realized that I really didn't know anything about her. I started to say something about Tatiana's two brothers and her father, but I stopped.

Simonian explained the seriousness of the allegation. "To be accused of cosmopolitanism these days is very serious. If convicted, you would face prison time."

This startled me, and Simonian also amazed me with how much knowledge he had about the Soviets. For wearing a necktie I could be sent to prison? I didn't believe it, and I told him so.

"There was a recent article in one of the newspapers related to this, to the harmful effects of cosmopolitanism on our people," Simonian continued. "Obviously, the article had been approved by the Politburo, or it would not have appeared in such a prominent place—the front page. The newly enacted law called upon all Soviets to sieve out those who glorify materialism, to fight against those who worship all things foreign, and to report to the state those who continue to idolize the bourgeoisie and the aristocracy."

Simonian's explanation seemed ludicrous and loutish to me. I would not accept it. It did not seem rational. "So, my tie represents all of the sins of capitalism, the aristocracy, and the bourgeois classes?"

"Correct!"

"And wearing one brands me as an enemy of the people?"

"Exactly."

"Oh, God forbid!"

"No. The Communist Party forbids."

"Then who are these zealous servants of socialism who are purchasing all of my ties at the *sev shuka*? These people buy them up quicker than anything else I have, except maybe for the chewing gum."

"The ties are cloth, and the purchaser could be making stockings or clothing out of them." He glanced at his watch. "I've got to get going. I have to open up the shop. I cannot be late."

I should have know better than to ask him why the hurry. He donated everything to the state. Was it a crime to be late for work, too?

It was.

Simonian got up from our makeshift breakfast table, went into the bedroom, and got dressed for work. As he left, he asked, "Am I ever going to meet this young lady?"

"I don't know her. I don't know if I will ever see her again."

"It's too bad. You could learn a lot from her."

Chapter 27

STANDING IN THE RAIN

I stood in the rain outside the opera house and waited for Tatiana. If I agreed with anything that Mr. Simonian had told me at breakfast, it was that Tatiana was someone special whom I should get to know better.

I wasn't thinking romance. She wasn't beautiful in the stately, elegant style of Kiva. And there I was again. As Kiva had predicted, I was comparing all women to her.

Tatiana's years of brutal practice to become the ballerina she desired to be gave her an exquisite body that was graceful and sleek and legs that would be the envy of any model. Her skin was creamy white, so coveted by the darker-skinned Armenians of the mountain range. And her eyes, Armenian eyes, large and dark and mysterious, sparkled purple or deep blue and lured one to them immediately. The eyes sparkled but told nothing. She knew how to keep her secrets. Tatiana had the perfect figure, a regal carriage, and the swan's neck of a prima ballerina. She would have drawn attention on the Champs-Élysees or on the catwalk of La Croix, but fate placed her in the Soviet Union at the height of Stalin's power. Tatiana never realized just how exquisite she was. She was on the stage for the public to see and admire, but what she really wanted was to be touched and loved by someone who did not wear a military uniform and did not know war.

There I was, standing in the rain, thinking of her and asking myself where she was.

Did she confide in her mother that she had met a stranger, an American who wore a necktie? And did her mother remind her daughter that coming into contact with a repatriate, especially an American, could be dangerous, could endanger her father and the family? Did her mother tell her that some had even been arrested and exiled for mere contact with foreigners?

I stood there waiting, soaked in rain, reflecting on how most of the Russians—not the Armenians—I encountered on the streets of Erevan did not even make eye contact with me. I suspected that they feared that someone was watching. Always in a glass house. But there were those who willingly risked it. I suspected that Johnny's nurse and Garo's bride were among the exceptionally brave. Raised a Soviet, married to an American, outcasts of their society—how much worse could it get for them?

In less than five weeks, I would be in Moscow. Why did I want to be involved with anyone? I wanted to hear the soft voice of a woman, a voice other than Johnny's and Simonian's. I wanted to do something in the evenings other than gather around the bonfires and reminisce about a life lost. Karibian, Sourian, Papazian, and I had agreed that the best strategy before we implemented our planned trip to Moscow was to refrain from visits to one another's apartments. Limited contacts made me stir-crazy. The four bare walls of the room had become a chamber of ennui. I needed to escape. Tatiana would be a reprieve.

Simonian, of course, suggested books. And I read his books, Bernard Shaw and his Fabian Society and Oscar Wilde's *The Soul of Man Under Socialism,* Hemingway and Jack London and Theodore Dreiser. I had read them so many times that I had memorized entire passages.

Tatiana was so much more pleasant to look at than a printed page. Where was she? She must come! What did I say wrong?

The rain had seeped through my jacket and soaked me. I was numb. I waited for what seemed like hours and decided that it was futile. I should have known. She wasn't coming. I turned and headed out of the park. I wandered in the rain, walking in the direction of Abovian Street. I didn't want to go back to the apartment. I decided that it was time to write my family and let them know that I was still alive.

I covered the several blocks to Lenin's Square, stood before his

mammoth statue, and bowed gracefully to him, uttering a few expletives as he quietly looked down upon me. Then I continued the few
yards to the Central Post Office, purchased some postcards, and
retreated to one of the stalls to write. I wrote several cards with photos
of historic sites, terse notes stating that I was well and healthy and that
I missed and loved them. Nothing political. Never anything political. I
approached a window and handed the clerk the cards. He looked up,
stared at me, and gasped. My rain-soaked clothes, my hair dripping
water down my face and into my eyes, water on the marble floor, and
my face as white as a ghost's—it was no wonder he thought he had
actually seen the ghost of Rasputin emerging from the cold waters of
the Neva.

"I would like to send these cards to America," I announced, half in
English and half in Russian. He continued to stare. He nodded as if he
understood, but I knew he did not understand a word I had said. "I
would also like verification that these beautiful postcards have reached
their destination," I added.

The postal employee nodded. He still did not understand.

"Ya vas ne'panee my you." He finally spoke, but I didn't understand.

There was a wall of silence between us. Someone behind me tapped
my shoulder. I turned and looked at someone about my age, bronze-
skinned, with curly brown hair, who topped my six feet by four or
maybe five inches.

"May I be of any assistance?" he asked in a British accent.

I started to explain the situation, but he had already overheard my
dilemma. In a few words, he explained to the clerk, who immediately
began processing the cards.

The stranger looked me over and said, "You're Tommy, that bloody
American, aren't you?"

I said that I probably was, but I definitely was not bloody. "How did
you know my name?"

He introduced himself and explained that he had been looking for
me. The clerk handed me a slip to fill out. It was in French and Russian.
I looked at Abraham, who said that he could take care of it. With me
providing the answers to the questions on the slip, Abraham filled in
the blanks, I returned the necessary paperwork to the postal clerk and

paid him, and my postcards were on their way to America. If only *I* could have been dispatched home so easily, I thought.

I thanked Abraham. As we walked out of the post office together, I asked how many languages he knew.

"None," he said with a smile. "Does anyone really know a language?"

"So, you're a philosopher, too?"

"No, I'm a basketball player."

"You're a what?"

"I play basketball for a living."

"You're a professional basketball player?"

"No. There is no such thing as a professional athlete in the Soviet Union." And then he listed the languages he spoke: Arabic, Armenian, French, English, and some Russian.

I was impressed.

Abraham continued, "Those documents won't guarantee that your letters will reach America."

I knew that, but I wanted to hear his explanation and asked, "Why not?"

"Since your cards are going to the United States, the NKVD will look at them, and if they believe there is a secret meaning in what you have written, the cards will be destroyed."

He also cleared up the mystery about how he knew my name.

"From the *sev shuka,*" Abraham said. "One of the other Americans was selling something, and we began to talk. He told me about you. Your family is in America. He told me that you had come to this country by yourself and that you know basketball. You are a fool, you know."

"Why?"

"If I have to tell you, then you are not as smart as some people have said."

I pushed for an answer.

"I'm here with my father and mother and two brothers and sister. We are from Port Said."

"Port Said?"

"Yes," replied Abraham. "Do you know it?"

"Yes. It was one of the ports we stopped at before we came here. But we were not permitted to get off the ship, so I did not see the city."

"Oh." Abraham sighed ruefully. "Too bad. Egypt has so many beautiful places. You would have liked it there."

"When did your ship arrive?" I asked.

"We arrived in Batumi after you bloody Americans left. We were quarantined aboard ship."

"Quarantined?"

"Typhoid. There was typhoid on our ship."

"My God. You're lucky they didn't send all of you back."

"No, you mean unlucky, right?"

We laughed. It was the beginning of a lifelong friendship.

Chapter 28

FINDING A FRIEND

I personally had never heard anyone with a British accent. There was, of course, Churchill and English actors in war movies. But those weren't real people to me, not like the bronze-skinned, dark-haired, Egyptian-born Armenian who was as good-looking as those stars. He had learned to play basketball from American armed forces personnel stationed in Egypt. He would later prove to me that he was as fluent in basketball as he was in languages.

Life had changed for the better for him and his family once the Soviets discovered how proficient a player he was. Recruited to play basketball in Leninakan, he was about to change jerseys to play for the Institute of Physical Culture and Sports in Erevan. He urged me to participate in a scrimmage.

"Before, we had nothing. Now, my family has bread and sugar and butter on the table. Sometimes even chocolates."

I sat with my mouth watering, eager to hear more about sports.

We were on a rain-dampened bench in Weepers' Garden, adjacent to the post office at the foot of Abovian Street. I forgot about my wet clothes. I listened while Abraham filled my ears and my mind with the benefits of playing ball for the Soviets. Some people did profit in this amalgamated nation of fifteen republics whose rulers claimed it was an egalitarian state. The question was, could I be one of them?

Chocolates. The word made me dream of Hershey's and Mars and Mounds and Milky Way candy bars back home. The thought of sweets awakened in me the delights my tastebuds had indiscriminately enjoyed at one time.

"Chocolates? I haven't seen anything that resembled a chocolate bar since I left America. Where are they hidden? Under what counter? Where do they get the sugar to make them?

"Play basketball, and it can all be yours, too."

"I don't believe it," I said.

"It is true," he replied.

Abraham knew I was drooling. He had been there, aching for some comforts of back home, and was tossing me a life preserver.

Visions of sugarplums danced in my head. I turned what he had told me over and over in my mind. And the only thing I could think about was that I had written a letter to the U.S. ambassador, and I was going home.

"And we get a voucher for meals when we prepare and when we play in tournaments," Abraham was telling me.

"Do you also get paid?"

"You mean in rubles?"

"Yes, money. Like dollars. Do you get financial compensation for playing?"

"No, no," Abraham protested, shaking his hand in front of my face as if he were guarding me. "No money. No rubles. I play basketball, and they give me a stipend and food." But there was another benefit if one proved good enough to make the republic's team. "You can travel."

Abraham had really piqued my curiosity. "Travel? Where?" I asked.

"We will go to Moscow this summer. Then Leningrad and maybe Kiev. They played against the Lithuanians last year, and it was bad."

"You mean the Armenians were badly beaten?"

"Yes, very badly. That is why the Institute is gathering new players from the repatriates."

"I see."

If the Armenian team could travel around the country, could it also travel to Europe and, possibly, the United States?

Abraham knew immediately what I was driving at. "No. No Europe. No America. Just the Soviet Union. If you make the national team, the NKVD must give approval to travel—you, me, they never approve. If you were the best in the world, you would not be allowed to travel outside the Soviet Union unless the NKVD had a hook on you to pull you back into the bread line."

"But Moscow?"

"Moscow, yes. No Europe. No United States. Do you understand?"

I understood him well.

Abraham was quick to point out that there were other stipulations to qualify as a member of the traveling team. "We must first win the championship of Armenia. Leninakan and Kirovakan have strong teams. If we defeat them, we will go to Moscow this summer. If not, we will beat them next year. We must play together as a team to become a team."

I did not like all that I heard. I didn't tell him that I didn't plan on being around Erevan for much longer. But I considered the possibilities. There was the thorn of an athlete's doubts about being able to play against a caliber of competition he had not seen. I would not want Abraham to have high expectations of my talents. If the ambassador told us that there was nothing he could do for us, I would surely look Abraham up.

"I have not touched a basketball for more than a year," I told him. "And, besides, physically, I do not think I could run up and down a court without looking like a steam engine." I explained how incompatible Soviet food was with my body. These statements surely conveyed a message of insecurity, but I had to remain uncommitted. I had other things on my mind.

"Abraham," I finally said, "I am not as good as you may think I am. I am very sick. My stomach . . . Maybe someday, you and I could team up."

Abraham took a long look at me before he reassured me that he understood.

"When our boat reached Batumi," Abraham related, "I thought we would all die. With the typhoid and the quarantine for almost three weeks, we were all ill. And the food? Very bad. I know how you feel. I have walked in your shoes. But we have survived. There is a reason why we are here. There is a reason why I met you in the post office. Can you see, it is *jagadakeer?*"

I laughed. Was there any Armenian in the world who didn't believe in fate?

"You will attend practice, yes?"

I refused to commit myself.

Abraham pressured me. "All of these people in this park—all repatriates. No *teghatsis*. Look at them."

I did. I saw what I had seen throughout the city: people in need.

"All of these old people come here every day. They have little to eat. But they share their miseries with one another, and that gives them hope. They eat their black bread when they sell something. That is all they have. Maybe some cheese. They have nothing else to do but wait . . . wait and die. They try to forget. They play backgammon. They dream of how it was back in Greece and Egypt and France. You now see people and things differently from when you were in America. Watch. Look closely at the old men; they will die here. We won't. Believe me, you and I will live."

As we stood up to leave, Abraham said, "We practice tomorrow at six. I will tell the trainer you will be there. I will come and get you so that we can go together."

He was persuasive, but I knew I wasn't going to go. I had other plans.

"Abraham, you don't know where I live." I threw it out as a joke.

Abraham remained determined to get me on a basketball court. "You are in American House in Yeroth Mas, no? Erevan is not too big a city. Not like Cairo or Alexandria. I will find you. We will make a good team. You'll see."

"Abraham . . ." I started.

"Yes? More questions?"

"No, not really. I just want to thank you for everything. I am sincerely impressed by you. In America, we say first impressions are very important. And you really made a great first impression on me."

"Merci, merci beaucoup," he replied with a smile. Then his face

grew solemn. "We, from the Arab world, also have a saying: Not only first but all impressions are important."

It was confirmation for me that Abraham was, indeed, a philosopher.

Chapter 29

THROWING DOWN THE GAUNTLET

I still hadn't made up my mind, but the next day, I scrounged through my trunk to see what I could wear for the scrimmage. I found an old pair of gym shoes, the ones I had worn the year we beat Miller High School for the city championship. I had kept them for good luck. I had T-shirts and a pair of shorts and some sweat socks, so I had most of the gear I needed. But then I ran into a big problem: no jock. I kept looking. Nothing. As I scraped the bottom, tossing things around, the letter to the ambassador surfaced. I quickly stuffed it back into the corner. Seeing the envelope shocked me to my senses. What I was doing was ridiculous. I tossed my gym shoes back into the trunk and slammed the lid.

There was a knock on the door. I opened it, and there stood Abraham, all smiles. He had found me as he said he would.

"Are you ready?" he asked.

"No," I replied. "I'm not going."

"What do you mean you're not going?"

I was trying to drum up an excuse. "I don't know how to play. I never played basketball in my life," I lied. I hoped that Abraham would understand.

He wasn't deceived. "I know you can play basketball," he said.

Now he'd become Sherlock Holmes, too. "OK, Abraham, how do you know I can play?"

"Your eyes. They light up when we talk about it. The way you walk, all of your moves. It is basketball."

"Damn you!" I shouted at him. "Leave me alone."

"No, damn *you*. Now, tell me, what is wrong?"

I couldn't tell him. I couldn't tell him how homesick I was. How I was going to Moscow. About the others involved. About the letter.

"You bloody Americans are crazy." Abraham was disgusted with me, and he was justified. His bronze face turned red. He had begun to leave but then turned and yelled, "No! No! You will come. I promised the trainer you would come. I cannot break a promise."

"Abraham, please, I can't! Please understand. I can't. I mean it."

We stood there sizing each other up. I felt like shit having to lie to someone who obviously had my best interests at heart and who wanted to be a friend. Suddenly, there was noise in the corridor, and the doorknob turned. Simonian entered. I was as surprised to see him as he was to see Abraham.

"What's all this shouting about?" Simonian asked. "You can be heard all over the building."

"Nothing. Nothing's wrong. My friend and I . . ."

"Friend." He took a good look at Abraham. "I didn't know you had a friend."

Abraham reached over, shook Simonian's hand, and introduced himself. Without a second's hesitation, they continued their conversation in Armenian. I assumed that Abraham explained the situation.

"I thought you were at work," I said bluntly.

"I have the day off, and I was visiting with Sabu. He's under the weather. By the way, Momigon would like to talk to you when you have a few minutes."

"About what?"

"He didn't say."

Abraham had explained everything to Simonian. He immediately aligned himself with Abraham. "It would be good for you, Tommy. Unless . . ."

"Unless what?" I asked defiantly.

"Unless, of course, you have been exaggerating your athletic abilities all these months."

That was the last straw. I turned to Abraham and said, "I'll go. Let me get my things."

I gathered what I needed, stuffed it in a duffel bag, and marched out of the room, with Abraham a foot or two behind. I didn't say goodbye.

We headed for the tram stop. Abraham wouldn't stop talking about basketball. I kept silent, fuming over what Simonian had implied. I could hear Abraham talking, mentioning that there would be other repatriates—from France and Egypt and from Rumania and Bulgaria—at the practice. "Now we will have an American, an international team."

Chapter 30

THE PIONEERS' PALACE

The Pioneers' Palace gym occupied most of the second floor of a three-story white-stone building on Moskova Street. The gym had a squeaky-clean polished parquet floor, high ceilings, huge twelve-foot windows protected by mesh wiring on three sides of the walls. A series of bars were attached to the fourth, interior wall. They were used for gymnastics and ballet. All of the gymnastics equipment—the horizontal and parallel bars, the pommel horse, and the rings—was stashed in a corner covered by gym mats. In one of the other three corners was a piano, also covered with mats to protect players who might slam into it. The piano was only a few feet away from the baseline, and the far-end windows were only a few steps away from the other baseline. A player could mangle himself if he drove in for a layup and didn't stop immediately or was followed by a defender whose momentum carried him into the shooter and pinned him against the wall. The gym was suited for gymnastics, not basketball. It might work for basketball practice, maybe a light scrimmage, but not for a full-blown game between adult opponents, which I believed was the purpose of this meeting.

The Pioneers' Palace was the best indoor gym facility in Erevan at the time.

I had played in smaller facilities and the Olympia Stadium back home. That evening, I would have played outdoors in a blizzard to prove myself. Not to these people but to Simonian, for I knew he would be inquisitive the next day.

I could see no locker rooms and asked Abraham, "Where do I change?"

"Right there," he said, and he pointed to an area cordoned off, with thick red carpeting running the length of the hall and a draped entrance.

"And where do I put my street clothes?"

"On the floor. Nothing will happen to them."

I felt uneasy, rubbed my forehead in wonderment, but didn't say anything. Then I remembered I didn't have a jock strap and mentioned it. He laughed so loudly that it drew attention to us.

"That's OK. They won't notice."

I looked at him.

"OK. Wait here." In a few minutes, he returned with a triangular cloth and handed it to me with the suggestion that I should "just tie up the strings and hope they stay tied."

I eyed the cloth suspiciously but took it and put it on. Was there an alternative? I changed my clothes under the close scrutiny of the other players, who did not say one word that I could understand. I felt coolness from them, but that was to be expected; after all, I was the newest player on the block.

Basketball had been a part of my life since I was six or seven. I knew the game well. And I knew locker-room antics and practical jokes. I was prepared for anything. I did not need to prove myself to these players. I wanted to know how they played the game and by what rules.

In America, I had played against some of the finest high school players in the country, and I had held my own. I did not know how much strength I had, and the long trip and stress had taken a toll on my body. But as soon as I saw the ball, the backboards, and the baskets and heard the sounds of shots bouncing off the rim and sinking into the net, I felt that I was back home. This was the perfect escape.

I strolled onto the floor, grabbed a few rebounds, and took a few shots. This was my home turf. My problems dissipated for the moment.

But basketball is a team sport, and the other four on the floor could make you look good or bad. I wasn't sure how I would fit in. I knew how to communicate, pass the ball; make the play so that my teammate would get the easy shot, the basket. I could get back on defense and, above all, get that rebound.

There was a fierce suspicion, almost hatred, between the *norkaloghs* and the *teghatsis*. I had to bridge that animosity.

I knew what prejudice was, but Armenia and the Soviet Union had taken it to a level that I had never seen before: fierce nationalism. When Lithuanians, Latvians, Estonians, Russians, Georgians, Ukrainians, Azerbaijanis, and Armenians clashed in an athletic sport, it was all-out war.

In Detroit, I never felt I was playing against a particular ethnic group. I was competing against a team of Americans playing Americans.

In Detroit, I knew most of the players on the team. Many rival teams knew me. I knew who smoked, who drank, and who was sleeping with whom. They knew me. That was a key in a team sport, to know yourself as well as your teammate. That was what made a team. In a team sport, championships are won by the team and their coach and every member of the team on the bench. They are also lost by the team and their coach and every member on the bench.

As I warmed up for the scrimmage, my goal was not to embarrass myself or Abraham. This was not supposed to be a long-term relationship. All I wanted to do was forget, for just an hour, the problems that were weighing me down.

Counting the players and coaches, there could not have been more than twenty-five people in the gym. It was not basketball country, I was sure of that.

"Aren't you going to dress? I thought you were going to play, too," I asked Abraham, as he stood there watching me warm up.

"Coach wants me to officiate. Come, let me introduce you to him."

As I walked over to the bench, I had decided that the coach had made the decision to sideline Abraham so that I would stand alone, on my own merits. He didn't want Abraham feeding me easy baskets and making me look good.

The coach—the Russians call their coaches trainers—was Konstantin Nikitich. He wore a military uniform over a slim figure. His blue eyes were looking as nervously and awkwardly at me as mine were looking at him. A faint smile played on his lips. It was probably the first time he had ever met an American-born Armenian. After exchanging the usual greetings, with Abraham translating, I was teamed up with four *teghatsis*. We would be the skins, playing without jerseys. I took a few more warm-up shots, dribbled, passed, and smiled at my teammates, hoping that they would get the message that I was not an alien.

Abraham summoned the teams to midcourt, and I stepped into the center circle for the opening tipoff, since I was the tallest on my team. Then came the opening jump ball. It felt great, like old times. I was back in America, even if only for a brief time. But my gym shoes and the polished floor were incompatible. I slipped all over the place. I had played on slippery floors before, so I knew I had to make an adjustment, no driving in for layups, concentrating on set or long shots. It was strange how those unused skills came back after only a few minutes. I made tap-ins under the basket and could pass out whenever the opposition piled up on me. I hit a few from far out that had to have impressed those on the sidelines. I may have been weak physically because of the lack of food, but I could play. One doesn't forget a game that one has spent a lifetime learning. I made my share of baskets and made sure my teammates had their opportunities to shoot and score.

At one of the breaks, Abraham called me to the sidelines.

"Konstantin Nikitich," he said, "wants to see your gym shoes."

What a strange request in the middle of a scrimmage. But he was the coach. I untied the shoelaces to one of my shoes, slipped it off, and handed it to Abraham. Abraham looked at it first, then handed it to the coach, who looked it over, bent it, turned it over to look at the rubber imprints, and touched the grooves. The only thing he didn't do was kick the sole.

They sure made a big deal over a gym shoe. But then, when I took a closer look at what the others had on, I understood. They wore low-grade sneakers, made of cloth that had a thin layer of rubber for soles. How the players managed to stay on their feet and on the floor was beyond me. The coach said something in Russian to Abraham. Abraham told me that the coach wanted to know if I had any more shoes like the ones I was wearing. I told him that I didn't, that the ones I was wearing were the only pair I had brought with me from America.

Remembering how Russians liked to say that anything the repatriates were selling on the black market could be purchased in Moscow cheaper, with a chuckle in my voice, I told Abraham to tell the coach, "There are a lot more like the ones I have in Moscow."

Abraham groaned at what I had said and told me to shut up. "This is not the time to be smart."

The coach asked him what I had said. I was certain that Abraham would modify as he translated. But the coach immediately exploded in laughter. The laugh was sincere, and a warm smile crossed his face.

Later, I asked Abraham, "What the hell did you tell him?" He said nothing. "Come on. What did you say?" I pressed.

"I told Coach you said that if you made the team, you would write home to your parents and have them send over several pairs of shoes and American basketball uniforms."

I was embarrassed. "You really didn't tell him that, did you?"

"Of course."

"Abraham, believe me, I will never use you as a translator again."

"But you have no one else. Besides, I work for free."

The scrimmage resumed. It went well, I thought. During the game, I would pat some of the members of my team on the butt after they had executed a pass or made a basket, a tradition among American athletes. The scrimmage ended before I knew it, and I was still in one piece. I felt I had played a decent game, under the circumstances. Abraham supported my feeling. But the coach didn't say a word to me afterward, so I was left in limbo. Abraham's smile was as huge as a full moon after he chatted with the coach. When he approached me, I asked him what the coach had said. He said he'd tell me later.

"OK, where's the shower you promised?"

"Follow the others. They will lead you to the shower room. I will wait here for you."

"Thanks."

I showered for more than an hour. I loved every moment of it. There was a layer of dirt under the sweat. I just stood under the shower, letting the warm water wash everything away. But my sorrows refused to leave. I felt as if I hadn't showered for years. I could see other players glancing furtively at my body. I wanted to turn around and ask them if they hadn't seen one before. Then I realized that it was probably the first time they had seen an American naked. As long as it was only their curiosity that was aroused, I didn't mind.

It was good to shower. The warm water splashing against my body invigorated me. It was like the sacrament of baptism. Born again. I thought I would have played for anyone if they would only allow me to take a shower afterward. When I got back to my clothes and began to dress, I looked for my wallet and discovered it was missing. I dressed hastily and raced back to the gym floor to tell Abraham. He asked me if I was sure that I had the wallet with me when I had left home. I was sure. I remembered that I was going to give it to him to hold but had decided against it, since Simonian had assured me that there was no theft in the Soviet Union; it was a capital offense to steal. Stealing bread was stealing from the state, and if convicted, it meant either a long stretch in Siberia or even death by execution. Of course, I hadn't believed him.

"What did you have in the wallet?" Abraham asked.

"Seven dollars."

"American dollars?"

"Yes. And a few rubles and photos of my family. They can have the money. It's worthless. But I want my photos, Abraham, I want my photos back."

He again asked me if I was certain that I had the wallet with me. He suggested that it was possible that it might have been stolen on the tram.

"It was taken from my pocket in the dressing room," I said. I was visually angry, irked that he did not believe me. I repeated what Simonian had told me about theft in the USSR.

"Simonian lives in a world of makebelieve. He should come live in our dormitory. Wait here." Abraham disappeared.

I stood there as the gym emptied, looking rather foolish, resigned that I would never see the wallet again.

As I waited, a slender man in a jogging suit, with white hair and a receding hairline, began moving mats around and getting gymnastic equipment ready for the next class. He was having trouble moving one of the pieces of equipment. I went over and helped him. He looked at me with a strange grin.

"Where? Where do you want this?" I asked.

He replied in Armenian, then pointed to the spot. I helped him gather up the basketballs and put them in a box. I assumed he was the building custodian.

About a half-hour later, Abraham returned with a big grin on his face, waving my wallet in his hand over his head.

"Where did you find it?" I asked, my face lighting up.

"Oh, someone who knew who took it went and retrieved it," Abraham said nonchalantly.

I could not believe he had gotten the wallet back, money and photos intact.

"How did you find it?"

"We know who the thieves are and who can talk to them in their own language. Once they get to know you, they will not bother you."

As we gathered our things to leave the building, I asked Abraham how he thought I had played; his answer was ambiguous.

"Just like an American."

I didn't know what that meant, but I wasn't going to ask. Then he calmed my fears.

"Tommy, Konstantin Nikitich wants to see you in his office tomorrow. You must be there."

I had mixed feelings about meeting with the coach. I was getting too involved in something I had no business doing. "Why? Do I get my box of chocolates?" I finally said.

"You must ask him, not me."

Abraham gave me directions to the university and told me the time of my appointment. He retrieved my wallet and encouraged me to play. I needed to back away. I did, after all, have other things on my mind.

"Will you be there?" I asked, for no other reason than to keep the conversation going.

"Of course. Who will translate?" Abraham apparently remembered another message from the coach to me, but he didn't appear eager to convey it. He looked uncomfortable.

"Is everything all right, Abraham?"

"Yes . . . and no."

Had I offended my new friend?

"OK, as you Americans say, I will fess up. You must not touch players on the . . . *vor.*" Abraham put his hand on his butt to make sure I knew what he was talking about.

"You mean their asses?" I asked, not knowing whether to laugh or be embarrassed.

"Yes, their asses."

"Why?"

Before he answered, I told him that in America, when players made great shots or executed good plays, we always patted them on their butts. It was our way of saying "Nice going."

"Yes, yes. I understand. But you are not in America. They think you are . . ." He paused to pull out the right English word, but apparently it was not part of his vocabulary. He said, "The *teghatsis* think you are a *getveron.*"

"A *getveron?* What the fuck is a *getveron*, Abraham?"

"You know, you know," said Abraham, insisting that I should know.

I tried unsuccessfully to reassure him that I didn't. His face flushed redder than a Soviet flag.

"*Getveron* is a *xhraoll,*" he said, replacing the Armenian word with its Arabic counterpart, as if I would understand the Arabic.

I continued to shake my head. Then, suddenly, the light went on. I asked very cautiously, "Do you mean they . . . they think I am a homosexual?"

"Yes, homosexual."

"You're kidding."

"No, I'm not."

Abraham sighed in relief that he had finally gotten the message across. I assured Abraham that I preferred women and that I was not a homosexual.

I learned that evening that the butt is a no-touch zone in the Soviet Union.

184 ~ THE REPATRIATE / Book II

Chapter 31

IMPROMPTU ENTRANCE EXAM

With trepidation, I prepared to set off the next morning to meet with the coach. But before I left for the nine o'clock appointment, I had to answer a slew of questions from Mr. Simonian and Johnny about how the scrimmage had gone.

How did I play? "Don't really know."

Who won? "It was a scrimmage; we didn't take score."

Did I make many baskets? "Wasn't counting them."

Was I accepted by the other teammates? "Can't say yet."

Would I be playing for the team? "Don't know, but the coach invited me to meet with him this morning to discuss that, and if I don't leave, I will never know!"

"Good. Very good news," offered Simonian.

"How much are they going to pay you?" asked Johnny.

"I don't know if they are going to pay me anything. And if I don't get there, I will never find out, will I?"

Simonian repeated his words of encouragement and said he was very happy for me. He was sincere. I guess he was happy because I was going to be involved in some local organization. I promised that I would tell them what happened after I met with the coach.

After taking my last swig of tea, I stuffed a piece of black toasted bread into my pocket so that I could have something to munch on, then left the apartment with my two roommates looking contented. I raced down the two flights of stairs and walked into the sunlit courtyard. A few of the French repatriates, in their berets, were already on their way to work, walking slowly to the artel, which was at the other side of the courtyard. They were surprised to see me up so early. One shouted, *"Bonjour,* Tommy, where are you off to so early in the morning?" I recognized him as David, who, with his wife and their eleven-year-old son, had repatriated from Nice. "To Nice," I shouted back. "Do you want to come?" He and the others laughed. He shouted back, "Only in your dreams, Tommy, only in your dreams."

I caught the tram to the city. According to Abraham's directions, I was to get off at the Kolkhoz Shoega, the open market, and from there, I was to proceed down a winding street behind the market until I came to an open field. There would be workers in the field, digging the foundation for a sports coliseum, ultimately the home of the Dynamo Stadium. North of the construction site, in perfect view of Ararat, there would be a dairy factory, which sold ice cream. My instructions emphatically included that I should not buy ice cream. It would make me sick. Directly across from the dairy was the Institute, a three-story grayish-blue building. If I went beyond the Institute, I would have found many deaf and blind children playing in the fields, Abraham had noted, for there was a school for them nearby. If I deviated from the directions, he had warned, I would wind up in a weeded maze where I would never find my way out and might step on a land mine because I would be too close to the border. "Continue westward, and you will come to the Turkish-Soviet border."

"Is the border that close?" I had nervously inquired.

"Yes," he had said, raising his voice. "Very close. But for you and me, it is a million kilometers away. It is well guarded on both sides of the border. An ant can't crawl across without a passport. Remember that."

Abraham knew that if I got off the trail, I would find trouble, not only for being a *norkalogh* but for being a *norkalogh* who didn't speak the language. I would have been immediately taken into custody by the patrols.

My first basketball scrimmage had convinced me that I could play for just about any basketball team in Erevan, for the Physical Institute team was considered among the best in the republic, even though the cities of Kirovakan and Leninakan had claimed the championships in recent years. But I didn't know the caliber of basketball they played in the other cities or in the other fourteen republics. I hoped that I would never need to find out, because I expected to be home by then.

The truth was, I was scared. Very scared. And I didn't have my older brothers to turn to, to advise me as they had before the war. I really had no one. But I still trusted everyone. I needed someone, however, to get me out of this minefield. Sympathy was useless. Like charity, it was not a cure. The antidote for what ailed me had to come from within. I suppose that was why I had accepted the invitation to meet with the coach. If everything else failed, as it had over the previous year, maybe basketball would lift me from the bottom of the pit.

I got off the tram just past the Kolkhoz Shoega, as Abraham had instructed, and zigzagged my way down a winding, narrow cobblestone street. I followed a dusty path that I was certain the Roman legions had trampled upon on their way to conquer Asia Minor and that the apostles Bartholomew and Thaddeus must have traveled up from Constantinople en route to Erevan to convert the idol-worshipping heathen Hittites. My head and shoulders stood above the flat mud roofs with piles of straw on them. Adjacent to those one-story homes were cakes upon cakes of mixed manure and straw, used, I assumed, as fuel to warm the houses and in stoves to cook food. The ovens were usually holes in the dirt a few meters from the homes. There were no chimneys that I could see. That was how my forefathers had lived for centuries, and that was how the people lived now. Because their needs were minimal, they survived wars and revolutions, plague and famine, and the harsh Soviet life. It was a miracle that life, any form of it, survived in the slate and lava that had drained the soil of its fertility.

I walked past a large rectangular structure, which stood on a rotting foundation, again no higher than my shoulders. Intrigued by this strange structure, I peeked through the crevices of the boarded-up windows. An arctic breeze from inside chilled my face. The cracks revealed blocks and blocks of solid ice, piled from wall to wall, from floor to ceiling. I wondered what the cavernous receptacle was. It could have been a man-made icebox or, perhaps, a mortuary.

I walked farther and farther away from the center of the city, increasing my stride for fear that I might be late. Mount Ararat loomed closer. I convinced myself that I was lost. Somewhere, I must have taken a wrong turn. I became concerned that if I continued on my path, as Abraham had warned, I would encounter border patrols, probably in time for their target practice.

Then I heard loud sounds of metal crashing down on rock. The noise got louder with each step. Soon I arrived at a field where men and women in rags, knapsacks wrapped around their feet for shoes, duplicate portraits of others I had seen on my walks in other sections of the city, were bent over, pounding boulders into rocks and stones with their crude tools. Armed guards atop huge rocks turned their attention from the prisoners to me as I came into view. They tightened their grips on their weapons. My weapon was a smile. The guards motioned me to move on, swinging their rifles in my direction to make their point. I had seen scenes like this in movies. It was different in real life.

No one seemed to see these people; no one seemed to care.

This was the site of the sports coliseum Abraham had mentioned as a landmark, so I knew that I was on the right path. I was not lost. My next landmark was the dairy factory, and I soon came upon it. With nothing but a plaque on the side of the front door identifying it, I found the Institute of Physical Culture, a bluish-gray, three-story building.

There were no paved roads or cobblestones, just dusty, potholed dirt roads and, beyond, fields of wildflowers and a sea of bushes fluttering in the wind. This was a painter's paradise, but it was obscene to think of it as a proletariat's utopia.

Abraham was waiting impatiently for me at the front door and greeted me quickly with a few terse expletives that the British apparently used to describe Americans when their allies angered or frustrated them.

"I thought you were lost," he said before I could greet him. "I was about to organize a rescue party."

"I thought I was, too, until I saw those workers."

"Never mind them! Come! We can't be late," he said in an agitated tone. "I will explain everything some other time. Right now, come!" Abraham grabbed me by the arm and led me into the building. We trotted up a flight of stairs. And the race—it seemed like one—ended in front of an office door.

During my brief sprint up the stairway, I couldn't help noticing the differences between the Institute and the schools back home. Unlike the schools I had attended in America, where chaos reigned in the hallways, where students skirted around, over, and under others to get to where they were going and the halls were filled with litter, the Soviet Institute had a morguelike silence. Within and outside the classrooms, the floors were immaculately clean, and the only sound was the droning of some professor's voice addressing his students in a nearby classroom. All was quiet on the scholastic front.

The door looked so familiar to me. It had a square glass windowpane that allowed one to peek in. It was an admission clerk's office, to be sure. A wave of homesickness wafted over me as I gazed inside, seeing an image of myself in bygone days sitting on one of the benches, waiting for an administrator to mete out punishment for one or another of my misadventures. I could see only one figure at a desk as I glanced into the office area. Without knocking, Abraham entered. I was a step or two behind him, and I closed the door quietly. Sitting behind the desk was a robust woman, not much older than thirty, if that. She was fanatically flipping the counters on an abacus, a calculating instrument I had only seen in history books. She wore her black hair straight back in a bun, and when she lifted her face from her accounting chores, her dark Armenian eyes, warm smile, and wrinkled brow put me at ease immediately. She wore a simple brown dress, the hem falling far below her knees. Although she did not look like a typical one, she played the role of the ultimate babushka, who cared for each and every student as if each was her adopted child. She immediately stood up and shook Abraham's hands and waved Abraham into the room after exchanging a few words. The coach was in and was waiting for us.

As I passed her desk, I could feel her eyes on my back. She left me with a feeling that she knew me, or about me, probably more than I realized. Although I was not prepared for what happened next, I should have seen the handwriting on the wall.

We entered the room. It was a simple, no frills except for the usual portraits of the founders of the Soviet Empire. Konstantin Nikitich stood at a window overlooking the dirt road I had just walked and the dairy factory. His arms were folded at his chest, his back to us. He wore the military uniform I had seen him in the night before. The coach turned, greeted us cordially, then dropped a hand into his chest pocket and pulled out a package of cigarettes. He took one out, lit it, and began nervously puffing away. The signal was clear: something was wrong. Abraham and the coach chatted for a while, and the conversation appeared to be serious. They were waiting for someone.

That someone soon entered the room. Barrel-chested and muscular, he looked like either a boxing coach or a wrestling coach. He was bald, and his stony blue eyes took a long look at me, as if to say, "So, this is the *norkalogh* from America. America is our enemy; therefore, he is the enemy. He is a danger to our Institute, to our students. Make short work of him." Abraham was not spared this man's icy glances.

Oganoff's broad shoulders were accentuated by the black suit he wore. It was atypically minus military medals, a rare sight on the streets in the Soviet Union after the war. Although I later learned that he was Armenian, not Russian as I had originally believed, he spoke only Russian and knew about as many Armenian words as I did. Like most of his ladder-climbing Communist colleagues, he had Russianized his surname, which had been Ohanesian. Because the Russian alphabet doesn't have an *h* sound, it became Oganoff. I was certain that even if we spoke the same language, we would not be able to communicate. Abraham, sensing that I might execute a fast break to the door, gave me a *Stay put, everything will be all right* look.

Oganoff's monologue, primarily directed at me, was political, beyond even Abraham's comprehension. All in Russian. All loud, as if the Politburo had convened in that room to hear him. I knew I was the main topic—that is, capitalism was the main topic—but I didn't know what he was saying. Sometimes there was an advantage in not knowing a language. If I had understood, I am not sure how I would have reacted. Abraham would fill me in later. Oganoff and the basketball coach became involved in a heated discussion.

The door opened again, and the abacus lady entered. Oganoff said something to her. In English I barely understood, she said to me, "My name is Anahaid. I will be translator."

I asked her why Abraham couldn't be the translator.

"No, not Abraham, I," she replied.

She was Mr. Oganoff's secretary, and she was learning English. She spoke it as if it came right out of a Russian textbook. Her stresses in the English words were misplaced, and my ears were not attuned. What I heard her say sounded like a new language. I listened, but with the exception of a word or two, I could not make sense out of what she said.

"Please softly speak, I understand," Anahaid reassured me with a smile.

I nodded and asked cautiously with a bigger smile, "I think it would be better if Abraham translated instead."

Before she could respond, Oganoff demanded a translation of what

I had said. The administrator and the secretary had a lengthy dialogue before she turned to me and explained, "I will to be official translator." She tried to explain that the Institute would need an official record of what was being said. I had thought the purpose of the meeting was to meet with the coach to find out when the next practice session would be held and where I could pick up my chocolate bars. There would be no chocolate bars that morning. I shrugged my shoulders, smiled at everyone, and tried to appear calm. I wasn't.

Oganoff directed a series of questions to his secretary, who translated them for me, hoping that I could provide her with a simple-sentence answer. I answered the best I could. I didn't challenge her or ask her to repeat, for I did not want to impugn her integrity as a translator in front of Oganoff. I did not need to make any enemies.

The confusion that followed taught me new respect for those who had created the United Nations. I glanced at Abraham in hopes of support, but I knew I was knee deep in shit's creek when his glances were directed the other way. He left me with the impression that he could not get involved, that I had to get through this alone, and if I passed the test, the battle would be won and the war over. This was my Borodino. Napoleon stood before me. How could Abraham know that I hadn't studied Kutuzov's tactics of retreating to fight another day? Stand or fall was the call of the day.

Oganoff had a prepared Party propaganda sermon for me. He need not have taken it out of his black suit jacket. Anahaid really did not need to translate. I had heard the words before. "Capitalist war Mongols," "American imperialist pigs," and "the Party's righteousness" were repeated several times during his soliloquy. I had seen the slogans painted in red and black on billboards and on the banners on the gates to factories and institutions across the city, and I had heard the propaganda blaring from radios wherever I went.

He asked Anahaid to ask me my reasons, the word was "motive," for repatriating to the Soviet Union and why my parents hadn't repatriated with me and why I was not working as all patriotic Soviets were. He reminded me, via Anahaid, that those who did not work in the Soviet Union did not eat. I wanted to tell Oganoff that from what I had seen in Armenia, those who worked didn't eat, either. Instead, in a slow, methodical tone, I asked Anahaid to tell her boss that I thought the reason for this meeting was to find some sort of employment for me so that I could eat and become a productive citizen of the Soviet society.

Disgusted, I told Anahaid, in first-grade English, to inform her superior of whatever she believed he wanted to hear. Her eyes opened wide, and I was left with the feeling that she did not want to navigate the uncharted waters, that she feared repercussions. I was surprised when she shook her head and said she would not do so.

Oganoff fell short a centimeter or two of accusing me of being a trained FBI agent, taught to play basketball so that I could infiltrate the Soviet Union, an American spy who had a secret mission. I begged Anahaid to translate: "Does Tavahrishch Oganoff believe the NKVD is stupid?"

Anahaid's face flushed. Though she was embarrassed, she complied. Oganoff said nothing.

That final remark ended the political-indoctrination portion of the meeting, it seemed, for Oganoff turned to questions about my education and my qualifications. How many years had I attended school? Had I graduated? Did I play basketball professionally? I gave Anahaid all of the answers and hoped that she would make Oganoff understand that I had had twelve years of formal education. I didn't think she understood what I meant when I said I had "dropped out" of college. I told her that I had not played professional basketball; I was too young and never thought I was that good.

Oganoff demanded proof that I had completed twelve years of schooling. Soviet pupils spent their first ten years in school studying the same courses, and then, upon successful completion, they moved on to either *teknicum* (technical training) or a university. *Documente* was the only word Oganoff used during this phase of the examination that I fully understood.

"I left my transcripts back home," I told Anahaid, who I was sure did not understand what a transcript was.

"Documente?" Oganoff demanded again. *"Diplom,* yes?"

I repeated that I had graduated from high school.

Oganoff insisted that he needed proof. "How do we know this to be fact? Do you have *documente, diplom* to show this?" The argument continued. My nerves were on edge by now.

"No, I don't have any damned documents with me. I left my high school diploma at home, in America," I said, with growing irritation and a louder voice than usual. "Miss Anahaid, I have no reason to lie to you or to him or to anyone. I can write home and have them send the documents if he wishes." Better still, if the Institute could arrange it, I would prefer returning to America and mailing the necessary papers they wanted. I would also throw in a couple of dozen gym shoes, if they so desired. I didn't say it. I only thought it.

We were deadlocked.

Konstantin Nikitich, too, was losing patience with his colleague. He had invited me in good faith, and it was turning out poorly. He lowered his *katyushas* at the department head and launched a verbal assault on my interrogator that startled Abraham and shocked Anahaid. But when the smoke cleared, it was Oganoff who prevailed. He still sought proof that I had completed my primary and high school education. He would require that I present positive proof that I had completed the required courses to the university administration's satisfaction. I did not understand at the time how the Soviet system worked, but I concluded that if I were to be hired as a university employee, I would be eligible to play for the college team. That would have been prohibited under collegiate rules in the United States.

It was Anahaid who broke the deadlock with her resourcefulness. She whispered something to Oganoff, who, after mulling it over, nodded approval. Anahaid quickly left the room, and I waited in suspense. Minutes later, Anahaid returned, accompanied by a short, scholarly man whose flowing white hair reached well below the ears. He was wearing a white smock over an old wrinkled plaid suit jacket and a worn-out pair of trousers. He walked in with a noticeable limp, shook Oganoff's hand, and smiled at Konstantin Nikitich. He acknowledged Abraham's and my presence with a slight nod of his head. There was an eerie silence, heightened by an invitation that we all move next door, to his classroom. I was confused. I mumbled something to Abraham. He was as confused as I but whispered back, "Stay the course."

Anahaid introduced Professor Stepanov as the head of the chemistry and physiology department at the Institute. He had been an assistant to Ivan Petrovich Pavlov in Sokhumi, Soviet Georgia, before the war, and he, the professor, would administer a test. All I knew about physiologists was that they dissected frogs.

The professor questioned his colleagues, not raising the tone of his speech. After the exchange, he looked at me and in a calming voice, without once looking at Anahaid, asked me something in Russian. I quickly shook my head. Then he asked me something in Armenian, and again I repeated my movement. He tried German, Turkish, and French. I acknowledged that I did not know any of those languages. My fortune—or misfortune—was that he didn't speak English. He paused briefly. I wondered what would come next. All I could do was bite my lip, pray, and wait.

He paused, looked at me, turned his back on us, and limped his way to the blackboard. He picked up a piece of chalk and began scribbling something on the board. It wasn't clear to me at first what his motive was. He finished writing, turned to me, and invited me to join him. He handed me the chalk and pointed to the blackboard. I understood my task. He wanted me to complete the chemistry equation he had written. I did. We exchanged quick smiles. The equation was correctly completed. I must admit that I was enjoying every minute of this impromptu exam. I furtively glanced over at Oganoff, who was standing with his arms folded over his chest. His face was purple. Stepanov continued with what I considered would go down as my unofficial college entrance exam. He wrote several other problems, each progressively more complex. I took my time and finished them, but finally he wrote what I believed was an organic chemistry problem. That one perplexed me, for I never had organic chemistry. It was beyond my comprehension, and I quickly but sadly handed the chalk back to him. He patted me on my back. *"Harashol. Ochin harashol,"* he said. Then he turned to Oganoff and in a slow and deliberate tone, said something to him in Russian.

Stepanov asked Anahaid to relay a message to me. "Professor Stepanov is looking forward to having you in his classroom in September."

I knew I wouldn't be in his classroom, but I told her to tell the professor that I thanked him, my mother thanked him, my father thanked him, and the Detroit Board of Education thanked him, too. She didn't understand a word I said. I didn't mind.

Professor Stepanov slowly walked toward the door. Anahaid rushed to open it for him. He disappeared from sight. I didn't know whether to rejoice or retreat from the room.

Oganoff, who seemed to have softened his stand about documents, told Anahaid to tell me that he expected me to report to her the next morning. She was assigned to teach me the language. The coach did not say anything but conferred with Abraham. Abraham's face reminded me of the Cheshire cat as we left the building.

Once we were outside, I took a deep breath and asked if he had gone through the same kind of crap.

"No," he said.

"Why not?"

"Because I speak their language. And I have all the necessary documents."

"Who is this Oganoff guy?" I asked.

"He's a big shot. When you get to know him, you will like him. His daughter Irina is one of the most beautiful girls in all of Erevan."

"You're kidding."

"No. You will see."

"I hope so."

As we began our long trek back to the city, I thanked Abraham again profusely for what he had done for me. We talked for a few minutes, and then I asked, "What were Oganoff and the coach being so vocal about?"

"Oganoff has this fear that if you disgrace us while you're a student at the Institute or playing as a member of our team, it will come back and haunt the entire staff."

"Can that happen? I mean, if I, say, try to go home, try to cross the border over there." I stopped and turned around, looking west at Ararat. "Would the secret police take it out on the Institute?"

"Yes." Abraham's answer was plain but terrifying. "It would be worse than that. Many would suffer for your actions. You must not even think of it."

"But Abraham, my mother and father are back there . . ."

"And you are here. This is not like America. Believe me."

We continued to walk in silence.

"I don't. I can't believe it."

"Believe me, Tommy. It will be a big mess. I know. If you try to escape, even your teammates will suffer. Me, too."

Chapter 32

SABU AND MOMIGON

I sought the shelter of my apartment to sort out my feelings about the meeting with the school officials. On one hand, I was elated; I had passed my "test." They wanted me to return and play. On the other hand, was it wise? Abraham's sermon had left a chill running down my spine. I had heard rumors from the French of what happened to repatriates and their families who had attempted, but failed, to get across the border. No one could have been fooled or deceived by my intentions. That was probably why Tavahrishch Oganoff didn't want to have anything to do with me. I certainly could not blame him. The Institute was taking a big risk by even inviting me back. I had no roots in Armenia or in the Soviet Union. If I bolted when I was associated with the team, the school officials would have to answer to the NKVD. I tried to brush that aside, but I couldn't.

I knew I did not want to stand in long queues the rest of my life, waiting to buy whatever might be available. Nor did I want to try to eke out a living in a society where a necktie branded the wearer as a traitor and associating with a foreigner was an invitation for a midnight knock at your door or a predawn raid by the NKVD. What a tragedy it was that Stalin, a xenophobe who saw enemies under his bed and in the doctors who treated him, ordering their executions as if they were flies, was the ruler of the USSR. He was even preparing to go to war against an invisible enemy, because, he said, they were entrenched at the borders and had encircled his domain.

Events across the Atlantic were being played out in federal courts by federal prosecutors; these would decide my course of action. It would be only a matter of time before all I had brought with me had been sold. Except for George's ring—I would never part with it. There were no options but one: to go back to the Institute. I knew that I could contribute to the success of Konstantin Nikitich's team, which had never been invited to compete for a USSR national championship or in a major Soviet tournament. If I played on the Institute team, I would have to give up my plans to leave the Soviet Union illegally. That was the bottom line.

~ THE NEXT DAY, I paid a visit to Momigon. Simonian had told me that he wanted to see me. I found him and his roommate, Sabu, in their room. Sabu was in bed, with his coat over him for a blanket, and from the wheezing sounds I heard, I could tell that he was having difficulty breathing and wondered why he didn't seem to be getting any medical help.

"Let's get him over to the hospital," I said.

"He won't go. He says he'll be all right."

Momigon did not look well, either. He had lost weight, but he had pounds to spare, and Sabu didn't. He was not the roly-poly man I had seen aboard the *Rossia*. Unshaven Momigon could have easily been mistaken for a *teghatsi*. He had been taking care of and feeding Sabu since we had arrived at the apartment complex.

"I have news for you from home," Momigon announced after I had settled down in one of the two chairs in the bare room. "It is about your mother and father."

"Are they all right?"

"Yes . . ."

"But?" I was worried about my mother. She had always complained about her heart, and this separation surely compounded the stress. "It's not my mother, is it?"

"They are well."

I gave an immediate sigh of relief. "Then what?" I asked.

"Your mother and your father and your sister—they're coming on the next boat."

"Impossible!" I shouted. "They would never do that!"

"If you can read Armenian, here it is in black and white."

"Did my father write you?"

Momigon shook his head.

"Then who?"

"Do you know Oksen Selian?"

I shook my head. My heart began to pound in my ears.

"He's the publisher of the *Lraper* newspaper. The letter is from him."

I knew of the newspaper but not the publisher. Distributed from New York City, the four-page broadsheet devoted three of its pages to Soviet news—propaganda—and the back page was usually in English. The paper was circulated to the pro-Soviet Armenian community throughout the United States.

"Oksen is being deported; he's not an American citizen. He visited Detroit and stayed with your mother and father." Momigon thought it strange that I had not met the publisher, because he had frequently stayed at our home during fundraisers and meetings in the Detroit area.

"Momigon, a lot of people visit my father. He raises a lot of money for various causes. I don't know all of the people who come and go at our house. There were so many."

Momigon nodded. "Ah, yes, your mother is such a wonderful cook. We could use her here, couldn't we?"

"She won't come, Momigon, she won't leave Robert or George," I said, more to convince myself than him.

Sabu's wheezing suddenly stopped. I got up from my chair and moved over to his bed. I looked down at him and touched his forehead. It was cold. His hands were icy and shaking.

"Momigon, we'd better get him to the hospital."

"He won't go. Let him be."

"He'll die!"

"Most of us do. Don't you want to hear the rest?"

I looked down at Sabu, and it occurred to me that this was the first time in my life I was looking into the face of someone who was dying. My first impulse was to tell Momigon that I had heard enough, that the letter writer really didn't know my family. But I could not stop him. He had to give me all of the details.

"Oksen should be arriving here in Erevan soon. He has written me in advance. We were pretty close back in the States. One of the things he said in the letter was that he wanted you to know . . ." Momigon paused and looked straight at me. "That your father and mother and sister have signed up for the second caravan, and they want to know if there is anything you want them to bring."

"Yes, Momigon, tell them to bring their tombstones. That's all they will need. Can you do that for me?"

He understood. "I will get the message to them."

I told Momigon that I had mailed some postcards home a couple of weeks ago, that I had told my parents that I was well but never received a response.

"They're worried about you, and that's probably why Oksen dropped by. He'll fill you in when he gets here."

"Are you sure?" I asked. "Are you sure my folks will be on that second caravan?"

"I am only telling you what is in the letter. If I am not mistaken, Oksen should be here by next week. His family is also coming in the next caravan."

I turned to say good-bye to Sabu. He looked up and forced a smile. I asked if there was anything I could do for him. He could barely shake his head. He waved his hand as if he wanted me to get closer. I bent over him. He whispered, "Take good care of yourself. The cat has nine lives. I have lived all nine." He reached out and grabbed my hand with both of his. They were cold, very cold, and they trembled uncontrollably. "Good-bye," Sabu murmured. "I will see you in Detroit . . . at your father's coffee shop."

"Momigon!" I shouted. "Let's get him to a doctor!"

"No!" Momigon said in a raised voice. "He doesn't want that. He wants to die. Leave him be." Momigon shook his head. "I can't even find an aspirin for him in this godforsaken city. They can't do anything for him at the hospital. They stick leeches on people and bleed them to cure them. Believe me, it isn't easy to see a friend I have known a lifetime go."

I opened the door, walked out, and closed it behind me. I leaned against it as Momigon's words sank deeper. My mother and father and sister were coming. I prayed, "God help us. God help Sabu."

He did.

That night, Sabu got his wish.

Chapter 33

ANAHAID THE TEACHER

I did not know at the time that I had reached a crossroad—one street led to survival, the other to my grave. Within the next thirty days, a decision would be made about whether I would live or die.

Anahaid was waiting for me. Her abacus had been put away for the day. There was a notebook and a pencil on top of her desk, and she handed them to me as soon as I appeared before her. She motioned for me to sit and immediately cleared the air about what kind of relationship there would be in her classroom.

"This is no time for misunderstandings. No political confusions. Let us begin. We must not lose time. I will teach you Russian and Armenian; you will teach me English. Yes?"

"*Da,*" I answered in one breath. "*Ayo,*" I answered in the next.

"Good." She paused for a moment, then burst into laughter as she realized that I had answered in both languages. "*Harashol.* Very good," she answered.

Laughter is always a good way to begin a relationship.

I was back in kindergarten again, learning this time not the ABCs of English but the Russian and Armenian alphabets. Armenian would come easily, for somewhere in the back of my mind, the seeds of the words had been planted by my parents. Russian would take longer to learn.

Anahaid was a capable teacher. I spent most of the morning with that benevolent dictator, who went out of her way to be nice to me, even sharing her lunch of cheese, black bread, and tea, with hard candies as sweeteners.

She kept reminding me that Russian was a universal language and therefore must be mastered.

"But we're Armenians," I argued. "Should we not devote more time to Armenian?"

She put her finger to her lips for silence. "That is nationalism. No politics! You are from America, yes?"

"Yes."

"Why you learn English, not Armenian, in America?" She had made her point.

Before I left her office, as she would do each day thereafter, she tore out a page from an old calendar, circa 1946, printed in both Russian and Armenian, which highlighted historic Soviet and Armenian events. It would be my homework to translate the information on the page and return and recite what I had learned.

"Impossible."

"No impossible. We have students from Stalingrad here. Tell *them* impossible!"

I begged her to settle for either one or the other, not both languages.

"You must do assignment, or I must report this to Tavahrishch Oganoff."

"OK, OK," I replied. "I will try."

"What is this OK business?" she asked. "This not in English book."

I tried to explain, but I am sure it did not register. "OK means all right, you win; it's slang." Then I realized that she probably didn't understand the word *slang,* either, so I took out my handkerchief and waved it as a white flag. "You see, you win. OK, I surrender. I agree. I will do what you say." *Just don't get Tavahrishch Oganoff involved,* I thought.

"OK. I understand OK," she said. "I like OK."

"But you don't use it all the time, Miss Anahaid."

"What you mean?"

"Well, if someone says, for example, let's have sex, you don't reply, 'OK.' You say, 'No.'" I knew I wasn't getting through to her, so I dropped the subject until a future lesson.

When she wanted to stress something and make sure I understood it, Anahaid would ask, "OK?" and I would either shake my head or answer, "OK."

If only world politics were as simple.

I tried only once to convince her that America had many advantages over what I had seen in Soviet Armenia. She cautioned me that she would have to report to Oganoff any disagreeable discussion, so I quickly backed off.

Finally, she announced, "Now we must go to the opera."

I didn't understand. I asked her to repeat.

"Opera? *Culturney.* You learn language at opera. You been opera?" she asked.

I nodded.

"Good, then I have tickets. Eight o'clock. Understand? You be there tonight."

Students usually didn't date their teachers, I thought, but then, this wasn't a date. It was a command appearance. The purpose, as I understood it, was to introduce me to the language, the mores, and the culture. I also thought I might bump into Tatiana. I accepted the invitation.

"What opera will we see?" I asked Anahaid.

She understood the question, but I did not understand the answer: "Cio-Cio-San."

I had never heard of that opera; I thought it might have been Russian. She read the confusion in my face. Her attempts to explain were equally frustrating.

"Pinker*ton* . . . Pinker*ton,*" she said, accenting the last three letters of a name that she hoped I would recognize. "Pinkerton and Cio-Cio-San have baby." Anahaid began rocking her arms as if she were rocking an infant in them. Then she formed a fist as if she had a dagger in it and plunged the imaginary dagger into her heart. "Puccini . . . Puccini. *Ne'culturney* not to know Puccini."

"You mean Giacomo Puccini . . . the story of the beautiful geisha who falls in love with Lieutenant Pinkerton and commits suicide. You mean *Madame Butterfly?*"

"*Da, da.* OK, OK."

Chapter 34

BASKETBALL, SOVIET-STYLE

That afternoon—for better or for worse—I officially joined the Institute's basketball team. The game that was conceived for recreation in Springfield, Massachusetts, by Dr. James A. Naismith in 1891 and became a popular national winter pastime, exported to Europe and Asia in the 1930s, remained almost in its original form on the Armenian plateau as preached and practiced by Soviet Armenian coach Konstantin Nikitich Vartanian.

In America, my coaches had taught me to enjoy the game, to respect the opposition, to compete fairly, and to congratulate the opponent when the situation called for it. In Soviet Armenia, it was not a game; it was war. Nationalism was at stake. Ethnic prejudices and hatred, passed down from generation to generation, amplified by Soviet occupation, were renewed within the borders of the 94-by-50-foot court.

~ I RUSHED from practice across town to the opera house, where Anahaid was waiting on the steps, standing as teachers do when irritated, arms akimbo, right foot tapping the indisputable message of her impatience. Her face was flushed, her left hand holding the two tickets, her right hand raised with her index finger pointing at me while her head shook like a metronome. I was out of breath. She immediately commenced chastising me. I did not understand a word. Then she did mutter something familiar: *"Ne'culturney, ne'culturney."* And she added in English, shaking her finger at me, "Tommy, no good be late."

I apologized profusely. "I had to shower," I pleaded in vain. She seemed not to hear me. "If I had not showered, I don't think you or anyone else would have wanted to sit next to me." I added, *"Ne'culturney* not to shower."

Soviet citizens had been trained; there were severe penalties for tardiness. No excuses were accepted. This Soviet woman had been given a mission to baptize me as a Soviet—to Sovietize me—with the blessings of her superiors. Failure to do so was unacceptable. She knew that; I didn't. I was the dog; she was Dr. Pavlov.

"Must hurry," Anahaid repeated over and over as she grabbed me by the hand and quickly ushered me through the door. She presented our tickets and led me through a maze of hallways and up the stairs as fast as Jesse Owens would cover the 100 and 200 meters in Berlin, mumbling, *"Eta ne'culturney,"* several times until we had reached the mezzanine.

I sank into my seat, relieved that the opera would soon start and I would not have to listen to what a cultural shock I was. Anahaid talked to herself, looking around to see who was and who was not in the audience. She told me that mezzanine seats were the best for opera, because one could see the entire cast as the music rose melodiously in waves from the orchestra pit and united with the voices from the stage. She bent over the railing from our first-row seats and began searching the crowd below, naming names that meant nothing to me.

Attending the opera was considered an obligation for the "New Soviet Man," almost mandatory for any aspiring Komsomol, or member of the Young Communist Organization, who wished to move on into the elite circles of the Party.

"One must know the classics," said Anahaid, using simple Russian sentences. "For we are a cultural people, yes. Tolstoy. Dostoyevsky. Must read. Must learn. Turgenev, Gogol, Pushkin. You must read." She had not named a single Soviet writer; those she had listed had all written during the czarist era. I was proud of myself for not pointing that out to her. But I had to mention the names of Hemingway, Mark Twain, Jack London, Sinclair Lewis, and Theodore Dreiser, all American authors who were familiar to the Soviets.

Many Soviets attended the opera not because they necessarily loved opera but because they needed to see and to be seen by those who counted. I, too, looked over the railing and down to the main floor. It appeared that every officer in the Red Army was there that night. I wondered why, and it made me a little nervous. As the opera unfolded, the answer became clear—in my mind, anyway.

Madame Butterfly is the tragic love story of a beautiful geisha, Cio-Cio-San, told through the transcendental beauty of Puccini's music. Warned by her uncle that her love affair with Pinkerton, a U.S. naval officer assigned to Nagasaki, could only end in tragedy, Cio-Cio-San does not listen, refusing to believe that her lover's great affections for her are not pure and sincere. The affair is interrupted when Pinkerton is ordered to return to his ship and sail home to the United States. Unbeknownst to the handsome lieutenant, Cio-Cio-San is pregnant. Before Pinkerton leaves, he pledges his undying love and vows to return to her soon. Cio-Cio-San has their baby, a son. When Pinkerton's ship enters Nagasaki's harbor a year later, Cio-Cio-San believes that her lover has come back to make an honest woman of her. She prepares herself and their son to meet him. But Cio-Cio-San's dreams of a wedding turn into a nightmare. Pinkerton steps off his ship to the music of the "Star-Spangled Banner" with his American bride. (I almost stood up when I heard the national anthem, then remembered where I was.) When Cio-Cio-San learns that her lover is married, she decides she cannot live with the disgrace that has befallen her family. As she prepares to plunge a dagger into her heart, she sings, ending one of the most memorable scenes in opera history.

At the intermission, Anahaid invited me to become part of the current that flowed in streams up and down the main foyer, to see and to be seen.

"Maybe," she said, "we visit the buffet, no?"

We walked down the staircase and stepped onto plush red carpeting that led to a hallway richly painted in royal greens. The foyer buzzed with people, chatting between puffs on their cigarettes, making the rounds of the rotunda.

Anahaid was a step or two ahead of me, and as we strolled, she nodded to several people, even greeted one or two, in Russian or in Armenian. She did not attempt to introduce me. My anxiety level doubled as the crowds increased. When we reached the rotunda, my eyes caught a glimpse of a young woman, her back turned to me, revealing the nape of her long, swanlike neck. She was standing next to a silver-haired, distinguished-looking officer in a military uniform. For a brief second, the woman with the officer looked strangely familiar, but I decided it was my imagination working overtime. She had to be a repatriate, I told myself. A *norkalogh*. For no *teghatsi* would appear in public in that kind of dress. It revealed too much of her body. She would be branded a prostitute or, even worse, a cosmopolitan. The gown was blue silk and ended just above her knees, displaying shapely legs. She had a superb figure, thin at the waist and broad and strong at the shoulders. Unlike the skin of the mountain people, which was scorched by the sun, hers—what was revealed of it to the public—was creamy white. She wore no jewelry, however. With a necklace or a bracelet, she would have been a genuine cosmopolitan.

As we neared the couple, the officer, who seemed to age as we got closer, looked up at Anahaid, then at me. He studied me from the curly black hair on my head to the dust on my shoes. A slight nod of his head brought two young officers to his side; they exchanged words, and the younger men left. The young woman turned her head stealthily toward us. She glanced at Anahaid, then stared at me. I returned the courtesy. I did not recognize her at first. She had on a touch of lipstick, not the orange some of the prominent women in the city used but red, probably imported.

I said and did nothing. The young woman in the blue silk gown placed her hand in the crook of the elderly officer's arm, turned away from us, and whispered something into her companion's ear. I caught one word: *"Amerikanetz."*

The officer replied, *"Da, yazniyu.* Yes, I know."

I stopped and turned around. I knew the young woman's voice. It was her voice. It was Tatiana's. I stared until I felt Anahaid tug on my arm.

Tatiana looked much older. Was it the dress? The body? The lipstick? Was this the same girl in pigtails and a jogging suit I had met in the park?

Anahaid and I returned to our seats.

She looked at me suspiciously from the corner of her eye. She asked, "Do you know her?"

"Who?"

"Tatiana." She knew her name.

"No."

"Strange. She looked at you as if she knew you."

"No. I don't know her."

"That is good."

I wondered why but instead asked, "Do you know her?"

"Yes."

"That's good."

"Why?"

"I would like to know her."

206 ~ THE REPATRIATE / Book II

There was a pause, then Anahaid said, *"Neleeza."*

"What does *neleeza* mean?"

"It is forbidden."

I shook my head, wondering how Tatiana could be forbidden and wanting to ask more questions, but the lights dimmed, the maestro entered the orchestra pit to the applause of the audience, the tap of the baton echoed through the hall, and the curtains parted for the final act of *Madame Butterfly.*

Chapter 35

AROUND THE BONFIRE

A rriving home late from the opera, I strolled into the courtyard and found Karibian and Papazian standing around the fire, talking in subdued tones. The first of May was ten days away, and they needed the solitude of night to talk things over without children or wives overhearing them. Doubt, the enemy of most decisions, accompanied by an unexpected new caveat had stirred questions about the wisdom of our actions.

Instead of heading for my room, I violated the agreement that those of us involved in the Moscow mission would not meet or be seen together in public if we could avoid it. We needed to talk, and this was as good a time as any to finalize our plans—in the open, under the stars, around a fire.

The flames, fueled by crates marked "USA to Erevan, Soviet Armenia," cast an eerie, almost surrealistic portrait of the other two men. From where I stood, I could read the doubts on their faces.

I was not kept very long in suspense. As soon as I joined them, Papazian said, "I saw Selian today."

"Selian? Oksen Selian?" I asked.

"Yes. You know him? You know the son-of-a-bitch is here?" Papazian said, speaking in anger of his former fellow traveler.

His tone made Karibian uncomfortable, and he raised a finger to his lips to indicate that we should keep our voices down.

"Momigon told me the other day that the U.S. had deported him and that he was on his way," I told Papazian. "I did not know he would arrive so soon."

"Well, he's here. We saw him. Talked to him. They've already given him an apartment near the opera house, and he has an office on Abovian. His family is packing up and coming with the next caravan."

"Must be a pretty important guy," I said sarcastically.

"Back there. Not here. Just wait a few weeks and see. They'll cut him down to size. They don't appreciate American Communists. Just our money."

"Did he have a lot to say?"

"Plenty. But did you know that he stopped over at your parents' home in Detroit? Did you know that your parents signed up for the next boat over?"

I shook my head. "And?"

"And Harry and I were talking, and we figure that you'd want to stick around, since your mother and father are going to join you, that you may not want to go to Moscow."

I shook my head again. "You're wrong, Eddy. First, I don't believe they will come. Second, if they choose to, there's nothing I can do about it, is there? Unless you want me out, I still want to go to Moscow. It's my life, isn't it?"

"Then you're still in?" Harry asked.

"Of course."

Harry gave Papazian an *I told you so* look during the awkward silence that followed. But I still felt I needed to convince them that I was committed to go to Moscow no matter what happened.

"Let's face it," I said, "if my father decides to pack up and bring my mother here, there is nothing I or anyone else can do about it. It's his choice. No one stopped me. Sure, they tried, but I wouldn't listen. Did you? The truth is that once the mind is set, it will fight any sort of evidence to the contrary. It isn't age that makes us vulnerable; it's lack of experience, no matter what age. The Selians of this world can dupe us because we don't have the patience or are not willing to listen to an opposing view. I know I didn't."

I was guilty of ignorance, but so was everyone else on that ship.

Karibian spoke next. I think that he wanted to lift the guilt from his conscience if anything were to go wrong. "If you want to back out of going to Moscow and wait until your folks get here and see them, I can understand that. I would not have you do anything that you may later regret."

"If I don't at least try, I may regret it later. I won't back down now. In fact, I think we should go as soon as possible. Tomorrow, if we can get our tickets."

Both men appeared uncomfortable about the change of plans. They argued that we should still stick to the May 1 date. I said that I felt time was against us, that the longer we waited to act, the more likely it would be that someone would discover our plans.

"Can either of you give me a reason to wait?"

It was Karibian who spoke. "I thought we agreed that the first of May would be the best time. That we could mingle with those who would be celebrating May Day and slip into the embassy under the guise that we were Americans."

That seemed a reasonable course of action.

"Then we wait," I said.

Papazian bemoaned the fact that there was no telephone communication between the Soviet Republic of Armenia and the United States. In Moscow and Leningrad, you needed a special permit to make a call to the States, and no Soviet in his right mind would place such a call. It would be a call straight to the NKVD. If only the mail could get through, but that wasn't to be. It was obvious that my attempts to veil my letters with allegorical messages, trying to get past Soviet censorship, had failed. The censors seemed to be masters at decoding covert messages to loved ones about the true nature of the beast.

My brothers did not like to write, but I knew that my sister would definitely try to keep in touch. Letters—both ways—probably had been scrutinized, censored, sent on to their destinations or, if the censors found anti-Soviet propaganda, destroyed. If the NKVD found anything in a letter that was incriminating, maybe something that could be used in the future to intimidate, they filed it to be used by the secret police either to blackmail the repatriate or to use the letter writer and his family to fill their quota of shipments to Siberia.

I did not think of myself as a courageous hero. I was afraid, definitely afraid, to go to Moscow, for Moscow now represented the epitome of clandestineness. The Soviet capital was the vortex of repression, secrecy, and oppression, and rumors about the NKVD's persecutions and arrests of repatriates had multiplied during the winter of 1947 and the spring of 1948. Whether these rumors were true or just propaganda spread by the secret police to ensure that the *norkaloghs* toed the line, I did not know. I did not care. But a day did not pass without my hearing yet another story of outspoken repatriates disappearing. None had vanished yet from the Armenian American ranks. Most were old and feeble and, like aging elephants smelling death, had come home to die. One of the prime candidates from our flock, someone the NKVD had to be looking at, was Alice Papazian, Ed's outspoken wife. She continued stepping out onto her balcony, her cup of tea in one hand and a lit cigarette in the other, looking down at the long bread line, and shouting obscenities about the Soviet system. Her husband knew that it was only a matter of time before the NKVD would step in. His only hope was that bribes would delay the inevitable.

"Then it's all settled. The plan remains unaltered," I said. "In ten days, Harry and I will celebrate May Day in the U.S. Embassy in Moscow."

If we had had a bottle of wine—we didn't—it would have been passed around.

"Ten days that shook the world," Papazian mumbled, making a reference to an American journalist's account of the overthrow of Czar Nicholas and the Bolshevik Revolution.

Papazian, who had been staring at the fire, turned to me. "Oksen told me he had spent a week with your folks and has some letters and a package for you. You should see him. Hear what he has to say."

I said that I would. "But let's get this straight—there isn't anything he could tell me that will change my mind. If my mother and father want to live here, that's up to them. I choose America. And damn it, I will get there one way or another. Right now, nothing else matters."

Harry whispered hoarsely, "Keep your voice down, Tommy. Someone may overhear you."

Karibian left a door open to me. "For our wives' sakes, we are committed to do this. You aren't," he said. "If you decide after meeting with Selian that you want out, we will understand."

I saw Papazian give Karibian an uncomfortable look, then cautiously remind him, "It's not that easy, Harry." He turned to me and said, "Without you, Tommy, we can't pull this off. Harry, Joe, and I were born in Turkey, and the embassy would probably laugh at us if we showed up at their doorstep with a petition in our hands. They'd probably direct us to the Turkish Embassy. They don't need to create an international incident over a few malcontented former American citizens. But you're different. You're young and American-educated. You were born in America. And youth does have its advantages. I don't see the embassy laughing at you. If you're not in this, then—I can't speak for Harry here or for Joe—Alice and I probably would have to back out, and I would have to tape her mouth shut for the rest of our lives. I don't think it's in you to betray us. But some people wouldn't hesitate a second—think of some of the loot they'd collect after they seized what we brought with us. Yes, we must all be careful."

Papazian lowered his voice almost to a whisper, "There is a slim chance that you and our wives and Harry's kids will get to go back. It is a long shot, but if we don't go through with this, we will never know. Even if they refuse to take us back, at least the word will get out. It will bring attention to our situation. And maybe we can stop some of our friends and other families from making the same mistake."

Standing there with these two men who were more than twice my age made me feel old, very old. I had so many dreams, and they had been swept away. How could one decision accelerate into something like this? I was angry. Not at the men around me or at my parents. I was angry at myself.

Karibian and I went over our plans. We would take separate flights out of Erevan to Moscow. I would get a message to him about when I was leaving, and we would meet in Moscow on Red Square.

Karibian asked about my copy of the petition. "You have it in a safe place?"

"It's safe. Nobody will find it."

"Good," said Karibian. "Very good. Don't trust anyone. Not Johnny or Simonian."

The three of us stood around the fire for a few more minutes without saying a word, each with his own thoughts. Then Papazian smiled, his face suddenly reflecting relief from the tension he had felt before our talk. I asked why he smiled.

"Just wondering where all of us will be six months from now."

"Back in the States," I said.

"I pray to God for that," Harry murmured.

Staring into the beauty of the star-filled night, I happened to gaze at our third-floor balcony. I don't know whether it was the flames casting shadows upon the glass or my imagination, but I thought I saw a face at the window.

Chapter 36

THE DEPORTED COMMUNIST

The next day, after spending most of the morning attending my language class with Anahaid, I rushed to the office of Aeroflot, the Soviet passanger airline, next to the Intourist Hotel on Abovian Street. I was greeted with a big smile by a pleasant, helpful young female clerk, who asked simple questions in simple Russian: name, destination, purpose of trip. The first two were easy, the last one I thought unnecessary but answered anyway. I was going to Moscow to view the great May Day parade and visit the historic and heroic city.

She acknowledged my answers with a smile that did not leave her face until she requested my passport.

"My passport? What passport?" I had already taken some rubles out of my jacket pocket and was preparing to pay her for the ticket.

She repeated, "Passport, *pajalsteer.*"

She must have thought I was an American. I informed her that I was an Armenian American repatriate.

"Yes, I know that. I can see that. I need passport. Soviet passport!"

She rattled off her pitch. All Soviet citizens must have passports in order to buy plane tickets or train tickets, to travel between republics or even between cities and towns in their own republics.

I listened impatiently, in something of a daze. I would learn later that passports had to be produced on demand, even in the street, if requested by the authorities.

After I explained the obvious, that I was a repatriate and that I didn't have a Soviet passport, she slowly canceled the ticket and gave me a strange look. I did not retreat. I needed more information.

"Where do I get my Soviet passport?"

"*Militzia.* Go to *militzia.*"

"How long will it take?" I asked.

She shrugged, and I didn't know if she was trying to tell me that she didn't understand the question or that she didn't know. She produced hers. It looked like an identification card: bearer's name, father's name, birth date, nationality. There was no photo on the ID.

I told her that I would be back. She gave me a look as if she doubted it. I stuffed my rubles back into my pocket and left the building in anger, not at the clerk but at the system, slamming the door behind me.

As I stepped out onto the sidewalk, undecided about what to do, where to go, I almost bowled over an old man with rounded shoulders, who was wearing a black overcoat, though it was a warm and sunny day. In the collision, the man almost lost his eyeglasses.

"Whoa, young man, take it easy. I expect something like this in New York but not in Erevan," the stranger said in distinctly American English, not out of a Russian textbook.

I started to apologize, but when I looked at the man's face and examined his demeanor, I immediately knew who he was. "You're Mr. Selian, aren't you?" I said.

"Why, yes," came the immediate answer. "I'm Oksen Selian." He stared at me for a moment, then broke into a pleasant smile. "And your high school senior photo is still on the radio in the living room. You're Tommy, aren't you?"

I nodded and began to apologize again, but then I remembered who he was and what Papazian had said about him the night before.

"How are you?" Selian asked sincerely. "Your folks are worried to death about you." Extending his hand and shaking mine firmly, Selian began to unleash a barrage of questions about my well-being and didn't wait for answers before asking others. "Come, come," he said, grabbing me by my arm without allowing me time to object. "We must go to my office. It's nearby. We have a lot to talk about."

He was pleasant and did not fit Papazian's description of him. As we walked up Abovian toward his office, Selian told me about his stay in Detroit, my mother's hospitality, my father's dedicated work for the cause, and how life in America had changed. He was a strange messenger, but he had a bubbly personality. I remained suspicious of his motives; after all, he was in the business of generating positive stories about the Soviets and the Soviet regime, propaganda, and I had now had my eyes opened. What I saw was not what he was writing about as the truth.

From his mind and his pen had come the potent words that had swayed and persuaded hundreds, if not thousands, to support Soviet Armenia. I reminded myself that he was the Goebbels of the Armenian American community, and he must have been good at what he did, for if not, why would the United States have deported him?

He was a nonstop talker. He talked all the way from the Aeroflot office to his own, which was across the street about a block away.

Selian had set up office in one of the older two-story buildings on the city's main strip. It was bare, except for a desk with one ancient typewriter, three chairs, and writing paper. The portraits of Lenin and Stalin were already on the wall behind his desk. I was sure he did not know that Karibian and Papazian lived in the same building as I did.

"We're just getting started. There is so much work to do," he said as he settled in behind the desk, which also held copies of the *Daily Worker, Moscow News,* and the *Lraper.* There were no telephones on the desk. A special permit was needed to install one, and it usually took time.

Selian's three-piece suit hung from him. I didn't know if he had lost weight during the legal ordeals leading up to his deportation, but I knew he would have been worse off if he hadn't visited Detroit. Mother usually stuffed guests with chicken and pilaf and dolmas and followed that with all kinds of Armenian desserts. Whatever his experiences, he appeared, I thought, pleasant, wearing his gray hair with dignity. One could not help but notice the white hands and the very white, almost anemic-looking complexion.

"How are my parents?" I asked.

"Fine. Everyone is healthy. They miss you, of course, but that will all be taken care of once they get here."

"Then they are coming?"

"Definitely."

I wanted to contradict him, but I didn't.

"Why haven't you written them?"

"I have. Several times. I have sent postcards and written letters. They don't seem to get them."

"Ah, yes, yes, the American censors. They won't allow anything positive about the USSR to get through. Nothing good about the Soviets ever gets through."

I suspected that it was the Soviet censors, not the American ones, who were holding up the letters, but I said nothing. I didn't want to start a political argument. I wanted more information about my family and why my father had suddenly decided to repatriate. Selian kept to politics. He told me that war was imminent in Palestine, that the UN was about to vote on the Partition Resolution. There would undoubtedly be a State of Israel, and war would erupt as soon as that happened. Attached to the Palestine question was a resolution that the UN would vote on, involving the return of all Armenian lands seized by the Turks after World War I. There was a crisis brewing between the Allies and the Soviets over the control of Berlin. And Congress was about to approve the Mundt-Nixon Bill, which would require all Communists in the United States to register.

Then he answered the question I had on my mind.

"That is why your father and many others have signed up for the second caravan. There is a red scare in the United States. Your father knows that as soon as the Mundt-Nixon Bill is signed, he'll be out of a job. He will be on the black list like so many others. And he won't be able to find another job."

"Then my father is definitely coming."

"Oh, yes, and so is your mother and Rose."

I asked, "And my two brothers?"

"You know better than that," Selian said. "They are not friends of our cause."

I did not know that he knew my family so well. "Did you see Robert or George?" I asked.

"No. I spent a week with your parents before I left for New York. My wife and children are still in California. George and Robert did not step into the house while I was there. That reminds me . . ." He opened the top drawer of his desk, pulled out a small gift-wrapped box, and handed it to me. "Your sister asked me to give this to you."

I pictured Rose tying the ribbon around the box, and I ran my fingers over it reverently. I wanted to open it immediately but decided to wait until I was alone. As I started to rise to leave, Selian stopped me. He came right to the point.

"We will be publishing some feature stories in English about Soviet Armenia and the many opportunities the youth have here, and we will need some bright young men and women on our staff who know English well. Rose told me that you wrote for the high school newspaper and were an honors student. Would you be interested in writing for our English publication?"

I knew what I should have said but wouldn't. He wanted me to join his propaganda machine to churn out more lies, more fluff, to lure more Americans and Armenians to that hell. If it had been anywhere else, in America or France or Italy, I would have jumped at the opportunity to write the truth. But I knew that he would not let me write my truth, only his—theirs. I would not be allowed to write about my experience at the Aeroflot office, about needing a passport to travel from one city to another within the Soviet Union. Nor would I be allowed to write that there was not enough bread to go around or soap to cleanse the body, that people were afraid to ride the tram because they ended up with lice. I wanted to set him straight about where I stood and how I felt. Instead, I told him about the university, about the basketball team, and then I excused myself.

"I have to be going. We have practice this afternoon."

"I understand, I understand."

I extended my hand and shook his, saying, "Thank you."

Before I left, Selian said, "Now, don't be a stranger around here. If there is anything I can do to help you, let me know."

"I will."

"My wife and kids will be on the same boat with your parents. If you want, we can travel to Batumi together."

"That would be fine," I replied

We parted. I never saw Oksen Selian again.

Chapter 37

LETTERS FROM HOME

T here was an uneasy, almost painful feeling in the pit of my stomach as I walked out into the bright sunlight after meeting with Mr. Selian. I knew that I had to get to Moscow, with or without Karibian. I needed to make phone contact with my family.

I walked slowly, deep in thought, toward Lenin's Square and reached Weepers' Garden. What an appropriate name, I thought. I found an unoccupied bench under some trees and sat down. As I did, I felt the small box. I took it out of my pocket and untied the ribbon. Inside were a wristwatch and two letters. I turned the watch over. Engraved on the back were the words "Come home. Love, Rose." One of the envelopes was addressed in my sister's handwriting, the other plainly said, "To Tom, from his history teacher." I opened my sister's letter first.

"Dearest brother, we miss you tremendously. You promised me you would be back in a year, but now I fear that Dad is going to force Mother and me to go with him to Armenia. I won't go, and I am trying to persuade Mother to say no. But I don't have to tell you how much control Father has over Mother. If Mother loses the fight, then I will accompany her. I shall not allow her to go alone. I know it must be hell, for if it were not, your mail would be getting to us. Please keep on trying. I understand, even though Dad doesn't. We miss you so. Love, Rose."

I sat and thought about the letter for quite some time. What a mess I had made of things. She didn't need to carry that load during her senior year in high school. My body collapsed on the bench; I was engulfed in despair.

Then I remembered the second letter. I tore open the envelope and began to read.

"Dear Tom, I admire your courage, and I want to take this brief opportunity to wish you all the luck in the world. As you probably know, you were one of my prize students, and our discussions about the Soviet Union, its form of government, the dictatorship, and the purges may have stirred you to seek firsthand information about the country. Therefore, I feel that I, too, may be at fault in your decision to leave the United States. You were and are a brilliant student and excellent athlete—and I have a feeling you'll be able to take care of yourself.

"But Tom, I sincerely fear for your life. If only one-quarter of the things we hear about the Soviet Union in our newspapers are true, then an American-born will have trouble there. The secret trials, mass deportations, executions, etc., have been documented by people who have survived. Please, please consider again before you leave.

"And whatever you decide, may God be with you always. Sincerely, Wixon, your teacher.

"P.S. You know I'm a stamp collector—please write."

I got up from the bench, put on the watch, and stuffed the two letters into my inside jacket pocket. I walked out of the park to the nearest tram stop, where I boarded the next streetcar headed for Yeroth Mas. I needed to get to the district police station as soon as possible, fill out the necessary paperwork for a passport or ID card or whatever the damn Soviets called it, and return to the city to purchase my plane ticket to Moscow.

Chapter 38

CHAPTER FROM CHEKHOV

I presented myself to the regional office of the *militzia* in the Yeroth Mas and stood at a counter waiting to be issued a Soviet passport. One officer, an elderly man whose striking white handlebar mustache complemented a trimmed goatee, was seated at a desk chatting with a young woman. The woman, a *teghatsi,* seemed distressed. The officer listened to her complaint, filled out a report, and told her not to worry, that everything would be straightened out. She didn't seem convinced as she walked away from the officer, brushed past me, and left.

The officer approached the counter and asked how he could be of service to me.

"Passport," I said. "I have no passport."

He seemed surprised, but he invited me to come to the other side of the counter to his desk. If not for his uniform, he would look like a Cossack or as if he had just stepped off the stage after playing a role in a Chekhov drama. After I explained my purpose, he asked my name, my father's name, and my date of birth. He jotted the information down, twirling the ends of his mustache after each question and response. I watched him glide his hand over the paper, and I was impressed by his stylish handwriting.

The officer, who until that point had seemed to regard me nonchalantly as just another *norkalogh,* a newcomer from who knew where, raised his eyebrows and took a long look when I said I'd been born in Detroit in the United States.

He asked, "You are one who came from America, then?" He studied me as if with a magnifying glass. I figured I was in trouble. I wondered if my place of birth would delay my application, if he might find some excuse not to issue the document until he'd consulted a superior, because I was from the enemy camp. But the other Armenian Americans must have gone through here, too, so why the delay?

"Yes," I said hesitantly. "I am from America."

"Detroit?"

"Yes. I am from Detroit, Michigan. You know of the place?"

"Ford? *Auftomobile? Da."*

"Ford. Automobiles. *Da."*

I felt as if a cultural curtain had fallen between us.

He proceeded with the interview. "Employment?"

I was not exactly employed, but I felt that if I gave that response, the interview would end. "I play basketball for Institute . . . Physical Culture and Sports." Then I pulled on the shirt of the blue warm-up suit I'd worn from practice. I moved my hands as if dribbling a ball, shooting at an imaginary basket. "Basketball. I . . . basketballist."

The officer smiled. I didn't know whether it was because of my animation or my acting or because I had found my first fan.

"Basketballist? Hmmm. Good. Very good." He wrote the information on what I thought was the application for my passport. There was more to come. His next question caught me completely off guard. "You are physically fit to serve the fatherland? *Da?*"

"Of course." I pulled back my shoulders, stood erect to show my physique, and smiled.

He seemed impressed. "Very good. Father work what factory?"

"Kelsey Hayes."

"Kelso Gayes? I do not understand."

"In Detroit. Auto factory. He works in America. My parents are in the United States."

The officer shook his head in disbelief, then dropped the pen and began rolling both sides of his mustache with both hands. "Then you bring wife and children to Hyestan, *da?*"

"No. No wife in Armenia. No children. Only me." I pointed my index finger at my chest. "Only me."

"Interesting. *Ochen interestnaya.*" After another quizzical glance, he posed the sixty-four-thousand-dollar question. "Tom Boghosovich, what branch of Great Victorious Red Army would you like to serve if the bloodthirsty capitalists make war on us?"

Military service! He had to be kidding. Never in my wildest dream had I ever thought I would have to put on a Soviet military uniform. I would not serve in any branch. But I couldn't say that. I could not antagonize the officer. I suggested, "The Air Force. The Soviet Air Force. I have excellent eyes. Basketballist, *ochen harashol glazee.* A basketball player has excellent eyesight, you know."

The officer smiled. "*Da, da,* I know . . . but do you think me a fool?"

I didn't answer that. He wrote down infantry.

He finished filling out my application and, with a serious look, asked me one more question, a strange one, which I first considered an attempt at Russian humor: "Are there any donkeys in the United States?"

I was sure he was pulling my leg. I asked him to repeat the question. He did. A psychological ploy, maybe? I wanted to say the capitalists, the warmongers, the Republicans, but I was sure he would not understand. So I offered, "Yes, comrade, there were one hundred fifty-one donkeys in America at one time, but all of them were shipped here on the *Rossia* to Soviet Armenia in November."

It went right past him, thank God. After he had signed and embossed it with a red stamp of the hammer and sickle, he handed me my Soviet passport. Then he came around the desk toward me and, as he presented me with the document, announced, *"Mashala.* Great. You now official citizen of the USSR." With that, he gave me a bear hug and kissed me on both cheeks. He told me that there was a fee of ten rubles for processing the application. I said I thought the fee was five. Yes, he agreed, five for the state and five for his pocket, *paparck.* I gladly paid him the ten.

~ IN THE WEST, it may have been called a bribe, the cost of doing business, but in Soviet Armenia, *paparck* was a ritual for survival. Corruption, widespread among the vendors who peddled ice cream, mineral water, and juices to merchants in the market, reached the top officials in the factories and beyond, even though penalties were severe. *Paparck* was part of the way of life in the three Transcaucasian republics—Armenia, Georgia, and Azerbaijan. Although it was a blatant violation of the law, the leaders condoned it. They knew that if the system did not exist, the citizens could not survive.

An overcoat cost a worker three months' earnings, yet there was money when coats were available. It came from *paparck.* Everyone was involved, even athletes. Often we would exchange our twenty-five-ruble meal vouchers for twenty rubles, and the restaurant would submit them to the Ministry of Sports for full value.

When a passenger boarded a tram or a bus and handed the conductor a ruble when the fare was fifty kopecks, the conductor automatically pocketed the change. If the passenger insisted that he wanted the change, the conductor, and even some of the passengers, would ostracize him, and he would take his seat and keep his mouth shut. One soon learned to have exact change ready unless he wanted to hear the conductor's voice sing, *"Axhbar, axhbar.* Brother, brother. I, too, have a family and a boss to feed." And his song could be heard on the streets of Tiflis and Baku.

The vulnerable Western European and Armenian American repatriates fought the system at first but eventually consented to it. They had no alternative. The *teghatsis* had lived with it since the Bolshevik Revolution and knew of no other way to exist. They accepted the practice;

did not fight it. They even encouraged it, because without it, they knew they would perish. Ironically, the passenger who boarded a bus and softly whispered into the conductor's ear, *"Dram choo nem,* I have no money," would be allowed to proceed to his destination without abuse from the conductor or anyone else aboard. For even those who held the highest positions, from the university president to the president of the Soviet Armenian Supreme Soviet, at some time or other faced payless paydays. They had all been in the ruble-less passenger's shoes.

~ I LEFT the regional office of the *militzia* with a smile on my face and jumped a tram that conveyed me to the Aeroflot office, where I displayed, before the red ink had dried, my passport, handed over the rubles, and did not have any further problems purchasing my plane ticket to Moscow. It would be my first plane trip. With a deep sigh, I closed the office door softly behind me and walked into the street. I had no idea of the adventure that was before me.

Chapter 39

RIDE TO THE AIRPORT

The first of May fell on a Saturday in 1948, the year that brought two former Allies—the United States and the USSR—to the verge of returning to the battlefield to settle the economic, political, and territorial issues that separated them. At stake was whether capitalism or communism would be the driving force and philosophy of economics in the world during the second half of the twentieth century. One of the superpowers, the United States, was armed with nuclear weapons, and the other, the USSR, would shortly have the secret. The stakes were higher when both possessed weapons of mass destruction, and there were many on both sides of the Iron Curtain who believed that mankind would not celebrate the twenty-first century. The world waited for the first atom or hydrogen bomb to ignite World War III.

Already politically fragile, the relationship between the United

States and the USSR collapsed over the issue of Berlin. In March, the Soviets had walked out on a meeting with the Allies and in the following weeks imposed restrictions on travel from their sector to the American and British sectors of Berlin, blocking East Berliners from getting to the West by road, waterway, and air. The challenge of the Soviet blockade was met by the United States and England. The Allies organized airlifts of food and supplies to nearly 2.5 million stranded West Berliners to thwart hunger, famine, and typhoid. As East-West tensions mounted, the NKVD operated its purge of Soviets who had any foreign connections, especially connections with the United States. Russians suddenly did not dare to speak or to be in the same environment with a foreigner.

NKVD agents and their trucks were busy uprooting families on the pretense that family members had been Dashnak or former Trotskyites.

As the Cold War intensified and the Voice of America news broadcasts were jammed by the Soviets, little news from the Western world reached the repatriates, and those behind the Iron Curtain had to rely on one-sided Communist newspapers.

~ I HAD been up before dawn, quietly packing a small suitcase, tucking the petition into my suit jacket, and preparing to go to the Erevan airport.

I glanced at the ticket, written in Russian, and slowly deciphered it. Ticket 850086, from Erevan Airport to Moscow Airport. My name: Mooradian, T. B. The cost of the flight was 610 rubles plus a seven-ruble tax. Flight 244, on aircraft 1838, was set to take off at 6:10 A.M. for Moscow via Kharkov and Tula. There was no arrival time stated. As I secured the ticket in my wallet, I smiled. Anahaid had taught me well.

There were no round-trip tickets. I mulled over whether I should ask the embassy for political asylum. If my request were refused, I would ask the embassy officials if I could make a personal call to my parents. There were too many ifs; I needed some answers. In addition to the petition, I also tucked the recent letters from my sister and my history teacher into my jacket pocket. I was quite certain that there would be no search of my belongings or my person at the airport, for this was a flight within the USSR.

I was satisfied with my appearance in the gray double-breasted suit and white shirt. I left the collar button open but packed a black tie to wear to the embassy. Since Moscow was still cold in April and May, I grabbed a sweater and a raincoat. My black shoes were polished until I could see myself in them. Before I put on my new wristwatch, I flipped it over and read the inscription again. "Come home," I whispered to myself. "Soon."

During the late evening, I had slipped a note under Karibian's door, simply stating, "I'm leaving at daybreak. See you in Moscow. Inform the others. Pray for me and a successful mission."

Mr. Simonian stirred as I was packing, but he did not wake up, and once Johnny was asleep, it would have taken an earthquake to awaken him. I felt strange leaving them. I wondered what Simonian would say if he knew what my plans were.

Quietly, so as not to disturb the two men, I moved toward the door, opened it, and eased it back as I entered the corridor. I walked down the steps, praying with each step, asking the Lord to guide me—not for myself alone but for those who trusted me, who had placed their lives in my hands. It was pitch dark when I entered the courtyard and made my way to the street and the streetcar stop. As I approached the intersection at Ordzhonikidze and Kalinin Street, a truck rambled by, narrowly missing me. Not a good sign, I thought. I had to be more careful. I didn't think he even saw me, but the driver stopped his vehicle a short distance ahead, put it in reverse, and pulled back to where I was standing. Without any formalities, he got down to the business of the night.

"Do you want a ride?"

"You almost hit me!" I shouted.

"So I'll take off ten rubles."

"No, thanks, I'll wait for the tram."

"It may be hours before it comes by. They come when the operator feels like it in the early morning."

"I'll wait."

"Well, good luck."

As the driver gave me one last look before driving off, I rethought my decision. What if the tram was late? I could not afford to miss the plane. "Hey, wait!" I shouted. "How much to the airport?"

"To the airport?" He eyed me suspiciously. "You want to go to the airport?"

"Yes."

After a second serious look at me, the driver said, "Fifty rubles."

"You're crazy. It would cost me only fifty kopecks by tram. Goodbye."

"Harashol. How about twenty-five rubles?"

"And you'll take off the ten for the near miss? So it's fifteen, right?"

He shook his head at first, as if to say no. But fifteen was better than nothing. "Jump in."

I moved around to the passenger's side and got into the truck. I took out the rubles and handed them to him. He didn't even count the money but stuffed it into his greasy, short Chinese-knit jacket. He gave me the once-over again, took out a long Russian cigarette, and offered me one. I declined but thanked him. He lit it, and we drove along in silence.

The dark-skinned driver, who had a thousand wrinkles around his eyes, looked as if he hadn't shaved or bathed for weeks. Body odor and cigarette fumes filled the cab. Unlike most truck drivers I had seen from the trams and buses and during my walks, this one did not wear a black cap. He had on a French beret.

"You are a *norkalogh,* right?" he asked.

"Yes."

"From America, right?"

"Yes."

"And you're going to Moscow, right?"

"How did you know?"

"There is only one plane that leaves the airport early, and that is the plane to Moscow." Then, as an afterthought, he said, "It is usually filled with important Party figures."

I was curious, but I said nothing as I looked out the dirty windows into the darkness. I sat there quietly contemplating what I would do at the airport.

We had rolled along for a few more miles when the driver looked over at me and smiled. "You have nothing to fear from me. I am not NKVD."

"I thought we all worked for the state," I replied. "We all must be diligent."

"I am also a repatriate—like you."

"Repatriate?" I asked, emphasizing the word in Armenian.

"From Athens, in 1936. My father was a Communist, and they hanged Communists. So he packed up the family and brought all of us here."

"What's he doing now?"

"I don't know. They arrested him during the 1937 purges as a Dashnak. A truck pulled up one night. The Cheka came in, dragged him out of the house . . ."

"Cheka?" I asked. "Who are they?"

"NKVD . . . secret police."

"Oh."

"I am good mechanic, drive truck, make good *paparck,* you know."

"Have you never heard from your father after his arrest?" I asked.

"No." He shrugged. "He probably died somewhere in Siberia."

I tried to get a closer look at his face, but I couldn't in the darkness. I shook my head.

"Have any of your people been arrested?" he asked.

"What do you mean? Why would any of us be arrested? We have not done anything."

"*Axhbar,* you don't have to do anything here to be arrested. They have quotas to fill."

We were nearing the airport, and I could hear the drumming sounds of aircraft in the distance. "If there is only one flight, why so many planes?" I asked.

"Ah, my friend, to the north of us is the military base. There you will find many military planes. Turkey, you know, is just over that hill." Pointing to Mount Ararat, he continued, "The enemy is on the other side of that mountain." Then he asked, "Why are you going to Moscow?"

It really was none of his business, but despite his appearance, he had been so friendly that I gave him my practiced pitch. "I'm a history student, and I always wanted to see Moscow and the May Day parade."

A cynical smile crossed his face.

"You don't believe me?"

"Of course, *axhbar,* I believe you. Why should I not?"

I didn't answer. I continued to gaze out through the windshield, hoping to spot the airport. There was a streak of light across the horizon, and it would be daybreak soon. I wished I were aboard the plane, off the ground, at peace in the air. Suddenly, the lights of a small building came into view. The driver pointed them out to me.

"There, over there, that's the Erevan airport. We'll be there in a few minutes."

The airport building was impossibly tiny. I asked the driver if he was sure we had come to the right airport. Perhaps there was another place I should be flying out of?

He laughed and said, *"Axhbar,* we are a small republic. We have only one airport for public use."

There were very few passengers and fewer vehicles in the small lot adjacent to the building. As we approached, I could see men standing outside smoking cigarettes. We pulled up to the curb, and I turned in the seat to thank him, but he suddenly shifted into gear. My body was thrown forward, and I scraped my head on the windshield as he drove off.

"Are you crazy? You almost killed us!" I shouted.

"Axhbar, keep quiet for a minute. I shall explain."

He drove a mile or two down the road into a wooded area, then stopped his truck. I wondered if he knew I had a wad of rubles on me and was going to rob me. I looked for something to grab to hit him over the head with. Finding nothing, I tightened my fist and waited for an explanation.

"The men . . . did you see them?"

"What men?" I asked. "What's this all about?"

"The men in black, the canvas-covered truck . . . did you see them?"

"No! And what's this got to do with anything?" I was getting angrier every second.

"It is an NKVD vehicle, and the only reason those fuckers are there is that they are going to beat the shit out of someone. American, if you want to bet, it is you."

I knew he was crazy now. "What's wrong with you? I have done nothing! I'm flying to Moscow, fool!"

"I am not the fool, *axhbar.* You are, if you think the NKVD is going to believe that you're flying to Moscow to watch a fucking parade. You will disappear. Let me take you back where I picked you up. I don't want your money. But I am the last human being you will see if you walk through that door. Go back to where you came from. They will come for you someday, but I don't want the guilt on my hands that I delivered you into theirs."

I didn't know what to say. If he were right, I would not make it to the plane. But how could I know? "Please, take me back to the airport. Or I will walk from here."

He looked at me and took a deep breath. *"Lav.* Good. I am not the one who is crazy. It is your funeral, my brother."

Chapter 40

NALBANDIAN STREET

The driver didn't drive me to the terminal entrance but stopped about a hundred yards short of the door and ordered me out of the vehicle. I figured that if there really were NKVD agents stationed at the airport and I happened to be the reason they were there, he didn't want them to question him about his vehicle and why he was on the streets so early. And he didn't want to be seen with me. Before I could thank him, he sped off into the breaking dawn.

One could not have asked for a more perfect spring morning. The smell of budding flowers filled the air, and there was no reason to suspect anything or anyone as the sun's rays broke the darkness of the night.

I walked toward the building, reached the door, and glanced at the truck with the canvas top. I smiled at the men inside it before I opened the door and strolled into the small room. There were not many passengers that morning and, it seemed, no one to see loved ones off. I walked over to the counter to check in. An Armenian clerk, his head cleanly shaven, greeted me with a smile as I presented my ticket and passport. He wore a suit with a blue shirt open at the collar. After perusing the passport, he looked up and, giving me a smile, handed the document back to me. As I waited for him to process the ticket, I glanced around and saw nothing to make me suspicious. There were the usual portraits of the leaders, a kiosk in the far corner where a plump middle-aged woman in a white smock was busy sorting out editions of the daily newspapers and placing them on racks. There was no food counter, and there would be nothing to eat on the plane. I wondered how the food in Moscow would be.

I figured that the truck driver's imagination had been working over-time. I looked around the room for a place to sit. There were a few rows of wooden benches and only male passengers, no women. Shortly after I sat on a bench in one of the corners near the window overlooking the runway, a plane approached that resembled an old Douglas DC3. I got up and began to walk toward the clerk to ask him if that was our plane.

As I reached the counter, two men wearing black suits intercepted me. One asked in a friendly voice, "Tom Boghosovich?" I stared at him and then nodded. "You must come with us." His pleasant smile did not leave his face.

"Why?" I asked. "Who are you?"

"Do not make a scene. We have some questions."

"I have a plane to catch. I am going to Moscow. I want to see the May Day parade."

"Good. Very good. But you will come with us. We will explain later."

"I don't understand. Who are you?" I repeated, and I looked to see if there was anywhere I could run to get out of their reach. Two armed men in military uniform had taken up position outside the entrance, the only escape route.

There was a nervous pause between us.

"Will you come now?" the man said.

"I do not know who you gentlemen think you are . . ."

And before I got out another word, the second man grabbed me by the arm and kicked me in the shins. I nearly fell. The two grabbed me and dragged me out of the airport building to the canvas-covered truck. None of the passengers in the airport moved, except to look the other way. They knew—I didn't—where I was going.

When we got to the truck, an armed officer appeared from within, leaped to the ground, and helped the others toss me into the vehicle.

The armed man and the one who had viciously kicked me jumped into the back of the truck, while the other man slipped into the passenger seat of the cab. The driver sped off. We drove toward the center of Erevan. As we approached Nalbandian Street, there was no doubt about where we were going.

I had few fears, though the pain from my shin was reaching my head. In my mind, I had done nothing. I had violated no laws. I felt that I could explain. I would not be overcome by fear. But the child who was driven into the NKVD building was not the same man who came out.

As I limped into the building with one of the plainclothes officers on each side and an armed guard behind me, I suddenly remembered what my history teacher had said in his letter about my always being one who was stirred to seek firsthand information.

I saw no crime in my actions. They would set me free once we had ironed this all out, I was certain. And they would put me on the next flight to Moscow.

But I could still hear the driver who had taken me to the airport. *"Axhbar,* it is your funeral."

They knew of the petition to the U.S. Embassy, who was involved, who had provided me with funds. The NKVD knew everything. The judge, the jury, and the verdict had been predetermined. All that was needed was an executioner—and he sat right across from me. Did he not pull the trigger? Had I not seen him slowly squeeze it?

Chapter 41

RETURNING FROM HELL

I was falling and drifting into a world of darkness. Voices cried out for help and water. I could not respond to them. I had become one of them. My body suddenly vaporized, but my senses alerted my brain that I would survive. I drifted from room to room, from cell to cell. Tossed down a narrow staircase, I felt my body plummeting, and I screamed as my body met the concrete. In time—I didn't know how long—I heard footsteps above me. I looked up and saw the soles of boots. I was in an oubliette. They had their mouse in the trap. Even if the mouse managed to find a way out of the labyrinth, where could it go but back to the hole?

I wondered if they had picked up Karibian and Sourian and Papazian. My head was pounding.

And suddenly, bright lights.

Hot and cold compresses upon my forehead and friendly voices and words that I thought I recognized. *"Asvasz, asvasz.* God, God. He is lucky."

Who were they talking about? Where was I?

My eyelids slowly opened. The blur before me took shape. It was Mr. Simonian sitting on the bed, shaking his head and placing hot compresses on my forehead. There was a person standing behind him, leaning over his shoulder looking at me. I could barely make out the face, but he looked familiar—the driver who took me to the airport.

Simonian turned and whispered to the stranger, "He's all right. Thank God. He's opening his eyes."

"Thank God," I heard the stranger say. "Thank God." Then, after a pause, "I'd better be going . . ."

Simonian put another compress on my forehead. He got up, turned around, and told the stranger, "If it hadn't been for you . . ."

The stranger said nothing. He moved away and walked toward the door. Simonian followed. They exchanged whispered words, the door opened, and the man left.

Simonian returned to the bed. "You're going to be all right, Tommy. Get some sleep."

I could barely understand his words.

I didn't know how long I had been sleeping or how I'd got into Simonian's bed.

When I finally was strong enough, I asked Simonian, "How did I get here?"

"We found you," he said, "in the Weepers' Garden, and we brought you home."

"We? Who?"

"The man who drove you to the airport."

There was a silence in the room. Everything remained a blur.

"How did I get to the park?"

"I don't know. Maybe you could tell us."

I couldn't. My mind was too hazy. "Who was he? The driver . . . I mean, why did he want to help me?"

Simonian told me how the driver had come back to where he had picked me up, made some inquiries about "the Americans," and was pointed in the direction of our apartments. "He thought he would find your wife or your parents and inform them that the NKVD had taken you into custody. He found me instead. I got worried after you didn't show up. At first, I thought you had found yourself a cute sleeping mate, like Johnny does. But as time went on, I knew better. We were on the lookout for you ever since. He found you in the park. You're alive, that's all that counts."

I was alive. I was at the apartment. But being alive wasn't all that counted. Why was I released? Who gave the order to release me? And did I say anything or confess to anything that could incriminate anyone? I searched my mind to put the puzzle together. Pieces were missing.

"Has Karibian been here?" I asked.

"Yes."

"And Papazian?"

"Yes."

"Has Sourian been around?"

"He was the first, when he learned you were here." Almost in a whisper, he said, "Yes, they and many others. They all have been worried sick about you. Even some of the French have been here. One old lady heard you were very sick, said a prayer for you, and brought you some chicken soup. We made some pilaf, but we couldn't get anything down. We really thought we had lost you, Tommy."

I looked at him and thanked him.

"No more talking. We'll have time to talk later. Just rest."

I tried to smile, but my jaw hurt. All I could remember when my head returned to the pillow was that Simonian's hair seemed to have gotten whiter and that he had not shaved for a couple of days.

Simonian said, "By the way, don't look in a mirror. You look a mess. I tried to clean you up and even tried to give you a shave. But . . . anyway, it was the best I could do."

"Thanks."

"Do you think you're strong enough for me to leave you? I need to get down to the barbershop and see how things are going."

"I'm fine, Mr. Simonian. I really am."

"Good. I know you are."

After he closed the door behind him, I buried my face in the pillow and sobbed for the rest of the day.

Chapter 42

CONFRONTING THE *TROIKA*

As I looked out our window into the courtyard, I saw the clouds coiled and rolling across a quickly darkening morning sky. I knew there was one more task I had to accomplish before I could get on with my life in the Soviet Union. I must confront the *troika*—Karibian, Papazian, and Sourian. Which one informed, and why? It would be heartbreaking but cathartic to learn the identity of the one who had performed the perfidious act. I must know, beyond a reasonable doubt, which of the three had tipped off the NKVD.

I had always respected my elders. I had been taught by my parents to respect the older generations, especially those who had survived the massacres, as people who had seen the worst of mankind and survived, thus learning about life in a way none of the *odars* could understand. My mother would never allow me to forget that family came first; she had lost so many of her loved ones. In our family and extended family, we looked to our elders for advice, and they were always there for us. Youth, although adventurous and carefree, is still the time of learning. Our elders had crossed the bridge, and they would extend their hands to us, if we needed their help, to guide us across. That is what I had been raised to believe—but no longer.

We met in my room, after Simonian and Johnny had left for work.

We sat on Simonian's unopened crates, and I didn't waste any words with them.

"One of us is an informer. And I know it isn't me. That leaves the three of you. Can anyone here tell me how the information of our plans got into their hands?" And before any of them could say a word, I made it clear. "They knew everything, even about the petition to the ambassador."

There was an uneasy movement of bodies on the crates, sending me the message that it was impossible for the NKVD to know. How could I accuse them of anything? Their silence, I felt, convicted all of them. None responded. Was it out of fear of what I might have done? Or was it because they saw the change in me as a result of the experience?

I changed strategies. "Did you get to Moscow, Mr. Karibian?" I asked sarcastically, looking directly into his eyes. "Or were you in the cell next to mine?"

"No. I was not arrested."

"Why not?" I growled. "I thought you were supposed to take the next flight!"

"Tommy, calm down, everyone will hear you. Please calm down. Listen . . ."

"That's one thing I'm not going to do. I did listen to you and the others, and I almost lost my life. And I still don't know why I'm here."

Karibian spoke. "When that stranger came into the courtyard the day you left and began asking questions, I approached him. He was asking around if anyone knew where a tall young American boy lived. So I asked him why he wanted to know. He said he wanted to talk to the boy's parents, maybe his wife. I told him that there were two young Americans living in our building. He described you. He began shaking his head. And he asked if there was anyone you lived with, and I told him Simonian and Johnny lived with you. I took him inside our building and led him upstairs, and I knocked on the door. Simonian had not left for work. He invited this guy inside the apartment. You know Simonian and I don't see eye-to-eye on a lot of things, so I left. But in the corridor, I overheard the man tell Simonian that you had been arrested. I didn't know how he knew, but that's what I heard." Karibian paused and looked at the others, who were nodding their heads. "I told

Joe and Papazian. In short, we didn't know what to do. We waited to see if the rumor was true."

"And what did happen to you, Tommy?" Sourian asked.

"I really don't know what happened," I finally said. "I know that I was at the airport ready to board. Two thugs approached me and told me that I had to go with them, and when I resisted, one of them kicked me in my shins." I showed them the deep gash, then continued, "And I was taken from the airport, dumped into the back of a truck, and driven to the NKVD offices and interrogated. They knew about everything I—we—planned. I didn't need to tell them. I didn't need to spill my guts out. They already knew!"

"Did you?" asked Papazian.

"Did I what?"

"Spill your guts out to them, and that is why they released you?"

"Fuck you. You son-of-a-bitch. I didn't need to spill my guts. One of you already did." I jumped from the crate and was about to attack him when Karibian and Sourian moved between us. Their immediate intervention prevented things from getting nasty.

Sourian paled. His hands were shaking, but he said nothing. I continued to lash out at them verbally, to humiliate them and demean them again and again, and yet they responded only with silence. In that silence that engulfed us, every noise sounded like thunder to my ears. If I had had a weapon, I would have slain all three men.

As if from a distance, I could hear Sourian plead, "Listen . . . listen to reason. Try to understand."

I couldn't understand anything.

"Calm down, please calm down, Tommy. For your sake, for all of us, calm down. Try to hear what I have to say." Again, it was Sourian pleading.

I didn't want to hear anything he or they or anyone else had to say to me. I hated them and everything around me.

"We all signed that petition, and we placed ourselves and our wives and Harry's children in jeopardy. Why would we betray you?"

I didn't respond.

"Believe me, we have as much as you, if not more, to lose by this. We're waiting for the other shoe to drop."

Karibian and Papazian nodded. "We don't know how they got the information, Tommy," Karibian said, "but my family is as frightened by this as Joe's and Papazian's."

"Yes, you had a lot to lose, but think—think—we do, too. Our families. What we worked for all these years—all lost. None of us would go to the NKVD, believe me," said Papazian.

I found it difficult to believe what they were saying, but if what they maintained was true, if it hadn't been one of them, then who? I wanted an answer, but I wasn't going to get one. Not there, not then, anyway.

"Tommy, Alice gets out there on the balcony every day and screams her head off. I tell her to shut up, but she won't." Papazian had regained his composure and started to talk. "I don't have a moment's peace and nowhere to turn except to Joe here and Harry. I—all of us—hoped that maybe the ambassador could help us. That door now seems to be shut. I told you, and I'll say it again, I would give these people the two cars, everything Alice and I have worked for all of our lives, if they would allow us to go. And I am sure Joe and Harry would, too. I know you want to go home. But let's not stab each other in the back. That's what they want us to do. None of us informed on you. You must believe me. You must believe us."

"Maybe someday we'll find out," Karibian pitched in, "but if we start pointing fingers at each other, we will never know anything."

Karibian pulled out his copy of the petition and asked, "By the way, where is your copy?"

"I don't know. I don't know." My mind flashed back to the airport. I tried to remember the events—giving my suitcase to the clerk at the airport, sitting on the bench near a window. Did I take my jacket off before walking up to ask the clerk about the plane? Or did I lay it on the bench next to me? "I don't know," I repeated.

"Where's your suitcase?" Sourian asked.

"I don't know. Probably in Moscow."

Sourian continued, "Where did you keep your copy of the petition before you left for the airport?"

It took me only a second to reply. "In the bottom of my trunk, in the other room. I kept the trunk closed, and the key was on me at all times."

Sourian stood up. "Show me."

I did, and he examined the closed lock.

"It wouldn't be hard to open. You could probably pop it open with a toothpick." Sourian's eyes darkened as he glanced at the other two men. Lowering his voice almost to a whisper, he said, "You locked your trunk when you left the building?"

"Yes, I'm positive I did. I would not want to carry that document with me anywhere." Anticipating what Sourian was leading up to, I added, "Simonian and Johnny and I shared a cabin on the ship. I may not agree with Simonian's politics, but he or Johnny would never go to the NKVD. Never! I am sure of that."

"But Simonian and Johnny had access to the room and the suitcase."

"Of course they did. They live here."

Sourian looked at me curiously. "There is a possibility, isn't there, that they may have seen you tuck something deep into the trunk and out of curiosity wonder what it was? Johnny's parents are coming on the next boat, and Simonian has signed up for life. It is something that all of us should consider in the future."

I didn't know what to think. I was so confused that all I wanted was for them to leave.

They did.

And an iron curtain descended between us. I had no more questions for them. It was time, I felt, to sever all ties—with them, with Simonian and Johnny, with any and all of the Armenian American repatriates. Sourian may have left me with doubts about who the informer was, but there was no doubt in my mind that the NKVD had successfully infiltrated the Armenian American community.

I realized that I needed to find another room, to distance myself from my friends. Unfortunately, there were no rooms to be had anywhere at the time.

My greetings in the courtyard and on the stairways to the other residents were now only courtesies, if not downright cold and terse. There would be no Christmas, Easter, or New Year celebrations or sharing of letters or news from America. We might have been in this mess together, but each of us would have to devise a separate plan for survival, even escape.

~ AS THE days turned into months and the horrific rumors of NKVD brutality became realities beyond a shadow of a doubt, I returned to the question that would haunt me the rest of my life: Why did the NKVD, which had the blood of millions on its hands, allow me to go free? There is no logical explanation, unless, of course, I was but a messenger to the others.

My mind would always return to the interrogation room. I would see the gun pointed at me. Why was my interrogator ordered to fire a blank?

But the NKVD did kill a part of me on Nalbandian Street. They tore out my heart. I would never believe in or trust people again, not even my closest friend. David had warned me aboard the ship that friendships meant nothing in the Soviet realm of reality. "Your closest friend will be your worst enemy."

The guilt of survival lived within me, depressed me, and overpowered me so much that at times, I sank into the corner of my room and refused to come out.

There were the endless attempts of do-gooders, who tried to justify my survival, who told me, "Put it behind you. Get on with your life. Chalk it up to life's experience. You'll forget." Or better still, "Find yourself a good woman, have children, raise a family." As if that would cure what was slowly eating away at my guts. As I put my head down on my pillow and waited for sleep, the pictures would come back and scream at me from the ceiling.

And there was the wise old woman, dressed in black, who came to my bedside, rushed there to console me, to ease my pain. *"Zavid donem,"* she murmured over and over. "Let me take your pain away." She urged me to believe in God. "He has spared you for a reason, for a purpose. *Derah, derah.* My son, my son. Your mission on earth is not yet ended. The Lord has other tasks for you."

I didn't want any other missions if they all ended the way this one did.

Eventually, I asked Mr. Simonian, "Why do you think they let me go?"

He answered, "For the obvious reason."

"Obvious to whom? Please explain, because nothing seems to me obvious these days."

"One of the higher-ups understood the ramifications."

"Like what?"

"That they could lose millions of dollars, millions. And they would have to explain it to Moscow and did not want to."

"What do you mean?"

"If you, or any of the American repatriates, were arrested at this crucial time and the news got back to America, what would happen to the second or third caravan?"

"I don't know. You tell me."

"Look around you. Look at all the goods we have brought here. There is much, much more coming. Their engineers are going over our refrigerators, tearing them apart, looking over our cars and the machinery we brought with us—looking over everything. They are making blueprints, and they will soon manufacture them. And what happens if you or any one of us ends up in Siberia? The repatriation program is torpedoed, the train is derailed, and the goods don't arrive. There are thousands of displaced Armenians who want to return to Armenia. I would not want to be the one to answer to Moscow for sinking the ship, believe me."

In the months that followed, events gave credence to Simonian's argument. In March 1949, thousands of Soviet citizens, including two families who lived in the French apartments across the courtyard, were rounded up in the middle of the night, herded into trucks, and never seen again. But not one Armenian American repatriate—not even Alice Papazian, who ventured precariously out on the limb one day when she shouted Stalin's name among her expletives—was on the list of victims of the mass deportation. The second caravan was on its way but had not yet reached the port of Batumi.

When the *Rossia* did dock, Johnny's father and mother and brother were on that ship. He and I went to Batumi together. His parents and his brother were among the repatriates; mine were not.

It was the last ship from the United States to carry Armenian Americans. The Iron Curtain would be tightly sealed in the years to come.

I would have to face Soviet life on my own. I got down on my knees and thanked God for that.

The Mooradian family, minus Tom, in the early 1950s, in their southwest Detroit yard. Pictured (from left) are Robert, Mother, Father, George, and Rose. Tom (inset) in 1946, when he helped Southwestern High capture its first city championship. A few years later (right), he was strolling down Abovian Street in Erevan, Soviet Armenia. In the background are two Soviet citizens wearing their military uniforms because no other clothing was available.

Photo courtesy of the Detroit Free Press

Abraham, from Port Said, Egypt, played a major role in Tom's life. He convinced Tom that playing basketball for the Soviets could help him make a living and survive in a society where people were conditioned to be suspicious of Westerners, especially English-speaking foreigners. The two helped Soviet Armenia gain respect in a sport that until that point was virtually unknown to Armenia.

Making his debut as player No. 11 for the Institute of Physical Culture and Sports, Tom did not know what to expect. As he nervously sized up the opposition, player-coach Konstantin Vartanian (No. 8) and Kolya (No. 3), a Georgian-born Armenian, helped him overcome his first-game jitters. One could have counted on one hand the number of fans who showed up to watch the opening game for the city championship. This was a far cry from the republic's championship game a year later (below), when the defending

champ Kirovakan clashed with the all-imported Erevan quintet, which defeated the champ and went on to capture ten consecutive titles and represent the republic in the USSR nationals for the next decade. After this championship match-up, a riot broke out between the locals and the repatriates, which left scores injured. There was no media coverage of the melee, so citizens never learned the extent of the personal injuries or property damage.

In 1949, Tom's first road trip outside Soviet Armenia was to Vilnius, Soviet Lithuania's capital. The team and the coaching staff were presented with flowers at the depot by the host republic, according to custom. It had taken about eight days to travel by train from Erevan to Lithuania, via Moscow and Minsk, and Tom (standing at far right) grew a beard for the first time in his life, because it was too dangerous to shave with a straight razor aboard the train. The Lithuanians did not respect the Armenian ball club and ushered them to a stable where cots had been set up. When one of the players informed the hosts that there was an American on the team, they were immediately packed off to the newly opened Vilnius Hotel in the center of the city.

An unidentified Lithuanian player makes an easy shot in a pre-Soviet gym that had been built to host the European Games. Lithuania's national sport was basketball, and the republic has produced some of the finest players in Europe.

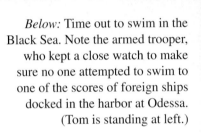

Abraham (holding flowers), Jeannot (No. 11) from France, and Tom (far right) teamed up with two locals to breeze to the intramural championship staged among the four grades. They were sophomores.

Below: Time out to swim in the Black Sea. Note the armed trooper, who kept a close watch to make sure no one attempted to swim to one of the scores of foreign ships docked in the harbor at Odessa. (Tom is standing at left.)

Above: Tom watches as one of his long shots descends from orbit toward the rim of the basket in Odessa. The Ministry of Culture and Sports had to be pleased with the influx of players from abroad. The team drew standing-room-only crowds in every game.

Abraham (left), Jak (center), and Tom got together on New Year's Day in 1956. That is not a Christmas tree, nor is it Santa behind them. Since they rose to power in 1917, the Bolsheviks had crushed all religion, saying it was the opium of the masses. Soviets did exchange gifts on New Year's Day and paid homage to the season by erecting "Father Frost" and decorating evergreens.

Tom (left) with teammates Abraham, Armenak, Jeannot, and an unidentified repatriate enjoy a sunny afternoon munching sunflower seeds while sitting on a fountain wall on Lenin's Square in Erevan.

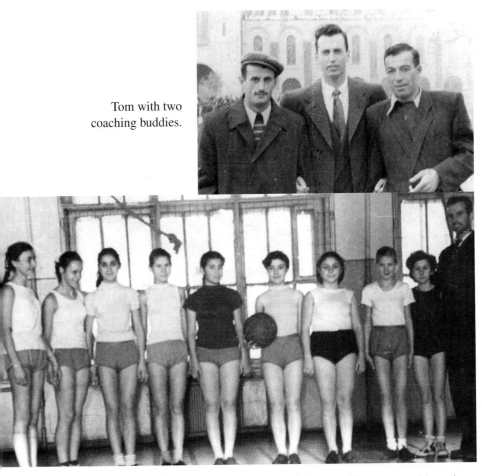

Tom with two coaching buddies.

How Tom managed to juggle his schedule to coach and play is still a mystery. Above is one of the girls' teams, coached by Tom and Jak, who won the city championship. The junior boys' team (below) also captured a city title.

Haratoun Simonian, the barber of Philadelphia, Tom's "guardian angel."

Tom with his aunt Ardemis.

Anahaid (left), Tom's Russian and Armenian mentor, and a coworker are pictured leaving the Etchmiadzin, the see of the Armenian Christian Church.

Tom (jacket over shoulder) with his teammates leaving a restaurant in Leninakan, a city noted for earthquakes and as the "ice box" of Armenia.

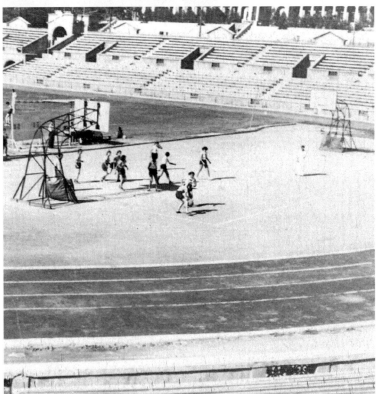

The Soviet Armenian women's basketball team practiced outdoors at Dynamo Stadium in preparation for a historic international game between the mammoth People's Republic of China and the diminutive Soviet Republic of Armenia. Thousands, including Politburo members, attended the match-up between the two Communist countries, which ended in decisive victories for both the Armenian men's and women's teams.

This Republic of Soviet Armenia's all-star team represented Armenia in most of the USSR's national championships. There were four foreign-born on the team, including Armenak Alajajian (left), Jeannot Makarian (second from left), Tom (fourth from right), and Abraham Hamamdjian (third from right). All four players eventually left the USSR.

Ереван. Спартакиада республик Закавказья.

Встреча по баскетболу между мужскими командами Армении и Грузии закончилась со счетом 59:53 в пользу команды Армении.

A Russian newspaper photo shows Armenak (No. 6) cutting through the middle of Georgia's defense for a layup during the finals of the Transcaucasus championship. Armenia destroyed Baku in the opening round and carved out a 59-53 victory over the Georgians, capturing its first Transcaucasus championship. Alajajian joined the Soviets' international traveling squad that claimed European championships and also played for the USSR squad that finished second to the USA in the 1964 Tokyo Olympics.

Above: Tom (second from left, back row) poses with other repatriates who attended the Institute of Physical Culture in Erevan. Paul Antaramian (far left, back row) and his brother were from Illinois. The rest of their family came in the second caravan from the United States.

Right: Tom with his friend and teammate Kolya.

he USSR, noted for spectacular sporting events, staged an Olympiad—or Spartakgeta, as they ere called—in celebration of Stalin's birthday. All fifteen republics participated, and the Soviet rmenian delegation, made up of its finest athletes, took part. Tom was among the more than ne hundred athletes who trained and participated in a parade that honored the Soviet dictator : Moscow's Dynamo Stadium. One of the tense moments of the Soviet Armenian presentation ame as the troupe stopped in front of the viewing stand, and world weight-lifting record older Sergei Hambartsoumjian, balancing an iron bar with a huge globe attached at either nd on his shoulders, walked up to Stalin and placed the bar before him on the ground. The vo globes slowly opened, and six small children crawled out, presenting the dictator with ouquets of flowers. The stadium exploded in applause.

Left: Flanked by two Russian players, Tom is photographed in the city of Kursk. It was there that the greatest tank battle in the history of warfare was staged. The trio is standing a few feet from one of the tanks that participated in routing the superior Nazi forces.

Below: In the city of Tiflis, two Georgians wanted to be photographed with "the Americanetz." Tom couldn't disappoint them.

Tom munches sunflower seeds (one of his favorite snacks) as Jak lectures him about being more respectful of his surroundings. On the right is the mausoleum where Lenin was laid to rest. There were always huge crowds waiting to see the remains of Lenin, the architect of the 1917 Bolshevik Revolution.

The Hotel National had such notable guests over the years as Prince Mikhail Romanov and his mistress, Natasha, as well as V. I. Lenin, Elizabeth Taylor, Van Cliburn, and Eleanor Roosevelt. Tom often wondered why he was able to book a room whenever he visited the city. After Tom received his exit visa, a KGB agent told him that the agency thought it best that he stay at the National, in the center of the city, where they could keep their eyes on him.

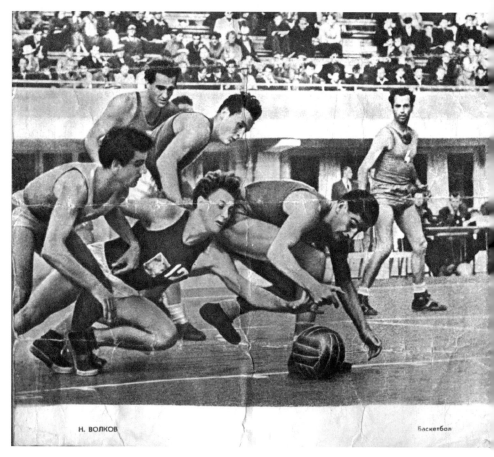

Н. ВОЛКОВ   Баскетбол

One of Tom's last appearances in a Soviet Armenian basketball uniform was at Dynamo Stadium in Moscow in 1959. His Soviet career spanned nearly a decade. In the photo, Tom (No. 4) watches as teammates scramble for a loose ball in a game against Riga, a team that represented Latvia in the nationals. The photo appeared on the cover of *Sovietski Sporta.*

Right: After a thirteen-year battle with the Soviet authorities, Tom was granted an exit visa and a passport to leave the country. Pages from those documents, along with pages from his American passport, are shown.

СВѢДѢНІЯ О ПРЕДЪЯВИТЕЛѢ
SIGNALEMENT DU PORTEUR

1. Дата рождения 31 июля 1928 г.
   Date de naissance 31 juillet 1928

2. Место рождения Соединенные Штаты
   Lieu de naissance les États-Unis d'Amérique

3. Семейное положение холост
   État civil célibataire

4. Специальность и род занятий
   Spécialité ou profession

5. Последнее местожительство в СССР
   Dernier domicile dans l'URSS

6. Документы, на основании которых выдан настоящий вид на жительство

МѢСТО ДЛЯ ФОТО

М. П.

Подпись владельца — Signature du porteur
Tommy Mooradian

	SIGNALEMENT	
Рост	180 см	Taille 180
Глаза	серые	Yeux gris
Нос		Nez
Волосы	черные	Cheveux noirs
Особые приметы		Signes particuliers

ВИЗЫ
VISAS

01 марта 60
492909
Мурадян
Погосович
один-

СССР ВЫЕЗД
03 АВГ 1960

января 1961 г.

DESCRIPTION OF BEARER

NAME OF BEARER Tom Mooradian   NAME OF WIFE, IF INCLUDED

MINOR CHILDREN, IF INCLUDED   DISTINGUISHING MARKS

HEIGHT 6 FT.   IN.   HAIR Black

PLACE OF BIRTH Detroit,   OCCUPATION Teacher (physical education)

DATE OF BIRTH July 31, 1928   SIGNATURE OF BEARER Tommy Mooradian

DATE OF ISSUED July 23, 1960

CANCELED

THIS PASSPORT IS NOT VALID UNLESS SIGNED BY
THE PERSON TO WHOM IT HAS BEEN ISSUED

I, the undersigned, John A. McVickar, Consul of the United States of America
hereby request all whom it may concern
to permit safely and freely to pass,
and in case of need to give all lawful
aid and protection to the above
named citizen(s) of the United States
of America.

Given under my hand and the seal
of the

Embassy
at Moscow, U.S.S.R.

Photograph of bearer

IMM. & NATZ. SERVICE
NEW YORK, N.Y. 26
ADMITTED
AUG 3 - 1960

CLASS
TO

Eddy and Alice Papazian (third and fourth from left) managed to survive the Soviet gulag and, upon learning that Tom had reached the United States safely in 1960, raised a glass of wine in toast to his unexpected freedom. The Papazians, along with Joe and Irene Sourian and the Karibian family, would follow in his footsteps and return to America. This photo was taken circa 1962 in a friend's apartment.

"When we learned that Tom had safely arrived in the United States, that he wasn't in some far corner of the Arctic Circle in a gulag, it gave the rest of us hope, hope that we, too, one day would be freed," said Massey Antaramian, a 1947 repatriate.

Most of the photos in this section are courtesy of Jean Alexanian, who, at the time, was a young Armenian French repatriate from Nice.

BOOK III

Chapter 1

THE AMERICAN RETURNS

T he child to whom the NKVD had given a second chance became the epitome of the new Soviet man. He trusted no one.

I presented myself to Anahaid at the Institute much like a mischievous dog with his tail between his legs. As soon as I opened the office door and walked in, she sprang from her chair, rushed from behind her desk, and ran to my side to plant a kiss on my cheek. The kiss was accompanied by the traditional Armenian bear hug. She stepped back a foot or two and stood before me, staring at me as if I were a long-lost son returning home safely from the Western Front. Anahaid told me that she had been concerned about me, and others had also expressed concern about my welfare and asked where that "wonderful American student" had vanished to.

"Tavahrishch Oganoff has made inquiries about you," Anahaid said with a smile, waiting for any response.

I did not have anything to say. As she pulled back to get a second look and concentrated on my face, her face grew pale, her eyes moistened. She knew but didn't say a word. She kept talking at a nervous pace to fill the void in the stillness of the room.

Anahaid repeated, "Tavahrishch Oganoff was concerned."

I tried to explain that I'd been sick. I had stomach problems. She accepted the excuse with a nod of her head but recognized that the young man who had picked up the chalk and completed the chemistry problem was not the man who was standing in front of her. Unlike the many she knew, this man was not in a rehabilitation camp or dead. Not even the passage of time would help.

I could hear Anahaid's questions, but I could not respond. "'Where is that American?' Oganoff has asked me. 'What have you done with him?'" It must have been difficult for her, too, to keep up the pretense, not to ask. "'He has not been to practice. Go find him.'" She expected a reaction from me, maybe even a smile, but there was none. Nothing. She spoke softly, in Armenian, to me. "When I told him I didn't know where you were, he became agitated. 'Make inquiries,' he demanded, but . . ." It became hard for her to continue.

"But?"

"It is OK. Everything is OK now. You are here, no?"

How many times had Anahaid said "Everything is going to be all right" to those she knew whose fathers and brothers had been arrested, knowing that it would not.

Anahaid walked behind her desk and gestured for me to sit in my usual chair. She sat down to discuss the day's lesson. I had not brought the calendar—the one I was obligated to translate a page from each day—with me. Again, it was "OK." Usually, she would have raised her voice, reminding me that "Oganoff would not like."

As we sat across from each other, my teacher told me that Konstantin Nikitich had reminded her that I'd missed too many practices, too many *trainerovkas,* as she put it. "Now you will explain to him? OK?"

I told her I would explain my absence to the coach and would get her off the hook.

"You must never again do this. You must report to me so school authority know where you are. Understand?"

I promised that I would and that I would be her faithful student. I pointed to my stomach to reinforce that it was my illness that prevented me from attending class and practice. Anahaid suggested an age-old Armenian remedy for stomach ailments. She ordered me to buy a pomegranate (and it took most of the hour for her to explain the prescription), peel it, and place the rinds in boiling water. "Drink—like tea—it will make you well. No sugar. No sugar," she said.

I tried to smile, but my face still hurt. Hell, I had not seen sugar since we left the ship.

"Why you laugh?" she asked. "You no believe?" She pointed to her own stomach, as if to say that she used the remedy when she had problems.

I told her that I was not laughing at her or the remedy but that sugar was as rare in the marketplace as smiles on faces.

"Soon you have sugar. Soon you will have butter and bread. You must work."

I didn't say a word.

How could I ever have thought that I could deceive her? She had seen my face on so many other faces, the telltale scars of a nightmare. She knew those scars would never disappear. They would be part of me every night when I lay down to sleep and every dawn of my life when I woke up. I was no longer the foreigner she was tutoring. Now I was one of them.

Anahaid was among those who struggled through sleepless nights not only in Erevan but throughout the Soviet Union, because one man had the power of life and death over each and every citizen.

Life did go on.

~ I BELIEVED it would be only a matter of time before the NKVD would take me and the others into custody and either put us on trial as agents or skip the ceremony and send us directly to camps. I was certain they had the letter I had written to the U.S. ambassador and that they had interrogated the other three. What cat-and-mouse game were they playing? I did not know. I was not trained to know. But I could feel the sharp razor's blade at my neck.

I could not concentrate on anything, let alone my lessons. My heart pounded every time someone knocked at our apartment door. The sound of a motor vehicle in the courtyard made my pulse beat faster, and sweat formed at the brow as I moved toward the balcony window to see what kind of vehicle was parked in the lot. My mind always returned to the airport, to the truck driver and the two men. I looked for them on the streets, behind me, and sometimes I thought I spotted one or the other, but it was my imagination. If I had taken the truck driver's advice at the airport, would I have been spared?

Only basketball gave me a few hours to return to another place. Another time. And another world.

With our first encounter, Oganoff laughed loudly and said, *"Americanetz, cock dela?"* But before I could answer *"Harashol"*—that I was fine—he pointed his chubby finger at me and shouted, "You are sick!

Lost much weight. I, Oganoff, will take charge now." He ordered Ana-haid to go to the buffet and bring back some rice and bread and butter.

"Go, quickly. Can you not see how frail this boy is?" As Anahaid ran to do her boss's bidding, he said to me, "You look weak, very weak. *Physiski ochen slava.* Physically very weak. You must eat."

I did.

And as I pushed down the food, I wondered what Oganoff would say when the NKVD presented him with my dossier, describing how I had attempted to go to Moscow to meet with embassy officials, that I wanted to go home. With evidence before him, what would he say? And do?

I was happy to learn in the course of my Soviet life that the NKVD answered to no one, except to Generalissimo Stalin and the NKVD chief, Beria.

Chapter 2

WAR ON THE COURT

I began my basketball career as a Soviet player.

Konstantin Nikitich, an avid reader and historian, was a decorated Red Army veteran of World War II. He was an atypical Soviet veteran. I had never seen him in a military uniform or with medals across his chest. He never talked of his war experiences or mentioned what battle-front he had fought on. The war was behind him, and he was happy to go home to a lovely wife and daughter. Before him lay the task of molding a group of young men who had, for one reason or another, left their native lands and traveled halfway around the world to become his charges. He desperately wanted not only to capture the republic title but to go on and become a force in the USSR.

Both of his goals would be accomplished sooner than he dreamed. The team eventually won ten consecutive titles in the republic and rose to become one of the best teams in the Soviet Union. The small repub-lic also hosted a national championship, unprecedented before the repa-triates arrived, and also hosted a historic game between the People's Republic of China and Soviet Armenia.

Konstantin Nikitich's coaching strategy was based on his war experience. Coaches with superior tactical strategies and technical weapons and numbers, the best-equipped manpower, would win the battle and walk off with the spoils.

A multipronged, well-thought-out assault, carried out swiftly against the enemy, would produce the necessary results, the coach preached. It would be best also if the assault were loaded with surprises that kept the foe speculating, guessing, and off-balance. Direct assault—through the middle of enemy lines—was the deadliest. Draw the enemy to you, by driving through the heart, and if they quickly close ranks to prevent penetration, then pitch out to the flanks, to the wings, and let the long-range artillery fire away. Those who were in charge of the long-range artillery fire—that was my forte—put in countless extra hours of shooting practice from the top of the key. The corners were to be loaded with accurate snipers who could shoot or, if challenged, drive the baseline to the basket, then feed the pivot man or center. If the base was blocked and the center guarded, and if there was no free player, they were to proceed to the other side. There was no twenty-four-second rule during this era. If the opposition chose to double-team one of our players, it meant there was a free man. We were to find him and get the ball to him immediately. Whether the enemy set up multiple zone defenses, and it was best not to allow them time to do so, or opted to confront us man-to-man, we were all to be deft in all of the basic skills—dribbling and passing and shooting.

But equally important, all must be physically fit.

There would be no retreat on the floor unless a basket was made. And retreat, as Kutuzov had taught Napoleon, might win not only the battle but, if well organized and planned, also the war. Defense would win games and championships.

"Volleyball," Konstantin Nikitich stressed, "is the ultimate stage of basketball."

I could not believe what my ears had just heard. What did volleyball have to do with basketball?

"Listen," Abraham reminded me over and over. "Say nothing. We do the playing. He does the coaching."

The ball, according to the coach, was to be moved among players like a bullet, was not to be given up aimlessly for a reckless shot at the basket. Those who hogged the ball, who believed they could penetrate enemy's lines and coveted glory for their individualism, were doomed to return to the bench and warm their butts forever. *"Bestra! Bestra! Bestra!* Fast! Fast! Fast!"*—the coach's call to arms—would echo in my ears in years to come. We were not to hang on to the ball. It was a sin to slow down the tempo by holding or dribbling the ball.

Outside the republic of Soviet Armenia, all teams north of us—the Ukraine, Russia, Georgia, Lithuania, Estonia, and Latvia—had an edge in height, so we had to rely on our speed. Convicted of any infraction of the coach's plan was, he would remind us, a direct invitation to sit beside him and watch from the outside, a player's nightmare. Since we had no player taller than six feet, five inches (Abraham was the tallest), the team had little, if any, alternative but to adopt the coach's strategy.

Abraham became the coach's Murat, acting as advisor and marshaling the cavalry during the toughest campaigns; Armenak, his driving force, whose pinpoint passing and speedy drives to the basket would have fans up on their feet, shouting "Hoorah," as if they were praising Stalin. And I served as his long-range artillery, having developed a deadly long shot. Alas, there were no three-pointers during my era. That came much later.

Since Konstantin Nikitich knew well that an army travels on its stomach, he made sure we were well fed and also well compensated. Since there was no professionalism in sports, in order to be paid, I had to coach youngsters, and I also received a student stipend when I enrolled in classes. I would receive money from the Institute on the condition that I maintained passing grades. A failing grade in any subject during the semester would automatically cancel my monthly stipend. In the USSR, ball clubs competed twelve months a year, and games were played on outdoor courts.

Not a womanizer, as many of the other Soviet coaches were, Konstantin Nikitich was apparently happily married, and he had married well. His wife was the daughter of a former president of the Soviet Armenian Republic. They had one preteen daughter. Sometimes when we were on the road, the coach's wife and daughter traveled with us. The wife, slim and attractive, with dark hair, was an intellectual who loved to play the piano. Their daughter mingled with the players, played pranks on them, and taunted me constantly. She asked—no, she demanded—that I read stories in English to her before she would retire to her berth on train trips. Every one of his players was "family" to this man, whose entire life was devoted to the sport.

One would think that with Konstantin Nikitich's knowledge of the game and strategy, he and the Institute would have received recognition and fame throughout the republic and the Soviet Union. That was not the case, however. First, the war, which claimed an estimated 25 million Soviet lives, took a heavy toll on Armenia's finest and robbed the republic of its youth. Second, the available reserve of young athletes preferred, with the exception of soccer, individual sports such as gymnastics, wrestling, boxing, and weight lifting—traditionally popular sports among the mountain people. They shied away from team sports, especially basketball. Armenians, in general, were small, muscular, and steadfastly stubborn individualists to the point of arrogance. They did not work well together as a unit or a team. Hitler, who knew Armenia and the Armenians (his brilliant field marshal Heinz Guderian commanded the 2nd Tank Division that reached the gates of Moscow in the first months of the war), observed, "One Armenian soldier is worth one hundred German soldiers; but one hundred Armenian soldiers are not worth one German soldier."

Give an Armenian an impossible task, and he would perform the miracle or die trying. It was a question of honor for him and his family name. Give a group of them the same task, and mayhem would certainly follow.

Upon Konstantin Nikitich's shoulders fell what most of his college comrades considered an impossible mission: to train twelve independent, talented Armenians who had assembled on his back porch from around the world. He mixed that talent with the *teghatsis* and found the right combination, the right chemistry, among the twelve that would produce a winner.

The lineup that came from his labor changed the face of basketball not only in the republic but throughout the USSR. Because of the unique makeup of the team—players from France, Egypt, Bulgaria, and the United States—the team attracted huge followings wherever it played. What Konstantin Nikitich did not know—though he may have suspected it—was that, if given the opportunity, all of his players who came from Western cultures would execute a fast break across any border that would get them to their native lands.

Russian-born Armenian Stefan Spandarian, who coached the national Soviet team and prepared it for the European Cup, European championships, and the Olympics, had the pick of talent from all fifteen republics, while Konstantin Nikitich, thanks to the repatriation program, had the pick of Western nations.

Before the 1949 season got under way, he lured Abraham from Locomotive to the Institute. Other Egyptian Armenians who followed included Armenak Alajajian, a future Olympian and European champ, a Bob Cousy-style ballplayer, and Jeriad "The Enforcer" Minassian, along with handsome and suave French repatriate Jeannot Markarian. I represented the United States. With this nucleus of Western players and local talent, Konstantin Nikitich eventually brought respect to the university, to its coach, and to the Soviet Republic of Armenia.

Soviet Armenia's immediate neighbor to the east, Soviet Georgia, had dominated the Transcaucasian Games for years thanks to two of the finest ballplayers in the world: burly six-foot-eight center Korkija and six-foot-five forward Dzordzikija. The two were members of the USSR's national team that finished with the silver medal at the 1952 Olympics in Helsinki. The USSR lost the Olympic gold, 36 to 25, to the United States.

In basketball, before the repatriation program, Tiflis (Georgia) and Baku (Azerbaijan), with a strong contingent of Russians in the lineup, buried any team that ventured out of Armenia.

To get them, and eventually to defeat other neighboring republics, Konstantin Nikitich showed us little mercy. His practices were grueling, literally kilometers of uphill, steep mountainous running, situps until you couldn't stand up, and pushups until you cried for mercy. For relaxation, he had us enrolled in wrestling, boxing, and weightlifting classes, as well as ballet classes—for some. It is a miracle we had enough strength to play basketball. We did what he said, because we all respected him. We toughened up and learned to play together.

The coach occasionally had to remind us of how much hate there still was among the different races. Hate between Christian Armenians and Moslem Azerbaijanis, akin to the Turks. Hate between the Baltic countries of Lithuania, Estonia, and Latvia and the Russians. The Baltic people looked upon the Red Army as an army of occupation. Their athletes played relentlessly to beat any team from Moscow. It was war, and the referee's whistle was the signal to commence firing. But it was not the best team or the best athlete that was left standing; you could not get an unbiased referee to officiate a sports event. NKVD officers, sitting among the fans, often intimidated the officials, demanding that their team win.

As an American, I had difficulty understanding all of it. I was taught to play fair the first day I walked into the Delray Community Center as a child of eight. I was expected to live by the athletes' creed, that sportsmanship reflects on you, your teammates, your coach, and your family. When any player fell or got hurt, I was to extend a helping hand to lift him off the floor, ask if he was hurt, ask what I could do. Making the basket didn't count; making your teammate look good did. Basketball in the Soviet Union was a game of sharp elbows and short fuses, nothing like anything I had seen before.

"If you are not physically prepared for combat, you will pay a price," Coach warned us when we'd attempt to hedge on his brutal drills or groan about them. I would be glad that I had heeded the warning in the years to come. A broken nose, a shattered wrist, a fall on my back caused by a zealous rival who collided with me in flight are some of the reminders that the weak or the meek do not inherit the earth. As in chess, we were to negotiate from a position of strength, not weakness.

I never received any reprimand from my coach, not once, only encouragement to do my best. And that was about all my coach asked of me and the rest of my teammates: to do our best, win or lose.

Konstantin Nikitich even learned to pat me on my butt, which usually was accompanied by a *"Harashol."* He knew I didn't have anything to prove to him, yet he also knew that as an American born, I had a lot to prove to the ballplayers and the Soviets.

With no one waiting for me in my Soviet apartment room and with little reason to be there, I was usually the first one on the basketball court and the last to leave. I cleared snow from the outside clay basketball court and shot baskets in subzero weather to perfect my shots. I shot blindfolded in the Pioneers' Palace, where I was assigned to teach until I knew every sound, every niche and alcove of the gym, and made shots from the key. When a Swedish delegation of educators paid a visit to my classroom, I put on a shooting demonstration for them after they observed my class. The Swedes did not know I was an American, but they suspected that I was not from the local populace.

Basketball was not just a part of my life; it *was* my life. It saved my life.

There was one crucial credo of the coach that I violated. That was about dating women while training and on tour. He maintained that it was not an option for players. He believed that women were distractions, therefore taboo. I suspected he knew we violated the rule, for he, too, was young once.

~ ON THE DAY of his arrival in Leninakan from Port Said, Abraham signed on and began playing for the Locomotive squad. He had not received a release from that organization to play for the Institute, but there was an understanding that if he were accepted by the Institute the next fall, he would receive his unconditional release. He spent most of his time in Erevan, "because there is nothing to do in Leninakan." Later, I would understand what he meant. It was extremely difficult for him to adjust to an extremely cold climate after being raised in the shadows of the Nile and on the fruits of Egypt.

Before we became teammates, however, we met as opponents. Our two teams, the Institute of Physical Culture (Erevan) and Locomotive (Leninakan), met twice for the championship. Then he and I became and remained teammates and almost inseparable friends for the next decade.

The Institute of Physical Culture, a four-year institution that prepares educators for elementary school, middle school, and college, produced some of the finest athletes in the USSR and the world. During the decade I was associated with the Institute, its students included Olympic gold medalist gymnasts Hrant Shahinian (Helsinki) and Albert Azarian (Melbourne); light welterweight boxer and gold medalist Vladimir Yengibarian, who won the title in his division at the 1956 Olympics in Melbourne; and Igor Novikov, an outstanding all-around athlete who was named a member of the Soviet team that placed second to Hungary in the pentathlon at the 1960 Olympics in Rome.

But basketball was still in the Jurassic age when I made my debut on a clay-based field, named for the athletic club Spartak. It was in the center of the Velodrome in Erevan. I had never played basketball on an outdoor court and found it difficult at first to focus on the backboard. Wind became a factor, and I had to make adjustments. I quickly got into the flow of the game.

There were only four fans in the bleachers. After the Institute destroyed a team that represented the Polytechnic Institute of Erevan in the opening game of the tourney, the first fan, who had been standing on the sideline, approached me and introduced himself as Alec Mouradian. He wondered if we were related. (We were not.) He was a chubby, fair-skinned, broad-shouldered, Russian-speaking Armenian repatriate from Iran, who carried a raincoat in one hand and a lit cigarette in the other and considered himself a heavyweight boxer. He had stopped by the outdoor court because he had heard that an American with his surname was on the Institute's team. A second fan sat on a railing high above the circular track. She was a young lady in a blue jogging suit, and I paid little attention to her at the time. Initially, I thought she was there for cycling practice.

With the opening tip, I began my new life.

We blew the Polytechnic Institute away, along with every other team in the tournament. We earned the right to play for the republic's championship to be staged in early January in Leninakan. There would be nine other teams, including Kirovakan, the defending Armenian Republic champion.

When I glanced over at the coach after the first win, he was all smiles. No words needed to be spoken. He was pleased, a new era had begun, and I had found my escape.

Chapter 3

A SURPRISE ENCOUNTER

After showering and dressing, I left the stadium. As I reached the street and looked for the tram to go back to my apartment, I heard a familiar voice. I turned around and standing before me, in front of a blood-red sunset, was the silhouette of a shapely young woman dressed in a blue jogging suit. The second fan from the Velodrome.

"*Drazvouzi,* Tommy." Her voice was soft and friendly, accompanied with a smile.

"Hello, Tatiana." So much had happened since the last time I saw her that I didn't know what to say or do. "What brings you to this part of the city?"

"To watch a friend of mine play basketball." I was trying to figure out just who the friend was when she provided me with the answer. "He attends the Polytechnicum." That would have been a player on the team we had just beaten. "You play well. Do all Americans play basketball as well as you?"

I forced a smile. "I am just an average player, and I do need to work, do I not?"

"Yes, you must work. But you do play well."

"Thank you." It would have given me pleasure to tell the military brat and all of her anticosmopolitan, tie-cutting friends where to go, but it would not have been me. It was difficult to explain that I wanted her to go away and leave me alone, yet I wanted her to stay. I wanted to talk to her. I told her she had looked very beautiful at the opera.

"You noticed me, then?"

"How could I or anyone not have noticed?"

"Thank you." She observed me closely. "You look different."

"How so?"

"I don't know . . ."

"Maybe it's my broken nose?" I said sarcastically. I regretted my tone immediately. She took a closer look and asked how it had happened. I lied. I was getting pretty good at that. "In practice," I told her.

"It doesn't look too bad."

"I know. But I am aware of it." Then, remembering how I had gotten the injury, I felt a surge of anger rushing to my head. I wanted to ask her about all the military officers who had surrounded her at the opera, but all I could do was stare at her. I missed Kiva tremendously, but she was becoming only a lovely memory. I knew Tatiana could make me forget, but to touch her would have invited trouble. I had found my escape. I did not need any more problems. Instead, I asked, "How's your ankle?"

"Fine. I'm dancing again. Will you come to the opera?"

"Maybe. I have to practice, you know."

She nodded, then asked with a smile, "Are you going back to the Institute?"

"No. To the market, see if I can find some fruit."

"Do you want me to help you shop, maybe?"

I would have said yes, a thousand times yes, to the girl in the sweatsuit standing before me. But my eyes saw the woman in a revealing blue grown, surrounded by Red Army officers, whispering something about "an American." I decided I didn't want anything to do with her, any part of her or her world. When the time came and I felt comfortable in this country, I would date only the *norkaloghs*. I told her I needed to go. My heart broke as I said it.

"I understand," she replied.

I knew she didn't.

Chapter 4

CAPTURED AMERICAN FILMS

The Institute of Physical Culture swept all five of its games in my inaugural city tournament and captured the city championship without sweat. It was easy. Too easy. And although the coach was all smiles after the final game, I knew that anything that came easily, especially in sports, had some hooks to it. But, for now, we celebrated.

The Institute had qualified to represent Erevan at the republic tournament. The winning team there would advance to contend the national championship. The team also would have the option of picking up two other players from any team in the republic.

The republic's championship would be decided in late December or early January in the city of Leninakan. Because it was a border city and there was a large number of military stationed there, Leninakan had a sizable gym facility. It could easily accommodate a multiteam tournament. Erevan was restricted to summer games, because it did not have a large enough gymnasium for winter team sports.

Leninakan was also an icebox, and the Soviets were not noted for heating their apartments, let alone their gyms. During the winter months, arctic winds swept through the city, and temperatures in the region fell well below zero.

There would be ten teams competing to advance to the national championship round, and the coach warned us that the stiffest competition would come from the host team, Locomotive, whose lineup included Abraham. It would be his final appearance before he moved to Erevan and enrolled at the Institute. Kirovakan, the defending champ, would also field an excellent team, thanks to a six-foot-four center, Shora Sagetelian, who had a supporting cast of several Red Army players. Team members were stationed at the nearby garrison.

There was a concern hanging over me despite the fact that I was now part of the Institute's team: Would the NKVD allow me to leave Erevan with the team and travel to a border town? If we should win, would they allow me to go to Moscow? I actually feared a repeat of the airport scene. I realized I had no say in the matter. It would be the coach's responsibility to convince the NKVD that I was not a flight risk. All the secret police needed to do was review the dossier they had compiled on me.

At each game I played, I found myself occasionally glancing up to the top tier of the Velodrome, hoping to see Tatiana. I tried to put her out of my mind, but to no avail. My game didn't suffer for it. I did. I guessed you shouldn't tell a girl who wanted to go shopping with you that she couldn't.

Although the winter was mild, the summer was hot, and with the warm weather appeared in the stalls of the city market the fruits and vegetables that grew on the plateau: mulberries, melons, cherries, peaches, the grapes that Armenia is noted for worldwide, along with tomatoes, cucumbers, onions, and lettuce. Life seemed better. One could survive.

And the warm breezes also blew away the long, grease-stained, dirty coats and wool jackets that the *teghatsis* wrapped around themselves to keep warm.

I began to notice the bodies of younger women, their breasts and their legs. If I was not afraid to die, surely I must not be afraid to live. Even though I still could not get to sleep without seeing the gun pointed at me, I would not allow it to stop me from living.

My Soviet life had become rather predictable. I was up at dawn, leaving the apartment before anyone stirred and walking over to the tram stop, where I hopped a tram, no matter how packed it was, and went to the Institute. Those guarding the prisoners who worked on the stadium were accustomed to me, and the armed men actually waved at me as I walked past them.

At the Institute, I worked out in the weight room for about an hour. I got tips on how to strengthen my body. As soon as the cafeteria opened, I rushed to it, purchasing *kasha* (a poor cousin to oatmeal) and *smetana* (sour cream), along with tea, black bread, and grape jelly, which I mixed with the tea to sweeten it. Sugar was still rationed. I stayed away from milk, even though it was plentiful. It seemed that milk and water gave me the runs. After breakfast, I grabbed a basketball and strolled out to the outdoor court to practice my shots. The court was adjacent to the Institute. I worked diligently on my set shots, especially from around the key, and developed a shot that proved deadly.

When Anahaid showed up, usually at around nine, she greeted me, watched me go through my moves, and reminded me that I must attend our language sessions. I showered, dressed, and raced up the flight of stairs to her office, where she always greeted me with a smile and a hug.

"You are making very good progress with your Armenian," Anahaid told me one day. "Yes, you need more *practika* in Russian. But that is understandable."

Armenian had come naturally to me; I must have heard many of the words as a child, spoken by my parents and filed somewhere in the back of my mind. Russian, for me, was a much more difficult language.

"Maybe you find a Russian-speaking Armenian girl, no? She can teach."

I politely agreed. "Yes . . . someday. But not now. I'm just not interested." I wondered what she had on her mind. It wasn't uncommon for Armenian women to broker marriages.

"Why not now?" she said, shaking her head as if I had said something blasphemous about Armenian women.

I needed an excuse so as not to offend her. "Konstantin Nikitich has cautioned us about getting involved with women. They distract from our goal."

Anahaid's face lit up as if she were holding her first newborn. "You have learned our ways well. I need not worry about you anymore." Her English was also improving.

Then, with a sad face, she reached out and took my hands in hers. She said that I had graduated. "Comrade Oganoff believes that these lessons should end. That you should proceed on your own now. Of course, you will enroll in the Institute in September, in the Armenian sector."

I was a free man. I didn't have to report to her, although she had been the kindest among the *teghatsis*. I thanked her for her confidence in me and her patience.

"And we must celebrate," she said. "We will go to a movie."

I moaned, "Please, Anahaid. Not a movie. Anything but a movie. I prefer the opera."

"Yes, opera is *culturney.*"

"Then it is the opera?"

"Yes, opera, if you not want to see American *kino.*"

"An American film!" Impossible. In Erevan, USSR? I almost jumped to the ceiling.

"OK. OK. Do not shout, please. No raise voice. We no go to *kino,* we go to opera."

"No! No! Anahaid, you misunderstand me. I would very much enjoy seeing an American movie." Then followed a litany of questions. "What film? Where?"

She pretended to understand all of my questions but answered only one. "Good. You will meet me at the Central Post Office. Yes?"

"Yes. What time?"

"Movie to start at eight. Do not be late." Anahaid appeared amused when I replied in Russian that I understood. "To be late is *ne'culturney.*"

I was at the Central Post Office at seven and waited eagerly for my surrogate mother to appear. The last American film I had seen was

Duel in the Sun in New York, the night before I boarded ship. I wondered what film we would see. Would it be current or ancient? Anahaid walked up the steps to the post office, and I realized that I had not given her a gift to thank her for all of her kindness. I didn't know what she would like. I knew nothing about her family. I did not even know if there was a man in her life. I had been so wrapped up in my world that I had not really thought of others. And here she was purchasing tickets to the opera and to the *kino* and never asking for compensation.

She saw me, stopped, and nodded approvingly. I had no necktie on. I was wearing an open-collared white shirt with my sleeves rolled up to my elbows, black pants, and shoes shined until one could see one's reflection in them. And I was cleanly shaven.

"You are *internesnaya,* Tom Boghosovich," she said. In Russian, that translated to "handsome." I thanked her for the compliment and returned it. She laughed. "You are too young to need glasses. Come." She grabbed my hand, as a mother would a child's, and marched me down Abovian Street, past the Weepers' Garden. We stopped in front of the Red Army Officers' Club. The two-story square block of a structure looked like an outpost in the Sahara Desert. Military officers and their dates were milling around and waiting to go into the building. I started looking for Gunga Din with his leather pouch to offer Cary Grant a cup of water. We walked in, made our way through the lobby and up the stairs to the balcony, and took our seats in the front row. She loved the view from the balcony. It wasn't long before the lights in the auditorium dimmed and the projector's lights flashed the film on the screen. A late-arriving couple brushed our backs as they hurried to their seats. I couldn't see them in the dark.

"This film," the Russian prologue began, "was captured by the victorious Red Army as it marched through Germany to Berlin. Look carefully, comrades, at how the Imperialists exploit the black peoples of Africa." It was opening night of a series of old American films that would fascinate the Soviet people and fill movie houses throughout the USSR over the next five years.

Then the familiar cry of Tarzan the Ape Man filled the auditorium. The movie was the 1930s version of *Tarzan and His Mate,* starring the sensational Olympic swimmer Johnny Weissmuller and the beautiful Maureen O'Sullivan. The subtitles were in Russian, the dialogue in

English. I was in seventh heaven, about to see a film that I had seen as a child. Unfortunately, this time there was no popcorn or Coke.

As the film progressed, in whispers, I explained bits and pieces to Anahaid, but at one point, I apparently became too loud, and the officer behind me tapped me on the shoulder and kindly said, *"Teeah."* I turned to apologize and encountered a familiar face.

"Tatiana!"

"Tommy!"

"What are you doing here?" It was probably the stupidest question I had ever asked, but it was too late to retract. Our faces were so close that I could have kissed her.

I could barely make out her face in the darkened balcony, but I smiled at her words: "Learning English."

Chapter 5

THE TANTALIZING TATIANA

Tatiana and I exchanged glances several times as we left the Officers' Club. I wanted so much to approach her, but I didn't dare arouse the ire of the officers or of Anahaid. I had no idea what she would say or do if I did. Besides, I would have had to penetrate the defenses of the Red Army. I was not ready to do that. At one point, I stopped and stood staring at her, and she stared back at me. Under different circumstances, we might have been able to talk. But not here. Not in the Officers' Club. Not with Anahaid lingering so close. If Tatiana and I were ever to meet and chat again, she would have to pick the time and place.

I was certain that if Anahaid sensed some kind of attraction drawing Tatiana and me together, she would try to neutralize it. Not for Tatiana's sake but for mine. My language mentor apparently knew something I didn't: in her world, if East and West met, it would mean our doom.

Tatiana stood so erect, so graceful in a simple white dress, a princess protected by her Red knights. She did not need Paris's latest gowns or the crown jewels of the Romanov dynasty to look regal. The dress does not make the woman; the woman makes the dress. In Tatiana, there was that rare combination of innocence with the beguiling beauty and frustrating complexity of Scarlett O'Hara. Was that what drew all the military officers around her?

The opera house was closed for the summer and not scheduled to reopen until mid-September. The park near the building was not. In the evenings after basketball practice, I was drawn there in hopes of seeing her again.

On one warm August night, as I sat on a bench debating with myself the futility of it all, gazing at the stars and full moon that mocked my very presence, she appeared out of nowhere.

Alone.

"It must be lonely sitting out here every night," she said. I looked up, stood, and stared at her.

"It is."

"Why do you sit alone?" she asked.

"I have no one to sit with."

She asked in Russian, "Are all Americans as strange as you?"

"No. I am in a class all by myself."

She laughed. "At least you are honest. May I sit down . . . until that someone you are waiting for appears?"

"Please do. I think she has just come along."

We looked at each other, gently caressing each other with our eyes. I wanted her to know how sorry I was. I wanted her to know me. I longed to tell her everything—about my life in America, about my world before entering hers—but I couldn't find the words, not then. I wanted to tell her how much I hurt, how I hated her government and the injustices of her society, but not then. I wanted to tell her everything, but not then.

The night belonged to us. Only us.

I did apologize for my coolness toward her at the Velodrome. And I admitted that I had occasionally looked up during games at the very spot where she had stood, hoping to see her there again.

She gently put her hand in mine. "I understand. I get angry often. We cannot change what has happened. You have come from another world that I desire so much to understand; you are in a world you don't understand. I hope we will have time together for me to help you understand."

I wanted to know everything about her, and she wanted to know all about me.

There were silly questions. Were Tarzan and Jane ever married? Did they have children? And there were serious ones. Why did Americans want to war against the Soviets? Why were Negroes slaves? Even the czars had freed the serfs.

"But they are free, Tatiana, and Americans hate war as much as the Russians. Believe me. I had two brothers who went to war, and they came back, and one is happily married. My brothers are like all Americans. We don't want war."

"I, too, had two brothers, but they didn't come back. They died at Kursk. I hate guns. I hate weapons. I hate soldiers!"

"But you seem to always be surrounded by men in uniform."

Tatiana looked at me and hesitantly said, "They are just friends who served under my father. Some of them knew my brothers."

I accepted her explanation. I remembered how, after the war, many of George's and Robert's friends, who had served together, dropped by the house to talk, drink, and share their war experiences in a smoke-filled room. Usually, however, it ended with talk about women.

When she asked about the time, I told her it was well past midnight. She immediately stood up and moved as fast as Cinderella from the ballroom, saying, "It is late. I must go. My mother will be concerned."

"But wait," I said.

"I cannot. I must go."

"Can I walk you home?"

"Yes, but you must hurry."

I knew that Armenian mothers were pushovers and that it must be her father whom she feared. I asked, "It is because of your father that you need to rush?"

"No. No. He is not here. He is in Keytai."

I thought it was some far-off place in Siberia. "Keytai?"

"Do you not know Keytai?"

I shook my head.

She used her fingers to slant my eyes. "Keytai. Keytai," she repeated.

"China? You mean China?"

"Da. Da. China."

"What's he doing there?"

"I do not know. I must go now."

We walked out of the park, onto Bagramian Boulevard, toward the apartment building directly across from Simonian's barbershop. As we reach an archway into the courtyard, Tatiana turned to me and said, "You must not come any further." She reached over and kissed me on the cheek. "Please . . . no questions."

"Just one. Will I see you again?"

"Yes, tomorrow night, in the park. I will see you there. We will talk again."

Like in a dream, Tatiana vanished as suddenly as she had appeared, into the shadows of the candlelit courtyard.

Even the Soviet elite, at times, must survive without electricity.

Chapter 6

THE PLEASURE OF HER COMPANY

T atiana and I shared every free moment of every evening. Nothing else mattered or existed, except being together. We shut out the rest of the world and all of its people.

At dusk, we would take off toward the neighboring hills and explore. We did not plan our destinations. She would point to a far-off hill, and off we would go. It was on one of these journeys that we spotted an ancient church, standing alone on the rocks and lava, and made our way to it. I marveled at her vitality. She raced me to the top and laughed all the way.

"You see, Armenia is not so bad." She pointed to the plateau below us. "It is beautiful, is it not? Look. Look at the birds . . . how free they are."

I wanted to tell her that people in America were as free as birds, free to fly anywhere they pleased. "I wish I was as free as the birds," I said.

Looking through my eyes and into my heart, she said, "But freedom is nothing if you have no one to share it with. Even the birds will find their love." She whispered quietly, reverently, "Are we not free? Look around you."

It always depressed me when Tatiana talked about her kind of freedom. I could not tell her about my nightmares.

We paused before the door to the church on the hill. It had been boarded up, but the boards had been removed, and thieves had taken whatever metals they could salvage, leaving the rest for vandals.

I looked at the ruins in awe. This ancient edifice where my ancestors fell to their knees to worship would soon be gone from the landscape. I wanted her to understand that the desecration was not only of our church but of our people and our ancestors. All around us was our history. Tatiana admitted that she had never been inside a church before. I was raised a Presbyterian, for it was the Presbyterian missionaries in Turkey and Asia Minor who had saved my mother's life. They had taken in my orphaned mother and raised her until she was fourteen.

We strolled into the ruins.

The church had been ransacked of all of its religious icons, and the rafters looked as if they would cave in at any time. Because of the danger, I considered leaving, but Tatiana had spotted a stone stairway that led to the belfry. She rushed to the steps. "Let us go up," she said. I explained that the floor and the ceiling could be dangerous. But she pleaded, and how could I deny her? We carefully negotiated our way.

We climbed a stairway of rock and glanced down at the rotunda below. Its ceiling contained faded paintings of the Incarnation, by some ancient artist whose name had been lost in time. I stood in awe, wondering how it all had survived. I tried to explain to Tatiana that we were in a sacred edifice, and she responded with some ridiculous Marxist saying about religion being the opiate of the people. I did not need to argue. I just held her close to me, kissed her, and whispered that I hoped she would understand someday. She responded that someday I, too, would understand. We sat on the ledge beneath the archway of a window looking out to the valley, facing each other, trying to take it all in.

Why were we two, from such different worlds, brought together in this place? Were the fates mocking us? Or were they spectators seated comfortably in the amphitheater, watching the drama unfold?

There was still enough daylight to see, and both of us knew we would have to leave before nightfall to make it down safely. We sat in silence, holding hands, with our own thoughts. I dared not close my eyes, for I knew I would be transported back to the world I was afraid I would never know again.

We were young. We wanted more from our lives. We wanted each other. But did we dare? When I attempted to say something, she put her fingers to my lips. "Stay here with me in the present. Don't think of yesterday or tomorrow. This is what we have." I was a child of the Great Depression, she a child of the greatest war ever fought on earth. I did not feel or understand her pain; she would never understand mine.

In the ruins of the church, we made love.

And we vowed to be true to each other.

No secrets then.

No secrets.

We walked out of the church and down the cliff without another word between us, until we reached Abovian Street. It was dark now. I continued with her to her apartment complex. When we reached the archway that led to her apartment, I said softly, "Tatiana, I love you."

She looked at me strangely, then kissed me once more. "Someday, I fear you will return home to your America. That is my greatest fear."

She disappeared into the darkness of the courtyard.

Chapter 7

BECOMING A SOVIET

L ate fall and winter in Erevan were the worst for the masses. Food and heat were scarce and costly commodities.

Wicked winds swept down from the perpetually ice-capped pyramid of Ararat, scooping up sand granules and pebbles and whirling them into snowballs that unmercifully pelted unprotected faces. When there was no snow, those who knew the signs of the impending storm quickly sought shelter, and those on the streets prepared to battle a formidable wall of sand that, like sandpaper, rubbed the skin from the face. The storm left an indelible mark on the victim, teaching him to stay indoors whenever the sand clouds appeared. Not only was this mountainous region sandstorm country, but it also had more than its share of earthquake tremors.

"When the Ararat awakens, its yawn can be heard on the highlands," warned the *teghatsi*. Though the sandstorms were tumultuous, they were but a presage to the long and cruel winter. Not only was food scarce, but buildings and apartments that had heating were not allowed to begin using it unless Moscow approved. Moscow was more than one thousand miles away.

My teammates were quick to advise that I invest in a Cossack coat, a loose-fitting, very long, and usually woolen overcoat that Russians traditionally wore to keep warm, to sleep in, and to sweep the streets with as they strolled down sidewalks and paths. Pointing to my unprotected head—I never wore a hat in those early days in the USSR—my teammates also suggested that it was time for me to purchase a Cossack hat, the sheepskin and wool hat that most men wore in that part of the world. I chuckled at their advice. I had never worn a hat, even during the severest of Michigan winters. My thick black hair had always been ample protection from the elements.

Thanks to the food provided at the Institute and the vigorous basketball practices, I had regained my strength. The stipend I received for being on the Institute team met my needs. I didn't care about predictions of harsh winters to come when I could jump off the tram, walk over to the marketplace, and purchase the sweet and delicious red, silvery, and deep blue grapes of Armenia, the staple of the Armenian child during the late summer and early autumn.

Basketball provided me with everything I needed, except for my freedom and a way to reclaim my life. I had everything I needed to exist in my new life. I was now a part of the system but admittedly still viewing that system from the sidelines. The lack of language skill and knowledge of mores thwarted the assimilation. I was rapidly acquiring the tools I needed to move with—or follow—the crowd. I needed to be part of them, I felt, if I was ever to understand them. Standing outside the circle had for too long made them suspicious of me; I must learn how to move inside, learn how they think, move among them, reject and disassociate myself from everything that was America and American, without arousing suspicion, in order to reach my goal.

And I had the most beautiful woman in the country to help me understand the Soviets. Tatiana's dancing now made our dates infrequent. She would tease that it was my zealous ambition to excel in basketball that separated us, and I would reply that she, too, was busy working to be the prima donna of Soviet ballet. She was reluctant to meet during the daylight hours, and I accused her of being a vampire. There was not one moment that we stole from our classes or work that we didn't enjoy each other.

I was embarrassed to open my mouth because of my inability to express myself properly in the two languages of the republic. If I tried to put a sentence together in Russian, a Soviet would immediately know that I was not one of them, but if I kept my mouth shut, wore the Institute-issued warm-up jersey and sweat pants, like so many students and athletes, and did not shave for a couple of days, I could move among the crowds without drawing attention. In physical appearance, I could be one of them. It would take more time—how much I did not know—to think like them.

I was astonished at how quickly I managed to slip back and forth from being one of them to being myself, and I liked that tremendously. I considered how difficult it was for someone to infiltrate a society—to spy, if you will—without prior knowledge of that society. How vast and extensive was the training and knowledge required to become the perfect mole. To me, spying was the ultimate impossible mission.

Smiles, acceptable in Western civilization, were rarely seen among the hardworking, pressured-to-fill-quotas Soviets. Whistling, usually an act of joy and praise in American culture, was frowned upon, the equivalent to booing at a sporting event.

It was all about survival. If I was not to become a victim of the Morlocks, I must know their weaknesses. And how would I know where they hurt most if I refused to interact with them?

Chapter 8

TYRANNY IN COACHING

B asketball practices increased in intensity as the playoffs for the title of the Republic of Armenia neared. The sessions were torturous—one in the early morning before classes commenced and the other in the late afternoon. The sessions were so physically demanding and tiring that I was convinced that Coach Konstantin Nikitich was a masochist. After the traditional warm-ups, drills, plays, and scrimmages, two hours long, team members had to run up a nearby steep, rocky hill, then return to the court and shoot free throws, fifty of them. If a player did not sink at least half of them, back up the hill he would run, then back down to the free-throw line to shoot another fifty.

The practices were so exhausting that the body wasn't worth much afterward, as I tried to explain to Tatiana on those rare occasions we were able to spend time together. Usually, players escaped to the *banya* for massage and mineral waters, a place to lie down and mend for the next session, hiding from the coach. I didn't care about the physical punishment—I could take it, despite my on-and-off bouts with the runs. As a teen, I had worked as a U.S. postal employee, in Woodmere Cemetery, and on the Ford Motor Company's assembly line at the Rouge Plant in Dearborn, picking up truck wheels off the moving line and placing them on the wheel drums, during the war. My mind and body had been conditioned for strenuous work.

There were some very talented players on this team: Markarian from Marseilles, Alajajian and Minassian from Egypt, Kolya from Soviet Georgia, and Hrant Simonian, born and raised in Erevan, whose parents had escaped the heroic city of Van during the genocide. All spoke Armenian fluently, all except American-born me.

All of the players, with their different temperaments and personalities, meshed into one unit when the whistle blew. We became like family, and, like most families, we had our differences, our squabbles, quickly resolved. But if someone from outside the group hurt one of us, he would soon regret it.

One evening, at a restaurant, I was surprised to see that the elderly woman who usually checked coats and hats had been replaced by an attractive dark-haired young lady, and I innocently flirted with her. Later, as I walk out of the restaurant after collecting my coat from her, three men greeted me on the darkened street. One held a knife in his hand.

"She is spoken for," the man with the knife announced.

I realized I didn't know what he was talking about.

"Our families have united us, you bastard of a *norkalogh.*"

OK, now what had I done? I prepared to defend myself the best I could without a weapon, when the knife-wielding thug's face suddenly froze as if he had seen a ghost. I figured it was a ruse to get me to turn my head and take my eyes off him so that he could plunge the knife into my stomach. I did not dare turn my head.

"G'net es, g'net es. I'm sorry, I'm sorry," the thug said over and over. "Kolya, I did not know you knew him." And he backed off. I turned to find Kolya, one of my teammates, standing behind me. He had been in the restaurant, heard that the *troika* was about to perform unscheduled surgery on me, and rushed outside.

"We have no quarrel with you, Kolya," the man holding the knife said. "Is he your friend?"

Instead of answering, Kolya lashed out at them in expletives that I soon learned were part of everyday common speech.

The men turned and ran. Kolya told me, "The girl has been promised by her parents to that young man at birth. Do not flirt with Armenians you do not know; it can be dangerous. Flirt with Russians. They will appreciate it."

I decided to accelerate my education in Armenian culture.

~ AT ONE practice session, I rebelled, and I managed to express myself clearly to the coach. I felt that his approach to training had negative, not positive, results on the team.

"Konstantin Nikitich," I said, as my teammates paused to listen, "there won't be enough strength in me—or any of us—to play if we continue to train like this. Can't we save some of this for our opponents?"

Konstantin Nikitich was impressed with my language. After he took the cigarette out of his mouth and flipped the butt to the sidelines, he said in a loud and clear voice for everyone to hear, "If you—or any of you—do not have the strength to play, then you can keep me company on the bench until the desire to play overcomes your weakness." He continued in a low, menacing tone, "I will find five players who will play forty minutes of the game the way I want them to. Do you understand me?"

The cliché was accurate: you could have heard a pin drop.

"Yes," I said.

"Yes," echoed the chorus behind me.

"Good, then." He pointed to the hill. "All of you."

Up the hill the team went, and with every grueling stride, my teammates cursed me, using words I didn't know yet. I had thought sports were supposed to be fun. That's what my coach, Lyle Van Deventer, at Southwestern High, used to remind the team. "Have fun," Van would say. "If you don't enjoy what you're doing, you won't do it well."

But Van had never met a Soviet coach.

There would be no violations or deviations from Konstantin Nikitich's dogmatic principles. He made sure of that. His preparation for a tournament was like a Roman centurion cracking a whip above the heads of hungry lions before they were turned loose from their cages into the Coliseum to feast upon the slaves.

"It is not fair," I muttered in Armenian under my breath as I returned to the foul line, believing that the coach was out of earshot.

"What was that, Tom Boghosovich?"

"Nothing."

Kolya pulled on my jersey and whispered, "Idiot. Can you not shut up?"

No more lip from me.

Konstantin Nikitich was apparently getting disgusted with my impudence. Before the scrimmage, he noted, "There are special rooms reserved in hell for coaches who lose. Give us the name of one coach who has ever been canonized for losing. They are sent to hell and quickly forgotten. I care about winning; you and everyone else here should care about winning, not losing. I do not want losers on my team. Do you understand, Tom Boghosovich? Is that clear?"

I nervously nodded.

"Harashol. Good!"

I tried to understand the coach's philosophy as one of my teammates stood under the board and fed me ball after ball to shoot free throws. Then we reversed positions. "Nobody loves a loser . . . nobody loves a loser," I repeated as I shot my fifty. Whether in capitalism or in socialism, I soon learned, winning is universal, the uncompromisable goal of any coach worth the title on any side of any ocean. Someone once quoted to me the legendary Adolph Rupp, who built the foundation of the basketball dynasty at the University of Kentucky: "I'd rather be the most hated winning coach in the country than the most popular losing one."

Konstantin Nikitich would soon be the most hated coach in his country.

What young man believes he needs to be taught discipline? I needed the discipline that this coach was meting out.

~ THERE WAS MORE. Something else kept taunting me as the team prepared to travel to Leninakan. I did not want to bring it up during practices. The answer would be only too obvious when the team boarded the train to Leninakan.

A stone's toss from the Turkish border, the site of the championship, was a Soviet military fortress. Red Army troops stationed there were always on alert, and I suspected that I was considered a security risk. No Soviet citizen was allowed in or out of the border city without a special permit. I felt certain that the coach would let me know before the team left, but he did not say a word. I braced myself for the letdown.

On the final day of regular practice, the coach asked me if I needed help getting to the station. Instead of answering, I said, "You mean I will be able to travel with the team?"

Konstantin Nikitich looked surprised. "Why not?"

I stuttered and took way too long to reply.

The coach asked, "Who would prevent you from traveling? Are you not a Soviet citizen?"

I did not know what to say, so I said nothing.

"Harashol," he remarked. "We will see you at the station at six. Bring with you a warm coat and hat. It is very cold there."

I nodded. He didn't know what the NKVD knew.

As I waited at the station, I caught myself carefully studying everyone, waiting for two thugs to approach me, tap me on the shoulder, and physically remove me from the depot. Each truck that pulled into the parking area spread tremors throughout my body. I was incredibly relieved when I saw my first teammate arrive, then the others, and then the coach and his family. I was more than slightly surprised that I was able to board the train and sit with my teammates with no incident.

As soon as we left the station, some of the players took out chessboards and decks of cards and began to play. I don't think they noticed how moist my eyes got as the train picked up momentum. Erevan was at my back, the snow-covered mountain was alongside the speeding car, and I felt a kind of freedom from my fears of oppression.

Chapter 9

THE BATTLE FOR THE REPUBLIC

As the train pulled into the Leninakan terminal and the platform came into view, everything and everyone looked as if a sculptor had carved them out of huge blocks of ice and snow. The landscape was covered with a shroud of gray, and the tree branches hung low with ice. From the depot's frosted windows, to the train engine blowing steam after its long haul, to the soldiers in long gray coats and fur hats with rifles on their shoulders, some kissing their sweethearts and wives farewell, it was a postcard view of a military post.

The civilians were dressed in layers of anything that would keep them warm, their breath sending icy snowballs into the arctic air that seemed to float before them, then dissipate as the next one appeared. Icicles clung to beards and mustaches. Snow, like cream cake, lay on the sidewalks, and the frozen sun bounced its shivering rays over the landscape, making me blink my eyes. In the distance, outlined by the sun in the January sky, the mammoth Ararat stood, closer than ever.

As I walked up the aisle of our car toward the gated exit door, my nose and cheeks felt the sting of the arctic wind. My eyes roamed the platform and stopped at a corner of the terminal building. There stood a familiar figure, stamping his feet, jumping up and down to keep warm, looking at each car of the train, his head above the shivering crowd, in a jacket, without a coat or a hat. It was the man who worshipped the sandy beaches and tropical weather of Port Said: Abraham.

"Tommy, Tommy, over here!" he shouted over the sounds of the steaming engines. "Welcome, welcome, Tommy!" he shouted. "Welcome to Armenia's Siberia."

"Abraham, you're crazy. Where's your coat?"

"I don't need one."

I was dressed appropriately. I had to thank Simonian for that. He had given me his fur coat and warned me, "Leninakonzis are noted for their thievery." It did not take long for the arctic cold to seep down deep into my throat and lungs. It hurt. Michigan was never like this.

"I have been waiting for you. Come. My mother wants to see the foolish American boy who comes to this country alone."

"Don't show me off to anybody. Get us where we can stay warm."

As soon as the military guards permitted, the conductor opened the gate so that the passengers could get off. I tossed my rucksack over my shoulder and got off the train. The palm of my hand almost stuck to the iron railing as I descended.

Abraham rushed forward, grabbed me, and hugged me. "It's great to see you again. Come, let us go inside before you freeze to death. It is a little better there."

"I hope it is much better."

It wasn't. People were coiled into balls on the few benches there were, trying to keep warm inside the building, which appeared to have central heating but was still cold. The hall was filled with cigarette smoke, a scene I saw repeatedly throughout the Soviet Union.

"You will come to my house. My family is waiting," Abraham said.

Abraham and I stood there shivering and waiting for the rest of my teammates and our coach to gather.

"I know your strategy," I said. "You want to catch pneumonia so you won't have to lose to us. That's why you don't have a coat on."

Abraham retorted, "Bullshit. We will kick your asses." He tried to laugh but couldn't. His lips had turned blue.

"Don't they heat this place?" I asked.

"Yes, yes, but it never gets warm."

I spotted my team gathering in the center of the depot and moved to join them. The coach was counting heads, and mine was missing. He looked around, saw the two of us, and walked over to greet Abraham. After the cordiality, Abraham told Konstantin Nikitich that he was taking me to his home and later would bring me to the hotel.

"Abraham, it is best that Tommy remain with the team, and you can invite him over after the tournament."

Although Abraham put up a mild objection, the coach overruled him.

"He must stay with the team," he stressed. "Later there will be time to visit."

"I'll see you in the gym," I told Abraham. "And you'd better wear something warmer than what you have on now."

He laughed.

The hotel was only a block from the train station. By the time we reached it, we were all frozen stiff.

Konstantin Nikitich outlined our practice schedules and said that we would be dining together at the hotel restaurant. Then he looked directly at me and said that I must not leave the hotel without telling him or without the company of Kolya or Spartak, both of whom knew the routine well.

"I don't need to go looking for you, do you understand?" Konstantin Nikitich said.

I nodded. I did not need an explanation.

It was not going to happen in Leninakan. But on later team trips to almost every corner of the USSR, walking alone in an American-manufactured suit would be a direct invitation for me to be picked up in a black car for a free trip to the NKVD offices. The coach would have to come and explain who I was. During those dark and ominous days, in Odessa, Kiev, Leningrad, and especially Moscow, as well as Vilnius, Kaunas, Riga, and even as far away as Stalingrad, I would be questioned and later released thanks to the coach. Following Stalin's death in March 1953 and after Khrushchev assumed power as chairman of the Communist Party, the madness would end. It had gotten so bad that once in Baku, after I'd been swept off the street, Konstantin Niki-tich arrived at the NKVD offices shouting obscenities at the officials, accusing them of deliberately arresting me, harassing me so that I would not be in the lineup against the home team. It took years for the secret police to accept my explanation that I was in their city as a member of the visiting Armenian basketball team, that I was truly a Soviet citizen.

~ OUR TEAM did not win the championship in Leninakan.

All three favorites—Erevan, Leninakan, and Kirovakan—coasted into the semifinals without a sweat. It was in the semis that the sweat turned literally to blood.

Abraham was right: it would be a dogfight between them and us and between Kirovakan and us.

We eliminated Leninakan, but barely. We needed an overtime to advance. Abraham did not yield, even though his one-man performance was no match for our balanced assault. He brought his team back time and time again with his tap-ins, jump shots, and superb defense. The versatile captain of his team was all over the floor, directing his team-mates, following up their shots for easy put-backs, and grabbing rebounds out of our hands as Konstantin Nikitich sat there helpless. I unsuccessfully tried to guard him one-on-one. We double-teamed him and sometimes triple-teamed him, fully realizing that this left the cre-ative Abraham a field of unguarded players to pass off to. But his supporting cast was weak, and he knew it and couldn't do anything about it. His last-ditch tap-in tied the score at 41, sending the game into overtime. At the end, two free throws in the extra three minutes by Minassian sealed Locomotive and Abraham's fate, 43–41.

In the championship round, Kirovakan was waiting to ambush us. In the other semifinal match-up, Kirovakan had clobbered Stepanagon to set up the boxing match to follow for the championship.

We did not expect the crowd—mostly men in uniform—to support the *norkaloghs*. Our lineup consisted mainly of repatriates, while Kirovakan had home-bred players. Our coach had warned us that it would be a more physical game, not one of finesse, and that we should be prepared. He decided to lessen the contact by playing a two-three zone, with Alajajian and myself in the front and Kolya, Minassian, and Spartak forming the line behind us. He hoped to stop Kirovakan's Sagetelian from putting his hook shot into orbit.

I found out just how physical the game would be when I drove in for a lay-up on my first attempt and was hammered by the defense. There were no whistles or fouls called, but I came away with a bloody nose and was forced to the sideline briefly. I sat out a few minutes before I returned eagerly to the battlefield. The officials—one from Kirovakan, the other from Erevan—allowed the game to get out of hand. Midway through the first period, both sides began swinging away at anyone who was around. Only the refs managed to separate the players. I took a few steps back and watched. I felt as though I had rebroken my damn nose; I hadn't. It was my eye this time.

Kirovakan reclaimed the title, and I walked with my teammates into the locker room, feeling that we had disappointed our coach. It was a Kutusovian setback, and I felt that I was to blame. Finesse didn't count when fisticuffs were the order of the day. It was a lesson well learned. We would regroup, the coach told us, and return to the battlefield another day.

It was the end of an era for the older Kirovakan team members and the beginning of one for Erevan. We looked forward to acquiring Abraham, who turned down an unprecedented offer of an apartment and other financial rewards from Locomotive. I did not meet his parents on this trip, because I didn't think they would want to see someone who looked as if he had just had plastic surgery on his face. I would visit them on later trips.

~ THE MINISTRY of Culture and Sports in Moscow heard of the influx of players from the West and extended an invitation to the republic's champion, Kirovakan, to play in the nationals, thinking that there were repatriates among that team's members. The nationals would be staged in Moscow sometime in the summer. Kirovakan, which would represent the republic, was allowed to pick up players from across the republic. They chose to add repatriates Abraham and Armenak to complete the all-star team.

My name was noticeably missing from the roster. At first, I believed the NKVD was involved in the selection process, but later I would learn from others that Kirovakan just didn't want an American on its team.

Konstantin Nikitich only laughed when he saw the roster. "They are fools. They will pay for their foolishness."

Kirovakan did. When Abraham and Armenak returned to Erevan from Moscow, they did not discuss their experiences with the all-*teghatsi* ball club.

Some might call it sour grapes, but I was happy not to be among the chosen, for I still did not trust myself. If given the opportunity to travel to Moscow, there was the possibility that I might bolt as soon as I stepped off the train and head for the U.S. Embassy.

~ IT APPEARED that my performance had not been overlooked by the Institute's administration. I was awarded the "consolation" prize a few days after the team returned from our trip to Leninakan. I was summoned into Oganoff's office, and he proudly informed me, "Great news, Tom Boghosovich. You have been selected to be among those who will visit our great leader's birthplace."

Several other students and I were going to visit Gori, the small hamlet outside Tiflis where Stalin was born. Our guide, instructor, and chaperone would be none other than Tavahrishch Oganoff.

Chapter 10

ADJUSTING TO MY WORLD

I n the fall of 1949, as the free world cheered the end of the Berlin blockade and yet another explosive military confrontation between East and West was defused, I was officially enrolled at the Institute of Physical Culture as a freshman. As one of the 250 million Soviet citizens at the time, I had slipped into my daily routine, saying nothing of a political nature and committing nothing to paper that might incriminate if seized. I rose at the crack of dawn, listened to the one government station piped into the neighboring huts, homes, artels, offices, and trains across the vast nation that covered one-sixth of the earth—a broadcast direct from Moscow. It began with the chimes from the Kremlin's Sassky Tower, immediately followed by the reminder, as if we needed one, that *"Gavarit Moskva. Moskovski vryemya shehst chisoff.* This is Moscow speaking, Moscow time is six A.M." and the national anthem. We didn't touch that dial. There was no other national program to listen to, and if we dared to turn it off, we could be certain of a late-night visit from the NKVD.

So the world turned, I knew not which way.

To say that all of this had no influence on my psyche would be a mistake. Inarguably the events around me were influencing my unconscious mind, forcing it to reprogram my thinking to express myself first in Armenian, then in Russian, and then to attempt to process it all in English. I was conducting a losing battle to preserve my English. No new English words were being added to my vocabulary, and those I had had so little difficulty pronouncing and calling upon were slowly slipping beyond the retrieval zone. The inner conflict would divide me for many years and cause irreparable damage to my psychological stability. I wanted to please. I became conciliatory. Rather than voice my true opinion, I learned to subdue my individuality in order to fit in. I had made my bed, and I would sleep in it, despite the fact that I had to share that bed occasionally with lice.

There were numerous compensations for being a Soviet student. Food served cafeteria-style was the major one. But also, if I maintained passing grades (based on a scale of one to five), I would receive monthly stipends. If I failed one course during a semester and did not make it up before the next began, I would forfeit the stipend and face a board of inquiry made up of a student and two faculty members, to explain my poor grades. I would face expulsion if the board felt I was not worthy of continuing my academic career.

Classes at the Institute were conducted Monday through Saturday, and after classes I was obligated to attend basketball practice. The seventh day was set aside for rest—of a sort. Even though the doors to the Etchmiadzin, were tossed open on the sabbath, I knew of no one—not even the *norkaloghs*—who attended services. I believed they were afraid of probable retaliation. Sunday was reserved to rally the armies of volunteers for what we in the West would call community projects, helping with road repairs and construction, with no compensation except that we were serving the motherland. I helped to repair and extend the tramline on Abovian Street to the foot of the cliffs, which is called Nor Arapkeir.

It would be stretching the truth to say I had an easy time in the classroom. My first-semester curriculum included such subjects as "The Origin of Marxism and Leninism," political economics, Russian, and physiology. To ensure that I aced at least one course, I took English as a foreign language. (This was also out of curiosity about how the instructor would teach the course. Anahaid was the instructor, and I was able to pay her back by helping her in the course.)

I loved academia in America. I loved the classroom in the Soviet Union less. The difference between the two was the difference between sunlight and moonlight. In America, students could challenge the text and the instructor and ask questions. There was no debate about the text between the professor and student in the Soviet classroom. All was accepted as the gospel truth. Once in a great while, you would find a Natasha, rare indeed, one student who had a gleam in her eyes but no smile on her face, who questioned the establishment. The Soviet classroom during the Stalin era was as silent as a mausoleum. As soon as the professor entered, all were expected to stand and greet him. Students sat for the next fifty minutes to listen to the gospel according to Marx, Engels, Lenin, and Stalin. The students, though they answered questions put to them by the professor, never seemed to express their own opinions or ask questions. All would answer, "According to Stalin," or, "According to Lenin." If on Monday Stalin issued a *ukase,* or dictate, declaring that the earth was flat, I was quietly confident that no one, including the learned members of the Academy of Sciences of the USSR or any student in my classroom, would dare challenge it.

A great surprise came to pass when, during one of our dullest Marxian theory lectures, Natasha, a classmate of mine in political science, raised her hand. The professor had been having a field day ripping apart the decadence of American society and the bloodthirsty American capitalists' wanting to wage war against the freedom-loving people of the Soviet Union. He reminded his devoted class that the USSR was surrounded by its enemies. I had heard this many times before. The professor continued to denounce everything American, including hot dogs, apple pie, Chevrolet, and motherhood. Natasha, the darling blue-eyed, blond member of Komsomol (the Youth Communist Organization), raised her hand and said to the professor, "But Comrade Professor, if the Americans are so evil, monsters with bombs in each claw, how, then, can we account for Comrade Tom? From where I am sitting, he doesn't look that bad."

There was a deathly silence in the classroom as we all cringed in our seats and waited for the professor's response.

"But you must remember . . ." The professor paused to make sure he would choose the right words, which the Party would approve. "In every capitalistic country, the Soviet people have friends. His parents are working-class people like us. They have taught him well."

Not one word came from my mouth.

The professor resumed his lecture and changed his topic to support his argument. It was inevitable that the world, as our neighbors to the east had shown us, would soon raise the red banner. *Look, see and read, what is happening in Keytai today.* (*Keytai,* the word Tatiana had introduced me to, translated as "China.")

The professor went on to explain that Communist forces, led by Mao Tse-tung, had defeated the nationalists and Chiang Kai-shek, despite all of the aid the American capitalists had provided him. The People's Republic of China would soon be established. With the fall of China to the Communists, bringing into the Communist camp nearly one billion people, the Soviet Union and the People's Republic of China would forge an invincible alliance that no capitalistic power could defeat.

I knew nothing about the world and was slowly wondering if the Communists would eventually accomplish what Hitler had set out to do in 1939.

As the professor spoke, I turned and looked at Natasha. She smiled. I acknowledged it.

～ THAT FIRST semester, I passed each of my initial courses with a grade of four. I had thought I would be able to breeze through Professor Stepanov's class. My nemesis was physiology. That damn cat, that damn frog, that damn dog—I could not dissect them. The text was too difficult for me to understand. And Professor Stepanov would not tolerate my insolence when I told him I had difficulty understanding him.

He was the first teacher I had ever studied with who gave me a failing grade. Though I deserved it, I was still shocked. I probably could not have passed the subject in English, either. But Armenian and Russian had made it impossible. If that grade was not changed, I would be on the outside looking in. The failing grade would disqualify me from receiving my monthly stipend and could make me ineligible to play on the Institute's basketball team—though not the all-star team that represented the republic.

My first thought was to rush to the coach and solicit his help, but I was too embarrassed to admit my failure to him, although I suspected he already knew. My second thought was to go to Anahaid. I knew she was the perfect emissary. She could fix anything. But no, that, too, would embarrass me. Going directly to Professor Stepanov was the only course of action.

I met with Professor Stepanov, one-on-one. He immediately made it clear that I was not going to fast-talk myself into a passing grade. As soon as we sat down in his office, the professor charged that I was a disgrace as a student, to my parents, to my fellow students, and, specifically, to him as an instructor.

"I will not perpetrate a fraud upon this Institute by giving you a passing grade when you don't deserve one," Professor Stepanov announced. "I don't care if you are the best basketball player in the world, you have an obligation to study and to learn and to pass the subject. There is no reason for you not to achieve a passing grade. You have wasted my valuable time and this Institute's finances."

I shrank into my skin. I dared not plead ignorance.

The professor continued, "How long have you been in the Soviet Union?"

I told him it had been two years.

"Two years! Two years!" he shouted back at me. "You speak Armenian and Russian as if you just got off the boat yesterday. *Stytna! Stytna!* Shame on you! Shame on you! Do you understand? You should be able to speak five languages fluently by now, not only your English. Enough of this foolishness. Learn or leave this institution so that those who want to learn may take your seat."

I was thoroughly embarrassed. I had no response.

"I see that you have passed Marxism-Leninism and political economics with good grades—and your other subjects. Why are you having such problems in physiology?" the professor asked in a softer tone. "What is the problem?"

I wanted to tell him that I had breezed through the political classes by adding to any test or paper I submitted that all-important phrase that is never to be challenged: "According to Lenin" or "According to Stalin." But I knew better. I implored him for a second chance, believing that the failing mark would make me ineligible to play basketball. There was no room for bullshitting in Professor Stepanov's world or in his physiology class. No room for "according to Lenin or Stalin" the heart or the nervous system did this or that. You either knew the subject matter or you didn't. Even if I knew it, I couldn't explain it in plain Armenian.

"I wish I had an English textbook, so that I could at least try to understand what you're talking about, Professor Stepanov," I finally told him.

"You are saying that if you had an English textbook, you'd do better?"

"I believe so."

"Good. Good. We shall see." He got up from his chair and gestured for me to follow him. We walked over to the shelves, and in a short time he found what he was looking for. He pulled the book out, an English book on physiology, and handed it to me. "Here, then, prove to me that you can pass the subject, and I will change your grade."

I thanked the professor, but before he gave me permission to leave, he said, "You will be at Daracheechak for skiing, yes?"

"I believe so," I replied. "It is part of my mountain-climbing course."

"Good. I will be there also to conduct tests. You have until then to read and explain the material we have covered this semester. It is all there—in English." Then he added the caveat, "You will not receive your stipend until you can prove to me that you comprehend the material in this book. And you must explain the material in Russian, not English. If you are successful, I will change the grade. In the meantime, I will inform the administration that you have been placed on probation. If you fail again, I will recommend that you be dropped from the

Institute. I do not believe that a student who does not have the desire to learn should take up space here. There are so many other sincere young men and women who wish to attend our Institute. Do you understand?"

I nodded.

"Then you are dismissed. Remember, in Russian, not English. This is not America." Those were Professor Stepanov's parting words.

I thanked him for the second chance. But as I stood up and left the room, I wondered how the hell I would learn the text in Russian.

And I had another concern. I had never been on skis before, let alone done any mountain climbing. As a student, I was required to do both and to do them with passing grades.

If the mountain and the skis didn't get me, I was sure that Professor Stepanov's high-altitude tests and his physiology exam would.

Chapter 11

AN OLD MAN WHO WASN'T

S tripped of my student stipend, placed on probation by school officials, and with little hope of making up a failing grade in physiology that would restore my academic standing, I again found myself in financial straits and standing in an office at Pioneers' Palace, waiting to see Tavahrishch (Comrade) Abrahamian. Konstantin Nikitich had told me to report to Pioneers' Palace for a possible coaching position.

As I waited in the office, staring at the usual portraits of Lenin and Stalin, I wondered where I would find the time to coach. Tatiana and I were seeing less of each other with each passing day, and I was tired when I did see her.

The Pioneers' Palace, established to train preteen and teenage children in the arts and sports, was east of the central business district on a street adjacent to the NKVD headquarters and the medical school. Its director was a *matrushka*-doll kind of a man, with rosy red cheeks and pasty white skin. His protruding Santa belly was draped with a white cotton Ukrainian shirt that had multicolored flowers embroidered on the collar and sleeves. In his mid-forties, he was as bubbly as champagne, and he greeted me as if I were a potential son-in-law.

A second gentleman, with trimmed white hair, in a dark suit much too big for his small frame, sat on a couch and was observing me closely. The director invited me to sit in a chair, one of six that framed a rectangular table abutting the director's desk. Covered with a green tablecloth, the table held a water pitcher and a glass and several Armenian and Russian newspapers.

I sat facing the older man. The seating arrangement was awkward. When the director questioned me, I had to turn my face toward him. As the interview progressed, the older man on the couch seemed to ask more questions than the director, so I found myself facing him most of the time. The man who did most of the questioning had a stream of deep wrinkles flowing from the corners of his eyes. I dared not guess his age. Because of the dark suit and the blue open-collar shirt, I suspected that he was NKVD. The contrast between the two men fascinated me.

The director said, "We have been expecting you, Tom Boghosovich. May I add, you come highly recommended to us."

The comment caught me off guard. "Highly recommended? By whom? Konstantin Nikitich?"

"By me," responded the man on the couch.

I turned to face him. I was flabbergasted.

"We need your skills here," the old man continued in a low, quiet tone.

He paused, and I took a closer look at him. I had seen that face somewhere, but where? I could not be sure.

"I was at Leninakan, and I wish to commend you for your excellent performance. I thought SKIFF had the best team." SKIFF was the acronym for the Institute.

"Thank you. But best teams don't always win."

"How true . . . how true."

Where had I seen this man before? The thought kept rolling over in my mind. I could not place him.

He reached into his jacket pocket, pulled out a small white pouch filled with tobacco, and reached into another pocket to take out what appeared to be newspapers that had been cut into small squares. He filled one of the squares with tobacco, rolled the tobacco in the paper, lifted it to his lips, wet the end with his tongue, and offered it to me. I gestured with my hand to indicate that I didn't smoke. He proceeded to light the cigarette and smoke it.

"I have asked for you," the old man said in a soft voice, "because our children need to learn how to play basketball the way you play." As he spoke, he blew smoke rings that floated to the ceiling.

I thanked him for the compliment and was quick to tell him that I had never taught or coached children before. I didn't have the confidence to coach. "If I were to coach, I would prefer to teach adults, for I am sure that you can detect from my speech that I don't speak the language well, and children may not understand me."

Both men nodded their heads.

"But I believe you are willing to give it a try, or why would you be here?" the director said.

I nodded in response.

"Most of us don't understand children. Just ask any parent."

I suggested that they find a coach who had the appropriate language skills, since children also needed to learn language.

"True," agreed the director. "And Jak Simonovich," he continued, using Jak's father's name, "will be there to help you overcome any obstacles."

"And who is Jak Simonovich?"

The director's eyes turned to the man on the couch. "This is he, Tavahrishch Sarkissian."

It was difficult to mask my surprise. That old man a basketball coach? Was he going to retire, and they were looking for his replacement? Was that why they wanted me? He reminded me so much of the older men who had gathered at my father's coffee shop, rolled their own cigarettes, played *tavloo* (backgammon) or cards and drunk their Turkish coffee with gusto. And when they left for the night, they would dig deep into their pockets and come up with a penny to hand to this six-year-old and tell me to put it in my piggy bank and that one day I'd be rich. I had really wanted to use the money to buy a Baby Ruth candy bar, for Babe Ruth was my baseball hero.

I asked the usual questions, and the two men answered them all.

They knew there would be problems, but nothing that "the collective" couldn't overcome. I was a student, and I was also a member of the team at the Institute, so I asked whether I would have a lot of time available. It was my last-ditch effort to get them to look for another candidate. I waited for their response.

The telephone rang. Abrahamian picked up the receiver, said a few words in Russian to the caller, then motioned to Jak Simonovich to take me up to the gymnasium and show me around. We left the office and headed up the stairway to the gym, leaving the director on the phone. As we closed the door, the director's voice seemed to get louder. He appeared to be involved in a heated argument with someone. I asked Jak about the director's temper and whether he got angry often.

"It is his wife," Jak Simonovich replied. "She is a journalist and always calls him. They have problems. Serious problems."

"A journalist?" I asked, surprised.

"Yes. A good one. And very attractive. She writes for the *Sovietakan Hyestan.*"

I was doubly surprised. I could not imagine that Mr. Claus would be married to anyone but a Mrs. Claus.

"How long have you been coaching, Tavahrishch Sarkissian?" I asked, quickly changing the topic.

"I started right after the war."

"And before that?"

"I worked in the plant—we made ammunition for our troops."

Before I could ask him about retirement—retirement age was fifty-five in the Soviet Union—he said, "I am law student at university."

I was now completely confused. "A law student?" At age one hundred?

"Yes."

I gave Jak Simonovich a closer look. He must have thought he was going to live to be one hundred, which wasn't rare in that part of the world. My mind flashed back to the interrogation room, to the NKVD officer who had given me a simple but cryptic course in how the Soviet justice system worked. There were many questions I wanted to ask Jak Simonovich about Soviet law and Soviet justice, but this was neither the place nor the time. We continued to discuss my coaching responsibilities, and again I voiced my concerns about working with children.

"You have something to offer our children that neither I nor any other *teghatsi* can offer."

I believed he was referring to the basketball skills I had learned in America and asked him if that was so.

"Yes, but more important, you have come to us from across the ocean, and they will be seeing you, an American, as a human being. They will be much interested in you. In fact, intrigued."

I felt color rushing to my face. "Because . . ."

"They must know that there are people like you who are decent and helpful living across the ocean. People who do not want to make war. They will learn from you. I know this."

"And how do you know?"

By this time, all of the youngsters, boys and girls, about eight and nine years old, were bidding their good-byes to their gymnastics teacher. As soon as they saw my companion, they ran to him and surrounded him. *"Dasvidaneya,* Tavahrishch Jak." He acknowledged each one by name.

"They all seem to know you," I said.

"And I know each and every one of them."

But the children, like Jak Simonovich, seemed so serious. No laughing. No pushing. No boys pulling on girls' hair. How much time would it be before these children could be children? If Margaret Bourke-White could make Stalin laugh and carry her camera equipment, what would it take to get these children to laugh?

I finally asked, "How do you know I am the right person for this job, Jak Simonovich? There are surely better-qualified college students than I to teach them."

"And you are about to say that there also are qualified *teghatsis,* and you are a *norkalogh?* And why would I want to work with an American *norkalogh?"*

"Yes." I said, surprised that he had brought up the fact that I was a newcomer.

Jak Simonovich left my side and moved to the center of the gym, where there were several mats. I followed and offered assistance. It was then that I remembered that he was the janitor the night I had helped to move the mats after a scrimmage.

"Do you remember now?" he asked.

"Yes . . . of course."

"You helped me that night, as you are doing now. You played hard, yet, as tired as you were, you helped me, a stranger. It revealed much about you to me. Your heart is good. I want you to teach what you have in that heart to our children. They need to smile and laugh and be happy. They will learn basketball, but they will learn things from you that I cannot teach them. In my life, I have had little to smile or laugh about. I have a feeling that you are the right person for this job."

I learned in the days to come that Jak Simonovich had lost his older brother, Serosha, in the war. It was during the last days, when the Russians stormed Berlin. Yet there was no official notice of the death. Jak Simonovich said that his mother still believed her son was somewhere in the West. His mother had taken ill and was bed-ridden. She had a heart condition. He knew of, but did not talk about, his father. His mother rarely spoke of him—only of Serosha. And, of course, she waited patiently for Jak to marry so that she could hold her grandchildren.

I was bewildered. Impossible. I did not believe it. The hair was completely white, the wrinkles, the eyes—it was impossible for a man that young to look that old. I had read the horror tales created by the minds of Poe and Guy de Maupassant—how men and women, buried alive, would emerge from the grave looking as Jak Simonovich did. But Poe and Maupassant were fiction. This man standing before me brought those stories to life.

What tales did Jak Simonovich have to tell?

I would hear them on the many train rides we and our team would take across the USSR for tournaments.

"Then you will join our staff?" he asked.

"I will. And I hope you won't be disappointed in me."

"Good, then let us go and inform Comrade Abrahamian, if his wife has let him off the telephone."

"I do have one more question," I said.

"And what is that?"

"In a few weeks, I will have to go to Daracheechak for skiing. What will happen when I leave? Who will teach my classes?"

"I will take over the classes until you return. And when the Institute's team travels to the other republics, you will be free to travel with the team. There are no restrictions. I will be here. During the summers, if you are not away playing somewhere, and if our teams win championships, we would be obligated to take them together. I hope that you and I can coach a team that someday will win the national junior championship. If there are no conflicts."

"But when will I have time to study?"

"Now, that—that is your problem. Do not forget, I, too, am student. I find the time to study and work." He paused, then added, "There is one most important thing you must remember."

"And what is that?"

"When you are scheduled to work, you must be here before the students. You cannot be late for class. Do you understand this?"

"Yes, I know. It's against the law."

Chapter 12

THE BLIZZARD

A light, fine snow had fallen during the evening, blanketing the highlands on the eve of the students' departure for Daracheechak for skiing and mountain-climbing lessons. When I looked into the courtyard, I was overjoyed at seeing the snow. It brought back memories of Michigan and its natural vistas of snow-laden pine and spruce and frozen lakeshores.

"How long are you going to be gone?" Simonian asked from the other room as I finished packing.

"About four weeks, I believe."

Simonian walked into the makeshift kitchen to get a look at me, looking for signs of deception.

"You don't have any hidden plans, do you, son?" His face was full of concern.

"Honest, I don't. It's a class. I am obligated to take it as part of the curriculum. If I don't, I won't get credit for it, and I will have to make it up."

Simonian took a deep breath, then nodded understandingly. "Be careful. Skiing can be dangerous."

"Come on, Mr. Simonian, what can happen to me. It's skiing. I love the snow. I'm from Michigan, remember?"

His large hands held my shoulders as he searched my face, looking into my eyes with deep concern. "Knowing you, I'm sure you'll think of a way to get into trouble." He was not smiling.

When I arrived at the Institute, several groups of students, about sixty of them, were waiting to board open-aired trucks. I look around for Abraham, but he had boarded one of the four vehicles that had already left the parking area. The ski instructor assigned to my truck asked me if I had my skis. When I shook my head, he ordered me to rush down to the storage room and get a pair. He glanced at my shoes.

"Those will do," he said. "Just get skis and come. Come quickly. The others have already left. We must hurry. There is a storm brewing, and I hope we can beat it to Daracheechak."

Ours was the last of four trucks filled with students that had left the Institute's parking area.

Some fifteen of us, young men and women, packed like sardines, sitting shoulder to shoulder in the bed of the truck, our backs to the wooden sides of the vehicle, took off toward the northeast sector of the republic. Our trucks would climb hundreds of feet over unpaved ancient roads with no barricades to protect a skidding vehicle from plunging hundreds of feet into the snow-covered rocks.

I was warm enough, and, at the insistence of Mr. Simonian, I had a hat that I'd stuck into my fur-lined jacket. As the intensity of the snow increased, I considered wearing the hat but didn't.

There were several female Russian students in our group; most of them sat together on one side, while the males sat on the other. Our skis were placed in the middle of the floor. As the truck left the highlands and reached the hills, the girls began to sing Russian melodies. Nothing like the American songs of land and love, their songs and the music began in adagio, like moans carried in the wind from the top of a mountain, slowly gaining momentum and then coming to a tumultuous climax.

The truck's motor groaned as the vehicle struggled to make it up the snakelike deep snow path that would take us around our first mountain.

Dark clouds joined the arctic winds that greeted us at every turn. Like the Russian melodies, the whispering of the winds became a roaring sound, and we huddled close together to stay warm. Each inch of the road was a struggle for the truck motor, but, for now, it dutifully obeyed its driver. The whimpering winds began wailing, and I knew we were in trouble. I had been in Michigan blizzards. This was worse. The driver seemed to know every inch of the road, and he fought the elements bravely. It was near noon but as dark as midnight. My hands and my face were frozen, and I was sure the others felt the same. I asked the student next to me if there was a village nearby where the driver could stop until the storm blew over. What I saw was a reflection of my frozen face in a pair of the deepest blue eyes ever possessed by a young lady.

"Natasha?"

"Da?"

"What are you doing here?" Dumb question.

"I think . . . the same thing you are doing."

I felt a bit foolish, and it took me a few minutes to recover. "Do you think we will ever see Daracheechak?"

"Of course we will. Why not?"

"The storm . . ."

I did not want to admit my fear, so I leaned back against the side of the truck. When I turned again to ask another question, she had found my lips. I did not resist. As our lips parted, I wondered what had just happened. We sat there, the snow mercilessly barreling down on us, almost burying us. We obviously had problems.

I knew that Natasha specialized in gymnastics, but I had never seen her perform. Not like this, anyway. And I had never seen her at any of our basketball games. Except for the comment in the political science class, I didn't think she knew I existed. Thoughts of attraction were soon dispersed. The truck was having real difficulty cutting a path through the snow. The engine stalled, then stopped. As we waited for instructions, Natasha and I played an interesting game of words as the others pulled their coats over their heads to keep warm.

"What do you call these?" she asked, touching my eyes with a now-drenched glove.

"Eyes," I replied in English. "And in Russian, Natasha, what are they?"

"*Glasah.*"

"And this?" she asked, taking off her glove and softly touching my nose.

"Nose," I said.

"Nose? Then you Americans have stolen the word from Russian. We Russians also call *nos.*"

"I don't know who stole what, but that's what we call our nose." Then I took off my glove and touched her lips. "And this?"

"*Gubah.*"

"Natasha, I like the English word—lips—better."

"And this." She moved gently an inch forward, and our lips met again.

"And that," I said to Natasha, "is called a kiss."

"In Russian, it is *patsylooj.*"

I decided not to pursue the word game any farther at this point but realized with a quiet smile that I had found someone who could teach me physiology in Russian.

Chapter 13

THE NOVICE SKIER

The truck struck a snowdrift and sank into the deep snow. It refused to go another inch forward. Instead, with an attempt by the driver to free the vehicle by rocking it, the old piece of iron and steel just sank deeper. That was the old mule's grave until spring. We were definitely stuck in the wind-driven, heavy snow piling up by the second. I dusted the snow from my hair, took out my hat, and put it on, hoping in some way that it would protect me from the ever-mounting white mess. Because of the moaning and wailing of the wind, I could not hear what was transpiring in the cabin of the truck, where ski instructor and driver were holding an emergency meeting.

Man and vehicle had lost their battle against the forces of nature. The driver tried to open his door but couldn't. He pounded against it, but it was frozen. Our instructor, in the passenger's seat, was also iced in. Two or three of the students leaped from the truck, landed in about two feet of snow, waded to the driver's-side door, and began pounding on it with their fists in an attempt to free the driver. Cursing in Armenian, the driver got out, followed by our instructor, to assess the situation. I could barely make out their figures in the storm.

"We will have to proceed on skis," I overheard the instructor shout.

"Impossible! They won't make it. Best stay here and wait for help," the driver replied.

"The drifts, they are impassable!" the instructor shouted. "We can make it on skis. Stay with the vehicle, and I will send help. We can't be but five or six kilometers away."

Lord, help us, I silently pleaded. *I've never been on skis; I will never make it.*

"Did you say something?" Natasha asked.

"No, I was only talking to myself."

The instructor put on his skis and came around to the back of the vehicle. He ordered all of us to get out of the truck, put skis on, and prepare to ski the rest of the way.

"I need two experienced skiers to lead and open up the trail and another two to bring up the rear," the instructor shouted over the wind.

I soon discovered that most in our group had started skiing the day they got out of the crib, including Natasha, who was born in a small village just outside Moscow. I wondered where I fit into the scheme of things.

It became clear when the instructor called, "Natasha, stay near the American. Don't allow him to fall behind, or he will become fodder for wolves."

I was in deep shit—in deep snow, too.

Wolves? The word shook me from my visions of Natasha keeping me warm. Packed closely together in the truck and feeling particularly warm, I did not fully comprehend the power of the gale-force winds that roared over our heads. As I stood face-to-face with the snow and ice, it stung my skin, feeling as if waves of hornets were attacking it. I reacted instinctively by lowering my hat to my eyebrows and taking off my scarf to use as a mask across my lower face. Michigan winters seemed like summers by comparison. I was in a different world in more ways than one. Communication became impossible. The only word I heard after I strapped on my skis was *"Piedom!"* from the instructor. "Let's go!"

It came none too soon.

I could hear Natasha saying something behind me, but the wind drowned out the words. Despite my concerns, I was completely surprised at how I could stand and move on the snow, though somewhat awkwardly. If I did not have to fight the elements, skiing would be easy, I thought. I had yet to negotiate my first hill, up or down. As soon as the others made a track for me, like quicksand it filled and disappeared. I could not see the mountains or the valleys ahead—just wave upon wave of snow, riding the winds horizontally, hitting my face mercilessly.

We reached an incline, and somehow I made it to the top. I stood there to catch my breath. Natasha said, "Go! Do not stop." With that, there was a nudge from behind, and downhill I went. There was a striking contrast between walking on skis, cross-country, and skiing downhill, I quickly realized. Within seconds, I had lost my balance, lost my sticks, and tumbled over and over until I came to a stop somewhere in the belly of a strange, shapeless pit. Others, as if drawn by a magnet, came out of the wind to my final resting place. "The American is down," I heard in the winds. Natasha and the instructor were soon standing over me.

"Davahj, Tommy, *davahj.* You can't stay here. Get up!" Natasha was urging me.

I tried, but it was so comfortable in the snow that I didn't want to get up. They retrieved my skis and poles.

"Let him be!" the instructor yelled in a crude attempt to make light of my situation. "I'm willing to bet the wolves in these parts have never feasted on American meat."

Natasha would have none of the instructor's nonsense. She shoved him with her two hands, and the instructor fell down beside me.

"Piedom, Tommy, get up. We must proceed. It is not far now." She helped me get up and back on the skis.

Natasha and the instructor exchanged words, and she apparently convinced him that I could make it. The instructor returned to the group, and Natasha and I followed slowly. My baptism was not over yet. Going down a hill, I discovered, even tumbling, was faster than attempting to go up a steep hill on skis. Going up, I thought, was just walking straight up. Not so—it didn't work that way. As Lenin put it when implementing his so-called New Economic Policy, I, too, would take one step forward and two steps back. I was climbing up a step at a time and slipping down two, three, and four and not making any progress. I would never have reached the top if Natasha had not skied up and showed me how to move up the steep slope.

When we reached the summit, the winds suddenly died, and the sky cleared. We had an eagle's-eye view of the topography. The area was completely surrounded by woodland-covered hills, forming a bowl whose basin contained millions of puffed oats. There were barracks floating on top of the milky-white depression. I knew my next challenge was to get down the long, steep slope with dignity, for at the foot of the hill was a mass of humanity, waiting, wondering if we would make it.

People seemed to be pointing at the hill on which Natasha and I stood. I wanted them to clear out of the way for my soft landing. There were no ski lifts that I could ride down to avoid the humiliation that was certain. But I had made it through the storm—and on skis, at that. I could thank only Natasha for that. *"Spasiba,"* I said to her.

"Za shto? For what?" she asked.

I started to say, "For helping me get through the storm." Instead, without even trying to resist the temptation, I kissed her with passion and sincere gratitude, warming both of us.

After we caught our breath, Natasha looked at me and said, "Maybe the professor was right—you Americans are crazy!"

Chapter 14

BEAUTY ON THE SLOPES

T here was a jeering section waiting for me at the bottom of the slope. Students and ski instructors watched and waited as my body turned and twisted down the icy path, coming to a stop at the basin of the skiing camp. My skis and Natasha arrived ahead of me, my spill having occurred shortly after I left the summit. Those waiting had been recruited as a rescue party, but it had turned into a razzing party. Natasha came flying down the hill toward them, and she stood next to my aching and embarrassed body. The clowns stood above my frozen corpse, taunting me for my ineptness. I managed to keep a straight face, partially because it was frozen, and I acknowledged their jeers solemnly. I was, after all, fully content that my arrival, though quite unorthodox to them, was a small victory for me. I had survived the most severe snowstorm of my young life, and I had done it most of the way on skis. I had reached my destination in one piece. Broken but alive. As I lay flat on my back, with all of those faces looking down at me, my one wish was that everything from there on would not be downhill or uphill but on a level plain. That wish would not be granted.

Abraham and Armenak, my teammates who had arrived in the first truck, had missed the storm. They stood in the crowd but were not in the group who taunted me. They knew that their day on the slopes would soon come. I was happy to see their friendly faces in the motley crowd.

"We were worried," Armenak said, extending his hand to help me up from the ice as the crowd began to disperse.

"So was I."

"We have a fire going in the stove and tea waiting."

"Point me in the direction. I'm frozen," I said as I grabbed Armenak's hand and was lifted to my feet. I was soaked in snow and ice.

"Come," he said. "Follow me."

Abraham added, "You have to get into some dry clothes."

I told them that the truck carrying our things was buried under snow. I didn't know when I'd get a change of clothes.

"That's OK. I have things that should fit you."

Just then, Natasha caught up to the three of us, greeted my friends cordially, but looked at me. "Are you all right? You were not hurt, were you?"

"Yes, I'm hurt," I said woefully. "My pride has suffered irreparable damage."

"I can fix that. See you later, then?"

Abraham and Armenak exchanged glances, then looked at me as if they didn't recognize me. Abraham started to say something but was interrupted by Armenak asking, "Who is she?"

"Don't you recognize her? That's Natasha, the girl in my political science class."

"If I didn't know you, I would say you two have something going," Abraham observed.

"We do. She's going to teach me physiology so I can make up my grade."

"I don't think that is the only thing she has on her mind."

We strolled over to one of the rectangular buildings that had been assigned to the male students. There were more than a dozen cots, and a three-foot-high steel cylinder surrounded by logs stood in the center of the room. It served to heat the room and was a welcome sight to my eyes. Besides the clothes indiscriminately strewn around the room, hanging or tossed across bedposts, the room had little to offer in the way of conveniences. Abraham pointed to a cot that he had staked out for me. He and Armenak had claimed the next two for themselves. Armenak went to the stove to get me a glass of tea. I drank the tea slowly, enjoying every sip as it rushed down my throat. I tried to listen to what my friends were saying, but I couldn't. I was exhausted and quickly fell asleep. The last thing I saw was my two teammates finding some blankets to put over me. They had taken off my jacket and shoes and socks and were looking for places to hang them as I dozed off.

In this mountainous region of Armenia, there were no maps to indicate streets and roads, and I had no idea how high we were above sea level. The air may have affected the breathing of some of the students but not mine. And weather was definitely dished out in extremes. The lodges were protected by high hills, enclosing and enhancing the circle. For the next forty days, I would find myself standing on a merry-go-round, spinning under the canopy of a spotless azure sky and a radiant sun, listening to the music of songbirds that serenaded for the price of a few crumbs of my black bread. I enjoyed the ethereally magnificent natural vistas. I could not count the times, after my skis and I had become one, when I would climb the slopes alone into the wooded hills, despite the warnings of my peers and instructors, and enjoy beyond words the pastoral surroundings. I was lured to the hilltop, to be part of the silence of the forest, to watch the animals play their game of survival, to be free. A return to the dormitory or the cafeteria revived the images of the workers' dictatorship that were omnipresent in the cities and collective farms and factories. Standing alone on top of the hill, I would look toward the heavens and whisper, "Lord, you've surely done a great job here. Now, grant me my freedom and the freedom of these people, so I can bring others here to share your grandeur."

But before I got to the mountaintop, there were countless painful hours of practicing. My instructor and I managed to survive, although he occasionally would throw his hands up and shout, "Send this American back to America!" (I would secretly agree.) I passed my test—a grueling ten-kilometer race against time—with flying colors.

I didn't know which was harder, passing the ski exam or my makeup physiology exam.

But Natasha was a good teacher.

Each evening, after practice, I reported to Professor Stepanov. He took my blood pressure, told me to take a deep breath, and conducted his high-attitude tests, which I did not comprehend at the time. I would leave his office and find Natasha waiting for me so that we could study. But there was more on our minds than physiology.

She taught me that the heart had more than one chamber.

Chapter 15

THE HEART'S MANY CHAMBERS

T here are relationships between men and women that are endearing and enduring and remain unforgettable until the last breath.

And there are some experiences that are ephemeral, impetuous, and surreptitious in nature, ego building at the time but superficial and quickly pushed back into the farthest corner of the mind, intended to be forgotten but are not. They fade, yes, with time, but they never seem to die, recalled unsuspectingly by a whisper of the wind, a tune, a word, a smell, or another woman's touch. Those reckless deeds come back to haunt when displayed on the invisible screen of the mind. Events of the past alert most of us, as does a traffic light, to proceed with caution, to advance or to stop immediately, for there is danger ahead. When we need direction, we turn to the past; knowledge of the present is the sum total of one's past.

I reached for Tatiana, but she danced away. Natasha was sitting across from me, describing the heart and how it functioned in Russian.

Natasha knew I had something else on my mind as we looked at each other across the table in the cafeteria. Other students shuffled past with their dinner trays, looking for vacant chairs to sit in. We found it impossible to concentrate on physiology. There were no other rooms available where we could study. Natasha held a Russian textbook, and I had the English version given to me by Professor Stepanov. Each time I looked at Natasha, I saw Tatiana. I could not get Tatiana out of my mind. I had definitely made my mistakes with her. She had asked me if I would leave the Soviet Union for the chance to return to America. I paused before I gave her my answer. Our relationship was never the same, though we kept on seeing each other. Tatiana had bewitched and bewildered me, and I remained smitten.

There sat Natasha, so eager to please, to assist, so comfortable to be around, unscathed by criticism for hanging with an American. She was a joy to watch on the slopes. We raced downhill together. She was thoroughly amazed at how quickly I had learned the sport.

There was nothing scurrilous ever uttered from Natasha's lovely lips. Yet I knew she was not the one. Did she know that?

I wondered if Tatiana ever thought of me. Why could I not get her out of my mind?

Natasha and I were drawn to each other in this remote mountain region, in a land strange to both of us, and we found refuge in each other. She did not care that I was American-born, and I surely didn't care that she was Russian-born. Her slightly slanted eyes reflected her Tartar and Mongolian-Russian ancestry. She was, in many ways, more adventurous than I. She was aspiring to become a full-fledged member of the Party and knew the consequences of fraternizing with a foreign-born, but she apparently didn't care. She sought truth and asked me about many things, trying to determine the truths in the teachings of the Soviets.

She had a superb body, perfected by years of disciplined training in gymnastics. She was taller and more slender than she appeared at first glance. Her shoulders were straight, and her arms, though muscular, were slim, with the strength of one who was trained to execute the strenuous rituals and minute physical and coordinated details of a sport that required its disciples to train or pay the consequences. The palms of her hands—so callused, hardened skin sometimes bloody—were the price she paid for her calling.

"Do you understand the nervous system?" Natasha asked me, after reading from her textbook and breaking the train of my thoughts.

"Yes, yes, of course I do. It is simple," I replied with a smile.

"Good. Now, explain, please, in Russian."

I paused and tried to fake an answer, totally unaware of what I was saying.

"I thought so. You are not even listening to me. Am I wasting my time?"

"No! Honest, Natasha. Please forgive me. I just have so much on my mind. Please excuse me. Forgive me. I will pay attention. I promise."

She looked at me with concern. "You know, if you do not pass Professor Stepanov's course, there will be consequences."

I knew them well, fair Natasha.

"Then let us proceed . . . in seriousness."

I nodded.

She sat there, her eyes glancing at a page in the textbook and then at me to make sure that she had my full attention. "It is not a difficult subject," she said as she lifted a cup of tea to her lips, carefully studying me over the rim of her cup. "We are here to study physiology, *da?*"

I nodded again.

Her tone was serious. "You must remember that the autonomic nervous system is divided into two separate and very distinctive parts . . . and they are?" The quiz had begun.

I shook my head.

Natasha looked at me in disgust. "Professor Stepanov definitely will ask you this question. You must learn the answer."

I didn't have any idea what the autonomic nervous system was, and I really didn't care. I was doomed, I knew that for certain. I changed the subject. "Natasha, has anyone ever told you how beautiful you are? Your dark eyebrows, your lips, your blue eyes. American women paint their lips with tons of rouge; yours are red and so exquisitely sensuous."

"It is obvious you are not here to learn physiology. You will not pass the course."

If, instead of wearing the hand-me-down blouse and the ugly brown stockings that hid her shapely and strong long legs, she had worn the plainest of American dresses and silk stockings, no man would take his eyes off her. And there she was, sitting right across from me, teaching me something I didn't give a damn about.

She recited, "The two divisions are the sympathetic and the parasympathetic systems. Though they have separate functions, they coordinate their activities. Do you understand?"

I nodded.

"Does that mean you do or you do not understand?"

"Natasha, I apologize, but I just can't concentrate."

She broke into a strange smile. I moved forward in my chair to get closer to her face; she moved her chair back.

"Has anyone ever told you how beautiful you really are?" I said in a whisper.

"Not lately, but for some strange reason, I have the feeling that someone is."

"You are, you know."

"What?"

"Very beautiful."

"Thank you. Now we proceed with the lesson." She looked at me as if I were a lost cause. She quietly closed her textbook, stood, and reached for my hand. "Come. Come with me."

"Where are we going?"

"For a walk."

"In this freezing weather?"

"Yes! You have to cool off."

We grabbed our coats. I opened the door, and we walked out into the subzero weather. I took her hand, and she didn't resist. We slid across the frozen landscape, lit up by a crescent moon. We tracked through the freshly fallen snow, past huge pines and spruce.

As I looked around, I realized that we were heading toward Professor Stepanov's lab. With each step toward the hut, my fears mounted. Natasha was handing me over to my nemesis. She was going to rat on me and tell him that I was not taking my studies seriously. I jumped a step or two in front of her.

"Why are we going there?" I asked, pointing to the lab. "I promise to study in earnest."

"I have heard that before," she said with a chuckle in her voice.

We reached the lab. There were no lights on inside. She looked at me and I at her. She said nothing. She knocked on the door. There was no response. She turned the handle; the door was not locked. We walked into the darkened lab room, and I shut the door. Well, at least we could study in peace and quiet.

"Where is Professor Stepanov?" I asked, as Natasha took off her coat and unbuttoned mine.

"He has gone to higher elevations, for more experiments."

I didn't care where Professor Stepanov was, as long as he wasn't here. Natasha and I were alone. The room might have been heated, but as we touched and caressed and our lips met, who gave a damn? We dropped our coats to the floor.

I found Natasha's method of teaching the subject matter far more interesting than the professor's.

Chapter 16

THE PROFESSOR'S MYSTERY

A fter being away for a few days, Professor Stepanov was back in his lab, and he summoned me to make up my exam. It was strange standing before the professor, answering his questions, as recurring visions of Natasha and me making love in that very room could not be suppressed.

"Are you feeling well?" the professor asked, after I paused before answering the first question about the heart.

"I haven't felt better," I admitted. "I love it here."

"Good, then let us proceed. First the examination, then I wonder if you could help solve a mystery for me."

I rattled off some details, explained how the heart had four chambers, the differences between systolic and diastolic pressures, and I was about to continue when the professor interrupted.

"Good. Good. I can see that you have studied and that you are trying to learn. This is very encouraging. There is indeed progress. Noticeable progress. I will give you a passing grade and inform the administration about your progress. Your stipend will be restored next month."

"Thank you, Professor Stepanov. I really appreciate it. And I will try even harder in the future."

"Good. That is all I require, that you attempt to learn. Do not try to bluff your way through my class or through an exam." Then the professor added, "However, I am still not convinced that you are exerting yourself to the fullest of your potential. There is so much room for improvement."

"I am trying."

"Yes. That is good, as I have already noted. But let me ask, does your father speak English?"

My initial response, which I did not voice, was what did my father's speaking English have to do with this? Instead, I answered, "Very little. Broken English as we say back home."

"How long has he lived in the United States?"

I could not give him a definitive number of years, for I did not know when my father had actually left Turkey. "Twenty-five years, maybe."

"And he hasn't learned English because . . . ?"

"He has always dreamed of returning home to Keghi, I believe. He has always been surrounded by his old Armenian and Kurdish friends and countrymen from his village, and they only speak Armenian or Turkish."

"And he never spoke English fluently. Correct?"

"Yes, that is correct."

"And you, of course, you are dreaming about returning to your home in America, yes?"

I paused to let my mind process what the professor was driving at. It was politically dangerous to admit that a repatriate would ever want to return home. I went out on a limb and replied, "Yes, I do dream about that day, but it is only a dream of a youth. I enjoy my life here."

An impish grin crossed Professor Stepanov's face. "I understand. Better than you may think I do. And while you dream, the days are passing. Yes?"

Another pause. I wondered where this was going. Was this in any way connected with the mystery he wanted me to help him solve? "Of course, the days pass," I say, and finish by quoting some songwriter: "Time passes us all by."

"Yes, it does, and those who dream about tomorrow usually forget about today. Today passes quickly and sooner than we realize. We get old. One day, you will look back at all of your tomorrows and wonder where they went. Then suddenly, you discover life has passed you by and you have not even lived it. Do not allow what has happened to your father and his countrymen in America to happen to you here in the Soviet Union. Do not waste your talents. If you can play basketball the way I have heard some people talk, then you can learn our language and our customs. Do you understand?"

"Yes, Professor, I do."

"Good."

"Thank you." I was about to bid him good-bye when he said, "Do not go yet. Remember, I have a mystery."

"A mystery? Oh, yes, I almost did forget, Professor."

"Have you been sleeping well?" Another strange question.

"Why, yes, Professor Stepanov. In fact, I have been retiring early these nights. Our workouts on the slopes have been strenuous. I barely have time to study and sleep. I try to get to bed as early as possible. Why do you ask?"

"Interesting . . ."

"Why so, Professor?"

"Well, some of the students have informed me that you have been retiring quite late."

"Some evenings, yes. My studies, you know."

"Yes, I know."

Then I offered him a secondary excuse for my absence from the dorm. "I enjoy walking and the beauty of the mountains and the snow. It is gorgeous here. But what does my sleep have to do with your mystery?"

"I thought maybe you sleepwalk."

"I don't think so."

The professor got down to the crux of the matter, the mystery. "My dear boy, I believe I still possess all of my faculties. I still have a very good memory. And I would have known if you had returned this book." He picked up the English textbook he had loaned me from his desk and showed it to me. "Did I not loan this to you?"

I looked more closely at the book and knew it was the very same one. "Yes, you did."

"And when did you return it?"

"I don't think I did."

"Hmmm. Now, that is what makes the mystery."

"How so?"

"If you didn't return the book, as you said you did not, how, then, did the book find its way onto the cot over there? I found it there when I returned from my field trip."

I could feel the blood rushing to my face. I avoided his face and his eyes, wondering what I could conjure up as a plausible explanation. I couldn't think of anything. The professor, seeing the awkwardness of it all, gave me one. "Maybe you misplaced it in the dorm or lost it and one of the other students found the book and brought it here."

"I am sure, Professor Stepanov, that is what actually happened." I profusely apologized for my carelessness.

He dismissed me, but the smile did not leave his face.

When I closed the lab door behind me, I took a deep breath, a sigh of relief. I began walking back to the dorm. I didn't know which was tougher, the physiology makeup exam or the explanation of how the book had made it to the cot in the lab.

Chapter 17

A LITTLE OLD LADY

When I returned to my apartment that first week of February, Simonian was happy to see me. I thought he was more surprised and pleased that I had returned in one piece than anything else. There had been interesting events during my absence. Johnny had moved out, which meant that Simonian and I now had more living space. And there had been a little old woman to see me, according to Simonian. I knew that Johnny was planning to move in with his parents, but I thought Simonian was kidding about the little old woman.

"It was a tremendous experience. I love to ski. I want to go back next year," I told Simonian.

"I thought you would," he said. "Where did you get the tan?"

"On the slopes."

He laughed. "I bet you fell a lot."

I admitted I had. "But I learned to ski well. Even the instructor was impressed."

I tossed my backpack into one of the corners. Simonian had a fire going and put the teakettle on.

"This will warm you up," he said, pointing to the kettle.

"Want some real sugar?" I asked, and dug in my knapsack for the bag I had squirreled away.

"Real sugar?"

I told him that whenever I didn't use my allotment, I gathered it up and put it away to bring home with me.

"Ah, you're learning. You're becoming a true Soviet."

We shared a laugh together.

Shortly afterward, the teakettle began to whistle. Simonian poured the tea into a couple of mugs, and I tossed in two lumps of sugar each. We sat back to catch up on the news. The room looked much bigger since Johnny had moved his stuff out. More relaxed. Everyone in the building was doing fine, surviving, according to Simonian, and a French family—the Alexanians—had moved into one of the first-floor rooms vacated by an elderly Armenian American couple, who had moved to a village where they had built a modest stone house

"By the way, there was this woman—an elderly woman—asking about you. And she said she was going to come back to see you."

"Then you are serious. There was someone to see me?"

"Yes. I don't know who she was, but she definitely wanted to talk to you."

"About what?"

"I don't know. She wouldn't say. She showed up here one evening and said she wanted to talk to the American boy who came alone from America. It fit your description, so someone pointed her to our apartment. She came up here, and I chatted with her briefly."

"Did you get a name?"

"I asked, but she didn't say. When I told her you were not in, that you were away, and I didn't know when you would return, she said, 'I will come back. I would like to see this boy.' I asked why, and again she wouldn't say. I asked if there was a message. She said no."

"That's strange. I don't know any old ladies, except the ones who live in the French building. But you know all of them, I'm sure. This stranger probably has me confused with someone else."

"Maybe. But she was stubborn and determined to speak to you. I am certain we haven't heard the last of her." Simonian continued, looking at me over the rim of his mug, "I asked her to sit to see if I could pry any information out of her, and I offered her tea. But she just shook her head, said her visit was personal, that she only came to see and talk with you. Didn't want to inconvenience me. It was pretty cold outside, and I offered her one of my sweaters. She thanked me but refused to accept it. She said, 'I am not here for charity. I want to see this young boy.'

"I repeated that you might not be home for weeks. She said, 'I have

waited for many years; I can wait a few more weeks. I will be back.'
She's tough, tough as steel."

I laughed. "It sounds more like something my mother would say
and do than anyone else I know. And I know my mother is back in the
States. Was she a *teghatsi?*"

"Couldn't tell, but her clothes were—the traditional ankle-length
black gown, white knitted shawl over her shoulders, her white hair
covered by a black scarf. Her face had the brown, sunburned, leathery
look of one who labored out in the fields. She has had a hard life. Yet
she stood straight, shoulders back. Very proud. There was something
about her, her language, not the cultural Armenian spoken by the repatriates but the Armenian of the Turkish villager. When I spoke to her
in Turkish to find out if she knew the language, she scolded me for
doing so. 'You're Armenian!' she said disdainfully. 'Do not address
me in the language of those hyenas.' I am quite certain that she, too, is
from the other side of the mountain, but I cannot place the village or
the region."

"What did she want of me?" I pressed.

"I don't know. Guess we'll find out soon enough. She's not the type
to go away without answers."

"Do you know where she lives? Is she from Erevan?"

"She wouldn't say. But she didn't have any luggage. Just a small
leather handbag."

I tried to dismiss what Simonian had said as a case of mistaken
identity, but for some reason, I couldn't.

~ A FEW DAYS LATER, during the evening, there was a light knock
on our apartment door.

"I'll bet that's our mystery woman," Simonian said as he moved
toward the hallway door. He opened it, and I could barely hear what
was being said, but I could make out a soft woman's voice on the other
side of the door. "Yes, he's here."

I got up from my crate to investigate. Before I got to the door, an
elderly lady walked in. Simonian had described her perfectly. Once
inside the room, she walked right up to me and studied my face. Neither
of us said a word. Her eyes were frozen on me, investigating my features. She made me nervous, tremendously nervous. I was afraid to
move.

She took a few steps back, but her sky-blue eyes kept penetrating me. Her presence made me uncomfortable. I looked over at Simonian, and I could tell he was as puzzled as I. Moving a small step toward me, she gently touched my face with both hands. Her fingertips were as rough as sandpaper. I stood there, frozen by her touch. Then she kissed me on my forehead, and for what seemed an eternity, we stood there speechless. I finally got enough courage to ask, "Who are you?" I should have known.

A lightning-swift slap across my face startled me, stung, and left me dazed. In a reflex, my hand reached to soothe the rising pain. I was speechless, Simonian dumbfounded.

"I pray, wherever Dzovinar is now, that she felt my wrath."

I vaguely remembered hearing the name Dzovinar. I did not remember who it was.

I took a step or two back from her. "I don't understand. Why would you strike me?"

"You are Dzovinar's son," she said. "I do not doubt that now at all. I am the oldest of the Der Ohanessians. I am Ardemis, your mother's sister. And I am your aunt."

Chapter 18

ARDEMIS'S STORY

S imonian flipped on the light switch as darkness began to fall, but those who controlled the power that night had apparently decided not to provide us with electricity. I could see Simonian shaking his head in disgust, but he did not say a word. Instead, he looked around the room for the tin container where we kept our candles for such occasions. He took two out, dug into his jacket pocket, and pulled out some matches. After lighting the candles, he placed them on the small crate we used as a breakfast table. The candlelight flickered and danced to the moods of the drafts coming through the unsealed windowpanes behind me. He took a step or two toward the stove and lifted the lid with a stick, and flames rushed to escape their confinement. The red and orange tongues of heat licked hungrily at the cold air, warming us, but only momentarily, before retreating to their cell. After Simonian added wooden planks stripped from empty crates, the fire, fed with its new source of energy, crackled with contentment. Soon the thin sheet of metal on the side of the stove had a bright red glow. The heat provided a wall of comfort in front of us but could not defeat the chill of the cold February winds that battered the door and windows behind us.

Simonian carried in a chair, draped with a blanket, from the other room and placed it near the fire directly across from me. He stood with his back to one of the crates, waiting for a command, any command, from my aunt, who by now had settled into the chair. Ardemis removed her scarf and shawl and placed them on her knees. She sat rigidly, warming herself, not taking her eyes from me, in apparent disbelief that the encounter was actually taking place after so many years. Simonian handed her a cup of steaming tea. She thanked him and held the cup with both hands to warm them. Then, lifting it to her lips, she sipped the soothing beverage, but at no time did her eyes leave mine.

"Yes, I am your aunt," Ardemis finally said. "I have lived all these years in Salonike, waiting for a day like this one." She took another sip. There had been stories told among family elders that another of the Der Ohanessians, my mother's older sister, had survived the genocide and was living somewhere in Greece. It was said that before World War II, my father had sent her money to purchase passage to America for herself and family. I told Ardemis about the rumor.

"True, your father helped us. He has been very generous over the years. He did send us money and clothing, but my husband, may he rest in peace, found better use for your father's generosity." She paused as if she were prepared to explain but did not elaborate on what the "better use" was. I did not press her. Then she asked, "Do you know how your mother got her name?"

I shook my head.

"I gave it to her—Dzovinar."

"Dzovinar?" I said, glancing over to Simonian. "My mother's name is Sophie."

"No, it is not!" she replied, raising her voice defiantly. "It is Dzovinar. I gave her that name. And I watched her die before my very eyes!"

"Die?" I shuddered at the word. "Mother is not dead! She is very much alive. In Detroit!" I recovered quickly from the shock, because now I was certain that the person sitting before me was not who she believed she was. Simonian's facial grimace indicated that he, too, was bewildered by where the discussion was heading. Without speaking, we agreed that it would be best to listen rather than contradict. His message to me came by way of his finger on his lips. I furtively nodded and sealed my lips from that point.

"Your mother was born in the summer. I believe it was in August 1910. Before the Great War and before the massacres began. She was the last of the six Der Ohanessian children. I was seven years old at the time of her birth. Yervant was the firstborn; then came Miram and Ashot. I was the fourth, and then came your uncle Garabed, who, I believe, still lives in Canada. Your mother was next. I remember that it was very hot that day, so we decided to go to the riverbank. Mother and I had gone to fetch water for the evening meal when the pains began. I ran to get help. Your mother was born there on the riverbank. She was so beautiful, with her dark eyes and the fairest of complexions, just like yours. I told Mother, 'We must call her Dzovinar.'"

I saw a smile cross Simonian's face through the darkness of the room. "How appropriate," he muttered. "How very appropriate."

I look at him and then at Ardemis, not understanding the significance, but I said nothing.

"Yes, yes," she said. Then, to me, "Do you know what your mother's name means?" I shook my head.

"The name Dzovinar comes from two words, *dzov,* meaning lake or ocean, and *na,* meaning flower or rose. Mother agreed that this child, which would be her last child, would be called 'a flower that blossomed by the shore of an ocean.'"

"That is a beautiful name, Auntie."

"Yes, it is. Yes, it truly is." Ardemis became silent. There was a deep sigh, and she said, "Yes, but that was about all that was beautiful in our lives after that." Ardemis began to shake her head mournfully, as many of the older Armenian women did when they prepared to describe the events that intertwined with tragedy.

"Your grandparents on your mother's side were farmers who owned their own land in the province of Erzurum. We planted wheat and barley and had flocks of sheep. The doors to our house were open to everyone—Turks and Kurds and anyone who hungered for food. Mother was certain to have something for them."

"So that's where my mother learned her kindness and her generosity—from her parents. She, too, always fed those who came to our doors, relatives, friends, and strangers, though at times we didn't have much to share."

Simonian nodded. "She always had food for us. I sometimes wondered how she managed, even during the Depression."

"It is good to hear that," Ardemis said softly. "She, like myself, later knew hunger." She continued her story. "We played with the children of the Turkish and Kurdish families, and we shared our bread with them when they had none. Children were always accepted as family in our home. There were never any quarrels or fights, and the adults in our community talked about crops and harvesting. Not about war or killing. We may have prayed to different gods, but our gods taught us to love—not hate or kill. Religion didn't separate us. It united us. We were all like family.

"We had picnics together, sang together, bathed together in the hot springs, and there, in the village of Ileja, where the great Euphrates has its source, we truly enjoyed a good life."

She fell silent.

"Then what happened, Auntie, what happened? Please go on."

She leaned forward to study my face before she asked, "Has not your mother ever told you the story?"

"No, Aunt Ardemis, she did not. She never talked to me about her life in the old country."

"And for good reason. Listen closely, for I will, and you will never forget what I tell you here.

"Like a flash of lightning that strikes a field, setting it all ablaze, the war changed everything. The Turks called us traitors. Our Turkish friends first shunned us; our Kurdish neighbors warned us to leave. Leave! Leave our homes. Our lands! 'Never!' my father said. 'This has been my land and my father's land. We will never leave.' And I remember overhearing him tell his lifelong Turkish and Kurdish friends, 'In poverty and in wealth, in good times and bad, we have lived as one. And you tell me now to go. I will not. Bury me here, then.' And he, like most stubborn Armenians, refused to go. We had heard the rumors that Armenian villages were being pilfered, homes were set ablaze and the inhabitants slaughtered, but who would believe them? Not my father. And my mother, of course, was an obedient wife. It was propaganda, my father would tell us. The Turks and the Armenians had lived together for centuries, he said. Why would they want to harm us now?

"Your mother and I and Miram, who was pregnant, were playing in the fields when we saw the huge clouds of what we thought was dust in the direction of the village. It wasn't. It was the entire village of Ileja up in flames. We ran, but because Miram was pregnant, we could not run fast. As we approached our house, we stopped and looked and were shocked at what we saw. It was as if the earth had opened up and the flames of hell had engulfed the entire community. There were screams and cries for mercy. I can hear it now as we sit here. '*Azvas, Azvas, ohkney!* God, God, please help us!' But the cries and prayers went unanswered. Flames and smoke and cries and shots. The earth had swallowed up every Christian in our village. And in the smoke and the mayhem, you could see horsemen, sabers drawn, cutting down anything that stood in their way. I grabbed Dzovinar and held her tight, but Miram, shouting and screaming, would not be contained. She raced from the woods toward the house, and I saw one of the horsemen ride out to greet her and cut her down. I screamed and realized that during my shock, I had released your mother. She was running to help her sister. I watched as the horseman wielding his sword cut her down. That was the last I ever saw of your mother. There was nothing more for me to do but save myself. I retreated into the woods and hid. They did not find me.

"I knew they were all dead. But I had to be sure. I ran back to the river, followed the bank to the mountains. And I hid till nightfall. Then I slowly made my way down the mountain to the home of dear Kurdish friends, whom Father had befriended many times, and begged them to help me. They refused at first, because they feared for their own lives. I told them I had to go back, to find my father and my mother and my family. I told them that if they didn't help me, I would leave and tell others that they were harboring Armenians, that they, too, had Armenian blood in their veins. That persuaded them to allow me to dress in their daughter's clothing.

"I dressed as a Kurd, in their beads and veil, and went back to our home. I spoke only Turkish. The Turks had burned our house to the ground. They had slain my mother and father, and I found Miram, her body tossed on a heap of others. A bayonet had been plunged into her stomach. I knew that if I shed one tear, I would join her. As the Turks gathered around me, some became suspicious. I spat on my dear sister's body and shouted, 'Infidel!' and then I started to walk slowly down one of the streets. When I was sure their eyes were not following me, I made for the hills."

"And where was my mother all this time?" I asked.

"I did not see her body. I assumed that they had killed her, too."

"And Garabed?"

"I did not see his body, either. He, too, had to be dead. There were Turks all around me, looting Armenian houses, pilfering our churches, and taking from the dead what could be salvaged. I decided not to go back to the home of those who had befriended me. With what I had on, I began my journey to Russia, hoping to find other Armenians on the way. I was one of the unfortunate ones."

"And why is that, Auntie? You survived!"

"Yes, I survived . . ." There were no tears in her eyes, for, as she had said, there was none left in her. But when she next spoke, her voice trembled. "I should have been killed with the others. The pain did not leave me in Erzurum. I got to Greece, married the first Armenian who would have me. I bore him five sons—four were hung by the Greek nationalists as Communists, during the Civil War. I decided then that I had had enough. I left the country before they could hang my fifth and only other son, Arshavid. We came here to the Soviet Union."

"But why here and not America?"

"I did not want to beg your father for any more help."

"But your sister—my mother—you knew she would help."

"Your mother had suffered enough. She didn't need the additional burden of me and my son and my son's family. Arshavid is married and has three of his own children. They are in Kirovakan."

I had one more question that I longed to ask: "How did my mother escape?"

"I wrote to your mother several times before the Civil War broke out in Greece," Ardemis said. "It is my understanding that a Turkish family found her lying on top of Miram's body. They thought she was dead, for she was covered with blood. There was a deep gash on her wrist . . ."

I interrupted her. "Yes, it is on her left wrist. And many times I have seen her rubbing the area with her hand, as if she were looking back, remembering something, but she would never tell me what."

"It is the wound that the Turk inflicted. She has written me and related that a Turkish family took pity on her, kept her hidden for days until some British missionaries looking for Armenian children appeared. They handed her over to them, and she was placed in an orphanage, later transported to Constantinople, where your grandmother on your father's side picked her out as a bride for one of her sons."

"For my father?"

"No! For another. The family sent your father to greet her and bring her home. When your mother arrived in Kitchener in Canada, they fell madly in love. Instead of marrying one of the younger sons, your mother married your father, who was much older and could provide her with more security."

"And how old was she when she married?"

Ardemis laughed. "Why is that so important?"

"Because . . ."

Simonian asserted, "It is important to Tommy."

"Well, then, she could not have been more than fifteen."

"And she became angry at me because I wanted to get married at eighteen!"

"Ah, Tommy," said Simonian, "but you did not pick an Armenian. You picked an *odar.*"

Simonian and Ardemis exchanged smiles.

Chapter 19

UNFULFILLED WISH

O nly the crackling of the flames in the dying fire could be heard
as Ardemis finished her incredible story. I had questions—
many questions—but they were not answered this evening. My mother
held the secrets of her odyssey, her miraculous escape across her hostile homeland, into Europe, then Canada, and eventually America. Was
it a myth? I did not think so, but I would not hear the rest of her story
until I returned home.

I wanted to ask her now, but letters of any length or content were
out of the question. They were opened by the NKVD in search of
incriminating evidence, used against citizens to justify arrests or for
blackmail. The NKVD often misunderstood or misinterpreted secret
meanings in the letters; it would have been ridiculous if it were not so
tragic. Since my personal brush with death at the hands of the NKVD,
I was reluctant to commit anything to paper. Even in the classroom, I
attempted to memorize things, without writing them down—nothing
on paper, only in my mind. This would also prove beneficial when I
returned to the United States and the CIA and the FBI questioned me
about my life as a Soviet citizen.

I did write a brief note home and told my mother that Ardemis was
living in Kirovakan and had paid me a visit and that she reminded me
so much of her. It would be the last time I would communicate with
my family until I had an opportunity to phone my mother in 1956, long
after Stalin's death.

Tension between East and West were rapidly escalating in January
1950, as the Soviet Union walked out of the UN Security Council, and
Alger Hiss, a former official of the U.S. State Department, was convicted of passing government secrets to the Soviets. Both incidents
provided Joseph McCarthy with more fuel for his anti-Red crusade;
Communists had infiltrated the federal government.

Ardemis stayed with us for a week. Simonian gave up his couch to
her, and I turned over my cot to him. I put my bedding on the floor in

the kitchen area near the fire. Ardemis rose early in the morning, fetched water from the cistern, carried it up the stairs, made the fire, and boiled the water for tea without disturbing our sleep. Simonian and I found lavash bread and butter and honey on the breakfast table. While I attended classes, she and Simonian would set off to his barbershop. She continued to the marketplace, negotiated with vendors, and returned with her bounty. It was beyond me how she managed to pull off minor miracles, purchasing items that were never in view of the shopper, in a city of obvious deprivation. I was exhausted just watching her clean up the room, wash our clothes, and put meals on the table.

"How does she do it?" I asked Simonian.

"She probably deals with the Kurds," he answered. "They're nomads and don't give a damn about Soviet rule. They come out of the mountains, sell their wares, and go right back up. And Ardemis, having living in the mountains of Turkey, probably speaks their language. If you speak the native language, that alone will open doors for you. That is why it is important for you to learn Armenian and, especially, Russian."

"I am trying Mr. Simonian. Honestly, I am."

"I know you are, Tommy. A smile and a few words in their tongue opens doors, believe me."

After the one-week visit, Ardemis ordered me to pack my things. She said I was going home with her to Kirovakan. I laughed out loud, not realizing that she was serious. But she was. Once she had found me, she said, she wasn't going to let me out of her sight or leave me in the care of strangers. I told her that I could take care of myself. It went right past her.

"It is impossible, Auntie," I argued. "I cannot leave Erevan."

"And why not?" She wagged her index finger at me as if I were a child. "You will obey me."

"I attend school here. I work here." I was certain that she was not even hearing me.

"Do not be arrogant like your mother. You will live with us. I shall not leave you here alone. Do you understand this?"

"But Auntie, I . . ."

She answered with the Armenian equivalent of "No ifs, ands, buts, or becauses."

Simonian witnessed the confrontation between nephew and aunt and did not, at first, raise a finger in my defense. He listened to my aunt's argument and then to mine, and I could see a hidden smile on his face.

"Do you think that after all of these years," Auntie stubbornly continued, "that after I have found one of my sister's children, I would leave him among these strangers? In this hostile environment with no one to take care of him? You will come with me. I will find an appropriate young lady for you to wed. Do you understand?"

"Please, Aunt Ardemis, I can't leave here now."

"Impossible child! Your mother almost got herself killed because she refused to listen to me. You will come with me."

I was helpless, but I knew that I couldn't give in, and I did not want to sound unappreciative of all she had done for us. I needed Simonian to convince her that she was wrong, but his first words made me wonder whose side he was on.

"You are right, Madame Ardemis," he began. "You and your sister's son should not be separated again. Not after all you and he have been through. You need each other. He has much to learn from you and your experiences. You are, after all, family."

Traitor! I thought, but I said nothing. What Simonian had said was absurd. He knew it; I knew it. He could not be serious. He was the one who had advocated, pushed, for me to go to school, to learn the language, and he was the one who had challenged me to prove my basketball prowess. What would I do in Kirovakan, anyway?

Simonian continued, "If your nephew does go with you, however, he would have to drop out of school, and there will be much speculation, and maybe even an investigation, because, as is the case when students abruptly leave, it would cast an appearance over the school that the administration is not doing its job. The school also has a plan to fulfill. It could create problems, Madame Ardemis, for many people. You do not want this to happen, do you?"

Ardemis searched Simonian's face as if to question his motive.

Simonian went on, "This is not Greece, where there is freedom to do what you want. The government here has invested much in students like Tommy, and they are looking for dividends. You must understand this. Also, you know how Armenians gossip. If Tommy should disappear, even if I tell them he found a long-lost relative and went to live with you, some will think he had attempted to leave the country or, worse yet, had been sent away to a camp beyond the mountains. I believe you understand what I mean. It is best, taking all of this under consideration, that he stay here for the time being."

I nodded in agreement as Simonian continued, "And, then, of course, if he goes with you, he would never learn to write or speak Armenian or Russian fluently, because there are no institutions or universities in Kirovakan. Just collective farms and state farms. Do you want this young man, who has many talents, to work on the government-operated farms?"

"There's nothing wrong with farming. My mother and father were farmers. The soil would not hurt him but teach him respect."

"I agree. But look at him—look at his hands—they are not callused. He was not raised to work on a farm. I am sure his mother and his father had other plans for him. I think it would be best to allow him to fulfill his own destiny. You and I have lived our lives; his kismet is not ours to determine."

Ardemis did not want to yield, but she knew she had to.

"Besides, Auntie," I said, "I could always visit you, and you could visit me. When our team comes to Kirovakan, I will come and stay with you for a week or two. I promise. I cannot leave the team now. My friends depend on me."

That evening, my aunt and I boarded a tram for the train depot. When I handed the conductor a ruble for our fares, he didn't give me my change; it was part of the conductor's *paparck*. Aunt Ardemis refused to move; she would have none of this "bribe to ride" system. She stared him down until he reluctantly dug his hand into his pouch and pulled out the fifty kopecks in change. We took our seats. We talked in whispers all the way to the train about my mother and America. There were even some smiles on her face now. She reminded me so much of my mother, and I told her so. Before I put her on the train to Kirovakan, we hugged and kissed. She did not want to let me go. When she finally did, she touched my face with both hands, kissed my eyes, and said, "At least I have seen and touched a part of my sister, and I can see she is well and has done well."

For the first time since we had met, I saw tears streaming down Aunt Ardemis's cheeks.

Chapter 20

PUZZLE WITH MISSING PIECES

I t was hard to believe that I had been a citizen of the Soviet Union
for more than three years and had survived in a land where one
was either informed on or obligated by law to inform on others, where
a citizen who strayed off the path of socialism and communism fell
into a bottomless pit, never to be seen or heard from again. I had
learned from personal experience not to speak up or speak out against
the deprivation; instead, I, like millions of others, lived day to day just
trying to survive.

Time had not helped me to understand the government; it had kept
me apart from it. The more I tried, the more I misunderstood the con-
cepts of the proletariat dictatorship. Marx, the founder, after a lengthy
study of history, of the rise and fall of empires, believed that as capitalism replaced feudalism, it followed that socialism would replace capitalism. According to my professors, Marx and his colleague Engels
based their conclusions on "scientific and historic research." Soviet
students, like myself, were never allowed to challenge Marx's conclusions; it was Soviet dogma and was never to be challenged during
Stalin's era.

Perhaps the greatest lesson I learned from Anahaid, which I stashed
away in my survival kit, was the explicit warning that anything I did or
said against the Soviet regime would inevitably be reported to the
secret police, that the report would affect me and also harm those who
had helped me secure my job.

If I, somehow, miraculously managed to cross the line or climb the
mountain to the other side, those who remained on this side—including
Anahaid, my basketball coach, my teachers and professors at the university, even my teammates—would come under immediate suspicion
and would not escape consequences for my actions. No evidence
needed to be presented against them; it would be guilt by association.
A day did not pass that that warning did not surface from the back of
my mind.

The greatest crime I witnessed in the Soviet classroom was the denial of the right to express opinions. There was no toleration for any voice that questioned the power of the proletariat to govern. The tenets of Marx-Engels-Lenin-Stalin were dogma. Fear perpetuated the system. My lips were sealed; my eyes became my teachers.

The only place I really felt secure and safe was on the basketball court. And I was spending more and more time there. And with Natasha.

But in no way could I escape the pain of my lost freedom. It was what I cherished most—and had lost, as a citizen of the state.

~ RUMORS OF arrests never ceased in the early 1950s. From the crack of each dawn, news spread that the NKVD had been working overtime. Names were whispered of officials and citizens, unfamiliar to me at the time, who had been arrested as "enemies of the state." Although I didn't know them, I knew the pain of their inhumane, unlawful incarceration. Rumors were just rumors, of course, and no one from our apartments had disappeared into the night. The Armenian American repatriates seemed to be immune. That immunity was soon lifted.

I remembered a passage attributed to Martin Niemöller, a German pastor. He was warning the German intelligentsia specifically, and the world generally, of the consequences of avoiding involvement when observing injustices. "First they came for the Communists, and I did not speak out because I was not a Communist. Then they came for the Socialists, and I did not speak out because I was not a Socialist. Then they came for the trade unionists, and I did not speak out because I was not a trade unionist. Then they came for the Jews, and I did not speak out because I was not a Jew. Then they came for me, and there was no one left to speak out for me."

First they came for Harry Karibian, and his arrest sent a shock wave through the apartments, and the American and French Armenian communities did not say a word.

Then they came for Joe Sourian, a quiet, intellectual, gentle man, and some wondered why, but none dared to speak up.

Then they came for Eddy Papazian, and we all shuddered and asked who would be next.

I was certain it would be me.

But it was Alice, Eddy's wife. The morning after her husband's arrest, a sleepless and gaunt, ghostly figure of a woman, looking nothing like the elegant, well-dressed New Yorker who had come across the ocean on the *Rossia,* stood above the courtyard on her balcony and shouted to the bread-seeking crowds below, "You are all cowards! You will be next!" As many faces turned toward the balcony, fearing that she might leap from her third-story perch, with her long white hair blowing in the wind and wearing only a nightgown, Mrs. Papazian blasted the Soviet regime, in English, Turkish, and Armenian, using the names of Beria and Himmler in one sentence. She screamed at the top of her lungs, "Those bastards brought us here only to rob us and take from us what we worked so hard to earn in America!"

French repatriates hurried inside and closed their doors and shutters. They knew what the Nazis did to partisans. They wanted no part of this sedition.

"You are all cowards!" she continued to scream as the crowds opted to leave the bread line for the safety of their homes. "There isn't a man among you like Karibian or Sourian or my husband." She did not stop her anti-Soviet ranting until Jean Karibian and Irene Sourian pulled her off the balcony and into her apartment and remained with her the rest of the day.

When the secret police came for her later that week, she shouted and kicked all the way down the stairs and into the truck, shouting in English all the way, "At least I will not be branded a coward!" And she yelled in Armenian at the arresting NKVD officers, "Dogs! Bastards! Killers! Your turn will soon come!"

Like the other three, Alice Papazian disappeared into the night, and I would not see any of them again until Khrushchev rose to power.

The arrests deepened my depression. When I asked Simonian why this had to happen, he had no real answers for me.

"I feel like a coward, like Alice said. We're all cowards."

"Sometimes it takes more courage to keep silent than to act. Do not think I have no emotions. I, too, feel the injustice here. But to fight a battle against those who are well armed, when you have only words to shout at the enemy, is an effort of futility, bordering on insanity."

"What can we do?"

"Learn from what you see. And see it as a weapon. If you need to vent your frustration, then write to Stalin. Tell him what you saw, and ask him for help."

But I would not violate the vow I had made. I would not commit anything to paper. I suggested to Simonian that I should have gone to Kirovakan with my aunt.

"And do you think the NKVD's arm would not reach you there if they wanted you?"

During the month of arrests involving the Armenian repatriates, I continued, somehow, to function, attending classes and playing basketball. But in the evenings, when I returned to my room, I often saw the Karibian children or bumped into Jean or Irene. Pain overcame me. They said they were all right, but I didn't believe it. They lived by selling what they brought with them, and how they managed, no one knows.

My mind was not on what I was doing but on the three men who had been part of the plot to contact the U.S. ambassador. Again, some pieces to the puzzle were missing. I didn't know if I would ever put all of the pieces together.

~ ONE MORNING, Anahaid greeted me in the hallway of the Institute with a worried face. Concerned, I asked, "Is your mother all right?"

"Yes, she is quite well."

"Your sister?"

"She's doing quite well."

I expressed my worry that she did not look well. She told me that Natasha had transferred to Leningrad. I was caught completely off guard. I had no clue that Natasha was even thinking of transferring to another Institute. Why hadn't she told me?

"Anahaid, I don't believe it. She loved it here."

"It is true. They have informed me."

"But why?"

"I do not know. But officially, she stated that she felt that Leningrad had better opportunities for her, that the gymnastics coaches there had encouraged her to come, and she would have an opportunity to train under some of the finest coaches in the USSR."

I knew that was a ruse, but I said nothing. Natasha had loved her professors. The Institute had an excellent coaching staff and outstanding gymnastics coaches. It also had potential Olympic gold medalists among the student body. Natasha was now more than fourteen hundred miles away, and I knew of no way to see her.

~ IN THE DAYS that followed, Simonian did everything possible to cheer me up, but every time I glanced up to the darkened Papazian apartment, I could see mirages of Alice on the balcony shouting to all, "You are cowards!" And there was only silence in the room below us where the Karibian children and Jean now had to make a life for themselves without Harry.

I actually wanted to join the other three imprisoned men; I felt that I should be with them. Simonian knew of my role in the original plan, and I asked him why they didn't come for me.

"It is obvious that you have been spared because of your basketball talent," Simonian offered. "Your coach, even the Institute, may have defended you, told them they could not touch you."

I laughed. "Bullshit, Mr. Simonian, and you know it. The NKVD doesn't care one iota about me or anyone else. And they don't listen to anyone, either, except Beria and Stalin. Besides, they have arrested far better athletes than me and sent them away. I know. I have been talking with the others."

"Then you have a guardian angel in the ranks of the NKVD."

I gave him another sinister look, but that was all I could do.

"Tommy, I have tickets to the opera. Why don't you go?"

"How can you talk about the opera now?" I shouted. "People you and I know are behind bars, and you and I know that their only crime was that they believed in this system."

"Don't let your emotions cloud reason," Simonian retorted. "We don't know why they were arrested. Please, listen to me, in time everything will be revealed."

"And what will you do when they come for me? Will you speak out, say anything?"

Simonian didn't answer.

"And what will you do when they drag me out of here? Will you speak out for me?"

Simonian still did not answer.

"I thought so!" I left the room, slamming the door behind me. It felt as if the entire building would crumble under the impact. I headed to the Institute, to the Spartak Stadium to shoot baskets.

Chapter 21

BASKETBALL: AN ESCAPE

How quickly days turned into weeks and weeks into months. Like an autumn snowflake that falls prematurely from the heavens onto an earth that is still breathing its last warm breath of summer and disappears into the grains of sand, my youth was fading—and, with it, my memories of America.

I had little time to reflect on what had been; rather, I needed to address the present.

I would have pounced on any opportunity to escape. Like a tiger that paces back and forth in his cage, eyeing those who approach his pen, wondering who they are and why they have caged him, waiting for an opportunity to break loose and escape confinement, I, too, felt the pain of confinement. In America, if one did not like his supervisor or place of employment, he could just leave the job, sometimes without notice. In the Soviet Union, such a move was unheard of, for it would be considered an act against the state, a capital offense.

I did not know what freedom was until I was stripped of it.

I felt free only when I performed on the basketball court. There I knew the rules, the restrictions, and the penalties for infractions. As I played, the fans were not critical of me or where I came from. And there were times when they could have been. They applauded my antics, never resented where I had learned my skills, and smiled when I challenged the authorities when I felt their calls were biased. The crowd nodded graciously as I trotted off the floor and applauded gratefully when we defeated a neighboring republic. I hoped that one day I could convince them that I would do them no harm if they or their leaders would allow me to return home. But, alas, those who governed did not trust me.

Yes, there was safety inside the rectangular box that allowed me to move from sideline to sideline, from baseline to baseline, soar as high as I could toward the rim of the basket for a rebound or a tap-in. God, it felt good to be free on the indoor teak floors or the hard-clay outdoor courts. And if the region under the basket was occupied by barbarous Huns, who had orders to rearrange my face or body, I would avoid the conflict by a quick snap of my wrist, sending the ball into orbit like a rocket, soaring high above. The ball would twirl downward, as if by my command, until it swooshed into the net. I'd hear the "oohs" followed by the "ahs" after the basket was made. That was my revenge, for now, my only consolation against overwhelming injustice. On the streets of a nation purportedly created for the salvation of the working class, this foreigner displayed skills and abilities that they enjoyed, that did them no harm.

~ WITHIN THE Soviet glass house, movement was monitored, but the secret police did not restrain a person unless someone had aroused their suspicion. By now, my movements were predictable. The caricatures on public billboards depicted American capitalists as fat hogs, getting fatter by exploiting the workers, with blood dripping from their lips, an atom bomb in one paw and a hydrogen bomb in another. But I didn't fit that description. I, like most Soviet Russians, was a human being who loved life and wanted to live it as much as I could, given the circumstances. I had the same fears as they did.

And those fears came when the sun disappeared below the horizon and darkness set in.

The Soviets not only took away my youth, but they also made it impossible for me to sleep.

The worst part of the Soviet day was the Soviet night. The nightmares. The midnight pounding on doors that could be heard everywhere in the apartment complex. Waking up in a cold sweat, wondering if it was my door being hammered. Praying that they hadn't taken the elderly or the children. Not knowing until the mind and the eyes agreed that the whitewashed ceiling and the single light bulb hanging from it were in my room; I was not in a cell on Nalbandian Street.

So many times, I walked the streets of Erevan, searching the faces of those in military uniform, wondering if they were the ones who had tossed me into the NKVD truck. Was it that one or maybe that one? What did it matter? I tried to put it all behind me. I firmly believed that the cage door would open one day. That was what the men and women on the streets believed also.

The cold sweat on my forehead and the chill that extended to my very toes were telltale signs that I had survived yet another night; my number had not yet been called.

I was doing something that I loved, playing basketball and coaching children, and physically, except for the scar on my ankle, I survived those early years unmarked. The Armenians said, "Where there is bread, stay." At this point, I had bread, and I had no alternative but to stay.

Like most Soviets, I did not save a kopeck. The ruble was worthless. Why would one save in a society where the government owned the banks and could randomly, indiscriminately, without due process, accuse a citizen who had savings of stealing from the state or of specu-lation or profiteering or pilfering state goods and seize those savings? The less you had, the less chance you had of receiving a visit from the NKVD. A wise Soviet citizen knew it was not wise to bank anything. They lived from day to day. I followed their example, shelving Ben Franklin's philosophy that a penny saved is a penny earned, which had been stressed by both of my parents as far back as I could remember.

Every single kopeck of every single ruble I earned from the Pio-neers' Palace and as a basketball player was invested in wine and vodka, bread, and, later, women. There was nothing else to spend money on. Everything went to and for the military; it was a butter-or-guns economy.

Vodka soon became my best and most reliable friend, and most of my teammates agreed that it was the best escape a Soviet had from reality. We drank when we lost a game. We drank when we won a game. We drank when we tied a game. As soon as the game was over, we headed out to toast our victory or drown the sorrows of our defeat.

Our coach did not say one word, as long as we were ready to play the next game. Somehow I was always ready, although in one game, I was yanked from the floor when I began playing for the opponent by shooting for, instead of defending, our basket.

Thanks to the team Konstantin Nikitich had put together, there was really no competition for us in Erevan or in the republic. Even Dynamo—a team that conjured in my heart and mind all that was evil in the system, for it represented the Ministry of Security, the NKVD— was no competition. If there were a sadistic streak in me, if I really wanted to play dirty and maim a player, I would have picked any member of the Dynamo club. As Robert Louis Stevenson proposed with *Dr. Jekyll and Mr. Hyde,* most people have inherent good and evil.

Anyone who has played basketball knows that flying elbows can cut an opponent's face open like a knife. I have had my nose rearranged and my eyelids cut by opponents, but these were not deliberate assaults. It was chalked up as one of the hazards of the business. From the beginning, even when I was a preteen, my coaches drilled it into me that I was at all times to display sportsmanship, on and off the field, and that was the credo I lived by. If I used violence against someone who had done me no harm, was I not like the NKVD? The Nazis? I remained true to my beliefs until the end of my basketball career. I also worked to instill those values in the boys and girls I coached.

Once, long after Natasha had faded from my memory, I thought I saw Tatiana in the crowd at a game. I was certain that I saw her sitting there as we buried a Dynamo team that had made its way into the finals. I could not focus on the game once I believed I had seen her. I kept trying to catch another glimpse, forgetting about the job at hand. I missed easy lay-ups and passed the ball to where players were, instead of to where they were breaking. Something was definitely wrong.

Midway into the third quarter, the coach yanked me out of the game. "Where is your head? It surely isn't on this game!"

I kept looking into the crowd as my teammates made room for me on the bench.

I sat there, wiping my sweat with a towel one of my teammates had thrown into my face, scanning the crowd, but I did not see her. I felt her presence, though. Tatiana had to be there. I wondered why she continued to haunt me. It wasn't fair for someone to have that much power over another person.

The Institute retained the title, thanks to the exceptional perform- ances of Abraham and Armenak. I offered no excuses for my ineptness.

After we showered and dressed, I walked back into the stadium area and looked again, hoping to see her seated in the bleachers. She wasn't. The team left for the restaurant as I slowly returned to the locker room. They thought I wanted to be alone because of the lousy game I had played. What I needed was time to sort out my feelings.

As I packed my gear, I turned and saw a stranger with a smile on his face, standing a few feet away. Short and unshaven, the man wore a greasy black felt cap and had a cigarette dangling from his lip. The long sleeves of his grease-stained *busahlat* were spotted with oil, and the cotton lining showed. I was alone, and I was sure he wanted the ring on my finger. I tightened my grip on my satchel, preparing to use it as a weapon.

"You played excellent basketball" were his first words. He displayed a gold tooth, as most thugs do. "You do not remember me, Tommy?" he said as he stepped closer.

I couldn't place him, but he did know my name. He could have picked it up from the crowd while watching the game.

"I'm sorry. I don't. Do you want to refresh my memory?"

"Maybe you want a lift to the airport, no? Ten rubles—that's not too much. No?"

I looked again. It dawned on me. "You're the guy who drove me to the airport that night."

He smiled. "Good, then you know I am friend. *Ayo?*"

"Yes, and I owe you. I owe you more than a thank you."

"You owe me nothing. I enjoy watching you play here. Better here than in Siberia, no?"

"Thank you. If there is anything . . ."

He continued to smile. "My name is Bedros. Do you want to go for a ride maybe someday, and maybe we talk?"

"Where?"

"Where the NKVD dares not come."

"Where's that?"

"The Etchmiadzin."

"You tell me when and where, and I will be there."

Chapter 22

ROAD TO THE ETCHMIADZIN

We had been traveling southwest on a timeless, sleepy dirt road that led out of the city of Erevan into the ancient ruins and the hamlet of Vagharshapat. It was at Vagharshapat—Bedros told the story as he drove, smoking a Russian cigarette—that a saint had a vision. After he converted a pagan Armenian king to Christianity, he poured his heart and soul into making that vision a reality. The dream became known to the world as the cathedral of the Etchmiadzin. Armenia may be a divided nation, a divided people, its sons and daughters scattered to all the corners of the earth, but within the sacred compound of this cathedral there was unity. One God. One God they believed in, would live and die for. Within the walled, domed cathedral, there was still hope for the future. Within the walls were the palace of the Catholicos, the cells of the monks, a museum, a library, and a petrified plank from the holy Ark, brought down by explorers from Mount Ararat.

Though the monastery had other names in centuries past—Saint Kat'olike Ekelec'i, Mayr Ekelec'eac'kat'olike, and Solakat Astuacin—down through the 1,525 years of its existence, the name given to it possibly in the fifteenth century, Etchmiadzin, remained. It was built in praise of and as a tribute to the "Descent of the Only Begotten."

According to Greek and Armenian historians and ancient manuscripts preserved at the Matenadoran, an archive utilized as a depository of Armenian relics and ancient writings, it was Saint Gregory the Illuminator who, while traveling in the region, had a vision. In that vision, Christ descended from heaven with a host of angels and struck the soil with a golden hammer. Gregory saw a circular base of gold and tall columns of fire rising. It was a holy message that convinced him that he should build a cathedral on the site. He accomplished the feat with the aid of the Armenian monarch. The church was the first on the Asiatic continent and served down through the centuries as a springboard to spread the word of Christianity.

As we traveled the twenty-five kilometers from the capital, the land-scape became increasingly gentle, devoid of the lava, rocks, and stones that dominated the city and the scimitar-shaped ridges and hills to the northeast of it. Vineyards swallowed up the land. Peasants were busy harvesting the fruit Noah had brought down from Ararat and planted in the rich topsoil at the village of Arghuri, whose name means "the planting of the vine." This fruit was a national treasure. Life might have been hard then, but these people had enjoyed it through the centuries and were surviving on the lessons passed down through the ages.

It took hours for us to travel less than twenty miles, and I enjoyed the blue skies and the dazzling sunshine. Bedros made sure I would not be bored; he entertained me with his stories and Armenian folk songs of a brave people whose tears the world did not see and did not care to see.

The major delay was that Bedros kept making sudden stops to pick up peasants on the side of the road. He got out of the vehicle, walked over to a group, and negotiated a price for transporting them to their destination. Each time he returned to his vehicle, the word *paparck* popped up in our discussion. Most of his travelers were from the nearby *kolkhozes,* collective farms, and Bedros stressed that it didn't hurt to make a few rubles or exchange a few bottles of wine on the side. After all, there was "the boss" to be concerned about—*xhazain* was the Russian word he used. The factory director had given approval for the use of the truck, and he needed assurances that the trip would reap dividends, or how else could the director pay his boss?

Although Bedros's passengers were usually *kolkhozniks,* a few were on a pilgrimage to the holy see, and he refused to take anything from them, urging instead that they donate whatever they had intended to pay him to the church. A few had sheep with them. I asked Bedros why these travelers would encumber themselves by bringing animals along. He explained that the sheep were to be sacrificed, roasted on an open pit. The *shashliak* would then be offered to the hungry as *madagh,* in praise to the Holy One for answering a prayer.

Most of the pilgrims wore colorful rags. They were, on the whole, unshaven, and their weathered, unsmiling faces reflected their hard lives. These were definitely a tough and stubborn people. Throughout the centuries, all the kings, all the sultans of the Ottoman Empire could not conquer their spirit or bury their belief in their God.

Pointing to the cathedral of the Etchmiadzin, now in clear view, Bedros said that it was the reason we existed, our church. No power on earth could take that away from the Armenian people, though the Romans, the Persians, the Seljuks, the Mongols, and the Ottoman Turks had tried. As Bedros lifted his foot off the accelerator and placed it lightly on the brakes, the vehicle came to a stop before "Trdat's Gate." I looked at the edifice before me. It had been there for more than a thousand years, and yet I still knew so little about it or the heritage that was mine. My ancestors might have helped build it, might have prayed there, and might be buried there. Was this where I truly belonged?

There was a stillness in the air. Only the bleating of the sheep could be heard.

Chapter 23

DESECRATED SACRED GROUNDS

There were no hawkers on the grounds of the Etchmiadzin, peddling portraits or images of Catholicos Kevork VI. The Catholicos had ascended to the office in 1945, only after Stalin had approved an election to fill a vacancy that he had created himself with his purges of the late 1930s. Catholicos Khoren, Kevork's predecessor, was murdered in 1938, one of thousands of priests who either disappeared overnight never to be seen again, were slain, or were exiled by the paranoid Communist dictator during the Reign of Terror, apparently triggered by the assassination in 1934 of Sergei Mironovich Kirov, the first secretary of the Communist Party in Leningrad.

There were also no kiosks or pavilions with religious icons for sale on the church grounds and no beggars asking for a few kopecks. The Soviets did not tolerate begging. There was no feeling of anticipation or anxiety in the air surrounding the palace, where in the past, Bedros told me, throngs awaited the Catholicos's arrival, his appearance on the balcony, and his blessing.

The Armenian Orthodox Church was waging a life-and-death struggle to exist. Its future looked grim. It was losing the battle for the youth of society, and the older generation of worshippers was dying. The dropped torch could not be passed to the younger generations, for the Soviets had the minds and bodies of the children, who pledged their loyalty as Pioneers and as members of the Komsomol. The classroom in the seminary was empty, and no one could be found in the church library pondering the mysteries of creation and reading the Bible. The buildings were vacant, eroding, in disrepair. There were no Bibles in Armenian or Russian or any other language, no souvenirs or postcards I could purchase to mail home, no priests or bishops on the sacred grounds greeting us at the golden gates with smiles of welcome.

There were no worshippers or foreign tourists or other visitors on this sunny summer day that Bedros has chosen to show me the ancient hamlet. But then, there also were no portraits of the Soviet gods—Marx, Engels, Lenin, Stalin—on display.

After I strolled from one empty building to another, studying the paintings, the portraits, the frescoes, the mosaic etchings of the saints—Saint Paul, Saint Theola, Saint Bartholomew, Saint Gregory, Catholicos Komitas, and Catholicos Krimian Hayrig—I found myself alone in the chapel. Bedros had lingered in one of the alcoves to study some ancient Greek inscriptions he had come across.

Through one of the massive rectangular windows, I spotted an artist, sitting with paintbrush in hand and canvas before him, looking westward to Ararat. His back was to the church. His eyes moved from his canvas to the mountain and back. He was the only other person I had seen on the holy grounds. If there were others, they were in the catacombs or in the caves; they did not make their presence known. Even the pilgrims, once they had gotten off the truck, had disappeared from view.

In the summer of 1950, the bells in the towers of the holy Etchmiadzin tolled for no one, not for Bedros or for me. They had fallen from the tower, and apparently the church did not have the funds or the manpower to repair them and put them back in place.

As I walked the dusty paths from one building to another, I saw pile upon pile of human feces, either deliberately planted to desecrate the sacrosanct grounds or out of human necessity. I believed the former was true.

My Soviet professors had noted that in March 1921, Lenin was forced to implement a New Economic Policy, a drastic retreat from socialism and a return to private enterprise, in order to save the nation from starvation. The nation began to recover, but Lenin did not. After a series of strokes, he died in 1924. Lenin had warned the Politburo of Stalin's ambitions, but Stalin still managed to dispose of his enemies, consolidate his power, and take supreme command of the country. Even the then-powerful Russian Orthodox Church fell prey to Stalin's deceitfulness. As the Nazis closed in on Moscow, Stalin purportedly got on his knees and begged the high-ranking bishops of the church for forgiveness and asked for support against the invading armies, which he received unconditionally. Church officials wrongly believed that after the war, the Soviet dictator would stop his persecution of believers.

But the persecution continued after the Nazis' fate was sealed. Not only were Christians systematically and vilely attacked in the Soviet press after the war, but they were also physically tortured if they continued to profess their religion. As Christians had been taught to do, they turned the other cheek. They miraculously survived, but barely. They retreated into the catacombs and the caves and prayed in silence (only the very old prayed publicly) to escape the deadly Red plague. Was it any wonder that the bells of the Etchmiadzin were silent?

Only divine intervention could have turned the tide. The Bolsheviks were fulfilling the mandate that had been issued by Marx and Lenin. And it continued, even as I sat in the Soviet classroom. According to Lenin, the proletariat was "dispersing the fog of religion and liberating the workers from their faith in a life after death, by rallying them to the present-day struggle for a better life here upon earth."

Soviets saw the handwriting clearly written in red on the walls. Satanic Stalin, the ultimate hypocrite, contemptuously stood upon Lenin's crimson sarcophagus in Red Square and urged troops departing for the front to fight for Mother Russia and for the glory of God, and he would crucify those who returned to the homeland after the war. Ironically, Franklin Roosevelt and a reluctant Winston Churchill had agreed at Yalta to return any Soviet prisoner of war who had remained in the West to the Soviet Union. Unknowingly, the two Western leaders had signed the death warrants of all those they had forced to board trains to return to the Soviet Union.

Stalin's prayers were answered. The Soviet Union won the war, and the church was on the verge of extinction, as evidenced by what was all around me at the holy see. Each one of the gray blocks of stone I saw was put in place more than fifteen hundred years before, maybe by one of my ancestors. I was keenly aware of all that surrounded me; I felt myself part of it, yet I was not. I had an eerie feeling that I was visiting this place in another time, a parallel universe, perhaps. I found myself standing alone in the chapel before a carving of the crucified Christ. A thousand thoughts raced through my mind—the ultimate pain, the torture he had suffered. I stood there before him and prayed.

Chapter 24

MY PRAYER

My side of the conversation went something like this.

"Lord, you and I know that I have traveled down a separate path from yours since you and I last talked. I now realize that I should have talked with you first. I have never asked for anything for myself, as you know, for I feel that you have given me the strength and the intelligence to work things out for and by myself. I now realize that I have had a rich life, and every day of it was filled with love and happiness. I was raised in a land of milk and honey, and I tossed it all away for this. All I have to do is look around me to know how fortunate I used to be. But that—and more, the most important thing in the world, my freedom—is now gone. I have shed my tears. I am facing up to what I did. I will confess I never realized the value of freedom and justice before. Now I have lost them. Like most people, I didn't understand the loss until it happened to me. That is why I am here, kneeling and begging forgiveness for my impudence, my conceit. True, no one can see the shackles, the chains on my ankles, but they are there never-theless. They were placed there by a godless government that preaches to its citizens that you do not exist. And to accept you is to reject them—a sure invitation to persecution. They have replaced you and worship the one who betrayed you, Judas Iscariot. They reward those who would sell out members of their family and friends who do not follow the teachings of the Party.

"If you thought that Sodom and Gomorrah were wicked, look around here! You know what these people are doing. Is it not time for your return trip? That great Judgment Day some are predicting will be soon. It is long overdue. Man has walked hand in hand with evil for as long as I can remember. In the first half of the twentieth century alone, and during my lifetime, there have been two global wars, and some believe there will be a third one that will end all of civilization. I don't need to tell you what the Turks did to the Armenians, though the Turks continue to deny it, and what the Nazis did to the Jews. Tell me, how can mankind ever justify the killings, the incarcerations, the slave labor—where and when will it all end?"

I paused and looked out the window at Ararat, then asked quietly, "In the waters of another great flood?"

I continued to pray. "I am truly thankful that I am alive but remain mystified about why. If my greatest crime was deciding to come to this godless country, I am sorry, and I ask for your forgiveness. I exacer-bated things by getting involved in the plot to contact the ambassador, and I am willing to pay the price for my foolishness.

"But I don't believe—and this is why I kneel before you now—that the others involved should pay for the same mistake that I made, when I have been allowed my 'freedom.' Sourian and Karibian and Alice and Eddy Papazian are good people. Spare them, and allow them to return home safely to their families. Watch over them so that no more harm will come to them. And please, Lord, watch over my dearest family in America."

I opened my eyes, and as I slowly got to my feet, I smelled incense burning somewhere. I was alone, yet I felt another presence. I looked around. There was no one in sight, not even Bedros. I walked out of the church and into the sun-filled garden. I was hungry. The aroma of roasted lamb led me to an open pit, where several men, including Bedros, were feasting on *shish kebab.*

"I have been waiting for you," Bedros said as he sliced a huge piece of lamb from the skewer that was hovering over the flames of the pit. "You had a lot to say to God, huh? This meal is an answer to someone's prayer. Maybe someday he will answer yours."

Chapter 25

CHILDREN OF THE STATE

I was on a train traveling with Jak Simonovich and our junior basketball teams. Our girls' and boys' squads had earned the right to represent the republic at the Transcaucasian Games hosted by the Republic of Georgia. The tournament would be staged in Georgia's capital city of Tiflis and would include teams from Azerbaijan.

I was looking forward to the weeklong trip. It would give me an opportunity to get away from the apartment and Simonian and the rumors of another war.

Before the end of the summer of 1950, North Korea had decided to invade South Korea, and President Truman and the United Nations called upon General MacArthur to lead the UN forces.

It was strange how living with older people could work on one's nerves. Nightly news broadcasts from the Voice of America were interpreted differently by the French and American repatriates. Some argued that war was imminent and that the sooner the Americans landed, the sooner we would all be able to go home. Others said that a war with nuclear weapons would destroy the world; therefore, there would be no war.

I kept my nose out of politics and into athletics. Those who publicly discussed politics disappeared, and I would not be one of them.

The trip to Tiflis, though I personally would not be playing, presented a new challenge: coaching. I would be testing my abilities and strategies against coaches much older than I, and to my knowledge, they had never faced an American-born coach on the other bench. I knew nothing about the quality of either the coaches or the junior teams outside Soviet Armenia. It definitely would be a new experience for me.

I did not know if the news of an influx of Western European athletes into Armenia via the repatriation program had reached the sports communities elsewhere in the USSR. News did not travel fast in the Soviet Union, unless it came directly from the Kremlin. I didn't believe any of the repatriates, not even the excellent cyclists from France, had ventured outside Armenia. It was still a matter of trust; the Soviets just didn't trust us. In fact, most of the newcomers who managed to enroll in the colleges and universities, like myself, were not even allowed to attend classes that had a military curriculum, something like ROTC.

Jak had warned me that it wouldn't be easy in Tiflis. The Georgians had their own set of rules; the man who led the nation was a Georgian, and the Georgians believed that they were the chosen ones.

In Tiflis, old ethnic rivalries would also surface. We did not bring a ref, so both officials on the floor would be local, and we, the visiting team, would be at their mercy. Though Georgians, like the Armenians, were Christians, most Azeris were not. It was no secret, moreover, that the Armenians hated the Turks, and the Azeris were "first cousins" to the Turks. Jak had told me that our teams would run up against deep-seated hatred and bias, laced with vile and derogatory words on and off the court. Thank God my vocabulary was very limited, for if I could understand what they were saying, there certainly would be physical confrontations.

Azerbaijan had never lost in basketball to Armenia. Though the native Azeris, like the Armenians, preferred wrestling and soccer to basketball, they managed to field a competitive team, thanks to the Russians who had migrated to Baku to work in the oilfields. The nucleus of the Azerbaijan lineup was the Russians.

～ JAK AND I had developed an excellent coaching relationship. He managed to translate my thoughts to the kids, who, though at times they must have thought I was a bit weird because of the way I murdered their language, listened patiently. I thought Jak was telling them what

I said, but I couldn't be certain. Something is always lost in the translation. I would say something in all seriousness, but the kids would chuckle after Jak translated it. I still had problems finding the right Russian or Armenian words to express myself; my mind still functioned in English. When all else failed, I got onto the floor with basketball in hand and personally demonstrated what I wanted them to do. Sometimes I felt I was reaching my players, and then there were moments when I got so frustrated I would slam the ball into the wall with the sound of an exploding bomb that made the gym shake. That got their immediate attention but also seemed to send a wave of fear into the hearts of the youngsters. I eventually learned to control my temper.

Jak required our students to attend games at the Institute in which I played. He usually accompanied the boys' and girls' teams to the gym, the Spartak Stadium, and during a game, he would single out what he felt were some of the finer points. After the game, he walked the students home. If I didn't have a previous engagement, I joined them for a stroll back to the center of the city, stopping at the new juice store to enjoy a beverage. The camaraderie helped build understanding among us and make for a better team.

I could always depend on Jak to bring peace when turmoil was about to hit. In the years Jak and I worked together, not one of our players ever dropped out of our class or transferred to another basketball school. None dared ever to show up late for practice.

The boys and girls participating in the Caucasus Games were supposed to be between fifteen and seventeen years old. Birth certificates or passports were used to verify a player's age. Jak had made certain that all of the necessary documents for our players were in order.

We had gathered at the Pioneers' Palace early on the day of our trip. It was rare for a parent to show up at practice or a game, because both parents in a Soviet household usually had to work to make ends meet. There was no one to see us off.

We boarded a bus—not one of the open-air truck types that made up most of transportation in the city—and went to the train station. We took the morning Erevan-to-Moscow train. The Ministry of Education had purchased "hard reserve" tickets, which meant we would be traveling in compartments for four but with no sliding doors. We kept our eyes on the kids at all times. Jak noted that ours were the best accom-modations available for such a large group. He was very pleased, because he could monitor the players without running all over the train. Obtaining train tickets at any time during the 1950s was an all-day chore, and to get all of our players in one car had been almost impossi-ble. The Ministry had managed to do it.

The trip would take about six hours, I was told. It stretched to ten because of frequent delays. The train stopped for every shepherd and every flock of sheep that had to cross the track.

Since the train was bound for Moscow, there were much better facil-ities than usual. Although there were no private lavatories, there was a common washroom at the end of each car. An attendant was on duty in each car, ready to provide tea or hot water and assist travelers. Ours was a robust middle-aged grandmother type, with her white hair in a bun. She wore a blue uniform, with a white lab coat serving as an apron over it. She was very pleasant, and after Jak informed her that the children were "basketballists" and were going to Tiflis to compete in a tournament, she was all smiles as she fired up the samovar.

~ ONE LEARNS a lot from kids by traveling with them. For one thing, I realized just how mature my players were. They listened to Jak's instructions, every word. They respected him as if he were from the Politburo, in part because they all had experienced something that I would never understand. Only those who had been on the battlefield, lived through war, seen the pain and suffering and destruction, could understand. These were the children of men and women, some 25 mil-lion of whom had died during the Great Patriotic War. These children had seen their families disappear, their homes and schools bombed, their lands occupied by the invader. And during five terrifying years, they were lucky if they had a piece of bread to eat. It was not easy for them to identify with me, someone who had never heard a bomb or seen a body mangled by a bomb or flesh pierced by shrapnel. Was it any wonder that when I banged the ball against the wall, creating an awesome noise like an exploding bomb, some of the boys and girls cringed and the younger ones raced into the locker room? I was on the outside, trying desperately to look in, and I was an intruder. Some believed that the people I had grown up with were preparing to go to war against them. Yet they tolerated me, greeted me cordially, and welcomed me into their midst as their teacher, their coach.

I saw children well trained—perhaps conditioned would be a more appropriate word—from birth to believe that theirs was the best life and the only life. Soviet children, red Pioneer kerchiefs around their necks, were being prepared to serve the nation and to respect authority and authoritarian figures. Jak fit the bill. They were prepared to fight for the motherland and to sacrifice their lives because there were men of evil across the ocean who, for their selfish gains, were preparing to drop nuclear bombs on them.

As hard as I tried to make them understand that no one in America wanted another war, I usually walked out of the Pioneers' Palace gym discouraged. I was not reaching the kids; they were reaching me.

The youth in me, the American in me, was still there. The best I could do was try to make them understand me. Eventually, they would, years later, even though I had shouted at the top of my lungs, banged the ball against the wall, and spoken to them in their language with an accent.

The children who made up my first teams reminded me of the tragic Eloi in H. G. Wells's *Time Machine,* created for a certain purpose in life, to give up their lives for communism when the time came. Like me, they had lost their youth to a cause. They were Pioneers now, some already having joined the ranks of the Komsomol, and, if they were fortunate, someday they would be inducted into the elite Communist Party. Communism gave meaning to their lives; capitalism prevented them from realizing their goals.

The children studied hard, attending school six days a week, finding time for basketball practice, grateful to the Party of Lenin and Stalin. These were the children who sang and wrote odes of praise to their leaders, recited from memory scores of patriotic poems and essays praising the socialistic way of life and never-ending verses lauding Stalin. I never heard a child flub or forgot a line or a word in a verse that honored Lenin or Stalin. That would be inexcusable.

Whenever a question from one of them had a political aspect to it, Jak would quickly intervene and diplomatically dismiss it with "Tavah-rishch Tom is not a capitalist. He is one of us. He gave up his fascist country, his family, to live with us and learn from us, because he believes, as we all believe, that communism will bury capitalism."

Would I dare challenge him to say otherwise?

Chapter 26

A DISCRIMINATING GOD

I was fortunate to have Jak Simonovich at my side. I never would admit it to him, for the Armenian in me would not allow me to acknowledge that I was not a *dlramart,* a man who could stand on his own two feet. I would have appeared weak and incompetent. That was not the case; I was idealistic, maybe, but never a coward. Armenian boys were supposed to be men from the first day they could stand up. They knew how to hold their alcohol, for their veins were filled with grapes and wine at birth, suckled from their mother's breasts the day they were born.

Handpicking me, an American-born, to become his colleague, to work with him side-by-side, showed a lot of courage. Jak was a Komsomol; he had the support of three Party members and had applied for membership in the Communist Party. He jeopardized it all by associating with a foreigner. The wrath of the Party hierarchy could be brought down upon him. No matter what Anna Louise Strong wrote or said, the Soviet Communists laughed at the so-called U.S. Communist Party. The only true Communists were the Soviet Communists.

Jak knew many qualified college graduates who spoke and wrote English. He could have had his pick of them. He chose me. We were both obligated to present lesson plans to the administration at the beginning of the month. Needless to say, mine looked as if they were written in hieroglyphics—part English and part Armenian, with some words in Russian. It was a nightmare for me. Jak had to prove to the commissars that we could fulfill our plan, established by the Ministry of Education, and that our students would pass the nationally required standards, which stipulated that all Soviet citizens, even the severely handicapped, were to be physically fit and ready for work and defense of the motherland. If a citizen successfully completed the course, which was geared toward all-around physical exercise, including walking, running, swimming, skiing, and rowing, he or she was awarded a Badge of Distinction. No Soviet citizen was exempt.

Lesson plans were submitted, usually after Jak perused them, to the Ministry of Education, and the commissars did routinely approve them. I had no idea what criteria the commissars used. I felt that win-loss records should be important. Jak accepted that that might be the American way, but it wasn't the Soviet way. He said that personalities, negotiations, and changing statistics to appease the director usually determined whether an employee stayed on a particular job or was transferred to some remote village.

When it came to playing or coaching basketball or anything else I did, I never considered the consequences of failure. Losing was never an option in my book. I had too much pride in my work and the way I played. I didn't walk onto a basketball court or coach a team with the thought of losing in my mind. No decent coach or player ever did. But losing was not a disgrace if you played your best. Then again, if you played your best and the team still lost, *was* it your best? That question always lingered after a loss.

For the tournament in Tiflis, I gathered from Jak that our best shot at victory was against Baku. To finish second at the three-team tournament would be an improvement and would be acceptable back in Erevan. Finishing last would mean there had been no improvement, even if we managed to stay close. There was never a mention of victory over Tiflis. I didn't know why. Baku had a large population of Shi'i Moslems, eighty-five percent, whose sports of preference were wrestling and horsemanship. But our team would be playing against Russians.

It still felt strange to be coaching youngsters I didn't understand. It must have been the same for them. As I've said, they were learning to despise capitalism, the United States, and everything the country of my birth represented, and I was standing before them, teaching them how to play basketball, shouting orders at them from the sidelines, cheering or chastising them. I did not know what had made them choose to play for my team. Perhaps they had wanted to enroll in Jak's class and got stuck with me. There I stood with the ball in my hand, muttering words that they could barely understand. They gawked at first but never mocked. They were as bewildered as I but patient enough to listen.

In the very first class, when the kids gathered in a line to face me, a cold shiver took control of my body, and I wondered what I would say. I had forgotten everything I ever knew. Worse yet, I didn't speak their language. But I knew basketball, and that was why they were standing before me. In time, those emotions and feelings dissipated, and from that first class until my last class, they remained like family to me.

Tiflis would be my Rubicon, and what happened in that ancient capital on the Kura River would mark me for the rest of my Soviet life, if not my entire life.

~ AS THE TRAIN approached the outskirts of the city, the towering mountains remained in sight, but like a chameleon, the landscape suddenly changed its colors. The gray stones and the reddish volcanic rock of Armenia were replaced by the velvet greens of sloping valleys and meadows and wildflowers. Animals were scurrying about at the sound of the train's shrieking whistle as we raced toward the depot. Far below us, I could see the Kura carving its way through a valley and bridges that bound one bank to the other. Those bridges were built in other times by invitation from the kings and queens of Iberia, the Grouzeen Empire. Unlike Erevan, whose awe-inspiring biblical mountain had made it a controversial centerfold of religious history, Tiflis was masked by the mystique of its people. They enjoyed life and lived it to the fullest, accepting the stranger with open arms. Beware the dagger concealed beneath that Cossack coat, for if a stranger should dishonor or betray their hosts, the Grouzeen would not fail to use his weapon.

The Armenians say that God blessed Armenia with lava and rocks and told the Armenians to go carve themselves a living out of the abundance of stone that he had given them. Georgia was allotted the fertile valleys and the forests sandwiched between the Black Sea and the Caspian. God told them to go play and to enjoy life, for he had blessed them with food and drink to thrive. And he left the wealth of oil to the Azeris, and the Azeris laughed all the way to the banks of Europe and Asia while they hired others to do their work for them.

I had told Jak that I would not have minded the Lord's discrimination, but I wished that he had blessed our people with a little more height and a little less hair.

Because our team lacked height, speed was the fuel driving our pistons. To utilize our quickness and agility to its fullest, I had installed the full-court press, something that I had learned in high school but was new to the Soviets and needed fine-tuning. The team had learned quickly, and even Jak was surprised at how fast and effective the strategy could be. The first time I tried it, there was mayhem on the court. Jak had said the kids were not ready for such a radical change in the way we played defense.

"We must concentrate on beating Baku," he had said. "If we can come out with a victory, I am sure that it would put smiles on the faces of the commissars at the Ministry."

"Impossible," I'd replied.

"What? To beat Baku?"

"No. To see a smile on any of the commissars' faces."

~ THOUGH JAK had been to Tiflis many times, both as a player on the Armenian team and to visit relatives, this was my second trip to the city, my first as a coach. (The "repatriation train" also had made a brief stop at the depot en route to Erevan.) I had briefly visited the year before when the Institute had sent a group of us to tour Stalin's birthplace. I had discovered that though Stalin was Napoleonic in stature, his countrymen who passed me on the streets and on the main thoroughfare, Shota Rustaveli, were not. They were tall, many more than six feet, well-built, sturdy, robust men, and not one older than twelve was without a mustache. I was looking forward to learning more about these people.

After the stop at Tiflis, the train would continue on to the Black Sea resort cities of Sukhumi, Gargra, Adler, and Sochi, where many of the travelers were going on passes to rest. Then the train would turn north for Rostov, Kharkov, Tula, and Moscow. Although passengers boarding planes were scrutinized, even questioned, by the NKVD after they purchased their tickets, no one was challenged when taking a train. I realized why Bedros, the truck driver who had befriended me, had suggested that I take the train to Moscow. I might have had a better chance of reaching my destination.

There was a notable presence of troops aboard, however, assigned to border patrol, either returning to or being transferred from their positions on the Turkish border. The ethnicity of these troops was neither Armenian nor Georgian nor Azeri; they were blond, blue-eyed young Russians, there because they would not fraternize with the local population. It wasn't uncommon to see pairs of submachine-gun-toting soldiers, in their long brown winter overcoats (even in summer), weaving their way through the cars and past passengers, just looking, never asking questions or requesting passports. German shepherds accompanied their handlers and sniffed their way down the aisles of the train. Jak cautioned our team members not to pet the dogs.

It was comforting, all the same, to know that Jak had all of our players' documents, including a letter from the Ministry stating the purpose of the trip and our destination, and I kept my passport handy at all times.

By now, I had become accustomed to the *militzia,* which would stop me and request it. I was no longer fazed or frustrated by such requests, as I had been when I first arrived. Often, I wanted to blurt out, "It's a free country, isn't it?" before I realized where I was. Being stopped was an inconvenience, but, of course, it was a necessity according to the Soviets, because "Comrade, you know that we are surrounded by our enemies."

Wearing my Institute-issued blue basketball sweatpants and shirt with the athletic club's name across my chest in Russian helped thwart suspicion. All the same, even when I occasionally allowed my beard to grow, some of the troops would see something that others didn't. They would stop and question me. The ring I wore on my finger gave me away, Tatiana used to say, but I refused to take it off. Sometimes she said it was my fair skin and my dark hair that made them jealous. I had chuckled at her remarks and said they only stopped me because they wanted to talk to her.

A sure way to draw the NKVD's or the *militzia's* attention was for me to wear an American-tailored suit, white shirt, and tie. The suit was a red flag for the authorities to question me. When I was with the Institute team, I deliberately wore Western clothes, and then, during questioning, I would unleash a line of obscenities in both Russian and Armenian that floored even the investigating officers. After all of their taunts, they had become fair game for me. I did not really fear them.

What was there to fear? If Karibian, Sourian, and Papazian could survive in a slave-labor camp, so could I. Besides, I was already a prisoner of sorts, wasn't I?

~ AS WE got closer to the city, Jak said he needed to get some cigarettes, and I was surprised when he mentioned that there was a dining car where he could purchase some. I knew I had to investigate the restaurant. But I was concerned that if both of us left our charges alone, especially the girls, something could happen.

Jak only laughed. "They are more streetwise than you will ever be. They know more about danger than you'll ever know."

He turned and told the team where we would be in case of an emergency, and they seemed happy to get rid of us for a while.

We made our way through the cars, tossed and bobbing like bottles on the ocean by the turns and twists of the train, until we reached the dining car. I was acutely aware of the dress many of the passengers had changed into. In fact, I even ogled some of the women. The passengers sitting in their compartments, standing in the aisles, and walking around the cars were wearing their pajamas. It was midafternoon. I asked Jak about this, and he said that wearing pajamas in public, especially on trains and at the beach, was a common and acceptable custom.

"Not so in America," I replied. "We wear pajamas when we retire for the evening. Our pajamas are not for public display."

"You have some strange customs in America," he said.

We reached the dining car, and while Jak moved toward the counter to make his purchase, I looked around and was elated to see that "cosmopolitanism" was alive and well on the train. I wondered if it was because the train was going to Moscow or perhaps because foreign tourists were aboard—unlikely, though, since we were at the height of the Cold War.

There were lily-white tablecloths, polished silverware, pitchers of drinking water, and vases with ruby-red roses on the twelve tables in the car. I asked Jak if we could sit for a while. It was a pleasant change from the stuffy, sweaty, smoke-filled car we'd been in. He agreed but reminded me that we'd have to get back to the team in a few minutes.

We took a table, and a waiter approached and told us that the diner was closed until after the Tiflis stop. He could serve us drinks if we wished—vodka, Armenian cognac, Georgian wines, mineral water, or fruit drinks. Jak asked for mineral water. I ordered a soft drink. We fell silent for a moment, with our own thoughts. The dining car was clean and pleasant. I wondered if I could go straight through to Moscow.

I sat looking toward the back of the train and noticed that there was one more car. I wondered if it had passengers in it. I asked Jak. He glanced at the door and said the car was reserved for international visitors, maybe top Party members or the military brass. Before he finished his explanation, two officers opened the sliding door from that car and entered the diner. They noticed me and gave me the once-over. In military cadence, they walked down the aisle toward the counter. Not wanting to be unsociable, as they neared our table, I invited them, in my best Russian, to join us. Surprised, one replied, *"Spasiba.* But we are on duty. Maybe some other time." The other officer went directly to the counter and purchased a bottle of vodka. The first officer joined him and also ordered a bottle. They paid for their purchases, and when they reached our table, the officer I had spoken with placed his bottle before me on the table and said it was a *podahrak,* a gift. I tried to refuse it, and Jak, in Armenian, told me I couldn't. I was to accept it and say *"Spasiba."* I did as I was told. The officers left.

When they shut the sliding door behind them, Jak called the waiter over and told him to take a bottle of Armenian cognac to the adjoining car and give it to the officers who had just passed through. The waiter, an Armenian, understood the gesture. Jak tipped him generously.

"We need to leave. Put the bottle away. We will have it after the competitions. If we sit here, this exchange of drinks may go on all night."

I accepted what he said, though I didn't completely understand.

"It is tradition. And it will be worse in a Georgian restaurant."

Jak's face was flushed, and he was obviously embarrassed by my unorthodox behavior. As we got up to leave, the door to the last car opened again, and this time, a young lady in pajamas strolled into the diner. I froze.

"What are you doing here?" I asked her in a low voice.

She ignored the question.

Jak turned. There was a puzzled expression on his wrinkled face. "Tatiana Mikhailovna, my dear cousin, what a surprise."

Cousin?

"Jak Simonovich, my favorite cousin, it is always a pleasure to see you."

I was dumbfounded.

"Where are you traveling to?" Jak asked.

"To Tiflis, to visit Aunt Sonja. And you?"

"To Tiflis. Our youngsters will be playing there." As he turned to me, he continued, "My apologies. This is Tom Boghosovich. He is from America."

Looking directly at Jak, ignoring me, Tatiana answered sarcastically, "Strange. I thought this American would be back in his own country by now."

Suddenly, the train jerked and bumped, and I found Tatiana in my arms. It had been a long time. Pictures of her surrounded by Soviet officers, always and many, raced through my mind.

Caustically, I whispered to her, "And I thought you might be pregnant by now."

In one fluid movement, she pushed me away, looked at me, and slapped my face.

Jak looked at the two of us and smiled. "Oh, I see that you two are acquainted."

Tatiana rushed back to her car. I didn't think she had gotten what she came for, but perhaps she had.

Chapter 27

AN ELITE LIFESTYLE

All of the events leading up to the tournament went well, even the pairings for the tournament.

Young Pioneers, with the traditional red kerchiefs around their necks and white apron attire, accompanied by sports officials, greeted us at the train station. The children presented Jak and me with flowers, a traditional gesture by the host city that I would discover was practiced throughout the USSR. There were no speeches, just the customary handshakes and welcomes. Buses waited to take us the block or two to the stadium, but Jak opted for the team to walk, so that we could get the kinks out of our muscles from the long train ride. It did us good. There was a cool morning breeze, and as we strolled, I enjoyed the colorful, tree-lined streets. People stared, some even turning around after we passed to get a better look at us. Soviet citizens maybe, but this old Iberian nation was still proud, the people much happier and more pleasant to look at than what I had seen in Erevan and the sur-rounding villages. The Georgians looked at you when you walked by. They acknowledged you with eye contact. They were not afraid to look, smile, or greet you, as many of the Russians were. Georgians were better dressed and better fed, and there were more private cars—Moskviches and Pobedas, minivehicles manufactured in the USSR—on the streets.

Dynamo Stadium, walking distance from the train station and an equal distance from the central marketplace, was where our teams would be bedded down for the tournament. Though the stadium was quite far from the gym where we would actually play our games, the accommodations there were ideal for practices. They gave us an oppor-tunity to conduct morning calisthenics and use the outdoor courts for light scrimmages. The games would be played in an indoor gym, despite the heat and humidity of late August. There was no such thing as air conditioning in Tiflis—or in the entire Soviet Union at the time. We no sooner settled into our dormitory-style rooms than Jak announced he had to go over to the Central Committee for Physical Culture and Sports to present our credentials. The committee would peruse the documents, approve or reject them, and then issue our meal tickets, to be presented at the restaurant where we would dine. All of the coaching staff and players from Baku and Erevan ate at one restau-rant on the Rustaveli. I assumed that since the Georgians were on their home turf, they would dine in their homes, but I was incorrect. Their teams ate at a restaurant down the street from where we had been assigned, and we bumped into them as we walked the boulevard.

August was usually scorchingly hot in this subtropical region, but it was not so bad during the time of the tournament. We were fortunate.

Also, in the stadium, the layers of concrete and stone acted as an insulator and kept the corridors and our rooms cool.

Tiflis drew a first-round bye, so the host would not be playing in the opening game. Our boys and girls played Baku in the opener. This gave Tiflis an opportunity to scout us, but we would have a game under our belts before we met them, and we could get accustomed to the floor, the rims, and the overall feel of the gymnasium. I was not looking past Baku, but I felt confident that the kids we coached could handle any team in their age group.

We had prepared well for this tournament. I remembered urging Jak in those final practices back at the Pioneers' Palace to allow the girls to scrimmage against our second-string boys' team to toughen them up. Jak had raised his eyebrows and given me a look, questioning whether I had missed my biology and physiology classes.

"It would toughen up the girls, you say, make better players of them?"

I nodded.

"*Che!*"

"No isn't a good enough answer. Why?"

He shook his head. "What will it do to the boys who happen to innocently, or maybe deliberately, brush against the girls? Do you not think there would be a natural reaction?"

"Jak," I pleaded, "we are not talking about having sex on the gym floor; we're talking about improving the skills and the endurance of our girls' basketball team."

"No. Impossible."

But he acquiesced after I placed a bottle of Armenian wine before him and we shared a couple of drinks. The girls' and boys' teams did scrimmage against each other, which apparently was a first in the republic. I liked what I saw. Though he would not admit it, so did Jak.

Although both sides seemed reluctant, at first, to make contact, as the scrimmages increased in intensity and after the girls scored a few baskets, the boys were not going to allow their rivals to beat them. The competition became more aggressive, more physical, and that's what I was looking for. Not only did the scrimmages improve the quality of the girls' game, but they also fostered togetherness as a team, as a family. It was with that confidence that I had come to Tiflis, certain that we could play and beat anyone.

Jak was grinning like a cat who had cornered his meal as he watched our girls. With a small lead in the first period, they did not look back as they blew Baku into the Caspian Sea. Jak sauntered over to the Baku bench and shook the coaches' hands. I just sat on my butt and took it all in—an Armenian victory before two thousand Georgian fans. The jubilation was overwhelming.

But it also was short-lived.

The all-Russian Baku boys' squad plastered our team by fifteen points in the nightcap, and I was dazed, shocked, and stunned. Our boys were no match for Baku's stronger, more experienced ball club, which controlled both boards and dominated the game right from the opening tip-off. My inexperience as a coach showed. I should have slowed the tempo, even stalled, but I didn't. My inability to communicate under fire with the kids led to the debacle. Baku made one uncontested basket after another, and there was little I could do about it. We were no match for Baku or Tiflis, which also struck like lightning after the opening tip and buried us with an avalanche of baskets.

Tiflis went on to capture both the boys' and the girls' championships.

I had no excuses. I offered none. I learned a lesson, never to underestimate my opposition. I didn't want to hear any words of sympathy or condolences from Jak. I had failed him, and, more important, I had failed my players. They were in tears after the games, and I could not find the words to console them. Jak told them that it wasn't the end of the world and that there would be tomorrows. *For them, maybe,* I said to myself, *but not for me.* I told Jak afterward, in private, that my coaching career was over, that I was resigning as soon as we got back to Erevan. His response came in a surprised, strange, nervous laugh. He didn't believe me. He said I could not be serious.

"Our kids lost, and you wish to resign?"

"Not because of the loss but because of the way we were humiliated. And there is no one to blame but myself."

"But are you not forgetting that I, too, am responsible for these teams?"

"And I let you down, Jak, I let you down. I can't go back into the gym and look the kids and you in the face anymore. I am a player, not a coach."

He shook off what I said. "This feeling will pass."

I told him it wouldn't. He was silent for a moment, apparently searching for a way to console me. He asked if I thought our team at the Institute could beat the two teams we had just lost to. I replied that we would have had a heck of a time against them; they were that good. I told him that at one moment during the Baku game, I had considered getting dressed and playing myself.

He nodded understandingly. "And how old do you think our opponents were? Sixteen? Seventeen? Maybe eighteen years old?" His eyes darkened as he answered his own question. "Do you not know that our children were playing against those who could have been as old as you?"

"Impossible!"

"Impossible, you say?"

"They had birth certificates, didn't they? Documents. You saw them, didn't you? Why would any coach use ineligible players?"

I remembered watching the opposing teams warm up. I had thought the players on the Tiflis and Baku squads looked older, but I found it difficult to judge in a place like the USSR where so many looked much older than they really were. When I had first met Jak, I had thought he was an old man, but he was only a few years my senior.

"How could they get away with using older players?" I finally asked. "How could they present birth certificates that are fake?"

"No, no, that is not the case here," Jak said with a grin. "Their documents are as accurate as can be determined. And it would be useless to challenge them." Jak noticed the puzzlement on my face and explained, "Our cities were devastated by the war, and the records of millions went up in flames. Many of our children were left homeless, orphaned. Others don't know who their parents are." He paused to allow the information to sink in. Then he continued, "When it came time to round up these children and find families for them, our officials also had to estimate the ages. We had so many orphans, so many problems."

"And what about our children? Are their credentials valid?"

"We were fortunate. The war did not come to us; we went to the war. Our cities were not bombed or destroyed as they were in the north. We sent older brothers and sisters out to the battlefield, and some came back. I remember on one summer afternoon such as this, a German fighter plane flew over Erevan, and the pilot looked down at us. He didn't even waste a bomb or his bullets. He just flew past. The pilot must have thought, 'Why waste a bomb on rocks?'"

Jak's explanation sent me through a wide range of emotions, but it did not change my mind. I reiterated what I had told him earlier, that when we got back to Erevan, I would inform the director that I was resigning, and my explanation would be that I wished to devote all of my time to my classes and playing for the Institute.

"If this is your wish, then so be it. It is your life. But come, Aunt Sonja has prepared a feast for us. Let us get the children together and go."

"Aunt Sonja?" I vaguely remembered a comment about her on the train. But I was physically and mentally worn, not in a mood for meeting new people, so I shook my head and said that I would not be good company, that he and the kids should go without me. I wanted to be alone for a while to think.

"As you please. I will tell Aunt Sonja how impolite Americans are . . . but then, I am sure Tatiana has already told her about you."

"Tatiana? Will she be there?"

"I am almost certain that she will. Did you not hear her say that she was going to visit Aunt Sonja? I would think she would be helping her aunt prepare the food, set the table. But that is no concern of yours, correct?"

"Do I have time to shower and shave?"

Chapter 28

A TUMULTUOUS RELATIONSHIP

As we entered his aunt's palatial home with the entourage of excited and noisy players behind us, Jak took a deep breath as if he recalled other days. He searched the room and spotted his aunt chatting with a group of her guests. He called to her. She immediately left her other guests to rush to her nephew's side. She greeted Jak with a hug and kisses on both cheeks. During the traditional Armenian greeting, I overheard him whisper, *"Americanetz,"* as if it was not obvious. She winked to indicate that she understood and looked around for her niece. Tatiana was nowhere to be found in the crowded room.

Our team members filed in and were introduced to their hostess, but before they rushed to a table filled with every imaginable fruit, Jak made it clear that the vodka and wine were for adults and not to be consumed by them. It was a futile warning, for Armenian children, like the Georgians, were raised on red wines after they were weaned.

I stood at the entrance, my face reflecting awe at what I saw beyond the foyer. There was an immense dining room decorated with Persian and Armenian rugs, framed portraits of ancestors, paintings, and works of art in bronze. Wealth surrounded me, and, as unobtrusively as possible, I took it all in. Despite two world wars, a revolution that toppled a monarch, and a civil war that changed the face of the earth and the way mankind would act for decades to come, this house and its furnishings remained regal.

I did not remember when I had last seen a crystal chandelier in the middle of a dining room. Time had certainly stood still here, and it made me nervous, for I knew that it was said that the bourgeoisie were wiped out in the 1930s. Why was this house immune?

I could identify the languages in conversations that filtered out of the smoke-filled rooms—Georgian, Armenian, and Russian—although the only word I knew in Georgian was *genusvalli*, very good. The talk was nonstop. As soon as one speaker finished a sentence, and sometimes before, another jumped in, raising his voice a notch or two to ensure that those nearby would hear his views.

All had drinks in their hands, and as soon as they consumed one glass, they reached for another. The dining room seemed to attract most of the guests. The men were not wearing military uniforms, so prevalent on the streets of Erevan, in municipal offices, and at Armenian gatherings. Rather, these Armenians, Georgians, and a very few Russians wore open-collared white or blue shirts with their sleeves rolled halfway up, revealing hairy, muscular arms. They wore dark pants and shoes that were not locally manufactured but, I guessed, came from somewhere in Communist-occupied Eastern Europe. All of the men were without neckties, but mustaches were ubiquitous.

The women were well dressed and actually wore makeup. Their lipstick had an orange hue, but the cheeks had a natural rouge to them. I suspected that these women had devoted their lives to the stage and screen. They were fans of Sergei Mikhailovich Eisenstein, worshipped Diaghilev and the Ballet Russe, and knew that Fabergé created more than eggs for Nicholas. They not only read Pushkin, Abovian, and Tolstoy, but they could recite from their works. I looked for portraits of Lenin and Stalin but saw none on the richly painted royal-red walls trimmed with gold borders. I was confused; this seemed to be a direct invitation for a visit by the NKVD. It was obvious that these were not the muscle-bound, big-breasted women who heaved lumber onto trucks or put asphalt down on the roads, as depicted on the pages of European and American newspapers.

This crowd gave lip service to Moscow and Marxist philosophy but would die for anything Western. They had had enough of *"Zafrta budyet kharasho,* it will be better tomorrow." They had somehow made sure that they would have their share of the good life today.

The Georgians had two patron saints installed in the Kremlin— Stalin and Beria, both of Georgian birth—but I didn't think these people believed they needed them to protect their way of life. They felt that they were the chosen people. One did not sense fear of the NKVD in this crowd, as one did in any gathering in Erevan. Armenians shuddered at the thought of an NKVD investigation; Georgians viewed directives from Moscow as farce and did not tremble at Moscow's demands. Let the Russians dream about a better tomorrow; Georgians would enjoy it today.

Aunt Sonja's dining-room table was laden with food I had forgotten existed. The sounds of corks popping from champagne bottles, exploding like balloons at the touch of a needle, could be heard constantly. I wondered if this celebration was really for us and our basketball teams or just another excuse to celebrate.

There were so many questions on my mind, but this was neither the time nor the place to ask them. Jak or Tatiana might be able and willing to answer them later.

Aunt Sonja was dressed in an exquisite floor-length white dress, with diamond rings and a shimmering diamond necklace from the world that had ended on October 26, 1917. She had not been instilled with the proletariat Soviet spirit. She was her own person. And not only did she wear stunning bourgeoisie clothes and fine jewelry, but she also dared to reveal skin, something most Soviet women were reluctant to do. When she turned to me, she grabbed me by both hands, her eyes falling on the sapphire ring that my brother had given me, and she smiled approvingly. With a typical Armenian greeting, *"Pari kaloust,"* she welcomed me to her humble home—her words, not mine.

She whispered, "Do not let them change you, as they have the others." I knew immediately what she meant.

That welcome was followed by an Armenian bear hug and a kiss on the forehead. She stepped back and continued to study me, her dark, sparkling eyes seeking the answer to why I had defected from paradise.

She raised her voice and announced to the crowded room, "This is the American. This one will make the perfect husband for my Tatiana. You devious bitches will keep your hands off of him, do you hear me? Or never again will you be invited into my home."

I tried to control myself, but I couldn't. I burst out in laughter. Only Jak's eyes brought me back to my senses.

The women in the room laughed, too, and, despite the warning, began to approach Jak and me. Aunt Sonja's cautionary remarks, and her outstretched arms and palms, had failed to faze them. They wanted to hear about the United States and whether I knew any long-lost relatives of theirs. Did I know Hollywood film director Rouben Mamoulian? Was it true that Avak the Healer could cure any disease? Did everyone in America own his own house and car? It went on and on, until Jak pronounced, "Enough." He pulled me away, and we walked toward the table. Aunt Sonja accompanied us.

My eyes were drawn to a painting of a young girl. I stopped walking, caught up in her beauty. I thought I recognized the face. She was simply dressed in white, wearing a gold necklace. Her stance was graceful, delicate, and regal all at the same time, but the face held a coquettish smile.

Noticing the puzzled look on my face, Aunt Sonja said, "It's Tatiana. She is beautiful, isn't she? I painted it when she was about sixteen."

"You painted this?" I asked.

"Why, yes, I used to paint a lot—that is, before the war . . ."

"It really is beautiful. But the smile isn't hers."

"It should be sardonic?"

"Sort of."

"It's Tatiana. You can never know what is on that child's mind, and I tried to capture that part of her."

Before her aunt finished the history of the painting, Tatiana was with us. I could feel the blood rush to my face as she greeted us. This time, her smile reminded me of the *Mona Lisa*. In complete juxtaposition, Tatiana spoke caustically the whole time she was there, and when some of her friends walked in, she excused herself.

Although the exchange between us was hostile, I should not have been surprised. After all, we didn't part on good terms in Erevan. But I thought somehow I could make it up to her here, explain myself. She had made it clear that that wouldn't happen. She was cold, rude. I was learning, and learning fast, that men never will understand women. Tatiana had her aunt's good looks, but she did not have her gracious personality.

Aunt Sonja was a petite woman in her mid-fifties. Her obsidian hair had tinsels of white that had been dyed with henna. The red, rather than detracting from her appearance, enhanced it. She could have been a ballerina or an actress, but she had turned to painting, and she was apparently very successful at it. She was a brave woman. In a country where anyone with a foreign tie was suspect, Aunt Sonja had invited me into her home. Not many Soviets opened their doors to foreigners, especially foreigners from the United States. From what I could see, she was a woman who had never known what it was like to wear felt boots with brown woolen stockings and padded Chinese jackets, carrying a small brown net from store to store and standing in long lines for bread and butter. The marketplace came to her; she did not go to it. She knew the good life, no matter who was seated on the czar's jewel-embedded gold throne in the Kremlin or in Saint Petersburg. I could not help but admire her as she switched from Armenian to Georgian to Russian with ease.

But a mystery surrounded her: how could she manage to live in the glass house without the secret police hammering it to pieces? What or who gave her the protection and the privilege to live in splendor when other families, even those who held high posts in the Party, had to wait months, if not years, for living accommodations? And how could she put on the table the caviar, butter, jams of strawberry and grape and rose petals, watermelon rinds, breads such as pita and lavash and the traditional Georgian *khachapuri*, and figs, bananas, pineapples, and the rarest and most precious of all fruits in the Soviet Union, oranges? Oranges were exchanged between Soviet lovers as tokens of affection. There were salads with tomatoes and cucumbers, as well as cucumbers in sour cream, when most of the country saw them only in their dreams. Our hostess called to someone outside to bring us *shaslyk,* and before Jak and I knew it, the plates in our hands were piled high with roasted lamb, roasted tomatoes, and peppers.

As I was busy stuffing my mouth, Jak and his aunt disappeared. I was not left alone for long. Others filled the vacuum and continued to drill me about America. Someone asked if I would like to attend the theater to see an actor named Vahram Papazian in *Othello.* I thanked him for the invitation but explained that we were leaving the next day.

"Horava is the best. You must see him onstage. There is no one like him in the world," several of the guests insisted.

I asked if they had ever seen or heard of Laurence Olivier. None apparently had, but they had seen Tarzan and gangster movies.

I excused myself and made my way to a terrace that overlooked Tiflis. The sun was slowly dipping behind the mountains, casting a brilliant red light through grayish clouds. I loved it there, but I wanted to get back to Erevan, back to playing basketball.

I was mesmerized as I stood in a garden exploding with all the colors of tropical flowers that I had not even known existed. There was a path leading to a cluster of palm trees, and I started to walk toward it, but I stopped when I heard familiar voices on the balcony above me. Jak and his aunt were discussing Jak's mother's health. She was gravely ill, and the doctors had little hope for her. I knew that Jak sometimes rushed from practice to his mother's bedside, but I had never realized how serious the illness was.

"You have done all you can," Aunt Sonja was saying to Jak. "There is nothing more you can do."

I froze, unable to move, when I heard Tatiana's voice. I did not want to violate their privacy, but I couldn't move without being detected, so I stood there and heard Aunt Sonja chastise her niece for her rude behavior.

"Auntie, please," Tatiana said. "You do not understand."

"Understand what? He is a fine young man, and if I were younger . . ."

There was a brief silence, then Tatiana spoke again, softly this time. "Would you have me marry a man who lives in the past, who, if given the opportunity, would fly the nest like a pigeon?"

"A good woman will make sure her man stays home. He is brave, and he is good. How many men do you know who have given up their fathers and their mothers, their families, to make a new life in a strange and godforsaken country like this?"

"That's it, Auntie. He hasn't given them up. He is obsessed! Would you have me waste my life on a man who would turn his back on me as he has on his own family?"

I could feel the life drain from me. I wanted to run, but I could not move. I wanted to hide, but where? I knew Tatiana was right.

Chapter 29

A HOUSE DIVIDED

I sat alone in an open compartment on the train heading back to Erevan, waiting for the train to get under way, watching as passengers shuffled and scuffled in the aisle for the limited number of available seats and listening to their crowlike chatter. The fatigue, the weariness, and the embarrassment of the week were overwhelming. My eyes roamed the platform, for I still harbored an unrealistic belief that Tatiana would board the train to return with me. But all I saw from where I sat were clouds of gray smoke from the train's engine. In the coach, which was rapidly filling, I felt as lonely as I had ever been.

Tiflis had been a disaster, not only careerwise but also for my personal life. The pain of defeat on the basketball court would dissipate as soon as I played my next game. I would take my anger out on my opponents. But the pain that Tatiana had inflicted, her seething pronouncement, would never be erased from my mind. It burned like a branding iron on my skin. I was too self-centered to see the truth. Tatiana was right. I was living in the past. Not a second passed that I didn't think of home, of my family, of my country, the United States of America. I had been away for more than three years, and the only thing I could think about, when I had time to think, was America. I could not, would not, close that door behind me, so I remained a stranger not only in the Soviet Union but also to myself.

I had tried to adjust, to become one of them, but I couldn't, and I couldn't forget. I did not understand them; nor, seemingly, did they understand me. My view of life was vertical, theirs horizontal. I looked up at the stars and saw a universe filled with stars of hope. They looked at the horizon, at the sunrise or the sunset, and saw their enemies attacking them from all sides. They saw evil in everything from the West. Their political philosophy was dogma; they could not tolerate diversity of opinion. They were paranoid and could not understand why I chose to remain an outcast, a pariah in their society.

Jak spent most of his time with our players, who were in adjoining compartments, playing chess or talking about practice and their school-work. I visited and talked about the games, but they wanted to hear about America, a subject that Jak definitely wanted me to avoid. And I did. I just wanted to get back to Erevan. He did not bring up my decision to resign, nor did we discuss his cousin or his aunt. He knew that I had a lot on my mind. If only I had had Machiavelli at my side to guide me, advise me, to get me through that maze. My world was filled with Iagos, and I could not escape from the thought that even Jak could be an informer. It was that thought that he interrupted as he came back from the players and sat down across from me. I had been gazing out the window at the landscape.

"They're exhausted," Jak said. "They'll be glad to get home."

Turning from the window, I looked at Jak and asked sarcastically, "Are you and I friends or not?"

Jak gave me a strange look. He had not seen me in this kind of mood before. He did not answer but reached into his jacket pocket, pulled out a pack of cigarettes, and lit one. With the cigarette on his lips, he reached under his seat, pulled out his valise, and opened it. He took out a bottle of cognac and handed it to me, saying that it was a gift from his aunt to me.

He must have recognized that I was surprised, for I did not immediately respond.

I finally said, "Thank you." Handing the bottle back to him, I added, "Open it. I need a drink. Misery likes company."

He brought out a small jackknife that he always carried in his pocket and carved away the cork with the blade. He returned the bottle to me, and I took a sip, paused a second, took another big swig, then wiped the lip of the bottle with my hand and extended the cognac back to him. With his eyes fixed on me, Jak duplicated my gestures effortlessly. We looked at each other across the small table that was fixed to the window side of the compartment. His face was expressionless; mine quickly flushed. The alcohol had found its way down to the pit of my stomach and was preparing to make its journey back, when Jak, sensing my discomfort, took out some bread, broke off a piece, and ordered me to eat it. The bread plugged the eruption within me, and Jak appeared satisfied that there would be no more repercussions.

"They'll be asleep soon, and maybe then we can talk—that is, if you still want to talk."

"I have so many questions, Jak, and I feel so miserable."

"I understand. My words may not be of any help to you, but I think you should hear them. Where do you want me to begin?" he asked, lifting the bottle again to his lips. After taking another sip, he passed it to me, then relaxed into the seat.

I refused the drink, telling him I had had enough for the moment; there was still a burning sensation in the pit of my stomach. "Begin at the beginning. That would be good."

Chapter 30

QUITTING: NOT AN OPTION

In a very casual tone, which he maintained during the whole conversation despite some heated and emotional moments, Jak told me that I would not be able to resign my coaching position, even if I submitted the paperwork. It would tarnish the careers of several who had supported me. Before I could challenge him and ask the obvious, he leaned forward.

"Hear me out, then the questions."

I sat back, folded my arms across my chest, and pouted, but I did not say a word.

I could not resign, he said with genuine sincerity and concern, because it would reflect poorly upon the judgment of those at the Institute, including himself, who had recommended me for the position.

I snickered. *Bull,* I thought, and went on staring at him. I had suspected, with no clear evidence to support it, that there had been much politicking behind the scenes before the job had been offered to me.

Jak told me that the administration had wanted to appoint a *teghatsi* who had graduated from the Institute and who spoke the two languages of the republic fluently. Jak wanted and got me because he believed in me, he said. It made me uncomfortable to think that he had gone out on a limb for me, but it also deepened my suspicion that Jak was more than a basketball coach. I thought I had gotten the job on my merits; it had seemed that I had. But my ego deflated immediately after he told me otherwise. He reminded me that the approval had come over the vocal and recorded objections of several old-time Party members, who feared I would pollute the minds of the young. Even as he was speaking to me, the objections voiced by Oganoff at the Institute echoed in my mind. Furthermore, Jak said, the onus of my resignation would specifically fall on him, for he had convinced the administration that I was the best person for the job because my technical skills were superior to any he had seen, and "our children must learn from the best." Generally, the Institute's administration bowed to the Party, but Jak had stuck his neck out and told the Party that he personally would see that I would be indoctrinated into the working spirit of the proletariat. If I resigned and my resignation was accepted, it would be an admission on the staff's part, and his, "that we all have failed."

After some moments of silence, he said, "To instill in you the importance of work in our society, and to impress upon you the goals of our society, I am finding a bit difficult. But, given time, I am sure you, too, can learn. The Party does not tolerate failure." He paused, reached for the bottle, and took another drink.

My mind flashed back to the interrogation room, to the NKVD officer sitting across from me, who warned me, "To release you would be tantamount to an admission on our part that the NKVD has erred, that it has wrongly arrested a citizen, someone who was innocent. And the NKVD does not admit to or make mistakes." I could hear Jak's breathing as he sat back and allowed me time to think about the repercussions of my actions. I didn't believe he wanted to hear any reply from me right away, which was fine, because I had no reply at hand.

After a while, he broke the silence. "If this is what you want, then submit your resignation."

Thinking aloud, I said softly, "After what you said, Jak, how the hell could I do that?'

"You are frustrated by our losses in Tiflis. Back in Erevan, they knew what you and I were going up against. We have lost this battle, but there will be others, and now that you know what we are up against,

I am confident that we will prepare aggressively for it. Look at this as our Borodino. Let us retreat for now. The war is not over."

I opened my mouth to comment, but Jak showed me the palms of his hands, and, without losing a beat, he continued, "You may not realize it, but by your display on the playing field, and your coaching style—though a bit bizarre at times, I will admit—you have won over many. There have been Party officials in the gym, even some from Moscow. They came first out of curiosity, just to watch, but left without comment. That was rare, for Russians, like Armenians, like to put in their two kopecks' worth. They definitely liked what they saw, or I would have heard the criticisms from Abrahamian. There was none, except that physically you looked weak. Even when you play, crowds gather to see the American play basketball, to see what an American really looks like. In Tiflis, they didn't stop coming. The crowds showed up not only to watch our games but also to see the American."

"Then I'm a freak. Is that it, Jak?"

Without a change in his voice, he replied, "Yes, in a way, you are a freak. But personally, I feel that you are more like the ugly duckling. Someday, you will find your own way, but for now, you must struggle and adapt to our ways. No other American has ever come this far south in our time. The English and the French were here when Andranik, our heroic general, cut through the Azerbaijani-Kurdish forces. He was about to capture Shushi when they told him he must stop because the war was over and the Paris Conference would resolve all the problems. They said your President Wilson was committed by his Fourteen Points to safeguard Armenian sovereignty. The French and the British betrayed us.

"You have many admirers, and you are proof for many that, despite all of our propaganda, all of our caricatures in our newspapers that depict Americans as fat and ugly, ready to spit atomic bombs upon our cities, it isn't true. You want to live, just as we do. The diehard Communists want us to believe that you want our blood. Some do want your blood, and if you are not careful, they may yet have it. But watching you, knowing you, working with you, I know they are wrong. That they, too, are now convinced that you did not come here to do us harm but to try to understand us. These children you are teaching, coaching, love their country, for they know no other. As they learn from you, you must also learn from them."

Jak's next sentence startled me, for it came in the form of a prophecy, though at the time he said it, I did not believe it. "If and when you go back, I am sure you will go back as a friend of Armenia and the Soviet Union. You will never advocate war against us. The youth will reveal to the man in you that you did somehow change the lives and touch the hearts of many. Tommy, unwittingly, I believe you have put in motion by your presence among us something that only time will decide is important. My life, too, has been changed because of our association."

We were in the mountains by then, past the mile-long tunnel leading to Kirovakan. The shepherds and their flocks were still in the hills as the sun was setting before us. Nothing, except that tunnel, had changed over the years. The czar might be gone, and the Soviets might rule the land, but the mountains and the valleys remained the same.

"If I didn't know better, I would think you were as old as these mountains," I said, looking out the window at the snow-covered caps of the Caucasus.

"At times, I feel it. I grew up not knowing my father and losing my only brother to the war. We don't know if he was killed or was captured or is living in the West, but we assume he is dead. There is no word. Back then, when I was a child, we didn't have electricity, so in the evenings, I would go out into the field where the elders gathered around a bonfire. I heard the stories, mostly sad, mostly about the Turks, how they and we lived in harmony for centuries until those Young Turks ran through the streets of Constantinople shouting, 'Turkey for the Turks!' and Talaat and Enver Pasha inked the documents that sealed our people's fate. I heard of the slaughters, the death marches, and how some survived and reached the Etchmiadzin and Erevan. The death marches. How could they slaughter innocent men, women, and children? And I thought that someday I would raise an army and march back over the mountain and avenge our people. A child's dream. As I was growing up, my mother and father would talk, but when Serosha and I entered the room, they would seal their mouths. They didn't want us to hear about the genocide or the Turks. There was never enough food, never."

Jak reached for the bottle of cognac on the table, drank from it, and handed it to me. I refused and placed it back on the table between us.

"But you, too, probably have heard the stories," Jak continued.

I nodded in understanding.

"Does your mother remember her birthplace?"

"Yes," I said. "Erzurum."

"It is not far from here. Maybe someday you will go to visit."

I chuckled. "In my dreams, maybe."

"There will be a proletariat revolution there, too, someday. You will see. Revolutions and civil wars, that is what our century will be known for—go down in history for." He shook his head. "If only that mountain had not been there, our people would not have suffered so." Ararat was coming into view.

"You mean Mount Ararat?"

"Yes, the Ararat! It has been a curse across the forehead of our people since the time of Noah!"

"A curse?" I tried to study Jak's face to see if it was the cognac in him talking, but outwardly there was no change, and when he continued, his voice was as steady as when we had begun our conversation. All of the Armenians I had encountered to this moment revered Ararat; to curse it seemed almost sacrilegious.

"Don't you understand, that mountain divided us," Jak explained from the shadows of his seat. "It divided us, with half kneeling to the sultans of the Ottoman Empire and the rest kneeling to the czars of Imperial Russia. We were but half a nation. Look upon it as a long and sharp steel blade that has come down on the heads of our people, cutting them in half, spilling our guts and blood upon the soil. If we had been one nation, not divided, no force would have dared to threaten our sovereignty. We know how to fight. Andranik proved that."

"What happened? How could the Turks kill off so many without the West intervening?"

Jak answered, "In World War I, half of our men fought for the Turks, the other half for the Russians. And when the war ended, the Turks decided that we were traitors. And you know what they do to traitors."

I considered what he said for a moment, and it made sense.

Jak sighed. "Forget politics, for we Armenians have been reduced to philosophers and dreamers. Our men sit in parks twirling their thumbs on worry beads, and our women are afraid to come out of their huts. The agony of the past is perpetuated by the society of the present. And none can change it."

I bit my lip and waited to hear what would come next. I knew I needed to be patient if I was to get the answers to my questions.

"No help ever came from the West," Jak said. "It is no secret that our people will never trust them again. If we are to rebuild Armenia, we will have to do it ourselves."

I took the bottle and swallowed the last drop.

A surprised and smiling Jak congratulated me for finishing the bottle. "At least you have learned to drink like an Armenian."

When it came to romance, Jak admitted, he was on thin ice, but he knew his cousin Tatiana. He had watched her grow from a child into an attractive young woman. "From what I see and what I hear, Tatiana adores you."

By this time, I was drunk, but I held on. I figured Jak didn't know anything about Tatiana and me. "If this is true, she surely has a strange way of showing it," I told him.

"How else can you expect her to react to you? She is torn between two desires. She loves her country and has been taught to hate America because of what it stands for. She hates the American in you; even the opera *Madame Butterfly* is about American betrayal of love and honor. She is very confused. You, apparently, have said something that gives credence to what she believes about Americans. Why should she invest her time in someone who can only hurt her?"

I did not tell Jak that I had overheard the discussion in the garden.

Jak's eyes met mine. "But she continues to have feelings, or she would not be outraged when your name comes up."

"And what am I supposed to do, Jak?"

"There is nothing you can do until you make up your mind about who you are and where you want to spend your life."

I looked at him in surprise.

"It is indifference that crushes all relationships. Not love. Not hate. Indifference. Plain and simple. She loves and admires you one moment and hates and wishes she had never met you the next. Can you blame her? You can frustrate people! I believe that is why people are yet to understand you. What little I know of women—and that amounts to a drop of water in the ocean—is that in affairs involving passion, women usually pick their words to express their inner thoughts and their love, whereas men use words to conceal their true feelings. You, Tommy, frustrate her, and who wants to be around someone who frustrates them?"

"She frustrates me, too!" I replied.

"Then it's mutual, isn't it? You two have something to build on. Live a life of frustration! Can you two be happy frustrating each other?"

"I don't mind, but not here. In America!"

Jak showed no reaction to my flip comment; he seemed to have anticipated my response. I wanted to say something more, but he continued, "My cousin is suspended between two worlds. She has lived in one all of her life and is devoted to it. She wants to become a prima ballerina. And she has the talent to do so. She is familiar with the first world and has been taught to be fearful of, even despise, the other. The very mention of the world you come from makes her nervous. Yet, despite all, she must have pursued you and not you her. I say this because if she had approached her father on this subject, he would have immediately put a stop to this relationship. On the other hand, you pine for America, which is natural, and you do not understand the ways of our women. Time will correct that. Two determined people with two completely different backgrounds and ideas are brought together in one place, and . . ."

"And?" I asked, hoping, almost expecting, that he had some sort of solution to my dilemma.

"If you were nations, you would be at war, but because you are both young and beautiful, you try to hurt each other."

"And where will it end, Jak?"

"Ah, where will it end, you ask? I am not a soothsayer. Both smitten. Both confused. Both afraid of what a commitment to each other would do. She wants it her way, and she can't have it, so she seeks to escape on the stage. You rush onto the basketball court and into the gym and hope to forget her and the outside world. I cannot write the final scene. It will be up to you two to decide."

"Damn you, Jak. That's not fair."

He nodded. "Neither love nor war is fair."

His face paled as he went on to reveal that Tatiana had yet another obstacle: her father. "She loves and respects him, and she would never disobey his wishes. He has fought vehemently to defend the country from its enemies, and her two brothers, whom she adored, gave their lives for it. Do you think you can tear this little princess away from her castle without her father unleashing his fire-spewing dragons to destroy you?"

Jak leaned back against the wood of the bench but kept his eyes steadily on me as I asked him, "Who is Tatiana's father? Who is your uncle?"

For the first time, I could see a change in Jak's expression. His high cheekbones were flushed. I even felt nervousness in my stomach after I asked the question. I didn't even know why I wanted to know. This relationship had been doomed from the start. It could not get any worse. Why did I want to know about her father?

When Jak spoke, it was almost in a whisper. "There is something I would like to tell you so that you will understand that our discussion will go no further than this place. These are family secrets, and Tatiana probably has never heard them, unless, of course, my aunt may have revealed them to her. But I sincerely doubt that because of the nature of the conflict."

Jak reached for his jacket and his pack of cigarettes. After lighting one and taking a few puffs, he seemed to relax. He proceeded slowly, and I felt he was debating with himself about what he really wanted to share with me.

"Let us say only that my uncle holds a high post in the security sector of the government and that I rarely see him, even when he is in Erevan. My mother does not welcome him at our doors, but the doors of the Kremlin are always open to him. Moscow has always respected his work and his opinions. They have bestowed upon him many honors."

I reflected about the benefits one would have with ties to the Kremlin. "That is not telling me much, Jak." I began to think that Jak was trying to change the subject.

"Do you know what a Dashnak is?" he asked.

"Yes."

The word *Dashnak* startled me. It was rarely, if ever, voiced publicly in Soviet Armenia. My uncles were Dashnaks, and my father refused to let his younger brothers into his house. The Dashnaks believed in a free and independent Armenia.

Jak continued, "My father was a member of the Dashnakzagan Party and believed that all true Armenians should fight for a free and independent Armenia. His brother, Tatiana's father, happened to be a Bolshevik, and there was constant bickering between the two houses."

"Brother against brother," I interrupted, and added that it was not unlike the American Civil War, when some family members fought to end slavery, while others fought to defend the practice. The United States had been a house divided.

"Yes, it was like that here, too. Father against son, son against father, brother against brother. A house divided." He resumed his story. "My father wanted a free and independent Armenia, and his younger brother opposed it and favored having a 'Big Brother' over us, to protect us. Many believed that we did need a stronger nation to protect our interests after what the Turks had done to us. Our enemies were forty million strong at the time; our people had been scattered to the four corners of the earth. There were only a few left to fight, and they, brave as they were, were mostly without weapons. Uncle used to tell me that Armenians had become a bunch of philosophers, intellectuals, and hard workers but stupid when it came to choosing their leaders. They fought among themselves. So he turned north and went to Russia and became a Bolshevik."

"So the Bolsheviks won, and all is history, isn't it, Jak?"

"No, no, the Dashnaks won."

"The Dashnaks won?"

I thought the cognac had finally gotten to him, but Jak went on. "Armenia managed to establish a republic after the collapse of the Ottoman and Romanov Empires, but it was short-lived, 1919 to 1920. My father, for his dedication, was appointed to a key post in the newly formed government and was involved with much of the negotiations and setting up commerce and industry and seeking foreign assistance. Incidentally, America and Europe promised to assist us but never fulfilled their promises. While the Armenians on the other side of Ararat were being slaughtered by the Turks and trying to get over the mountain to Erevan, my father was busy helping with the rescue efforts.

"His brother, Tatiana's father, fled from the Caucasus, eventually reaching Moscow, where he joined the party of Lenin and married a Russian. He came back as part of the Red Army that fought Enver Pasha's invading armies. Yes, the Turks even marched into western Armenia. The Red Army eventually turned the tide, ousted the Turks, and crushed the Dashnaks, who were removed from government and replaced by the Soviets and their commissars. Many Dashnaks who managed to escape formed opposition parties; they organized groups abroad to fight the Soviet takeover. But my father refused to go. He stayed here. He did not fear the Turks or the Bolsheviks. My father paid the price for fighting on the wrong side. Tatiana's father went on to military school and became an officer and distinguished himself against the Nazis."

I tried to figure out a timeline of the events and could not.

Jak gave me an answer. "My mother was pregnant with me when the Cheka came and dragged my father out of our home. Yes, it was one of those night arrests. My mother refused to talk about it. Needless to say, she abhors her brother-in-law, for she feels he could have used his position to save his brother. My mother has been sick ever since. I never knew my father."

Did any of us know our fathers? I wondered. "You said you had an older brother." I was trying to put the pieces together.

"He never came back from the front. He died fighting the Nazis. Mother believes that God has sent you to replace him."

I felt a weakness come over me, unlike any I had ever felt. We sat in silence looking out the window.

Then Jak asked, "Do you have any other questions?"

"I have only one."

"And that is?"

"Your aunt didn't give you another bottle, did she?"

Chapter 31

A CALL TO THE EMBASSY

I stood in the glass-enclosed public telephone booth clutching several fifteen-kopeck coins. My hand trembled as I dropped the first coin into the slot and slowly dialed the number to the U.S. Embassy. I waited nervously for the voice on the other end. None came. I could hear ring after ring after ring, and no one picked up the phone. My anxiety increased. Did I dial the wrong number? I must have an answer. I hung up.

Seconds passed, and I debated whether I should try again. *I have to do this. I have to know.* I had overcome the fears of another confrontation with the NKVD. I knew, after three and a half years of Soviet life, that the NKVD monitored everything and that they would pay special attention to a call to the embassy. But I had to risk it. The rest of my life depended on it. I had to hear directly from the consulate whether there was even a slim chance I could return home.

Indeed, standing there, directly across from the Kremlin, I knew I was standing in quicksand. As prosecutor-to-be Jak, now a senior at the university majoring in law, repeatedly reminded me, "It is a serious offense for a Soviet citizen to contact a foreign power. You would get off with a lighter sentence if you were convicted of raping a woman instead of being accused of being involved in a political plot against the state."

After three and a half years of living among the Soviets, I still didn't consider myself a Soviet, and the Soviets with whom I came in contact, as well as my basketball fans, didn't consider me one of them, either. A sure sign was that they didn't address me by my first and patronymic names. I was always Amerikanski Tom (pronounced "tome").

In spite of all of Jak's and my repatriated teammates' warnings to stay clear of political discussion and entanglement, unless I was berating the United States, I still was determined to contact the embassy. My friends continued to tell me that I should feel fortunate, that I was living above the standards of a Soviet worker. They did not understand the value of freedom. I remained tight-lipped on all political issues and vented my frustrations with the world on the basketball court.

I still shared the third-story apartment with Simonian. My steel bed, with its razor-thin mattress, plus a chair and a table donated to me by the French artel, made up my modest area of the apartment. I was a bachelor who was strong enough to live the Spartan Soviet way with no serious romantic ties. I had rubles earned from coaching basketball and playing basketball and from my stipend as a student. But rubles were worthless when there was little to purchase, as foreign correspondents and Western European statesmen stressed in article after article about Soviet consumers. A typical observation was made by Frank Rounds Jr. in *Window on Red Square:* "Like silent, black, purposeful ants—lonely crowds spilling over from narrow sidewalks into the gutters. . . . They pack all the stores and shops. . . . Buying anything, everything in sight. But, actually, there is very little to buy in this entire array of retail trade establishments. . . . But the Russian, resigned as he is, always has hope that there will be a little more available on the shelf on his next visit."

If Moscow, the Soviets' showcase, had so little to offer its consumers, what did the distant regions of this vast country have to offer?

As a junior in college and now an established Soviet ball player, I vowed that I was not going to wait for that special day of Soviet salvation, *"Zahftra boodit harosho.* Tomorrow will be better." For the Soviet worker and farmer, it had not gotten better after the war or during the early years of the 1950s. Things were worse. Lend-Lease not only gave them tanks and guns but food. And when the USSR and the People's Republic of China signed a nonaggression and mutual cooperation pact, it put not more but less bread in the local stores. In the wake of the Berlin blockade, in the midst of the Korean conflict, with Russia now in possession of the atom bomb, the Cold War had intensified. American financier and philanthropist Bernard Baruch, chief of the U.S. delegation to the UN Atomic Energy Commission, put it this way: "We are in the midst of a Cold War which is getting hotter."

I was in the frying pan, set to jump into the fire.

My high school classmates and my relatives were fighting and being wounded in Korea. Why was I not with them? And when I got back, how would I ever face them?

While the fighting in Asia intensified, the repatriates were betting that the confrontation between East and West would lead to war between former allies. Americans were not only concerned about the "Red Menace," but they were standing in line to get copies of the Department of Defense's 438-page manual on how to prepare for an atomic-bomb attack. There were those who were also busy building what they thought were atom-bomb-proof shelters, right in their backyards. After all, General Hap Arnold, who had molded the U.S. Air Force into one of the most powerful striking forces in history, said, "Another war would be the destruction of mankind."

I was getting the news but was tight-lipped, for no one trusted anyone where Big Brother was alive and well.

French repatriates, who had lived through the Nazi occupation, again tuned their shortwave radios to the BBC and the Voice of America broadcasts, getting some information despite the jamming of the airways by the Soviets. They relayed the news to us from across the courtyard, and though Simonian urged me not to listen, I could not resist. Although many of the Voice's English newscasts were jammed, the Soviets allowed the Americans one luxury. The "Hit Parade" got through, and I would join the Alexanians—Dave, Takouhi, and their son, Jeannot—to listen to the songs. I reciprocated by giving them the flour, sugar, butter that I received as an athlete.

Athletes, who remained apolitical, and the elite intelligentsia, especially the artists, writers, and composers of the pre-Khrushchev period, knew they had to glorify Stalin, especially his role as the master architect of the victory in the Great Patriotic War, if they wanted funds to continue their work. The brave among the most talented, those who dared to deviate from promoting the New Soviet Man, at best found their careers in a bureaucratic maze never to move forward, ridiculed by the Party and the state-controlled press and having their work ostracized by those who knew little or nothing of art. These talented people became outcasts. If they persisted, they were dragged off to concentration camps for rehabilitation. If they survived in camp, they ended up painting portraits of dying *zeks* (political prisoners) or landscapes or tundra near the Arctic Circle.

What the NKVD saw in me that spared me from a one-way ticket to hell, why they allowed me to play before thousands and teach their children by the hundreds and move among their elite, I did not know, and I never would. The mystery might be hidden in some former KGB member's desk file. It left me tending toward mood swings; the scars and the pain would remain always.

I wanted a second chance, and I wanted to know if America would give it to me.

That was why I stood in the shadows of the Kremlin and the colorful cupolas of Saint Basil's, dialing the U.S. Embassy number again.

I waited.

~ THE INSTITUTE'S basketball team had been invited by the Ministry of Physical Culture and Sports to send a basketball team to Vilnius, the capital of Soviet Lithuania. We were to compete in a national collegiate tournament. I made the trip with the team. It would be my first glimpse of Moscow. We changed trains there to get to Lithuania.

On the return trip, I asked my coach, with other teammates present, for permission to stay in Moscow for a few days. I said that I had heard that I could call home to Detroit from the central telephone office.

I was not surprised when Konstantin Nikitich raised his voice and shouted in my face, *"Nyet!"* I needed and wanted that answer in front of the others so that he would have witnesses who would support his story. I repeated my request to stay behind as the train from Vilnius pulled into Moscow.

"I would like to call my parents," I explained to the coach. "I'm concerned. I have not heard from my family in years."

There were no direct phone lines from Armenia, or any other part of the country, to the United States. If I wanted to call home, I had to call from Moscow, almost two thousand miles from Erevan.

Konstantin Nikitich refused to yield. "You," he said, lowering his voice this time, "and this team are all my responsibility. You have come with the team; you will return with the team. There can be no further discussion of this."

"Yes," I retorted, and moved to get out of his way.

Thank God he said no.

If he had said yes, and my plan was successful, with the embassy helping me to return home, it could be construed by the NKVD that my coach had provided me with an opportunity to escape, and he would be culpable. I was determined to contact consulate officials and hear for myself the status of my citizenship, and I alone would have to suffer the consequences of my actions. The Soviets never saw things that way.

I intentionally missed the train to Erevan, hailed a cab, and asked the driver to take me to a centrally located hotel. I had ample funds and, by then, a solid understanding of the language. I would have no problem finding my way around any city in the Soviet Union.

The cab driver suggested Hotel National. That was fine. I tossed my suitcase into the backseat and jumped in. As we drove, he eyed me in the mirror. I assumed he wanted to know where I was from. I didn't offer any information. He was stumped. Our conversation was cordial, in Russian, and dotted with questions about me. My answers were polite and one-worded. Was I Lithuanian? "No." Maybe German? "No." First time in Moskova? "Yes." Then he described the Hotel National. Excellent hotel. Excellent restaurant. Great big windows facing the Kremlin.

"Lenin has slept there," the driver said.

"With whom?" I asked, recoiling myself at the absurdness of my question. One didn't malign a Soviet god.

The cab driver took his eyes off the road and turned to study me, and for a second, I thought he would pull over and invite me to get out of the vehicle. Instead, he burst out laughing.

"You American, no?"

"Yes. I am American." I did not feel that I was lying, for I still did consider myself American.

"Met many American *saldaht*, soldiers, at Elbe. Only American say that about Lenin."

I thanked him for excusing my faux pas.

We chatted all the way to the hotel about America, about the realities and the possibilities of another war, and about the Americans he had met.

"Do you have chewing gum? Maybe Camel? Smoke, no?" He put his fingers to his lips to indicate cigarettes.

"Sorry," I said, "but I didn't bring any with me on this trip. Maybe next time."

"Good. Next time."

We drove in silence for a few more miles, and then he reminded me, "We fought Nazis together. We not fight each other now. No more wars, right?"

"Right! Americans do not want war."

We reached Red Square and whizzed past Lenin's mausoleum.

"You speak pretty good Russian for an American."

I thanked him.

"You want vodka?" Before I could answer, he pulled a bottle from under his seat, popped the cork with his mouth, and passed the bottle back to me. "Take. Drink. Drink to peace and good health."

I did. I felt the sting in my throat and pretended that it was stronger than it really was. As I thanked the driver again and handed back the bottle, he nodded, as if surprised.

"You drink pretty good for an American, too."

When he deposited me at the curb of the hotel, I got out some rubles to pay him, but the driver refused to take the money. I felt guilty. Had I not given him enough? I added to the pot. He refused to take the fare.

"*Mir. Druzba*. Peace. Friendship."

I raised my hands to indicate that I wanted him to wait, took out my wallet, and pulled out one of the seven single dollar bills I had left. I handed it to him.

He looked at it, turned it over, and, with a wide grin on his face, said, "American dollar! *Spasiba*."

"Something to remember America by," I said.

He drove off, waving the dollar bill out the window

Moscow's not bad, I thought.

I looked around. There was the Kremlin. And from where I stood, I had a glimpse of Red Square. I turned to face a gray stone building on the corner of Gorky and Mokhovaya.

It was late afternoon when I strolled into the hotel lobby. A lone clerk sat erect in a black leather chair behind a grand mahogany desk at the far end of the lobby. Between us was an elegantly furnished lobby, the floor of which was marble, with several ornate Persian and Armenian rugs near arched doorways that led, to my delight, to a pastry shop at the right and a barbershop at the left. A gigantic crystal chandelier hung in the center of the lobby, and to the left of the desk clerk was a marble staircase adorned with a royal-red carpet that climbed like a vine to a mezzanine, from which soft chatter and clanking plates could be heard. My eyes followed the stairs to the second floor, where I expected to see Scarlett O'Hara waiting for me with arms outstretched. Instead, a dark-skinned sinister Boris Karloff look-alike with a clean-shaven head, dressed in a black suit, stared back at me. Upon seeing this specter, my first thought was that Hollywood was remaking *The Tower of London* there.

Though my clothes were superior to those of the Russian on the street, they still were the originals I had brought with me. They looked as if they belonged in a low-end resale shop. I was wearing a wrinkled, worn-down double-breasted gray gabardine suit that had not been to a cleaner in three and a half years and a grayish shirt that was once white, collar opened, no tie, of course. The shirt, too, had lasted since the day I stepped off the ship. I still wore my Thom McAn shoes, which had been repaired at least three times and would have been rejected by the hobos of the Depression; I refused to wear Russian felt boots. Usually, I wore gym shoes, but they were on their last leg, too.

I walked slowly toward the woman with the golden hair behind the desk and stopped before her. As she sized me up, I wondered why I was there.

"What do you want?" she asked in Russian as I put my suitcase on the floor.

"If you have any vacancies, I would like a room," I said in English.

She invited me to take a cushioned chair in front of her.

"Yes, of course. And for how long will you stay?" she asked, taking out the registration form that had to be filled out and forwarded to the local law-enforcement office. "We have not seen many Americans lately."

"A week. No more than a week."

"Business in Moskova, *gaspadin?*"

"No business, sightseeing," I replied.

She had addressed me as a foreigner, and I didn't offer to explain that I was a Soviet citizen, for fear that she might not give me a room.

"Tourist?" she asked.

"Sort of."

"We have very few American tourists these days. Very good."

My charade ended with her next request.

"Passport, please."

"Passport?"

"Da. Passport."

I dug into my inside jacket pocket, pulled out my Soviet passport, and handed it to her. Upon seeing the document, her face dropped faster than a falling star. She looked up at me, then stared down at the photo in the document, and raised her tone a notch as she declared, "You Soviet citizen?" More of a statement than a question.

"Yes," I replied. "I am a Soviet citizen who speaks English better than I do Russian. Is that a problem?"

She considered my answer. "No problem." But her blue eyes darted up the stairway to where the man in black was listening. She filled in the blanks on the registration form and paused at nationality. "You are Armenian, a Soviet Armenian. You reside in Erevan," she said. She seemed to doubt that the bearer of the passport was who he said he was.

"Look. I am Armenian. I was born in Detroit, in America. I repatriated to the Soviet Union. Are my rubles not as good as anyone's? If you do not want to give me a room, tell me where the nearest hotel is that will, and I will go."

My comments seemed to confuse her more than ever.

She leaned back in her chair, took a deep breath, and said, "This is unusual. Very unusual. We do not have many English-speaking Armenians staying with us. But, of course, you are welcome. But you do not look Armenian, and I have many Armenian acquaintances and friends."

"There is also another possibility."

She was now staring at me intently, perhaps thinking that I would confess to being an impostor.

"There is," I said, "the possibility that my mother may have fooled around with an American. Who knows?"

She nodded. I didn't like that she agreed. I waited nervously for her to say that the hotel was reserved only for diplomats, foreign correspondents, and *mizhdunarodnaya,* international tourists, and that I might have better luck at the Metropole, which was down the street. She didn't. She completed the necessary paperwork, reminded me that she had to forward my passport to the regional militia, and handed me the key to a room. I sighed in relief.

Before I went to my room, I asked where the Central Telephone Office was, and she told me it was close to the hotel. I should turn left onto Gorky, and it was only a few blocks. I did not dare ask her the telephone number of the U.S. Embassy, but she did offer me information. Only a few years ago, the U.S. Embassy had been housed in the hotel. The quarters had moved to some other location.

She glanced again at my passport and said, "Tom Boghosovich, you are very *internesnaya*. Maybe you can find time for us to talk."

I said I would be glad to.

"My name is Maria Petrovna. If I can assist you with anything, do not hesitate to ask," she said. "There is a *dejernia* on duty at all times on your floor. Tomorrow will be another administrator. I will be on duty the following day. Maybe then I will see you."

I thanked her again, and as I started up the stairs, I looked back at her.

She asked, "Problem?"

"No, but is there a shower or bathtub in my room?"

"Of course, of course. This is the National. Do you not know that Lenin has slept here?"

I smiled and climbed the staircase two steps at a time. I had a bathtub, a real bathtub, for the first time since I had left the United States.

Now, if only there was a toilet, too, I would be in paradise. There was.

I dared not call the embassy from my room. I was almost certain it would be bugged. A day or two later, I got the number from Maria Petrovna, who would become my patron saint and protector during my frequent stays in Moscow over the next decade.

I had walked from the hotel, to and through the GUM department store, looking for a secluded niche from which to made the call.

Now I picked up the telephone again, listened for a dial tone, dropped a coin into the slot, and hoped that this time someone at the embassy would answer. *Please, damn it, someone pick up the telephone.*

I broke out in a cold sweat as a woman's voice announced, "U.S. Embassy. Can I help you?"

I tried to say something, but my voice failed. The woman repeated the question. I had waited more than three years for this moment, and I had practiced over and over what I would say, and the words would not come out of my mouth.

"Can I help you?" the voice repeated.

"Please. I am an American living in the Soviet Union. I want to go back home."

There was a very long silence.

"You say you are an American?"

"Yes!" I said several times, raising my voice each time.

"Please wait on the line, and I'll get someone you can talk to."

Seconds later, I heard a man's voice ask, "May I help you?"

"God, I hope so." I told him my story, that I had repatriated with a group of Armenian Americans, that I had been nineteen at the time. "Please, I want to go home, back to America. My parents, my brothers, and my sister still live there. I want to come to the embassy . . ."

"Do you have your American passport?" the man asked.

"No. I was never issued one."

"And you say you repatriated?"

"Yes!" I took a deep breath. "In 1947. I didn't know what I was getting into. I want to meet with someone and discuss going back."

"Do you have an exit visa?"

"What the hell is an exit visa?"

"Permission from the Soviet government to leave the country."

"No. No!"

Another pause. Then he said, "If you don't have an American passport, and you haven't obtained an exit visa from the Soviets . . . You have been here long enough to understand there could be some serious problems if we met."

"I don't care! I want to go back to America!"

"You've been here long enough to know what can happen," he repeated in a more serious tone. "There is really nothing the consulate can do for you at the present. I'm sorry. Very sorry. Good luck." He hung up, and all I could hear was the humming sound.

Shaken, I stood in the booth, staring at the telephone. His words echoed in my ears. "There is nothing we can do for you, you have to get an exit visa." The words rolled around in my head and made me dizzy. I knew I had to get out of there. I knew that whatever an exit visa was, the Russians would not issue me one. I had about as much chance of obtaining an exit visa from the Soviets as I did of flying to the moon.

I was stuck in the Soviet Union, and only God knew for how long.

Well, fuck the USA, fuck the USSR, fuck the world!

I slammed the booth door, shattering the glass into a million pieces. For a second, I stood there stunned at what I had done. I remembered what Jak had told me during one of our chess games, that vandalism was a capital offense. Destroying state property could lead to long-term prison. And that was all I needed.

I ran back into the GUM, shoving swarms of people aside, and disappeared into the crowds.

My U.S. citizenship was not renegotiable. The Soviets believed I was a sleeper. Where could I go from here?

"Let me have a bottle of vodka," I told the Hotel National waitress as I slipped into a chair at a table next to one of the windows overlooking the Kremlin.

"A bottle?"

"Yes, a bottle."

"Will there be anyone joining you, *gaspadin?*"

"I hope not."

She returned shortly with the bottle and placed it and a glass before me. I poured myself a drink as she watched. It went down, and she moved away. The next and the next, and suddenly I was in Mrs. Hale's world literature class at Southwestern High School, standing before my class, reciting Sir Walter Scott:

> *Breathes there the man with soul so dead,*
> *Who never to himself hath said,*
> *"This is my own, my native land!"*
> *Whose heart hath ne'er within him burned*
> *As home his footsteps he hath turned*
> *From wandering on a foreign strand?*
> *If such there breathe, go, mark him well;*

For him no Minstrel raptures swell;
High though his titles, proud his name,
Boundless his wealth as wish can claim;
Despite those titles, power, and pelf,
The wretch, concentred all in self,
Living, shall forfeit fair renown,
And, doubly dying, shall go down
To the vile dust from whence he sprung,
Unwept, unhonor'd, and unsung.

I sat staring at my glass.

The waitress returned and asked, "Is there anything else?"

I looked up into her beautiful blue eyes and muttered, "Yes, please bring me another bottle of vodka. And if you can find me someone I can cuddle with tonight, I'd appreciate it. I don't want to be alone."

She chuckled and said in a soft, sympathetic voice, "I understand. I can arrange for someone to cuddle with you, but if you continue to drink vodka, that is about all you will be good for tonight."

Chapter 32

DROWNING MY SORROWS

During the day, I walked aimlessly on the streets of Moscow, and in the evenings, I drank myself to sleep. I did not know what to do and did not care what happened to me. The Soviets controlled the chessboard, and I dreaded the new reality that I would never be able to leave the Soviet Union and return to my native land. I had never wondered what it would be like to be a man without a country, but after that call to the embassy, I felt like one. I could not damn the consulate; after all, I was reaping what I had sowed. I had turned my back on the flag that my brothers fought for, the flag my cousin Dave was wounded on Iwo Jima defending. How could I have done that? And without even knowing it. How stupid.

I hoped that the NKVD would arrest me and put me out of my

misery. I was certain they knew my every movement. Ironically, the people on the street averted their eyes as I walked by, considering this foreigner invisible.

Twice I had walked past the Central Telephone Office on Gorky, and twice I hadn't entered the building. Reason buried emotion.

Call home, my feelings urged.

Reason answered, *Why? What would you say? Give them false hope, when you know you will never be free? You are trapped here behind this Iron Curtain. Have you not caused enough pain to those you purport to love so dearly?*

And when the vodka sank even deeper into my bowels, I became sinister. I saw plots. Why would anyone tell me to seek out the Soviets for a solution? The American consulate surely knew what happened to those citizens, Soviet and foreign, who expressed a desire to leave the country. Even some passport-issued American citizens who left the embassy had been swept off the streets, shoved into NKVD vehicles, and illegally detained for weeks, if not months and years. That advice from whoever was on the other end of the telephone would surely lead to my arrest.

I dreaded the thought of returning to Erevan

Would it not be far, far better for me to end it here? Only the will, drilled into me by my coaches back home, to keep on playing no matter what the odds kept me going. *I will win,* I said to myself. *I am not a loser.*

Back I must go to Erevan, where I knew I would have to answer to my superiors. I had alienated my coach by staying behind. I had disobeyed his orders. My job at the Pioneers' Palace was lost, and how could I ever look into the eyes of my teammates?

But back I must go.

~ FEELING AS if I were crawling on my hands and knees, I walked up the stairs to the second floor of the Institute, where I had been summoned by Konstantin Nikitich and Oganoff to explain why I disobeyed a direct order from my coach. Of course, they wouldn't buy "I missed the train."

I was willing to face any punishment but did not even consider that they might drop me from the team. I was wrong, as usual.

Anahaid, whose face was as white as a ghost's, greeted me. She spoke in an icy and hostile tone. "I have been asked to take you to the director of the Institute's office," she said. "I would prefer taking you to the gates of hell. You deserve no better, Tom Boghosovich, for you are an idiot!"

I did not respond. I expected the criticism.

"Konstantin Nikitich and Comrade Oganoff are also there waiting for us." Over and over, she asked as we climbed the stairs to the office, "How could you? How could you?"

We walked as if we were in a funeral procession—my funeral.

"Anahaid, I did not do anything to harm anyone but myself," I said. We stopped on one of the steps.

"Nothing? Nothing? Then why did they come?"

"Who?"

"You are an idiot to ask that question. They have been in and out of this building. Don't you understand what you have done? You would jeopardize the lives and welfare of all of these good people, these people who have befriended you. Do not think they do not know why you stayed back, whom you met, where you went in Moscow."

I was sure Anahaid was referring to the NKVD, but she did not use the agency's name.

"They have been crawling all over this place, asking questions. Your foolish, selfish actions have placed all of us under suspicion. Do not think that if Moscow believes this is a hornet's nest for student activists and foreign propagandists to hide, they would not exterminate us. Look what happened to the Chechens. To the Tartars. To the *kulaks!*" By now, she was shouting at me.

The door to the director's office opened. My coach stepped out into the corridor to see what the commotion was about. He greeted me coldly but cordially. It seemed a lifetime since I had last seen him. He spoke a few soft words to Anahaid, trying to calm her. He led me into the office and asked Anahaid to stay in the outer room.

She managed to whisper under her breath, "You keep your mouth shut. Say nothing, do you hear?"

I nodded.

I felt the tension in the room. The director told me to sit down and indicated a chair directly across from him. The coach and Oganoff sat to the right and left of the director.

"You have been a commendable student," the director began. "You not only excelled in the classroom but on the basketball court." Then his face turned grave. "But . . ."

I waited for the ax to fall.

"But you have violated a trust all of us have put in you, and you have put the Institute in a very difficult position." As he slowly sank back into his black-cushioned seat, he continued, "You were told, were you not, that you could not remain behind in Moscow by Konstantin Nikitich?"

I nodded.

"But you did, did you not?"

I nodded again.

"To be victorious in any endeavor, there must be discipline. On athletic teams, in our schools and factories, and in our society—I would say in any society—discipline is a key to success. Would you not agree?"

I didn't say a word, only nodded.

"Did you disobey a direct order given by your superior?"

I answered that I did.

"Then you admit that you disobeyed your coach's orders not to stay behind, when he told you that he was responsible for the team, the entire team, and that you must return home with the team. If something had happened to you in Moscow, how do you think your coach would feel? How could he answer to your family? To this Institute?"

"Yes, I did disobey him, and I am truly sorry for what I did," I said. Directing my eyes to my coach, I told him I was sorry.

"That is a good start, but it is not enough, I'm afraid. We understand that you have returned to the homeland without your parents. We have made allowances for you and your behavior, but we can't overlook what you have done."

There was silence in the room.

"You will be suspended from the Institute; therefore, you will no longer be a member of the team. We have no alternative but to carry this out immediately."

I stared back at the director, then at my coach, who glanced away, and then at Oganoff, who seemed sad.

I turned to my coach, who had taken out a cigarette and lit it, and apologized again. Then I did the same to Oganoff and the director.

The director looked at me and seemed sincere when he said, "Tom Boghosovich, I am truly sorry. But rules cannot be broken—by anyone. We hope that you can learn by this experience."

"I understand. I am sorry for the trouble I have caused you and everyone else."

I stood up and was about to leave the room when Oganoff asked, "Why, Tom Boghosovich, would you do such a thing? We have done everything to make you comfortable here. We understand you are a special case, but there is such a thing as loyalty."

My voice was trembling as I replied, "I deserve no less for what I have done. And I want to thank you for what you have done for me."

Then, somehow, these words came out of my mouth: "Is it wrong for a son to want to speak to his mother whom he dearly loves? To his father whom he has not heard from or seen for more than three years? Is it wrong for a son to want to be with his family? His loved ones?" I took a deep breath. "I have been an obedient son all of my life. I have obeyed my father and carried out his wishes. I am here; they are there, in a country you call the enemy. I have repaid my parents and my loved ones with tears and pain. I am sorry that I have disappointed you and my teammates."

I was weary. As I closed the door to the office behind me, Anahaid rushed to my side, and I brushed her away. I wanted to go back to my apartment. I wanted to nail the door shut, never to see or talk to another human being for as long as I lived.

Oh, God! You spared Isaac, why in heaven's name did you spare me?

Chapter 33

SOVIET PARADISE LOST

I had hit rock bottom—again. This time, there was no bouncing back. I submitted my resignation to the Pioneers' Palace, was suspended from the Institute for insubordination, and would not be eligible to play on the basketball team. True, there were other organizations, such as Locomotive, Spartak, even Dynamo, that could use my services, but that was unlikely, since they would face the wrath of the Institute and the Party.

I was sidelined, and the worst part was that I would have no income, and I did not know when I would be permitted to get back in the game. It also hurt that my former teammates kept away. I was certain they were doing so on directives from Oganoff. Guilt by association. I would learn later that each of them had been questioned by the NKVD, which was trying to determine whether they knew I had planned to stay in Moscow.

Haratoun Simonian, my wise and gentle roommate, still remained very much in my life. He looked much older and paler, and he moved much more slowly, and when I asked whether he was sick, his terse reply was, "It's these damned cigarettes."

"Why don't you give them up?" I asked innocently.

"Can't. They keep me moving. Keep me alive."

From where I could see, it didn't look as if they would be keeping him moving or alive much longer. But I never seriously gave it a thought. He was there morning and night; in between, he cut hair. At the break of dawn, Simonian got up and heated the water for tea. When the tea was ready and the toast was burned, he pulled back the covers on my cot and told me to get up. At first, I rebelled and asked, "What for?"

"Eat. Then go find work."

"I don't want a job." I pulled the covers back over my head. He just stood there waiting.

"You'll have to come up for air sometime," he said.

"Why?"

"You'll end up like Virginia Woolf."

"Who the hell is Virginia Woolf?"

"She's there, in those piles of books, with Henry James and Proust and Hemingway. You've neglected them, haven't you?"

I didn't answer.

"Read her, especially her, and you'll understand why you can't close yourself in." He got dead serious. "Tommy, you must find a job. I'm not always going to be here. It's time to grow up."

"And if I don't want to?"

Simonian shook his head, and I crawled back under my blanket. I could see him shaking his head as he closed the door behind him.

Simonian never once questioned me about my latest pathos, but I suspected he knew about the Moscow debacle, since some of my teammates got haircuts at his shop.

My world stopped when I stopped playing basketball. After three years, I still didn't want to play the game according to their rules.

Days were becoming a blur, and nights were worse—my nightmares had returned. I thought I might visit my aunt, but I saw myself as a burden on a family that already had enough mouths to feed. I knew I had to do something, but what was the purpose when the will wasn't there? And I had too much pride to crawl back and beg to be reinstated on the team.

I really didn't care about attending classes. I went through Simonian's books, a world of literature, found Kafka and Virginia Woolf, and my depression deepened.

I had retreated and was living in a box, refusing to acknowledge the outside world. And that world wasn't doing well, either. It was moving toward self-destruction. There would be no peace, as our Soviet professors had reassured us: "The capitalists dare not attack us Communists, for this time if they lose, it would end the era of capitalism."

Although the Korean conflict was winding down and about to end in a split decision, war had flared up in Korea's backyard. In a French colony called Indochina, later to be renamed Vietnam, Communist guerrillas had begun a life-and-death duel.

News, slanted by *Pravda* and *Izvestia*, was available at the kiosk, but I had to rely on the French Armenian repatriates, who continued to monitor the airwaves, for the other side of the story.

There comes a time when one gets sick of four walls and is ready to venture out of the cocoon. So, one bright autumn afternoon, tired of my self-imposed exile, I left my room, jumped onto a tram, and traveled into the city to see human beings and to be seen. I had not been in a classroom or played basketball for nearly two months. I had come out for a breath of air.

The tram was packed; that hadn't changed. Nor had the filth or the body odor. The bread lines were intact. But who was I to criticize, for had I not been eating off Simonian's tray?

I missed playing basketball and the showers at the Institute, especially the feel of water rushing down my back after a sweaty practice. I wanted to get back into the lineup. But I would not crawl on my hands and knees, and I felt I had wronged no one by contacting the U.S. Embassy.

I was happy when I reached the stop for the Pioneers' Palace, and I leaped off the tram. I found myself standing in the shadows of the building where I had spent most of the past two years, teaching youngsters how to pass, dribble, and shoot. *My God,* I thought, *I do miss it.*

Suddenly, the front door opened, and a familiar figure appeared in the dorrway. "I was wondering if that was you. I watched you from upstairs, and I wasn't sure. Welcome back, Tommy." Before I could say a word, Jak grabbed me and gave me a bear hug. "I have missed you, but I am not the important one," he continued in one breath. "The children talk about you every day. They ask when Tom Boghosovich will be back, and they want me to take them to your apartment. I say, 'No, he is ill.'"

Jak did not let me get one word in, and even if he had, I wouldn't have known what to say.

"I have informed the director that you are ill."

"What about my resignation?" I asked.

"What resignation?" Jak retorted, looking at me slyly. "You have not resigned. You have been ill. Very ill." Jak took a step back and looked at me. "Look at you. No one has lied. You look pale. Unfed."

I forced a laugh.

"You may laugh, but this is no laughing matter."

"But Jak, I didn't come here to—"

Before I could complete my sentence, Jak took me by the arm and ushered me into the building, up the stairs to the gym, where some of my older students were shooting baskets.

"Look! Look!" Jak shouted. "Look, the *varbed*, the pro, is back."

One spontaneous "Hurrah!" echoed throughout the gym, so loud that even Generalissimo Stalin would have envied it. The children rushed to my side. They wanted me back, but there was still the administration. Would they have me? Would they be permitted to rehire me?

"Come, we must go see the director," Jak said. "He will be happy to see you."

I shared my uncertainty with Jak.

"We all get sick, and all he has to do is to look at you, and he'll know. You must come back."

I did not contradict him. I not only needed to come back, I wanted to. If I couldn't play ball, maybe I could at least coach the kids. As we left the gym and walked down the stairs to report to the director, I asked Jak about his mother.

"She's fine. There is still no improvement. She is bedridden still, but she is fine."

"That's good."

"And . . ."

"And what?" I asked.

"Are you not going to ask about Tatiana?"

"Tatiana? What for?"

"Oh, you have forgotten her?"

I shrugged my shoulders.

"Well, she always asks about you, and I had to tell her that I had not seen or heard from you."

"Does she know about my suspension, that they kicked me off the team and out of the Institute?"

"Of course, the whole city knows that. Erevan is a very small community."

As we reached the door to the director's office, I asked, "Jak, what if he refuses to take me back?"

"He won't. We have talked about this, and he will take you back."

"I am so screwed up. Jak, my mind is so mixed up, so clouded, that if there were one psychiatrist in all of the Soviet Union, I would travel to seek him out."

"You know we do not believe in your Freud. What you need is a good woman; if not Tatiana, then someone. But Tatiana is strong, and you two would make a good team. I have her telephone number—do you want it?"

"She has a telephone? How did she manage that? Did your uncle get promoted to commissar of internal security?"

There was no smile on Jak's face when he clarified. "My uncle is a military man, not a politician." But he still did not answer my question.

I told Jak I didn't want Tatiana's phone number. She didn't need the baggage that I would bring to the relationship. Besides, if I wanted to see her, all I needed to do was attend the opera, and all she needed to do to see me was attend one of our games. We were people who were usually on public display. True, at the time, I was not playing for anyone, but then, I didn't know the People's Republic of China was about to change that.

Chapter 34

SHUNNING, SOVIET-STYLE

Suspension in Armenian athletics meant shunning. Everyone had kept away from me. They didn't talk to me or visit me, and they kept out of my space. All except Jak.

There was nothing in life that I loved more than playing basketball. It was all of my life in America, and it brought me back to life in the Soviet Union. There, on the court, I was someone. Someone who could dish out and take whatever the opponent dished out. And when I walked off the floor, my body dripping in sweat, there was a sense of achievement, of accomplishment. Win or lose, I knew, and my coach and my teammates knew, that I had given it my best effort. I could forget who I was or for whom I was playing and enjoy the thrill of the game. It was a way of life I had learned and loved in America. I knew the American way; I didn't understand the Soviet way. But I was learning.

There came a day when the Soviet Armenian political and athletic establishment seemed to need me as much as I needed them.

In the United States, when the team was not winning, the coach was usually fired. In pro sports, even if the team was winning, but the fans didn't fill the seats in the stadium or the coach didn't win the "big one," the coach's head would roll. Economics was ultimately the barometer for all competition in a capitalistic society. Without profit, no enterprise would long stand.

But what motivated the Soviet athlete, who purportedly was not a professional?

In a socialistic society, where all was owned, in theory, by the people—all means of production, industrial complexes, railroads, airlines, banks, mineral and land rights, and, of course, the sports complexes and sports institutes—who owned the athlete? Where did athletes fit in the wider view of things? They couldn't survive without the state, for it was the state that provided them with the material and also the spiritual reason for their existence.

Athletes in the Soviet Union were serfs serving the state and dared not utter even one word against their masters. Czar Alexander II may have freed the Russian serfs in 1861, and Lincoln's Emancipation Proclamation of 1863 may have ended slavery in the United States, but it would be more than a century before professional athletes could wheel and deal for themselves as free agents.

There was no such thing as a free agent in the USSR. One toed the Party line, or else. As Stalin simply put it: "An enemy of the people is not only one who commits sabotage, but one who doesn't believe in the rightness of the Party line." No exceptions. You did as you were told, or else. Lithuania's premier basketball player in the 1950s, Rosa, or Moscow's super soccer player, Starostin, or Armenia's then heavyweight boxing champ discovered that whatever the Party bosses said must be accepted. Their careers ended up somewhere on the steppes of Siberia behind the Ural Mountains.

Many young Armenian repatriates had turned to sports, for many believed that sports was a safe haven in their mercurial and dangerous political environment. The French turned to cycling, boxing, and ping-pong, while the Chinese Armenians were among the best gymnasts in Armenia, and the Egyptians took to basketball, volleyball, and soccer.

Sometime during my suspension, the Minister of Physical Culture and Sports in Moscow had informed the Minister of Physical Culture and Sports in Erevan that the Soviet Republic of Armenia had been selected to host the men's and women's national basketball teams from the People's Republic of China. This was part of an ongoing cultural exchange program between the two monolithic socialist republics.

Armenia, the message from Moscow went, should prepare its men's and women's teams and the city for this historic occasion. Soviet Armenia had never been the site of an international sports contest.

What Moscow didn't have to tell the local ministry but the Soviet Armenian Politburo knew from past experience was that Armenia must beat China. There was no other option, if the republic wanted to host other such events in the future. Armenia must not embarrass Moscow.

Most sports fans had heard the stories about how Stalin and Beria didn't like losing at anything, especially in sports or to women. Lenin was the only player who had reportedly beaten Stalin in chess and lived to tell about it. Then there was the other locker-room story that shortly after Stalin took power, he approved a sports commissar's request to send a national Soviet soccer team to play a match against neighboring Turkey. Not only did the game have psychological value for the Soviets, but, the commissar successfully argued, it would also send the message that the USSR was on the road to recovery from the war and was seeking peace with its neighbors. The world soccer community also would see firsthand how advanced soccer was in the USSR. The Turks, however, deflated the Soviets, and when the Soviet team returned at the short end of a hard-fought 2–1 setback, the Kremlin was red-faced and humiliated. Incidentally, the rest of the rumor was that the sports commissar who had organized the exhibition game in Turkey was banished to the Siberian tundra.

The Soviets had skipped the London Olympics but ended their hiatus from international games with a delegation of men who competed in the Helsinki Olympics in 1952. They finished second to an outstanding U.S. team. Even after their surprisingly excellent effort, those

Soviet coaches whose teams did not fare well at Helsinki were either reprimanded or relieved of their coaching duties.

Armenian officials knew the mentality of their counterparts in Moscow; they learned from them and practiced the same customs locally. If they wanted to keep their jobs and their heads, they could not, must not, allow China to leave the Armenian plateau victorious.

To prepare for the visiting Chinese, the Soviet Armenian all-star team, Sporniya Commanda Armenya, would spend the month of February 1953 in Leninakan to get in shape, then travel to Riga to compete in March for the national championship, and in the summer of 1953 take on the visiting Chinese team.

~ BEHIND THE political scenes, the suspended Tom Mooradian was dolefully shooting baskets from midcourt and practicing free throws blindfolded alone in the Pioneers' Palace gym while waiting for his students to assemble. When I believed no one was around, I would bang the ball against the wall over and over to strengthen my wrists— and to vent my frustration. The collision of the inflated sphere against a solid wall of concrete was deafening, but frustration, coupled with loneliness, does strange things to people. The noise drowned out the pounding inside my head.

Eventually, a stone-faced Jak would appear in the gym and rescue the ball and the wall. He would remind me that destruction of Soviet property was considered sabotage and was a capital offense. I never told Jak what I thought of Soviet justice; after all, he was really the only friend I had at the time.

During my suspension, Institute officials and Party members apparently mentioned my name more than once, stirred in a political cauldron spiced with the idea that a suspension could be rescinded and peppered with the fear that if the republic lost to China, their way of life would be lost. Would it not be better for them to reinstate the American?

But how?

The onus of reinstating me fell upon the shoulders of none other than my former coach. An unexpected development put it there. Oganoff, whom I had learned to respect by this time, had been awarded a high-level position in the Ministry of Physical Culture and Sports and had left the Institute. Konstantin Nikitich, the basketball coach, was moved into Oganoff's office. He continued to coach the men's team but also had the administrative duties of running the volleyball and basketball programs. He had a dilemma on his hands. How could he reinstate me at midsemester, get me into the classroom, and return me to the team without antagonizing powerful Party members and school officials? His search for an answer ended in a strategy universally accepted by the Party: public confession.

Confessions were used to cleanse the deviant, misguided reactionaries, like myself, of thoughts unbecoming a Communist or a young adult. If I apologized for my wrongdoings before a public assembly, there was still hope for my salvation as a Soviet citizen. This would show that it had been my youth, my inexperience, and my early education in a hostile and aberrant capitalist society that had led me down the primrose path. My salvation was my acceptance into Soviet society. I must pledge before Party and Komsomol members that I would no longer challenge the orders of my superiors and that I would accept the responsibilities of a Soviet citizen.

No problem, I informed the messenger.

There are events in one's life that are remembered at least until death, perhaps even after—the first kiss, the wedding ceremony, the first child, the first argument, the separation, the good-bye, the good-bye that is the final good-bye. And standing before a crowd of strangers, telling them with a straight face that you are sorry for disobeying a superior's instruction, should be included in that list.

I was told I would have to speak in Russian, for the majority assembled spoke only Russian and not Armenian. I gave it my best shot, but after I apologized in Russian for disobeying my coach, Chekhov, Gogol, Dostoyevsky, Tolstoy, and Turgenev must have rolled over in their graves, while the living, sitting on those benches, rolled over themselves and died laughing at the malapropisms.

The assembly rose to its feet and shouted in unison, louder, I believed, than the crash of the basketball against the gym wall, "Long live the great Stalin! Our glorious mentor! Our father!"

I smiled and bowed to the masses. None of us realized that time was running out for Stalin.

Chapter 35

DEATH OF A TYRANT

E ven the most powerful men on earth have an irrevocable contract with death. In death, the Soviets said, one found true communism. As for Joseph Stalin, who ruled the Soviet Union with an iron hammer in one hand and a bloodied sickle in the other for more than a quarter of a century, his contract was executed on Thursday, March 5, 1953.

The news of Stalin's death, at the age of seventy-three, attributed to a cerebral hemorrhage, struck like lightning across the mountains and plains of the Soviet Union, and the thunder was heard around the world.

The shoemaker's son had attended an ecclesiastical seminary in Tiflis as a schoolboy, had as a young man turned against the church's teachings and persecuted the teachers, had accepted the dogmatic doctrine of Marxism-Leninism, and had left a long trail of blood and misery in his wake. This ruthless ruler who butchered his enemies as well as those he considered friends, personified the Lord Acton philosophy: "Power tends to corrupt; absolute power corrupts absolutely."

Many of Stalin's Georgian countrymen did not accept that their god had died of natural causes; they wanted to believe that he was poisoned by a group of doctors on the orders of the Politburo. The talk on the streets was that the Brutus in the plot was none other than fellow Georgian Beria, chief of the NKVD, who had his eyes on the throne.

Months before his death, the Soviet dictator reportedly had assembled a host of Bulgarian doctors who claimed to have discovered a cure for old age and were attempting to prolong the inevitable, but they could not help the chain smoker and drug abuser cheat death.

Before the black steel doors to the red marble rectangular mausoleum on Red Square slammed shut for good on the dictator, Stalin's embalmed body, dressed in his military uniform, was entombed alongside Lenin's. He had led the USSR to victory over the Nazis and had surpassed even Ivan the Terrible's reputation for cruelty. His directives

sent millions of innocent citizens to slave camps, into exile, and ultimately to death. Those of us who survived during Stalin's sporadic
reigns of terror had lived in constant fear.

Stalin's hidden agenda had been no secret to the leaders of the Western world. Though he publicly advocated socialism in one country and
had disposed of his popular foe Leon Trotsky, Stalin's supreme goal
was to see the red flag fly atop every capitol building of every nation
on earth. He partially succeeded. Eastern Europe was forced to live
under Stalin's thumb, and China, one billion strong, established a People's Republic under Mao Tse-tung.

No one really knows how many actually perished during Stalin's
reign. They are still counting the bodies, in the forests of Katyn and
buried under the icy fields of the Solvetsky islands. Many were left for
the wolves to devour on the tundra of Irkutsh and Chita and Vorkuta.
No one knows how many were lost on the Siberian taiga.

No one—not even the best Soviet writers of the era, themselves
victims of Stalin's madness—has been able to characterize the terror
that struck the heart when there was a knock on the door at midnight.
I felt it. I heard it often at the American House, at 13 Kalinin Street, in
Erevan, Soviet Armenia.

~ OUR TEAM was en route to Riga, via Moscow, that first week in
March when, to paraphrase John Reed, the event that shook the world
took place. The music from the radio in the train corridor suddenly
went silent. After a brief break, instead of the resumption of traditional
Russian folk music, the somber voice of a Moscow commentator
announced that the general secretary of the Communist Party, Joseph
Stalin, had taken gravely ill. The words hit us like a bolt of lightning.

I looked up at Konstantin Nikitich, whose face had turned pale as he
reached into his pocket for a cigarette and nervously lit it. I asked him
to explain the news, but he didn't respond; he was deep in thought.
Time seemed to stand still as travelers turned to one another in slow
motion and spoke in whispered voices. No details about the chairman's
illness had been released, but it was the first indication to the masses
that all was not well inside the Kremlin.

There were not only tears but also fear on the Soviet faces on the train. They were worried about the power struggle that would occur after Stalin's death, a death they believed was imminent, or there would not have been a break in the radio program.

I did not believe that Stalin would die. Weren't the Bulgarian doctors working on a miracle pill that would restore youth and vigor to the aging Stalin, who then would live and rule forever? The chairman had the best physicians in all of Eastern Europe.

When we got off the train at the Kurski station in Moscow, the city was a ghost town. Few vehicles were on the roads, fewer people on the streets. All waited to hear the inevitable. Those on the street had somber faces, and there was no eye contact at all.

"Is he dead?" I asked one of my teammates as we boarded the train to Riga.

"No," he replied without looking at me.

"How do you know?"

"Because we are his heirs, and they have an obligation to tell us."

About a week later, the news of Stalin's death reached me in the strangest manner: a rock thrown toward my head from a distance of about fifty feet. As we left the gym after a game we had lost, a crowd began to gather and shout obscenities at us. The rock missed me. I turned around to confront the irate fans, not realizing that they were venting political, not sports, frustration. One of our players grabbed me by the arm and told me to run.

"Fuck them! I'm not afraid of them!" I shouted.

"You don't understand, Tommy. Run! They will kill you!"

Strong words. "Why the fuck would they want to kill us?"

"Stalin is dead. The Latvians think we're Georgians."

I ran as fast as I could back to our hotel.

Chapter 36

ATTACK OF THE SCORPIONS

A scorching mid-August sun spread waves of suffocating heat over the Armenian highlands as thousands of spectators jammed the Dynamo Stadium in Erevan to witness the first international basketball game between the Soviet Republic of Armenia and the People's Republic of China.

Though some were there just out of curiosity, others were forced to attend by the Party bosses, and a few were zealous basketball fans. All braved the torrid climate, wanting to be part of Armenian history.

Hundreds of red flags and banners representing the republics decorated the stadium. Quiet and dignified as usual, the spectators sat fanning themselves with the latest editions of newspapers. They waited patiently for the combatants to take to the field. For most, it would be their first glimpse of a basketball game. Many were there because they knew that officials from the highest echelons of the Soviet Armenian government and a few dignitaries from Moscow would be present.

This was definitely the biggest game I had played in the USSR. It would open doors for me that had been slammed in my face as an American-born. I had a problem. How would I play with heart before the hypocrites? This was not only an athletic contest but a political one as well. And the two, I had been taught, ought to be kept separate. In the USSR, everything was political. There were no gray areas.

How I performed and my persona on the court as I faced the enemy would be a topic of controversy in workplaces for days to come. I wanted to exploit the situation, but as any athlete would know, there were no guarantees that once I was in the battle, I would surface with my best.

I believed that my individual performance would influence the image these fans had of America and Americans when they walked out of the stadium. Their pitiless leaders vilified America in every speech, in every radio broadcast, in their literature and schools, and on billboards across the vast nation. They vehemently maintained that

America was the enemy and that the next war would be started by the capitalists in the United States. How could I prove to them that America didn't want war, that a difference in political ideology did not need to be solved on the battlefield.

I was known as Amerikanski Tom to them, and I was snubbed by the Soviet elite because of my birthright, but if I could win over the fans, especially the young ones, then I might inspire them to question whether Americans were truly as evil as their leaders depicted them.

I was scared as we worked through our warm-up drills. I had reason to be. Oganoff had booted Abraham, our captain and go-to player, off the team for this game. I didn't understand how this could have happened, unless Oganoff wanted to embarrass Konstantin Nikitich and sabotage his efforts. But I could not believe that was the case. Armenak Alajajian, a diminutive guard with excellent all-around skills, was named to replace Abraham as captain.

A bizarre incident on the eve of the big game added to our troubles. We had been lodged in a newly completed dorm at the outdoor stadium for almost a month so that we would be near the court. We practiced in the stadium mornings, afternoons, and at dusk, to get accustomed to the surroundings and the moods of the wind. Winds coming off Ararat at dusk could be strong. The game would be played in the cool of the evening, but in mid-August, there was really no such thing as cool, despite the nearby snowcapped mountain range.

Around midnight, as the team slept, an army of deadly scorpions invaded our dorm. Why they chose to reclaim their turf on that particular night was and would remain a mystery. Rafig, the only player who could dunk, was the first to sound the alarm. He leaped high into the air, almost hitting his head on the concrete ceiling, screaming, "Something bit me!" Lights came on, and there they were, scores of them, crawling everywhere. We leaped off our cots and ran for the exits.

Since we had no telephones and no way to get into the city, we were forced to sleep outdoors, under the stars on the concrete slabs that were the stadium's seats, and await the coach's return. When he showed up the next morning, he must have thought he was reviewing the remnants of the defeated army at Stalingrad. He knew we had a problem. We needed decent rest, and time was running out.

Instead of the calisthenics and light practice that he had scheduled for the final day, Konstantin Nikitich opted to bus us to Hotel Ani in the city, where we could get some undisturbed sleep. Then, two hours before game time, we returned to the stadium, where the coach gave us his final instructions.

Before we began our warm-up, the Party flunkies gave us their pitch on how important this game was to the people of Soviet Armenia.

I had breached almost every Soviet rule of the game and had known restless nights before, so I wasn't going to allow a bunch of scorpions and a sleepless night to stop me from performing at my best before this extraordinary crowd of fans.

We trounced the Chinese soundly and decisively. Alajajian starred that afternoon. But I seduced the crowds with awesome long shots and perfect pinpoint passing, and the usually sedate and passive spectators were up on their feet and shouting for more.

The Soviet Armenian basketball team made history that afternoon, and I found my way into the hearts of Soviet Armenian basketball fans—and back into Tatiana's arms.

Chapter 37

A VICTORY CELEBRATION

In the evening following the game, the visiting Chinese delegation, representatives of the local Party's establishment, our coaching staff, and team members attended a "friendship banquet" organized by the Soviet Republic of Armenia at the Hotel Intourist.

Beforehand, Konstantin Nikitich had called a team meeting and stressed that since most of the republic's top officials would be at the banquet, we should expect many toasts to the friendship between China and the Soviet Union. Then, as if directing the challenge at me, he had reminded the group that he expected us to be on our best behavior.

"You have made history, and our people are proud of each and every one of you. They will not soon forget your achievement, but let us not spoil it with any thoughts of your youthful foolishness."

Konstantin Nikitich had not exaggerated about the toasts. No sooner were we comfortably seated at the wall-to-wall rectangular banquet table, with the Chinese delegation and its basketball team members on one side and the Armenian Party elite and our team members on the other, than one of the members of the Armenian Politburo rose and offered a champagne toast: "Long live Mao and the friendship between the USSR and the People's Republic of China!" His voice boomed through the hall.

As that drink went down and the applause ended, almost before we had managed to sit down, one of the Chinese delegates stood and shouted, "Long live the Communist Parties of the USSR and China!"

That drink went down quickly, and the glasses were refilled by the waiters with Armenian cognac. "To the inevitable triumph of communism over capitalism," the next speaker sang out.

This continued for the rest of the evening.

Despite the delegates' ecstasy at the fact that the USSR and the People's Republic of China had combined manpower of more than a billion and a half people—though maybe not the weaponry—to take on the free world, this was a period of tense, suspenseful transition in the USSR. As Stalin's body lay preserved for idolatry, mistrust between the two great Communist powers was mushrooming. Some Soviets saw Tito in Mao and feared another defection from their camp.

In the banquet hall, as the toasts continued, none could forget the recent past; for them, Stalin still lived. His elaborate portrait, draped in black mourning cloth, hung side-by-side with Mao's and Lenin's in the dining room.

The time came when I, too, was called upon to offer a toast. As I prepared to stand, the Mr. Hyde inside me taunted me to propose a toast to Chiang Kai-shek and Madame Chiang, then sit back and delight in the commotion that would have followed such a tribute to the Nationalist Chinese leaders. Thank heavens my Dr. Jekyll prevailed. I slowly rose from my seat, and all eyes were upon me as I said, "We look forward to a rematch with a team that is a worthy opponent."

As I sat down, I heard, *"Ehta zamichahtilna,"* uttered by my coach, and from Oganoff, "Wonderful, splendid." I could almost hear their sighs of relief.

It would have been a perfect ending to a perfect day if I had not had to go to the restroom. My stomach rebelled against the undetermined amount of alcohol and the greasy lamb I had consumed. I stood up, took a few shaky steps to the hallway, and was walking toward the toilets when an elderly, much-decorated Armenian military officer came toward me. I recalled that he had made several short comments during the banquet, followed with toasts, even one in Chinese. I had not recognized him at the table, because I only got a glimpse of his profile. Now, as he strolled toward me in the hallway, my mind went over the memorable events of the recent past, yet it could not locate any concrete clues to where or when we had met. The uncountable number of drinks I had consumed at the banquet table had probably clouded my memory. But there was something about him, in his manner, in his walk, that convinced me that I knew him. He came closer, step by step. When our eyes finally clashed, all doubts vanished. A sickening sensation wrapped around my entire body. The pain. The suffering. The shame. I felt them all again. The degradation of the interrogation returned. This was not a nightmare that would dissipate with the first rays of dawn.

"Sir," I said, planting my unsteady feet in front of him, blocking his path. "Have we not met before?" I chose to speak in Russian, though I knew from his complexion that he was Armenian.

"We may have," the officer calmly replied. A strange smile crossed his face, and the mask was lifted as he said, "I see your Russian has greatly improved."

"Idi k choror-tu!" I screamed into his face. "Go to the devil!"

"I have seen the devil, my son, on the faces of the many I killed at the front. It would be wise if you moved aside."

"You had your opportunity . . ."

Before I could continue, Konstantin Nikitich was pulling me away, apologizing to the officer, and pointing out that I was drunk. I retaliated almost instantly, striking back at my coach, but I was in no condition to fight anyone. Swiftly, the coach grabbed my arm and led me through a maze of corridors to a rear door that opened to a patio and a courtyard crowded with hotel patrons.

"I must go back and apologize again," Konstantin Nikitich said. "You are a fool. I will send someone out to take you back to the hotel.

If you dare move, believe me, you will never play basketball for me again."

Even in my condition, I understood the seriousness of the coach's threat. I put my head under my arms on the table and sobbed. I could hear voices, cruel laughter, and jokes at my expense, before my body and my mind gave up on my stupidity.

Sometime later, I opened my eyes. My head rested on a fluffy white pillow in a room that was not my own or the hotel's. A woman sat on a chair near my bedside, but she didn't say a word. The ceiling moved in circles, and my head throbbed as if it would explode any second.

"Where am I?" I asked. There was no answer. Then I remembered the events of the evening before. I tried to get up, but my body would not respond.

"Where am I?" I asked again.

"You're in my cousin's house, my aunt's bed," I heard a soft voice reply. "There is nothing I can do for you. There is nothing anyone can do for a fool."

"Tatiana, what are you doing here? What am I doing here?"

And then I remembered the final moments before I'd blacked out and mumbled, "I am a fool."

"Yes," Tatiana concurred, "a big American fool."

Tatiana had made some dark tea and toast and ordered me to eat and drink. I shoved both away and tried to piece together what should have been the best day of my life in the Soviet Union. It had turned into one big headache and an unsettled stomach.

"How could someone loved by so many be so stupid?" she said as she filled in the details of the evening.

"Then you and Jak were at the banquet?"

"Yes, we were there."

"But I didn't see you."

"We were not in the main hall. After all, we were not as important as you. And then Konstantin Nikitich rushed to us after you revealed yourself in the manner of a drunken hooligan. He told us what had happened and told Jak to go to the patio and find you and take you home before you got into more trouble. I tagged along. He brought you here."

"Where is Jak?"

"He is teaching your class at the Palace. He asked me to stay with you until he got back."

"Then you have been here all night?"

She smiled. "Yes, I have been here through it all."

I was too embarrassed to say anything else until I remembered that she had said I was in her aunt's bed. "Where is Jak's mother?"

"You mean my aunt?"

Remembering the relationship, I nodded.

She looked at me sadly. "I thought you knew. She passed away while you were in camp training for the Chinese."

"He never told me."

"We are a very private family."

"And friends mean little to your family?"

Tatiana ignored the question as if I had not asked it.

By now, the pounding in my head had returned, intensified tenfold. I closed my eyes and put my head back on the pillow to shut off the world. A montage of images flashed across my mind and stopped in the hallway where I had confronted the elderly officer.

My eyes opened wide, and all the hatred I had for the Soviets and the NKVD was spewed at the lovely creature who was standing beside the bed.

"He's your father, isn't he?"

There was no look of surprise on her face. No denial.

"He's the one who built the wall between us, isn't he?" I continued, not allowing her a second to reply. "He's evil! He represents evil! And you are his daughter!"

"Are you done?" she asked patiently.

"No! I am not finished with him or with you! Why don't you ask him why he didn't kill me? As he probably has killed hundreds of others. Why don't you ask him what they do to people they drag off the streets and toss into trucks? And why don't you ask him what they did to Jak's father, your uncle?"

Instead of anger, I saw relief in Tatiana's face. She sat on the bed, leaned over, and kissed me on the forehead.

"My father is not an evil man. He is a servant of the state, a hero of the Soviet Union, and he has served his country well."

"I know how well. He's probably filled the gulags with more than his quotas."

Tatiana refused to carry on with the topic, refused to raise her voice or get angry. Instead, she asked something irrelevant. "She must have been very beautiful."

"What the hell are you talking about?"

"The girl you left behind in America."

"It is none of your business."

"Do you know what an Armenian—or a Georgian, especially a Georgian—or a Russian would do if he were lying there and looking up at me?"

"I am not an Armenian. Or a Georgian. Or a Russian. I am an American."

"And that is your problem. When I am on the stage, dancing before the crowds, all I can see is you. Have we not tortured ourselves enough?"

I didn't know what to say. I lay there watching her as she slipped off her dress and crawled under the sheet with me.

She whispered in my ear, "Don't worry, Jak won't be back until tomorrow."

Chapter 38

THE SUMMER OF '55

In the summer of 1955, our team had been on the road for more than a month, playing in tournaments in the cities of Kursk, Stalingrad, and Saratov, listening to rumors from players representing all of the republics that a political upheaval was about to occur. This was before the February 1956 political storm that would change not only my world but the rest of the world as well. There was evidence that change was coming—the number of tourists from the West had doubled, for instance—though my life had changed little.

The dual challenge of playing for what was basically a professional team and coaching junior boys' and girls' teams in my "spare time" so that I would not be considered a professional was taking a physical toll on me.

I looked forward to a reprieve from the environment of sweaty socks, locker-room antics, crowds, hotels, Russian cabbage soup, vodka, and, yes, the women who pursued young athletes.

After eight years of obedience to the state, I had accepted Erevan as my home and had partially accepted what my friends were saying: that I would never return to America. The flashbacks of my native country, though there were fewer with each passing year, were painful when they occurred. I avoided, the best I could, everything and everyone associated with America. But I could not sever ties with my brain, nor could I delete my memories.

And I could not avoid Mr. Simonian, with whom I continued to share the apartment, nor could I avoid American House, where I lived. Simonian knew me better than I knew myself. In fact, Simonian should be the narrator of this story. Unfortunately, he left me in the summer of 1955.

It was about then that I adopted Simonian as my father. One could easily express it the other way around: I was the son he never had.

Simonian was smoking more. Coughing more. He was sleeping less and eating less, despite the fact that I was able to bring to the table more of the "luxuries" from Moscow, such as oranges, bananas, sugar, butter, and decent bread.

On the other hand, he was talking more. Specifically, he was giving me more advice about how I should live my life. Our talks always turned to marriage and Tatiana.

"Get married," he would say. "It's time. Tatiana and you are a beautiful couple."

How did he know about my relationship with Tatiana? I surmised that a barbershop was the hub of all rumors.

~ TATIANA AND I were compatible in many respects and inseparable when we were not on the road—she with her ballet troupe, I with the team or coaching the Pioneers' Palace squads. But whenever we had a free moment, we would sneak off to the nearby hills, walk and talk, and argue about the simple things. Such as when she said that

Americans had stolen Alaska for the ridiculous price of seven million dollars, and it should be returned to the Soviets. Or when I mentioned the slave camps and said that the prisoners should be freed, and she reminded me that Negroes in America were still slaves, residing in slave camps called ghettos.

When we made up, though, it was bliss.

Love, I read somewhere, was not a guarantee of a happy marriage. How could I convey to Simonian my greatest fear, that our love could destroy us? Our love for each other united us, but our love for our two homelands kept us apart. There was and always would be an Iron Curtain between us.

Sometimes for months, we were in different parts of the country, performing for crowds and fans. When our paths would cross by chance, perhaps in Sochi, Sokhumi, Odessa, or even Moscow, we would be inseparable. We never wanted it to end, but the end would come.

In the summer of 1955, we thought our affair was still a well-kept secret. But everyone knew; we just didn't know that they knew. Despite our love, I believed she considered me a foreigner; to me, she had too much of the land in her. Sometimes I would joke that the Bering Strait or Sitka, Alaska, were the only places she and I could build a house where when she opened the front door, she'd be greeted by her Russian-speaking ancestors, and when I opened the back door, I'd find a handful of Americans to greet me.

As I debated with myself about the sins and virtues of marriage, Simonian did not allow me to forget the ancestral Armenian laws of dating. When a young man dated a young woman several times, he was obligated to marry her. In the eyes of the Armenian community, a date was a sign of commitment and announced that the two were spoken for. I told him that was ridiculous. He reminded me that Armenian divorces were extremely rare.

~ THERE WAS a reason Simonian wanted me to marry: the barber of Philadelphia was dying.

One night, when I had returned to the apartment after a tournament, I found the room in disarray. Simonian was not there, and he failed to show up that night. The next morning, I discovered that he had not slept in his cot and realized that some of his belongings, including his teapot, his toothbrush, and his shaving kit, were missing. I also noticed that his worn-and-torn robe was gone. My immediate concern was that he had been arrested, but I quickly dismissed the thought because of his silent approach toward politics and his longtime devotion to the Party.

The mystery was cleared up with the appearance of Mrs. Karibian, who lived in the apartment below.

"I heard footsteps," she said, "and I thought it was you, but I decided I'd better check to make sure." There was a nervous pause before she continued, "I guess you don't know, but Simonian is in the hospital. The one on Ordzhonikidze Street."

"He's OK, isn't he?"

There was an uneasiness in her face that suggested otherwise. "I'm not sure. You know we don't talk a lot." She looked at me sadly. "If there is anything I can do, let me know."

I nodded and thanked her, and she left.

Though I had never been to the hospital, I knew it well. I passed it every day on the tram. I rushed there, went to the reception desk, and explained to the nurse why I was there. She refused to let me visit Simonian.

"The patient is in an isolation sector. No one can visit," she explained.

I begged, but my plea was for naught. Finally, I said, "I am his son. I have come all the way from Moscow. Could you please get him a message that his son is here to see him?"

Moscow got her attention, for people from Moscow usually knew other people in the capital.

"If you wish to see your father, I do not see a problem, but you must go outside and look to the third-floor window. I will get a message to him."

I did exactly as I was told, returning to the street and waiting. Shortly, a thin, emaciated figure of a man appeared at the window. I did not immediately recognize him. But then his thick, now completely white eyebrows provided positive identification.

"What is this? I can't go away for a month without you getting into some kind of trouble?" I shouted to him in English from the street.

The eyes looking down at me widened and brightened. He recognized the voice, but without his glasses, I doubted he could see me.

"Is that you, Tommy?" Simonian called down, blinking to get a clear view.

"Who the hell do you think it is?"

"I don't know. The nurse said my son . . ."

"Well, hey, you've been a father to me all these years, haven't you?"

He still looked confused.

"I am your adopted son, aren't I?"

Now I could clearly see a smile on the deeply wrinkled face.

"Tommy, you must go home."

"Shit. Isn't that what I have been telling you all these years? I'll go. But I'm going to take you with me when I do."

He tried to find the strength to reply. "No. Back to the apartment. There is a book . . ." He looked confused again. "Bring it to me. Please."

"What book?" I could barely make out what he was saying. I figured he was sedated, but I shouted back, "I'm coming up!"

"Please don't. Please."

I stopped.

"Please leave the book at the desk. Come back tomorrow." He closed his eyes, and when he opened them again, he tried to say something, but I heard nothing.

I wondered what to do.

"I must go," he finally said in a quivering voice.

"I'm coming back tomorrow. Is there anything you want or need?"

There was no answer.

I visited him a few more times, but I was never allowed to go to his room. The conversations, yelled, were difficult for both of us emotionally.

One evening as I was preparing to leave, the nurse stepped in front of the window and closed it. I saw her take him by the arm and lead him away. A few seconds later, she returned to the window, opened it, and looked down at me.

"Your father told me to tell you that you . . . marry her."

"What?" I shouted. "What did you say?"

"Your father said you should marry her."

Those were Simonian's final words of advice to me.

No bell tolled for Mr. Simonian as we carried his crude wooden coffin to its final resting place among the volcanic rocks and stones on the hillside cemetery called Tokhmakhquel. There was no church service. No priests sang the hymns of the ancient Armenian church, beseeching the Lord to accept and welcome one of his children into his kingdom.

But there were members of the Communist Party of Soviet Armenia who reminded the large crowd of friends, workers, and Party officials that Comrade Simonian had fought against General Francisco Franco and his Fascist troops for the workers of Spain. He had stood up against Nazi Germany and had returned home to help rebuild his motherland.

There were cognac bottles popped and final toasts drunk to a brave compatriot. *"Sorgh leenank.* To our health." And "May his days be yours." Then each one bade Mr. Simonian a final good-bye. When they had all left, I remained behind to make sure that his clothes were cut to shreds and his shoes removed, so that thieves would not dig up the coffin and steal them.

I didn't want to return to the apartment, but I knew I must, for the state would soon come and claim what was left of Simonian's possessions. Back in the room, emotionally and physically drained and in tears, I remembered that Simonian had mentioned something about a book. I wondered why it was so important to him. I slowly took each book off the shelf and flipped through the pages, hoping to find what Simonian had wanted.

After an hour or so, a white envelope fell from one of the books. It was addressed to Mr. Haratoun Simonian at a Philadelphia address. I recognized the handwriting as my mother's and was puzzled. Though I had mentioned Simonian's name in the short notes and postcards I had mailed home, I did not believe my mother knew him. The letter was postmarked from Detroit in 1947. I opened it and read:

"My dearest Haratoun,

"I hope this letter finds you in good health. It has been so long since we have seen or heard from you, but news has reached me that you have decided to repatriate with the first group, and I thought you would be interested in knowing that my youngest son, Tommy, will be in that group. Boghos and I will not be on the boat. I will admit to you that I have dreaded this moment for a long time, for I have hoped and prayed that Tommy would reconsider. He hasn't. He is as stubborn as Boghos and is determined to go to Armenia. I do not know why. As a mother, I do not want him to leave, and I hoped, now that the war is over, that he would listen to his older brothers, Popkin and George, and join the Navy. But he won't listen. Once something is in his mind, he will never get it out until he does it. Before he graduated from high school he became engaged to his high school sweetheart. She is an *odar*. A very pretty *odar*. I was against this, but he went and did it anyway. They are too young, and I believe that they should be separated for a year or two, that this would do both some good. Thus, the reason for this letter. If you can, please keep an eye on him in Armenia. He is a good boy, but at times he has streaks of wildness in him.

"I realize this would place an additional burden on you at this time, but I beg of you, if possible, can you oblige this heartbroken mother? I have always admired you. I cherish the memories of the orphanage and the short time we shared together in France.

"My deepest respects and a safe journey. I shall remain, as always, a devoted friend, and if there are things you may have forgotten and will need in Armenia, please do not hesitate to write, and I will make sure they get to you. May God watch over both of you. And may God forgive me for allowing my child to return to a land where there has been so much bloodshed.

"Dzovinar."

I had never felt lonelier.

Chapter 39

POLITICAL UPHEAVAL

It was in 1955 that I noticed jokes starting to appear about the lack of consumer products or the shabbiness of Soviet-made products.

"Is this the shoe you wish to purchase, comrade?" the sales clerk asked the eager buyer.

"Yes," the purchaser said. "But where is the other shoe? I would like to try them both on."

"Oh, this left shoe is made in Leningrad; the right one is made in Moscow. We still have not received the right shoe. When it arrives, we will contact you. Do you wish to pay for this shoe now or when the other one arrives?"

Or, if you preferred politics, there was the one about a KGB officer assigned to patrol restrooms in Moscow, arresting those who were engaged in the art of political graffiti. Soviet restrooms lacked an essential, toilet paper, so users had to furnish their own, usually the daily newspaper. A man, so the story went, walked into a restroom with a copy of *Pravda,* used the facility, and exited, whereupon he was approached by the officer, who ordered him to hand over the rest of the newspaper. After closely scrutinizing the paper, the officer discovered that the page that had displayed a photo of Stalin was missing, and he immediately arrested the man.

"How dare you smear our leader's image? Off to Siberia with you," said the judge after hearing the case.

Later, a second man used the facility and was also questioned by the officer. Again, the officer demanded that the newspaper be handed over.

"Ha, you've used a piece of the newspaper with the Politburo's directives in it."

The second man, too, gets to ride in a *"stolypin* wagon" all the way to Magadan.

A third man, a wise curmudgeon, entered the restroom and stayed there for a considerable length of time. The officer waited and waited, then, losing patience, rushed in and found the man comfortably sitting on the toilet, humming a tune.

"What's holding you up?" the officer asked irritably.

The old man looked up with a smile and said, "I'm waiting."

"Waiting for what?" the officer demanded.

"Waiting for that sonofabitch in the Kremlin to die!"

As the thaw began and Western tourists flooded the USSR, the Soviets realized what the West already knew: Soviet life was drab, dreary, and draconian. The Soviets still feared change.

In the meantime, Soviet citizens, especially the handful of French and American Armenians who had family members in foreign countries and the Soviet Jews who sought to go to their homeland, slowly gained courage and began to petition the Office of Visas and Registrations (OVIR) for exit visas. Most were rejected and their paperwork turned over to the KGB for further investigation.

Members of the Soviet elite occasionally received approval for foreign travel, but only conditionally. A Soviet citizen had to have an unbreakable tie with the USSR in order for the state to approve travel. The authorities needed a "hostage" to ensure that the traveler would return and not attempt the unthinkable, defection. The diplomat corps, the political elite, had been traveling abroad for years, but their families stayed home. Now a select group of scientists, scholars, stage and screen performers, and athletes, who knew what would happen to their loved ones if they decided to defect, obtained visas—few did not return.

The choice between freedom and Soviet serfdom was no choice at all. Most Soviet travelers abroad had to choose serfdom, for the alternative was to sacrifice someone dear to them. I was glad I did not have to make that choice. Marriage and children were a liability if one wanted to leave the country.

Rare, indeed, were the Makarovas and Baryshnikovs who danced off the stage of the Kirov Ballet in Leningrad and into the hearts of the American people in New York. One can only guess at the number of heads that rolled at the Ministry of Soviet Culture.

Soviets returning from abroad remained tight-lipped about life in the West. Memories did not die overnight. Neither did late-night visits from the secret police. Fear seldom ever dies, for it is not a stranger but a silent partner that walks with us each step of the day, awakened by a scent, a sound, a word.

Beria was dead, but he still lived in the summer of 1955. He was victorious, for his legacy had been passed on. Just as Feliks Dzerzhinsky resurrected the Okhrana of czarist Russia in the Cheka, which evolved into the NKVD, the NKVD became the KGB. And the Cold War was still a cold war in the hot summer of 1955.

But a new and braver generation of Soviets joined the ranks of the former *zeks,* who had been released during the amnesty of 1953. They asked questions and demanded answers about the injustices they had suffered. They wrote books. They wanted to know why those injustices had occurred in a nation that had been founded on the pretext that the workers would never again be exploited by anyone, let alone their own class. The voices of the dead were heard in the poetry of the day and the preserved tales of the survivors of the camp, voices recorded on page after page where once only praises to Stalin and the Party were printed. Pasternak, then Solzhenitsyn, and later Yevtushenko told the story and changed forever the course of Soviet history.

Chapter 40

KHRUSHCHEV'S LEGACY

It was six P.M. on Sunday, August 26, 1956. I was sitting alone in a room, nervously waiting for the operator at the telephone office on Gorky Street in Moscow to say that my party was on the line. It was ten A.M. in Detroit. I was there because I was confident that I could now speak freely with my parents. Since April, when the director of the Sports School read to the staff Chairman Khrushchev's "secret speech" to the 20th Congress of the Communist Party, I had wanted to contact my parents and tell them that it was time for them to petition Khrushchev for my release. Our basketball team had played in a tournament in Stalingrad, and we were en route to Erevan via Moscow when I decided to call home.

It had been an unprecedented year in the history of the Soviet Union. And the month of February had been a month of revelation.

Joseph Stalin had been dead for three years, but his ghost still haunted the Kremlin. He remained a god to the people of the Soviet Union; after all, he did lead his nation to a victory over Hitler. But in February, monumental changes occurred. The evil that men do lives after them; the good is oft interred with their bones. So let it be with Caesar.

And so Nikita Khrushchev let it be with Stalin.

Of peasant stock, Khrushchev was born on April 15, 1894, in the village of Kalinovka in southern Russia. Nikita Sergeivich, as the people called him, walked with a wobble, talked with a lisp, and spoke his native language with a twist that Russian scholars labeled uniquely Khrushchevian, unlike anything they had previously heard. Stalin's accent was Georgian, and Russia forgave him (they dared not criticize him), but what was Khrushchev's excuse? It did not matter how he spoke but what he said.

Certainly, Khrushchev danced when Stalin ordered, he drank when Stalin ordered, and he slept when Stalin ordered, but what was the alternative? Join Trotsky, Zinoviev, and Kamenev before a firing squad? Be murdered in his sleep? It was time for the truth, and he spoke the truth. And the people listened. They believed in him. He became the first secretary of the Communist Party, and his longtime colleague in the farce that was the Politburo, moon-faced Georgi Malenkov, took over as premier.

The abuses Stalin inflicted were many, the scars too deep for Khrushchev to forgive and forget. The truth about the tyrant of Georgia had to be told. Round-faced, rotund, bubbly at times, vitriolic at others, the man who orchestrated the execution by firing squad of NKVD-KGB chief Lavrenti Beria, the most feared man in the Soviet Union during Stalin's reign of terror, and six of the KGB chief's longtime aides, Khrushchev did not allow the glorification to continue. Addressing the cream of the Communist leadership from the fifteen Soviet republics and the prominent leaders of the international Communist community, Chairman Khrushchev opened the Pandora's box of the former dictator, and the ghosts of Soviet past spilled out.

For more than four hours on February 14, the stunned two thousand delegates to the assembled 20th Congress listened in silence to the list of crimes Stalin had committed against the Soviet people and against humanity.

February 14 was a day that went down in history as the beginning of the end of the Soviet Union. How could anyone trust their leaders from that day forward? The Kremlin became synonymous with the Tower of Babel.

The first secretary's detailed accounts of torture, forced confessions, innocent men and women incarcerated and executed, purges of loyal and dedicated members of the military staff, Stalin's cowardice during the Great Patriotic Wars—he ventured only once to the front lines—shocked a nation whose people had suffered so long and so much. They would never trust the Party leadership again.

Khrushchev's victory was a Pyrrhic one.

The chairman had been warned by the old-liners—by Molotov, Malenkov, Voroshilov, and Kaganovich—that the people would not understand. And they also raised a good question: Were they not, as members of the Politburo, also culpable for the crimes committed during their tenure in the Stalin era? A courageous Khrushchev argued and won. The people, as heirs, had the right to know the truth.

Khrushchev gave a fifty-page speech and implored the delegates not to relay his words to the press. But they were eventually heard around the nation and the world, although they did not reach the shores of the United States until June. On June 5, 1956, U.S. newspapers picked up the story.

Meanwhile, in the provinces, East Berlin and Hungary decided that the death of Stalin and Beria's execution made it the right time to rise against those who had overstayed their welcome in their countries. They rebelled against their Soviet overlords, but German and Hungarian freedom fighters learned the hard way that handguns were no match for Soviet tanks. They had forgotten how mighty the Soviets were. Even the West cringed when, on August 14, 1953, the Soviet Union exploded a hydrogen bomb that, unlike the American counterpart, could be transported by air to a target.

The Soviets got down to the business of building Sputnik and Lunik and prepared to send a man into space. The Soviets' exploration of outer space and their development of missiles gave the Kremlin the psychological ammunition to promote communism worldwide. The world teetered as scholars in both camps debated whether the Soviet Union or the United States had the technological edge, and the world speculated about which of the two superpowers had rescued the most Jewish scientists from the concentration camps of Nazi Germany. The world also learned who was actually calling the shots in the Kremlin.

It didn't take an Einstein to figure out who was the Soviet boss. Khrushchev was the man.

For repatriates, like myself, the less we knew about Kremlin intrigues and power plays, the better.

~ "MR. MOORADIAN."

I did not hear my name called because I was deep in thought. The name sang out over the office speaker and was repeated several times, and finally I realized that the receptionist wanted to speak to me. I got up from the bench and strolled over to her.

"Your party is on the telephone."

I thanked her in Russian.

When I picked up the receiver, it was my sister-in-law Clara on the line. I had never met her. She had married George shortly after I left the States.

"I'm sorry that I missed your wedding," I said apologetically. "Maybe I'll be there for your next one."

She laughed and asked about my health.

"Fine. I'm in great shape. I'm been playing basketball and keeping out of trouble. How are Mother and Father?"

"Your father is as strong as an ox, but Mother has a heart problem. The doctors are prescribing drugs. But she'll be all right. When are you coming home?"

"It's still up in the air. Have you read about Stalin?"

"Yes."

I didn't think I needed to elaborate.

"But your father doesn't believe it. He says it is propaganda."

"Every bit is true, Clara, believe me."

The operator said that we had one minute left. I didn't waste any more time. I told Clara that I needed the family to write to the Soviet Embassy in Washington and to Chairman Khrushchev personally, asking them to allow me to return home, as a humanitarian, goodwill gesture.

Clara's last words to me were, "We will do that. But your brothers are also considering hiring an attorney to see what they can do through the legal system. You were just nineteen when you left. Why did you go?"

I did not answer her question. I implored her to make sure that the letters were written, signed, and sent to the Soviet officials.

"A lot has changed here, Tom, after you left . . ."

"And here, too, Clara. I am looking forward to returning home. Kiss Mother and Father for me."

I paid for the call and left the building.

On the street, I paused before jaywalking across Gorky. I sensed that I was being followed. I turned my head and looked back, noticing that someone I had spotted in the telephone office was a few yards behind me. My first thought was to bolt across the street and lose him. Instead, I convinced myself that it was foolish to avoid contact. I had approval to make the call, and I had not violated any law. Was this not what Khrushchev was talking about when he addressed the congress? Harassment by the secret police? Illegal arrest? Anyway, if the man was KGB, he could have me picked up at any time.

I crossed Gorky, and the stranger followed. He looked more Asian than Caucasian, but he was dressed in a European suit. When I reached the door to the ice cream shop, I lingered. The man caught up to me. We looked at each other, and he smiled. I thought I knew what was coming next: a black car and an invitation to get in. I was wrong.

"Who are you?" I asked.

The stranger did not answer my question but said, "I couldn't help but overhear your discussion back there in the phone room. Excellent English. Are you American?"

"No," I answered. "Why?"

He looked surprised, apologized, and was about to leave. He had taken me for an American, and there was ample reason to support his claim that I was. I was wearing an American suit recently sent to me from home, and if he had overheard me in the telephone office, he knew my accent was not Continental. He definitely wasn't KGB. A KGB agent would have ordered me to accompany him and would have had backup to force me to comply.

"You aren't Russian. Your English is impeccable," he said.

"No, I'm not Russian, and thank you for the compliment."

"I'm Roy Essoyan."

"Essoyan?"

"Yes."

"Armenian?"

He paused before answering. "Why, yes, but how did you know?"

"It takes one to know one."

"Then you're Armenian."

I introduced myself, and we shook hands. He took me by the arm and led me into the shop. He kept probing, asking questions. I explained the circumstances of how I had come to be in the country and in Moscow.

"Then you live and work here."

"Not here. In Erevan. I'm a basketball coach, and I also play for the national team."

"I'm with the AP," Essoyan said.

I was puzzled. I did not know what the two letters signified and asked him to explain.

"You have been away a long time, haven't you?"

"I haven't been home since November of 1947."

"Good heavens. That's incredible. I'm a foreign correspondent with the Associated Press, a news service."

"You're a writer?"

"Yes." He gave me a brief account of his work. He tossed out the names of some of his colleagues and told me that they were staying at the Hotel National. "Do you know where that is?"

I nodded and explained that I usually stayed at that hotel when I was in town. He seemed surprised.

I asked him, "Have you been to Erevan? There are a few of us repatriates left, but most have passed away. It was rough on the elderly. Especially the bread lines."

He shook his head and stared at me as if perhaps he understood. Then he continued, "No, I haven't been to Armenia. I've asked Mikoyan a couple of times to allow me to go, but he refuses, saying, 'Why do you want to go there? Moscow is where everything is.'"

I realized that he might write something about our encounter and asked him if he planned to.

"No. That is, not unless you want me to."

"Please don't. Right now, with so many things going on, I would prefer that my name didn't appear in any papers. I'm hoping to get out now that Khrushchev has denounced Stalin."

"Are you married?"

"No."

"Well, what I hear from the people who know is that those who have family ties here are permitted to travel abroad. The government knows they will return because there would be repercussions if they didn't."

Essoyan took a good look at me, and his expression changed. "You look like you're pretty well off. Why would you want to go back?"

For some reason, I resented the question. He should have known. "Why?"

"Yes, why would someone like you want to return? It looks as if you have everything."

"Everything except my freedom."

I knew that he had never experienced the chilling feeling of a midnight knock on his apartment door or what would happen next: men in military uniforms, armed with automatic revolvers, ordering him and his loved ones out to a black canvas-topped truck.

"Well, I hope you get back," Essoyan said, bringing a quick end to my thoughts. "But a lot has changed since you left."

"Strange. That's what my sister-in-law just said."

"There was a senator named McCarthy, who hates Communists and sees them crawling everywhere. The Senate censured him a few months ago. But there are a lot of others like him."

I had no idea what Essoyan was talking about, but I had a story of my own to tell. "And we had a guy here who was a sadist, who tortured and murdered millions because they were all enemies of the people." I don't know why, but I told him of my arrest for wanting to go to Moscow and present a petition to the U.S. ambassador. I paused and was about to continue when I realized it was useless. They would never understand. My father wouldn't even believe what they had printed about Stalin.

Somewhere between the fourth and fifth glass of wine (alcoholic beverages were served in ice cream shops, often mixed with the ice cream), I thought I'd had enough. I found I had been talking with myself. The American had left.

I had to go have a chat with Stalin.

I left the ice cream shop, strode boldly up Gorky to Red Square. Two young Russian guards stood at attention at the door to the mausoleum, protecting the Soviet rulers entombed within. I was an American and, therefore, was allowed to bypass the line of spectators waiting to pay tribute. Not so long ago, before the revelations about Stalin, the line would have stretched for miles.

I sighed in relief as I silently walked past the two bodies. Stalin, dressed in his generalissimo's uniform, was still there. He had not risen.

Chapter 41

TATIANA AND TOMMY

R arely was I in Erevan. I was usually on the road playing or coaching. When our team played in Moscow or when the junior team I coached had a tournament there, Tatiana would attend the games. And whenever she had a break from her strenuous and stressful ballet performances, she spent her free time with me.

Tatiana was our—no, my—biggest fan.

We enjoyed the museums or attended plays at the Maly Theater or headed for Gorky Park, where we could be alone on a park bench, with the rest of the crowd of young lovers. Even though I had attended two or three operas at the Bolshoi with her, Tatiana avoided Moscow's centerpiece, because, she said, it reminded her of work.

As intense as our love and our lovemaking were, we never discussed marriage. In body, we were one, but we were never one in mind—specifically when it came to politics—or in soul. We continued to disagree about capitalism and communism. Religion also was an issue between us, although I had become something of an agnostic.

If there was a merciful God, she argued, why did he take the young lives of her brothers who loved peace and life? How many young scientists, doctors, engineers, composers, and athletes had he harvested from the bloodstained battlefields of Stalingrad or Leningrad? How many lives had been lost in war, all wars? Why must twenty million innocent lives be sacrificed to appease one madman? If there was a God, he should see a psychiatrist.

I had no answers for her.

There were other quarrels—many—but I believed she never deceived me about how she felt about me, and vice versa. She and I learned to accept what Khrushchev was preaching to the world at the time: peaceful coexistence.

When it came to sex, the Soviets still lived in the nineteenth century, but you would never know it by Tatiana and me. We enjoyed each other, every inch of each other, and we lived every minute that we were together believing it to be our last. We knew it would end, but we didn't want it to. We could not, despite our efforts, bury our pasts. The fear that I would return to the United States on a second's notice would arise at the sight of each tourist. If they were coming, I would soon be able to go. But we shut out the world as soon as we slipped beneath the bedsheets.

I knew I would be there in the morning. She wasn't certain. We never dared to mention marriage.

My love for America and freedom was never ending. She loved me, as I did her, and my respect for her grew as we matured over the years. Youth ends and adulthood begins when one learns respect for another's opinions.

I knew she was inseparable from Soviet soil, for it held the memories of everything she had loved—her childhood, her youth, her love of family. It was also a land her brothers and ancestors had fought and died for. Her greatest fear—indeed, the fear of all nations at the time—was that the nightmare of the two superpowers engaging in combat would one day become a reality. And as those two superpowers stockpiled intercontinental ballistic missiles, it seemed that World War III was inevitable.

Tatiana and I decided that we would not allow the invisible lattice of Cold War missiles allegedly placed strategically around the world to destroy our love for each other. If anything, it intensified it.

We entered a covenant to dedicate ourselves to each other, during that unpredictable stroll through the labyrinth that leads most couples to the marriage bed. We feared that a legal and binding commitment would only bring reality into perspective and suffocate our love.

Chapter 42

THE ROOSEVELT INCIDENT

I stood in the doorway of the crowded dining room, the muted voices of diners wafting gently through my senses. Those were the sounds of my past, a language I now seldom used. English. American English. Russian and Armenian had become my primary languages.

How times had changed in Moscow at the Hotel National. Gone were the Chinese. Gone also were the *bushlats* and the felt boots. The GUM now displayed goods manufactured in the Hungarian People's Republic, the Czechoslovak Socialist Republic, and the German Democratic Republic. Tourists, entertainers, and politicians from all corners of the earth were flocking to the Soviet Union, and the streets of Moscow reflected the change.

The Hotel National also had changed. To accommodate the ever-increasing numbers of visitors, Nina and Marsha joined Maria at the front desk. Stalin's portrait had disappeared, and none took its place. The hotel's clientele were among the elite of Europe and North America. The restaurant catered to the Churchills, the Roosevelts, Gulbekian, Michael Todd, Ralph Bunche, and the cast of *Porgy and Bess*. Young Van Cliburn captured the hearts of the Soviets, and the prodigy became the first American to win the prestigious Tchaikovsky piano competition. Movies such as Todd's version of Tolstoy's *War and Peace* and the Oscar-winning *Marty* were being shown on Soviet screens.

Soviet teens were scrounging the streets of Moscow, seeking out American tourists to buy jeans and singing the latest Western tunes. Anything American they wanted.

Tourists came from all over the world, by the thousands, to get their first look at what was once a closed society. The corroded Iron Curtain still stood, as leaders on both sides of the Atlantic kept their missiles pointed at each other.

But those who came in those first waves, young and old, fellow travelers or McCarthyites, believed that their hotel rooms were bugged and that the KGB was following their every move. Freedom was still elusive for the Ivan on the street. The midnight knocks on apartment doors were now few and far between, but the threat remained.

Since Stalin's death, I had taken up my pen and had been writing to every member of the Politburo and every high-ranking Party member—Khrushchev, Mikoyan, Bulganin, Kaganovich, and Yekaterina Furtseva—urging them to allow me to return to my family. I never received one response. I knew that if the Soviets were allowing tourists into the country, eventually, inevitably, they would have to allow me to go home.

Or liquidate me.

I was willing to take my chances.

I did not know, as I waited to be seated in the dining room of the Hotel National, that one of the keys to my freedom might be in that dining room, on that particular night, September 5, 1957.

I had spent most of the month of August in Riga, where our team competed for the national title. After the tournament and on the way back to Erevan, I had decided to remain in Moscow, as I had done on previous occasions. Maria Petrovna always managed to have a room for me, even as the tourist trade became overwhelming.

My eyes fell on a threesome at one table. A middle-aged man, trim and well dressed, in a dark blue suit, with white shirt and blue necktie, wearing thick glasses, was speaking in Russian, though he did not appear to be Russian, to a waitress, turning and making suggestions to the other two at the table. We briefly exchanged glances. He turned to an elderly, white-haired woman sitting next to him and whispered something.

The woman had a distinguished air. A white knit cape was draped over her shoulders and came up to her swanlike neck. Saying nothing to him, she just nodded in response. I did not recognize her then, though I had seen her face in many newspapers and newsreels. She had been in the political spotlight during most of my "other life."

Next to the window, one that overlooked the Kremlin, sat a much younger woman.

It seemed unusual that they would prefer sitting on one side of the table facing the other diners and not across from one another. They sparkled in jewelry and rings. They were definitely not from the Eastern European bloc of socialist countries.

In the far corner toward the street side, at a window table, sat a young family. The father wore an officer's uniform, indicating that he was in the Red Army Air Force. I could not see the mother's face; she had her back to me. But the boy, sitting next to his mother, turned his head, and I guessed his age to be about eight. He had curly black hair and looked more Armenian than Russian.

I counted three KGB officers sitting alone at separate tables, with no food before them, and wondered why the KGB had assigned so many to the National on this specific evening.

Irina, a waitress I knew from previous visits, spotted me and rushed over. She was very nervous, and I reassured her that I was still madly in love with her, that I needed her smile to get me through the evening.

"Why are they here?" I whispered to her as she led me to my usual table.

"*Tikha,* Tommy, *tikha.* You know they still have ears."

"Nonsense. They are as frustrated as all of us. Send them each a bottle of vodka and my sympathies. That should loosen up their tongues."

She begged me to keep quiet.

For some reason, on this night, I just couldn't restrain myself. I felt like going over and sitting with one of the KGB officers and discussing the resurrection of their prick, Beria.

Irina whispered, "Tommy, I have news—very good news—for you."

"Ah, you have obtained passports so that we can run away to America, yes?"

"No . . ."

We reached my table, and I slipped into a chair where I faced a mirror. My back was to the rest of the dining room.

"Vodka?" she asked.

"Nothing better to drown my sorrows with."

"Ikrah?"

"Please."

"So, what's the good news?" I asked. "Has Nikita Sergeivich

decided to give us back the money the government takes out of our paychecks each month?"

She laughed and said, "Your president's wife is here, dining with two others." Her words did not immediately catch hold. She motioned with her head for me to turn around and look at the nearby table. I didn't.

"President Eisenhower's wife?" I asked. "Are you sure?"

She corrected me. *"Nyet, nyet.* Not Eisenhower. The good president's wife, you know, Roosevelt."

"Eleanor Roosevelt is here?"

"Da."

"In Moscow?"

"Da." Irina nodded again toward the table behind her. I followed her movement, and my eyes became glued on the threesome behind me.

"Eleanor Roosevelt," I said aloud. Too late to check myself, I was sure they had heard me.

"Da, da," crooned Irina. "Roo-see-velt."

I glanced into the mirror in front of me and stared at the table behind me. I confirmed who the white-haired lady was. So that was why the three KGB agents were spread out around the room, to shield her against people like me.

"Irina," I said. "Go get me a bottle of vodka."

"Of course, of course, but do not do anything foolish," she said, running off to fetch me what I needed to give me courage to get through the evening.

I continued to stare into the mirror, hoping that it wasn't playing tricks. It wasn't. Eleanor Roosevelt was sitting only two tables away from me. I needed to act, but only after a drink. It went down smoothly. I got up and sat down again. I needed another drink. I felt I was really ready.

My plan was a simple one. Just get up from my table, walk over, and welcome her and her party to the Soviet Union. I was sure she would invite me to sit down, and then we would talk. I would tell her how the Soviets refused to allow their citizens out of the country unless they left their families behind. How I had wanted to leave for more than a decade, but they refused even to consider it. How I had written to everyone who appeared to have power, yet not one had responded.

Surely, if Mrs. Roosevelt was in the Soviet Union, she was there to help ease the tensions. She would meet with Chairman Khrushchev. There could be no better goodwill gesture than to allow those who didn't want to stay to leave.

Would she need something in writing from me, and if so, what should I write? What would the KGB agents do once I moved toward the table? I did not think they would make a scene in front of her, right in the restaurant. I wondered if they would try to arrest me. I doubted it. Soviets idolized FDR, worshipped him as a god. The KGB would not dare intervene.

I learned later that her male companion was a longtime friend and physician, Dr. David Gurewitsch. Dr. Gurewitsch had accompanied her to the Soviet Union because of growing concerns for her health. The third person in the party was her personal secretary, Maureen Corr.

I chugged down my last glass of vodka, got up from the table, and made my move.

Was it the vodka, or was that Tatiana's face staring at me from the other end of the room? As if hypnotized, I walked right past Eleanor Roosevelt, stumbling on the leg of a table as I passed. I headed toward the end of the dining room and found myself standing face-to-face with Tatiana.

This had to be one of my nightmares.

"Tatiana?"

The air force officer stood up and started to leave. Tatiana waved him back.

"Tommy." She looked at me. I stared back at her. Then she turned to the man standing next to her.

"Lieutenant Pinkerton," she said, addressing me, "this is my husband, Captain Mikhailov."

She was speaking in Russian. Did I understand her correctly? Had she said he was her husband? I looked at her. At the man in uniform. And the boy with them. I didn't know what to say. What could I say? There was a moment or two of awkward silence before the boy's voice interrupted the drama.

"Mother," he said, "why do you play games? He is not Lieutenant

Pinkerton. He's the basketball player, you know, Amerikanski Tom. We have seen him play."

I looked at the boy, then at Tatiana, and my eyes returned to the boy, and his eyes, so much like my mother's, so much like mine. I stared, looking into a mirror. I could not take my eyes away. I shook my head, trying to clear it of the vodka.

"I apologize," I heard myself saying, returning my focus to Tatiana. "I . . . I must go."

Tatiana made a move toward me, and I heard her say, "You don't understand, Tommy, you don't understand."

She was right, of course. "Men never understand, Tatiana. All a man wants from a woman is the truth."

None of the three KGB officers in the room made a move to subdue me or to stop the scene. That didn't surprise me. I had played basketball in Moscow so many times that they knew who I was, and if they didn't, they should have.

I walked out of the dining room and reached the stairway, which seemed to be swaying like a suspension bridge during a storm. Down the first step, my shoes sinking into the plush red carpeting, then the next, and suddenly I could hear Maria at her desk. She glanced up, and I looked down. She had a strange look on her face. Then I was on my back at the bottom of the staircase, looking into Maria's deep blue eyes.

Maria gently lifted my head. *"Malchik, are you all right?"*

I didn't remember replying. I vaguely remembered her nodding and telling the *militzia,* who had stormed into the lobby when they heard the commotion, *"Nichevo. Nichevo. He is one of ours."*

Someone took me upstairs to my room and put me on the bed. I wanted to die.

Chapter 43

PLEADING MY CASE

T he next morning, as I slowly regained consciousness from a very deep sleep, I saw visions of Tatiana and Eleanor Roosevelt. I found myself doubting what I was certain was true. It must have been Mrs. Roosevelt in the restaurant. And I supposed it followed that that woman, that beautiful woman, was Tatiana, with a son . . . and a husband. I did not know which was most unbelievable, seeing Eleanor Roosevelt at the National in Moscow or seeing Tatiana with a husband and a son.

I forced myself out of the bed, managed to get to the bathroom, and looked into the mirror. The reflection was an appalling telltale story of my foolishness. I not only felt but also looked like hell.

Nevertheless, if Mrs. Roosevelt was not a dream, I had to see her and talk to her. Maybe she could help me return home. The only one who could confirm whether the former first lady was staying at the hotel was Maria Petrovna, the hotel's longtime manager. I quickly tossed on my sweatsuit, slipped on my sweat socks and gym shoes. I didn't take time to shave or shower. I rushed out of my room like a madman and raced down the stairs to Maria's desk. She wasn't there. Nina was still on duty. I was not close to Nina. I saw her as a direct line to the secret police. I nodded and greeted her with a smile, and she returned it. Then I turned and rushed up the stairway. Halfway up, I bumped into and almost floored an elderly woman.

"Young man!" she said, admonishing me as I hung onto her so she wouldn't fall. "You must be more careful."

As I looked into her face, newsreels flashed through my mind. I apologized profusely for my clumsiness and continued to stare. I was standing and holding the woman who, when the Daughters of the American Revolution had refused to allow a black American singer, Marian Anderson, to sing in Washington, D.C., at a hall the DAR owned, immediately resigned from the organization. Then she helped organize a concert for Anderson, which took place on the steps of the

Lincoln Memorial, where thousands showed up to pay tribute. It was this woman's husband, Franklin Delano Roosevelt, who gave a nation of 13 million unemployed workers hope by proclaiming, "The only thing we have to fear is fear itself," and then led the nation to prosperity and victories over Nazi Germany and Imperial Japan. I was staring into the face of Eleanor Roosevelt, and I started to plead my case.

"I am truly sorry," I repeated several times as I stood there, one step below where she was standing. She looked silently at me. What must she have been thinking, except what a rude and uncouth person I was? "You are Mrs. Roosevelt," I said, recoiling at the stupidity of the comment as soon as it came out of my mouth.

"Yes, and are you not the young man who made that scene in the restaurant last night?"

I nodded.

"I thought so. So, you are an American."

"Yes. I mean, no . . ."

"Well, young man, what is it, yes or no?"

I knew I had only a few minutes before Mrs. Roosevelt's friends or the KGB would intervene. I explained that I had left the States with a group of Armenian Americans, and though I couldn't speak for the others, I wanted to go home. But the Soviets would not issue me an exit visa. "If there is anything you can do so that I could be reunited with my family, I would appreciate it."

"What can I do?" she asked.

Honestly, I didn't know. For instance, I did not know at the time that in 1948, Mrs. Roosevelt had coauthored the "Universal Declaration of Human Rights," an amendment to the United Nations charter, approved unanimously by the UN, which guaranteed the rights of the individual. But I said, "Maybe the UN can help?"

She listened but didn't comment. Instead, she asked, "What is your name?"

I told her.

"And you haven't been home since . . ."

"Since 1947."

"That's a long time."

I nodded. Then I looked around, and I could see people gathering at the top of the stairway. I looked back at her and said, "I must go. I know you'll never realize how much hope you have given me, just standing here and speaking with me." I told her what the waitress had said last night when she told me that the president's wife was in the dining room.

She asked, "Will you have breakfast with us?"

"There is nothing in the world that I would like more. But if I did, I don't know what the KGB would do."

Mrs. Roosevelt nodded to show that she understood. "I will do my best to help."

I thanked her, stepped aside to let her by, and started back to my room. I felt her eyes following me as I continued up the steps. As soon as I reached my room and was inside, my body began to tremble. My mouth went dry. I was certain there would be a confrontation with the KGB. I waited for the knock on the door. It came shortly afterward. It was someone sent from the front desk. I must leave the hotel. There was a delegation from France, and the hotel needed my room. Things had definitely changed in the Soviet Union.

Chapter 44

THE HARLEM GLOBETROTTERS

Moscow had consumed me. The heartache of my breakup with Tatiana exacerbated my drinking. It was the first time in my Soviet life that I had wanted to get out of Moscow as fast as I could and return to the provincial life of Erevan. I wanted to get back to the kids at the Pioneers' Palace and to playing basketball and throwing the ball on the wall. I wanted time to think, maybe to talk to Jak. I knew I would never get the truth from Tatiana. The pain of seeing her with a son and a husband was excruciating.

Should I not have known? Were there clues that I hadn't seen, didn't catch? When did she marry? How could she have had a child and I didn't even know? I reflected on his face, especially his eyes. I could not help but wonder whose child he was.

Anyone who has been around the Soviet block as many times as I had should have known that, like everything else, love rarely had a Cinderella ending. Soviet life generally was built block by block on deceit, and relationships were as precarious as a Soviet-U.S. weapons pact.

I did not know how I would ever get her out of my mind. Although it was obvious that she was no longer going to be in my life, I knew that she would always be a part of me.

I knew that everywhere I went, there would be memories, years of memories, some of them more pleasant than others, many a combination of joy and pain. Wherever we were together—at museums, at the opera, or strolling down the ancient Moscow streets—I remembered the way passersby would glance at us. When we looked beyond the hatred reflected on the billboards and put aside the childish politics expostulated in the media by our two countries, we talked about the beauty and creativeness in life and in mankind. Nonetheless, we knew the reality that there would always be a wedge between us as long as there was a Soviet Union.

And as more and more tourists were coming and there were more cultural exchanges between the two superpowers, I knew it would be only a matter of time before I would be leaving.

But I still could not believe that she was married and had a son, maybe ten years old? I wanted to know the answers, but there are some secrets women will never share with men, even though they love them dearly. That was a lesson I paid a dear price to learn.

The flight from Moscow's Vnukova airport to Erevan was the longest in my life.

The struggle to maintain my sanity and attend basketball practices and classes drained me. I managed somehow to survive during the daylight hours, thanks to basketball. It was the evenings and nightfall that I feared the most. Returning to my empty and dark apartment was like returning to the silence of a grave.

Before dawn one day, I found myself on the balcony looking westward at the Ararat. A decade had passed since Simonian had awakened me from my sleep on the train, urging me to look out into the breaking daylight at the sacred mount. Ten years. Had it really been that long? God, how time had passed.

Simonian was gone. Johnny had married and moved out of the apartment. Abraham had married. And Armenak, also married, had left Erevan with his wife for Kazakhstan. I tried to date other women, but the relationships dissipated quickly, for Armenian women wanted to marry and have families. They were not interested in relationships that would not lead to the altar.

And there I was, in that apartment, on a balcony, gazing out at the snowcapped mountain, still pondering what I had done to my life because of one decision made ten years ago. What could I have become if I had remained in America?

The mysteries of life. I would never know. I was alone.

Would it not have been far better for everyone if the NKVD officer's weapon had been loaded?

As I pondered the mystery of the mountain that stood before me, whose ice-capped peaks pierced the clouds and reached the heavens, a mountain that had been a witness to all of man's history and still managed to keep its most holy secrets, I wondered what else this land had in store for me.

~ IN LATE April 1959, as our team competed in the Transcaucasian Games in Tiflis, news had spread among the players and coaches that the Harlem Globetrotters were scheduled to play in Moscow. There was no way I was going to miss the Globetrotters. By now, I was "free" to travel wherever I pleased in the Soviet Union, without having someone tail me.

We posted an easy victory over Baku and defeated the host, Georgia, to win our first Transcaucasian championship. Everything was going my way.

I promised Abraham that I would bring back some Globetrotters souvenirs, and my coach besieged me with requests for diagrams of Trotter plays and strategies so he could introduce them into our games. I did not have the heart to tell him that though the Globetrotters were great athletes, they were noted mostly for clowning on the court and that they "freelanced" more than they set up plays. They played the game to please crowds, have fun, and make money. They also did things on the court to themselves and to the refs that most players only dreamed of doing, such as smacking a ref's derriere with the ball after a supposedly bad call.

I flew to Moscow the week of the game. I had been given front-row seats, thanks to my contacts in the Ministry of Sports. They were not the best seats from which to study strategy, but they were great for being seen by the crowds. When "Sweet Georgia Brown" began its spin on the public address system, I felt as if I was back home.

The familiar drills of driving to the basket for lay-ups and practicing jump shots, along with spinning, twirling, and whirling basketballs, all part of the act to prepare for the game, were part of the routine. But the Trotters proved, to me, at least, that the laws of gravity could be defied. The players seemed to levitate themselves from the key toward and above the rim and stuffed the ball into the basket while their opponents were still rising to the rim and laying the ball into the net. Then came a phenomenon that I believed was the Eighth Wonder of the World: Wilt Chamberlain, the seven-foot utility pole, lighting up the gym as he walked onto the floor with a towel over his shoulders. "Man or beast?" some whispered. He strolled past, and we exchanged glances.

I was reminded of two seven-foot giants I had played against, though they were nothing like Chamberlain.

The two Soviet players could barely run and could not get off the floor. The muscle-bound Krumish, a woodcutter from the Latvian hinterlands, eventually developed into a so-so player for Daugava Riga and made his American debut in New York against the Phillips Oilers in 1960 with the touring Soviet national team. But seven-foot-two Akhtayev, a Chechnyan from Alma Ata in Kazakhstan, struggled physically to make it up and down the court. He never played outside the Soviet Union.

The first time I saw and played against Akhtayev was in Leningrad, where our team took part in the national collegiate championships. I was resting on a cot, almost asleep, when I heard the footsteps of what I believed was an elephant outside the dorm-room door. I opened my eyes and looked across the room at a rectangular window that was a little more than seven feet from the floor. I watched as the shape of a human head as large as a watermelon passed by. I thought I was dreaming. When I realized it was not a dream, for the thundering footsteps continued down the hallway, I leaped from the cot, rushed to open the door, and looked down the corridor. I could hardly believe what I saw: a huge mass of humanity, an escapee from *Gulliver's Travels,* who took up the entire corridor. Compared with that grotesque mountain of flesh, I had shrunk to the size of a Lilliputian. This thing turned and stared at me with eyes as huge as lightbulbs.

"*Yop vas mat!*" the creature growled at me, his voice shaking the rafters. His locker-room language did not faze me; my teachers, in a quick course of Russian expletives, had taught me well.

I was quick to respond. "And your mother's, too," I shouted back, tossing the gauntlet.

The giant took one step forward. I took two steps back. If he fell on me, I thought, my six-foot frame would be razor-thin.

"I'll step on you tomorrow and crush you like a fly, you fuckin' American freak!"

He apparently knew that we had drawn Kazakhstan in the first round of the tournament. I realized that he knew who I was.

"Freak? Freak?" I shouted to the mountaintop. "Look who's calling who a freak!"

We beat them 7–4. No, that's not a typo. We stalled for most of the game.

We developed a lot of professional respect for each other over the years. In fact, he wanted me to join his team in Alma Ata.

~ THE GLOBETROTTERS had a full house waiting to see their performance, and they were quick to disappoint the crowd. Fans had come to see an extraordinary group of athletes play basketball, not a bunch of zany grown-ups masquerading as clowns. Moreover, if the Soviets had wanted to see clowns, they boasted one of the finest in the world in Karandash and one of the best circuses on earth. When it came to clowns, the Globetrotters weren't in the same league as the Soviets.

In Soviet sports and theater, performers who disappointed patrons didn't get the shepherd's hook but were heckled by deafening, shrieking, whistling audiences. The internationally renowned Globetrotters were no exception. Their gimmicks of bouncing the ball off players and referees and stopping in midcourt to argue with the ref may have pleased American fans but not the Soviets. Soviet fans paid their hard-earned rubles to see the Globetrotters play basketball. When the Globe-trotters and the Philadelphia Warriors, the team that had accompanied them to Moscow, got down to the serious business of playing basket-ball, the way two rival teams usually played, the fans showed their appreciation and respect for the teams by applauding. And the applause shook the foundation of Lenin's Stadium that afternoon.

Of course, the Globetrotters won—but didn't they always?

The applause shook the foundation of Lenin's Stadium that after-noon, for the Globetrotters brought the game to a level never before seen in the Soviet Union. I was as drained as if I had played right along with them. Watching them pass, dribble, and drive to the basket brought back memories of home, memories that pierced my heart.

After the game, I got up from my seat and walked onto the floor. I wondered how I would have fit in if I had stayed in Detroit, if I had opted to stay in college and play in America. Almost in a trance, I meandered through the crowd, heading for an exit. Unexpectedly, I found myself face-to-face with one of the Globetrotters. We paused, sizing each other up. I introduced myself and told him I had played high-school ball in Detroit.

He smiled and told me he was raised on the east side of Detroit.

"Do you know Sammy Gee?" I asked.

"Sammy! Hell, we grew up in the same neighborhood. He played for us." He asked how I knew Sammy.

"I played against him in the city finals in '46."

"I heard a lot about that game. I'm Bobby Hall. They call me Showboat."

We could not stop talking. A crowd began to gather, and the fans asked what we were talking about. Deciding that it was not the place to reminisce, I asked Bobby where they were staying.

"At the Hotel Ukraine."

"How about breakfast, so we can talk?"

"Great."

"About nine?"

"In the morning? You must be kidding. We don't even open our eyes until noon. We party after games."

I laughed. "So do we."

"Then you're still playing?"

"Yeah."

"Who are you playing for?"

"The Soviets."

"You're kidding me, aren't you?"

"No. I'll tell you all about it tomorrow."

The next day, I took a cab to the Hotel Ukraine. As I entered the hotel lobby, I spotted Abe Saperstein, the Globetrotters' owner, at a table in a corner, leaning forward and chatting with another American. I later learned that Saperstein was conferring with Eddie Gottlieb, the owner of the Philadelphia Warriors.

I walked up to the desk and told the clerk that I had an appointment to meet one of the Globetrotters. He called up to the room. As I waited in the lobby, I was amazed at the number of foreign tourists in the lobby and the equal number of young Russians trying to hustle foreign currency from them. No KGB agents.

The Trotter came down for me and told me that the boys would like to meet me. If I didn't mind, we could skip breakfast and go directly upstairs. I was not hungry for food but for information about the States. There were several players, including Wilt, spread out between two rooms. We all sat around and talked basketball. Of course, when players get together, basketball is not the only topic. We also talked about women.

Were there prostitutes?

Yes, but they tended to shy away from foreigners.

Not even call girls?

Definitely not. There were usually hidden cameras in hotel rooms, so beware. Big Brother definitely was watching.

And why wasn't the most ancient of professions practiced here?

Where the hell were they going to shack up? There were families of six sharing one- or two-room apartments. There were no available rooms. The parks were crowded with *militzia*. Most lovers did it in the stairwells. And that was late, very late at night, when most had gone to bed. Very uncomfortable, wouldn't you say?

Did I speak from experience?

That was the only way I spoke.

And then someone asked me when was the last time I had been home.

Twelve years ago.

Silence. Broken by the question of why.

How naive, I thought. As naive as I had been. But I replied, "Because I can't get out. The Soviets won't issue me an exit visa."

Wilt said, "That's no problem." He was lying on the floor, his back to the wall, and I turned to look at him.

"No problem for you, Wilt. Big problem for me."

Wilt sized me up, then asked, "What do you weigh, about one-ninety?"

"Close enough. Why?"

He revealed his plan. He would stuff me into the ball bag and carry me aboard the plane.

"And the KGB is going to allow you to do that?"

"I would like to see them stop me."

I didn't say anything, but I thought about it. The reality was that I didn't want to stir up any trouble for them, and I felt that their visiting Moscow supported the belief that the Cold War was defrosting. There were more cultural exchanges than ever. Khrushchev planned to go to the United States later that year, and the Bolshoi Ballet had been touring the States while the Globetrotters were in Moscow. In 1960, President Eisenhower was scheduled to attend a Big Four Summit meeting in Paris with Soviet premier Nikita Khrushchev, France's president Charles de Gaulle, and British prime minister Harold Macmillan.

"Thanks, but no thanks," I told Wilt. It was too risky. Besides, I was not there seeking help; I just wanted to enjoy their company. I was convinced more than ever that since the Soviets had opened the door to tourists, it would be only a matter of time before they would allow me to leave the country.

I had waited so long; I could wait a bit longer.

Chapter 45

PAINKILLERS

I was back in Moscow for the summer. Jak and I were coaching the girls' basketball team. We had drawn Estonia in the first round of the junior basketball championships. I was designated head coach of Armenia's girls' team, and Jak served as my assistant. We might have been looking ahead to our next opponent, rather than concentrating on the first pairing. We were not prepared for an Estonian team that had upset on its mind.

Our team looked tired, played tired, and was quickly trailing by a dozen points. The burden of guilt fell on my shoulders, for I had taken the girls the day before to Sokolniki Park to tour the United States' National Exhibition. They enjoyed every bit of what they saw, and when it was time to leave, as kids will do, they begged to stay "just a few more minutes." I agreed. It had been an exhausting day, and it showed in the players' performances on the court.

We had more talent than Estonia. More experience. More everything. But we made early mistakes, turnovers, missed easy shots, and quickly fell behind. Playing catchup while making mistakes, feeling out of sync, could be fatal. In short, we allowed the Estonians to infiltrate our zone defense, allowed them to take unchallenged shots, did not go to the boards for rebounds on defense, and let them score on the easy put-backs.

I called more than one time-out in the first half and had already been slapped with a technical foul for challenging a ref's call. It wasn't too long after the first that—according to Jak later—I rushed onto the court and almost pulled one of my players off. Bobby Knight was a pussycat compared with me on a rampage. I was slapped with another technical. As I was ordered off the court, I told the ref I knew what his mother had done as a profession before he was born, and he immediately rushed me. Fists flew.

Jak separated the ref and me before my fists gave the idiot a facial makeover. But the official had the last say, as is usually the case in these kinds of altercations.

I was ejected. Jak took over the team. I told him that I was sticking around to taunt the refs from the crowd. He told me it would be best for all if I would leave the park and return to the dorm. I didn't say anything. I left the court to the jeers and taunts of the fans.

My actions were completely out of line, but they reminded me of my behavior the year I was on painkillers because of an injury I had sustained on the court. I had stolen the ball at midcourt from one of the guards on the Georgian team during a game in Odessa and was dribbling toward the basket for what I had believed would be an uncontested lay-up. I did not know that the guard was a step or two behind me. As I went up for the two-pointer, the other player caught my jaw from behind and pulled, and I plummeted, after flipping head over heels, onto my back on the solid red clay surface of the court. My head struck the surface, and I was knocked unconscious. Abraham told me later that he thought he would find my brains spilled on the surface of the playing field, but when I replied that that would be impossible because I didn't have any brains, he knew I was all right.

But I wasn't.

I might have survived the fall, but a few weeks later, I had excruciating back pains that would not ease with the local remedies of camphor rubbed in the area of the pain or hot and cold compresses or massage or the usual grandma's cure of bleeding with leeches.

Then a Bulgarian-Armenian doctor introduced me to a drug called Pervitine, a stimulant that appeared to give me some relief from the back pain—and everything else that ailed me that day. I had been sent to him by the Institute's medical staff, and when I explained to him about the pain and the spasms, he, after a thorough examination, prescribed something that he believed would take care of the pain and also enhance my playing skills and extend my career.

The doctor was right about one thing: the pill relieved my pain momentarily. When the relief disappeared, I would take another pill. And then another. It got so that I could not do anything without the pill. It made me sharper, faster, and more alert, not only on the playing field but also in my association with those around me. There was one drawback. After taking a pill, I couldn't sleep. I would lie down on my cot and close my eyes, but sleep eluded me. I often watched the sun come up without having slept.

Sleepless nights, I soon learned, made for jittery days, incoherent speech, broken promises, and severed ties with those I knew as friends.

It had been a more than a year since I had taken my first pill, and neither Jak, although he must have suspected something was wrong, nor my basketball coach nor my teammates knew that I was caught in a spider's web and that the harder I tried to break away, the tighter I became entangled. I would slip a pill into my mouth an hour or two before a game or whenever I had a problem, imaginary or real, to escape from the world I was in.

When I played the first game of a tournament, any tournament, I would play exceptionally well, but since there were six or seven games in a tournament-style format, in the next game, without sleep, I would look foolish on the floor.

The coach was perplexed and didn't know what was happening to me. I did not know, either.

And no one could stop me from using the pill, made available to me at the physician's office, on my command.

Soon I didn't care about basketball, playing, or coaching. About going back to America. About the way I dressed. About sex.

I went to see the American movie version of *War and Peace,* starring Audrey Hepburn and Henry Fonda. As I was translating, whispering into my companion's ear in Russian what Hepburn was saying in English, a cold sweat came over me. I stopped. My companion looked at me and nudged me to continue the translation. I couldn't. Suddenly, inexplicably, a series of buzzing impulses vibrated in my head, creating a tremendous headache. I could not sit still. She glanced at me again and asked what was wrong. Instead of answering, I got up and left my seat and the theater. I returned to my hotel room and collapsed.

Another time, I was sitting on a circular concrete wall, my feet dangling over the edge, on the third floor of a hotel in Sochi, overlooking the Black Sea. A crowd had gathered below and watched me as I recited something about Humpty Dumpty sitting on a wall. Someone in the group shouted, "Jump, Tommy, jump!" I looked down and stood on the wall. I was about to prove to them that I could fly, that I was indestructible.

One of my teammates snuck up behind me, grabbed me, and managed to subdue me.

And no one yet suspected that I had become addicted. They thought I was homesick.

I managed, miraculously, to make a comeback. I knew I had to. I couldn't allow myself to continue on the road to self-destruction. I returned to my Bulgarian doctor and told him what was happening. He wanted to put me in a hospital. I remembered Simonian's sunken eyes and pale face, standing before the window at the clinic, and I said to the doctor, "Never."

I would rid myself of the need for the pills. And I did, but there were still bouts of depression, and it would take time, much time, for the vibrating sounds within my head to be silenced.

~ WHEN I was ejected from the game, our girls were trailing by some fifteen points. There was, I believed, no hope that we could avoid the loss column and the disgrace that would follow me all the way to Erevan.

I walked through the park, toward the Moscow River, to a ferry stop where I planned to board a boat that would eventually dock behind Saint Basil's Cathedral. My destination was the Hotel National, where I knew a sympathetic mother figure, Maria, would soothe the pain of my guilt.

It was one of those unusual humid-free July afternoons in Moscow. The cool breeze off the river helped to settle my nerves. I found a seat on the boat's second deck. It was empty. A man, wearing a short-sleeved white shirt, dark trousers, and black Russian-made shoes, appeared at the top of the spiral cast-iron stairway. With so many empty seats, I thought it strange that he decided to sit right across from me. Then I remembered that most Russians preferred to sit with others and discuss life, as opposed to the American's preference for privacy. The man smiled as he took his seat. What better way to begin a conversation with a stranger than, "Fine day, isn't it?"

Still frustrated, I sarcastically offered, "Not if you're an Armenian basketball coach."

He kept smiling. "Armenian? But I thought you were an American."
That called for a closer examination. Dark brown circles underscored his blue eyes; streaks of white hair mingled with those of dark blond. He had a fair complexion, was solidly built, and had a body well maintained through vigorous exercise. It all led to a three-letter conclusion: KGB. I thought I had seen him standing behind our bench during the game back in the park. As he sat in front of me, I was not quite sure. His demeanor was more like that of a college professor than an internal security officer.

"We Soviets are very fortunate," the man said, continuing the conversation.

I thought to myself, *Here we go again with the propaganda bit.* "And how is that, comrade?" I asked.

"If all Americans had your temper, we would have had several wars by now."

I laughed and offered, "If Americans got the same kind of biased officiating as my team got, could one blame them for being angry? But war, Tavahrishch, is unjustifiable no matter how angry one gets."

He nodded in agreement.

Then I asked, "Do I know you?"

His response at first confused me, for I felt it was unrelated to my simple question—until I made the connection. He said, "I also believe that American cars are painted up to look like Easter eggs."

Sokolniki Park, only a few days ago, at the American exhibition. While Chairman Khrushchev and Vice President Richard Nixon were debating whether horse shit or pig's shit stank worse, I had struck up a conversation about cars.

"They're all painted up like Easter eggs," he had said.

And I had replied to that criticism, "It provides Americans with an option, something that Russians don't have. Like electing a president every four years, rather than waiting until a leader dies to replace him."

The man in the park hadn't agreed, and we had chatted as we strolled over to the Pepsi display.

"May I buy you a truly American drink?" I had asked the stranger in the park. I admitted that I had not tasted the drink for some time myself, but I thought he would enjoy it.

I'd asked the young lady serving at the display, in English, what the drink cost in rubles.

She had replied, "It's free, courtesy of Pepsi Cola Corporation." And she had poured the Pepsi into paper cups, handing one to me and one to the stranger.

He had tasted it and said to the girl, in Russian, *"Harosho. Ochen harosho.* Good. Very good."

I'd been surprised when the woman replied in Russian, then carried on a conversation with him.

I had drawn the man's attention to the paper cups—not glass, I pointed out to him, but paper, used and then tossed. Russian *kvass* and lemonade vendors used glass cups, then rinsed them in a basin of water and reused them over and over again, spreading germs from patron to patron.

"Maybe," I'd said, "when you file your report, you will note that Americans not only have excellent soft drinks but have paper cups that can be tossed after they are used, so they don't spread disease and germs from one mouth to the other."

He had offered a smile for a comment.

I had laughed, and shortly afterward, the man had disappeared into the crowd that had come to view what America had to offer. History would remember Sokolniki Park as the site of the "Great Kitchen Debate" between Nixon and Khrushchev.

But I would remember it as an introduction to a popular American singer named Elvis Presley.

I had strolled over to the book display and started a conversation with the attractive attendant. She had told me that if I came back on the last day of the exhibition, she could give me a few books free of charge. "After all, it makes no sense packing them up and shipping them back to America." I had told her I was American-born but had left the States and had not been back for some time. I did not mention, however, how long I had been gone.

Later, she had presented me as gifts *Peyton Place* and *The Bad Seed.* In return, she'd accepted my invitation to dine at the Hotel National.

During the meal, the conversation had been pleasant, and I had eagerly listened to news about America. All was going well until she'd asked, "What do you think of Elvis?"

"Elvis? Elvis who?"

"Elvis Presley, of course."

I had admitted that I had never heard the name.

She'd gazed at me from across the table, and suddenly her face had turned red. "I thought so! You are a KBG agent, aren't you?" She had stood up from her chair and stormed out of the restaurant.

That was my introduction to Elvis Presley.

The man on the ferry and the KGB agent in the park were one and the same.

When we reached the dock at the foot of Red Square, I figured the man, whom I had labeled "the messenger," for he did not reveal a name to me, and I would go our separate ways, he to Dzerzhinsky Square, to file his report and call it a day, and I to the National to drink the rest of the day away. But he stayed close by. It not only made me uncomfortable but began to annoy me.

When a taxi pulled up and the driver shouted, "Hey, Tommy, do you want a ride?" I was about to accept, but the messenger waved the driver off with such authority that it left no doubt in my mind what he was or what he represented.

"Our business, Tom Boghosovich, is not completed," he said, turning to me.

"And what business is that, comrade?" I asked.

"We're sending you back home, to your America."

I stopped in my tracks, turned, and looked at him. I searched his face for clues, something to tell me that this was just one of their mind games again. I saw nothing but sincerity. I asked him to repeat what he had just said, to convince myself that the pill was not at work. I had walked the road so precariously the past twelve months, and sometimes I was not sure what was real anymore.

He was. The same words came out, but he said them in such a serious tone that I was sure he was not playing games with my emotions.

We kept walking and talking.

"We are going to give you that visa you have been seeking. We're going to give you permission to go home."

By now, we had reached the Metropole Hotel, the KGB's favorite hunting grounds. "Let us go in off the street and talk." He took me gently by the arm. We walked into the hotel lobby, found a couple of chairs in a secluded corner, and sat down. No sooner had we made ourselves comfortable than a hotel staff member approached us. He apparently recognized the man I was with and asked him if he could be of any service.

"Please bring us a bottle of vodka," the man said, looking at me for approval. I didn't object. The employee disappeared and reappeared seconds later with the bottle and two glasses. The KGB agent opened the bottle and poured my drink. As he poured, he quipped, "Sorry, no paper cups. Vodka tastes better in a glass, yes?" Then he poured an equal amount into his glass.

"To your trip back to America," he said, lifting his glass and tipping it toward me. It went down very smoothly. He sat back and explained the process, that when I got back to Erevan, I was to report to the visa office, and they would provide me with the appropriate forms to be filled out and returned.

"And what if the officials refuse to comply?"

The messanger laughed. "I don't think they would dare do that."

As we enjoyed our first bottle, the messenger talked of the political changes that had come to the Soviet Union, how thousands of American tourists were visiting behind that Iron Curtain. That the Big Four would be meeting in Paris and that Chairman Khrushchev was preparing to visit the United States. He noted that Khrushchev was a man of the people and a man of peace. Had he not proposed peaceful coexistence?

I listened and said nothing.

He was serious. It was no KGB mind game to draw me to the edge. They really believed that they were the strongest nation on the face of the earth. And why shouldn't they think so? Under Khrushchev, on October 4, 1957, the Soviets had launched Sputnik, the first man-made satellite, into orbit around the earth. That shocked the United States and the world. Then, on January 5, 1959, they had followed up by sending a fuel-propelled rocket called the Lunik, a 3,238-pound satellite, on a cosmic journey to the moon, and when Lunik III took its photos, it was the first time in man's history that humans had a look at what was on the other side of the moon. And in April 1961, when Major Yuri Gagarin buckled his seatbelt on the spaceship *Boctok* and orbited the earth, the Soviets had taken the lead in space exploration and became the first to put a man into outer space. On earth, Soviet athletes not only managed to dominate the 1956 Melbourne Olympics, posting 712 points to the United States' 593, but four years later, they ruled Rome with 43 gold medals, 33 silver, and 30 bronze, for a total of 807 points to runner-up United States, which garnered 34 gold, 21 silver, and 16 bronze, for a total of 564 points.

Chairman Khrushchev may have disrupted the UN General Assembly in 1960 by pounding his shoe on the desk during one of its sessions, and he and President Kennedy may have jointly precipitated the Cuban Missile Crisis in 1962, but the peasant from Kalinovka was also brave enough to stand up when others feared to denounce Stalin and his henchmen before the world. He freed those who were wrongly imprisoned, restored the good names of the innocent, and took the first steps on a courageous road to *perestroika*. He lifted the Iron Curtain, enabling me finally to go home.

And I was going home.

I gathered all of the necessary documents, without encountering the usual red tape and without some bureaucrat demanding a bribe.

But there was still one unexpected obstacle.

It didn't come from the KGB. It involved an American-built spy plane, the U-2, piloted by American Francis Gary Powers.

Chapter 46

THE LONGEST WAIT

I could not believe how long and drawn out the procedure was for obtaining an exit visa. Perhaps it should not have come as any surprise, but twelve months was a long time. I was not allowed to speak with anyone about it but had to continue in my normal routine, coaching and playing basketball. Where did I get the strength to function?

And, of course, there was always the concern that the Soviets were playing another one of their mind games, as the days turned into weeks, then months, and there was no news from the visa office.

Jak believed that the source of my melancholy was my breakup with Tatiana. I didn't discourage that misconception. I wanted to tell Jak, but the messenger's warning held me in check. During one of our class breaks, Jak observed, "You're very distant these days, my friend. You seem to be carrying a heavy burden on your shoulders. Allow me to help lighten the load."

I apologized to him and tried to assure him that I would be all right.

"A friend close by is more valuable than a brother who lives on the other side of the ocean," Jak reminded me.

I thanked him again. "You have been like a brother to me all these years. I shall not forget you."

"You sound as if you're going somewhere, Tommy."

I didn't say anything. I couldn't.

As late as April 1960, there was still no word from the visa office. The unexplained delays heightened my anxiety.

Then, on a bright, clear May 1, International Workers' Day, when the twisted steel and debris that was part of the U-2 spy plane piloted by Francis Gary Powers plummeted to earth after being struck by a Soviet missile near the industrial city of Sverdlovsk, I knew the political atmosphere in the country would change.

The missile that brought down that U-2 also shattered my dreams of returning home.

Russians prepared for the worst. The U-2 was headline news in *Pravda,* and Jak rushed into the Pioneers' Palace office, reading the account.

"Any decent Soviet pilot would have gone down with his plane," Jak said with a smirk on his face. Then he gave me a blow-by-blow account of what was published in the official Communist newspaper and what we could expect, including a confession by the pilot himself.

"Then the pilot's alive?"

"Of course, or *Pravda* would not be printing these things."

The unthinkable had happened, and I could not find the words to defend the United States. I felt the humiliation that America must feel. But it was my country, right or wrong.

I had to assume that the United States had returned to the days of the Cold War, with the Stalin era resurrected. After listening to what Jak had to say about the spy-plane incident, a possibility crossed my mind. Perhaps it was the United States that was holding up my papers. Perhaps America didn't want undesirables, like myself, to come back.

In the days that followed the U-2 incident, Russians again refused to look foreigners in the eye and walked on the other side of the street when they saw one on the boulevard. *This is where I came in,* I said to myself.

If only Powers, as Jak and others noted, would have done what any decent Soviet spy would have done under the same circumstances and injected the poison-tipped needle into his vein, there would be little controversy. I, like most Russians, could not understand why President Eisenhower didn't apologize, as Khrushchev requested. The Eisenhower administration initially offered an inane excuse that the plane was nothing but "a weather plane" that had inadvertently strayed into Soviet territory.

But when the TV cameras were turned on in the Hall of Justice in Moscow and a bruised but very much alive Powers walked into the spotlight, the mystery of the international intrigue cleared in seconds. The Russians kept snickering and eyeing Americans suspiciously as Powers informed the world that his mission had been one of espionage, to photograph Soviet military installations.

President Eisenhower could do nothing but confess that the United States was indeed spying on its former ally. "We have been caught with our hand in the cookie jar," Eisenhower said. The political stupidity and flawed diplomacy on both sides of the Atlantic led to the demise of the Big Four summit scheduled in May.

The backlash of the U-2 incident created an aura of suspicion for anything American. The jeans, the chewing gum, the dollar seekers disappeared from Erevan's streets, and I was sure they also had disappeared from Moscow.

I had all but given up hope of ever returning home.

I tossed the messenger's warning to the wind and told all to Jak. His immediate response was, "If Moscow tells you that you can return to America, and you really want to go, then go back to OVIR and inform those incompetent sons of bitches that you have been given permission to leave, and that if you do not receive your visa within the next few days, you will have no alternative but to return to Moscow and report their incompetence to Chairman Khrushchev. And if they ask for *paparck,* inform them that you have an obligation to report that, too, to Moscow."

~ MY LUGGAGE was packed. My personal items, including many of my trophies, were sold. I was waiting with my walking papers in hand. I was going, by plane, to Moscow.

In the capital, I found the Russians in a festive mood. Powers had confessed his sins, and the Soviets were riding high on their success. America and the Americans, as Soviet Russians had painted them over the years, were the villains.

For some reason, I was glad when Maria told me she could not accommodate me at the Hotel National. I told her I understood, and she called Ostankino, a hotel in a nearby suburb, to prepare a room for me. I rode out there in a taxi. As soon as I settled in, I called the U.S. Embassy and set up an appointment to meet with embassy officials.

I was nervous, excited, scared, jubilant, and shaking inside and out as the taxi pulled onto Tchaikovsky Street and stopped in front of the U.S. Embassy. I was just a few steps away from American soil. I got out of the taxi and looked at the seal of the United States of America, then up at the American flag. Physically and emotionally, I was at my limit. I worked at maintaining control but found myself wondering what awaited me behind the door. I heaved a deep sigh, trying to calm myself, opened the door, and entered the lobby of the embassy. I was inside. It was true. It was no dream. I was going to make it—and not in a box.

The receptionist greeted me with a smile and, after I announced who I was, said I had an appointment to see Richard E. Snyder.

Snyder was counsel to Ambassador Llewellyn Thompson. I was ushered into Snyder's office, where, after preliminary introductions and chatting, we were joined by John McVickar. One of them asked me how long I had been in the USSR, and when I replied, they looked at me in disbelief.

"And what have you been doing here all this time?"

"Trying to get back to the United States."

They laughed.

I explained that I played basketball for a living.

Did I need any financial assistance to get home?

"No. I was paid as a coach and a player, and I have more than enough rubles to pay for the plane ticket back to America."

The interview was direct, simple, and very cordial.

"How old were you when you left America?"

"Nineteen."

"You were a minor, then."

"I guess so."

The two men looked at each other. I, of course, did not know that consulate officials had had a problem with a nineteen-year-old recently, an ex-Marine by the name of Lee Harvey Oswald, who had probably sat in the same seat I was sitting in, across from the same two men. Only a few months before, Oswald had angrily denounced the United States and announced that he wanted to renounce his American citizenship and planned to become a citizen of the USSR. And here I was, almost in tears because I was about to have my citizenship restored.

"We see no problems with your application," one of the men told me, and he asked how I could be contacted.

I told them where I was staying.

"We'll let you know in a few days."

After shaking hands and leaving the office, there was still the street outside the embassy that had to be cleared. I wondered if they would be there, or had times really changed? No, they hadn't. The KGB-assigned surveillance of the embassy was still roaming the immediate area. As I glanced down the street, I saw one standing at the corner with his cameraman, I guess, stationed somewhere across the way taking photos.

I smiled the best I could for the camera, hailed a taxi, and rode to the Hotel National. No incident.

In the next few days, I visited the Gosbank to exchange rubles for dollars and received the limit allowed a Soviet traveler to take out of the country, one hundred dollars, to be shown at the gate of departure. Ironically, it was about as much money as I had entered the country with thirteen years before. That left me with thousands of worthless rubles I had to spend before I left. Definitely party time. And party I did.

I spent my last night in Moscow at the National. I tossed a small party that got bigger and bigger as the night went on. At one time, I noticed at least six or seven Iranian pilots in my group. They were in the USSR training to fly Russian MIGs. We drank together until dawn.

At the break of dawn on August 2, 1960, I was on my way to Sheremetyevo Airport.

Chapter 47

YOU CAN GO HOME AGAIN

As I walked down the newly reconstructed concourse to the departure gate where I would board the Il-162 plane for Copenhagen, a thousand and one thoughts flared up in my mind, most of them shrouded in fear. Fear of the present—I was not home free yet; there were still customs and the KGB at the gate to clear. Fear of the past—had I betrayed my teammates or my fellow staffers at the Pioneers' Palace? And the haunting memories of Tatiana. Then, there was the future—what awaited me on the other side of the Atlantic? How much had I changed, and how much had America changed, during the last thirteen years?

A passenger carrying only one small valise, containing a couple of shirts, a necktie or two, and sundries, with one hundred dollars issued by the government, should not have any problems clearing customs, I repeated to myself. There, of course, would be the obligatory questions from the KGB agent stationed at the gate. He would focus carefully on my documents, but they had been issued legally, and I was not hiding anything. They surely knew who I was and where I was going by now.

I was going home, and that was all that mattered.

I greeted the customs official with a smile and obeyed his request to hand over the valise for inspection. He gave it a quick once-over and handed it back to me.

"Anything else to declare?" he asked with a smirk.

"These are all my earthly belongings," I replied in perfect Russian. He nodded for me to proceed to the next gate.

The KGB officer was next, and I had my documents in my hand, ready for him.

"And where is your destination?" he asked as he flipped the pages of my two passports.

"Home. To the USA."

The muscles in his neck and face tightened.

"CWA?" he replied, using the three letters of the Russian alphabet that translated to USA.

I nodded but didn't say another word. The officer beckoned another official to assist him, and someone in plain clothes came over and joined us.

Now what? I wondered. I had given him two passports, one in brilliant red with the seal of the Soviet Union. Before I had left Moscow, I was told that I had to surrender my Russian passport to the Soviet Embassy in Copenhagen, and then a Soviet official would accompany me to the U.S. Embassy. My second passport, in teal, with the emblem of the United States embossed on its cover, issued to me by the U.S. Embassy in Moscow, proclaimed that I was an American citizen. It would take me home.

Should I have presented the officer with only one? My Russian passport or my U.S. one? Perhaps the two had created confusion.

I stood, tense, waiting for the outcome of their whispered discussion. I was still vodka-driven by the party at the National the night before, and I was getting more anxious by the second. I sensed that my future was at stake. I repeated to myself that everything would be all right. For 4,750 days, I had waited for this day, for this moment, and nothing was going to prevent me from getting on that plane. Snyder and McVickar had assured me that there would be no problems, because I had regained my American citizenship and had been a minor when I allegedly renounced my rights, and my spirit had been bolstered by their words of confidence. To paraphrase Dorothy in *The Wizard of Oz,* I kept repeating, "I am an American, I want to go home. I am an American, I want to go home. I want to go home now!"

Thirteen years of my youth had been spent behind the Iron Curtain. And I knew these people. They would not let me go without a fight. There were more than 10,000 American tourists in Moscow. Why in heaven would they want to detain me here?

I waited to hear them say that I could pass through the gate to the plane. The order didn't come. It didn't come without raised voices and a scene.

Instead of allowing me to pass through after he returned my passports, the uniformed officer said I must show him the one hundred dollars issued to me by the Soviet government.

I sighed. It was all right. That was all they wanted. I put my hand into my inside jacket pocket, pulled out my wallet, opened it, and reached for the hundred-dollar bill. It was not there.

I desperately dug through all my pockets. The bill was nowhere to be found. Had I misplaced it? Where? Had I left it at the Hotel National? Had someone stolen it? Then I remembered that during the party, during all of that drinking, I had taken the jacket off and laid it across a chair.

All I could hear was, "Comrade, please show us the currency." But the money was not there. I looked at the officer, and he stared at me, waiting for my next words. I told him that I had lost the money. There was a strange smile on his face.

"Lost it?" he repeated. "You have lost the hundred dollars?"

I nodded.

"Follow me," he ordered.

I started to do so, but I realized that if I did, I would miss the plane.

"No. I am going to board that plane. I am going home. Fuck you. I am an American citizen, and I don't take orders from you."

The two men looked at me as if I had lost my mind. They stood there as other tourists began to gather.

"I am an American. You have no right to detain me."

The man in the black suit ordered me to calm down, to keep my voice down.

I shouted back in his face. "No! I am going home, either in a box or on my own two feet. I am going home! I am not going anywhere with you two!"

There was a deadly silence. The knot in the pit of my stomach had turned a thousand times, but this chess game was over. I had flipped the board and refused to budge.

"You are a speculator. You have sold the dollars for rubles," the uniformed officer asserted. "That is why you do not have the dollars."

"And you are a fool to think that!" My voice was getting louder, but I didn't care. "Why would I jeopardize my leaving this country? And where are the thousands of rubles I would have gotten for the dollars? In this valise, maybe. Here, keep the valise." And I tossed my valise at him. "Rubles are worthless in the West."

"Then where is the foreign currency?" the other one asked.

"I don't know. I drank too much last night with friends, and I may have misplaced it. Left it in my hotel room. There is no reason for me to lie. But I do not know where the money is."

They looked puzzled. I quickly cashed in on their indecision.

"Look, comrades," I said wearily. "Somebody will get very angry with you if I don't reach Copenhagen today. Your superiors have approved my departure, have issued me this passport"—I held the Soviet passport up to their faces—"and have provided me with an exit visa. Look at them carefully, understand, comrades, they have approved my departure. I must report to the Soviet Embassy in Copenhagen in a few hours, and if I don't appear, you two will have to explain. Do you want to explain to them why I didn't reach Copenhagen?"

After a brief exchange of words between the two, the one in the dark suit ordered the uniformed officer to escort me to the plane and make sure I got onboard. He turned to me and apologized for the delay. I thanked him.

"Have a good flight, Tom Boghosovich," he said with a smile. "You are free to go."

The uniformed officer led me through the gate, where an airport official took only a superficial glance at my ticket and allowed me onto the plane. My eyes became blurred as I climbed the steps to the cabin. I showed the stewardess my boarding pass, and she led me down the aisle to my seat. I stowed my valise, then sank into the seat. I was actually going to make it. I was going home. The stewardess asked me if I wanted something to drink. I shook my head. I tried to tell myself that men didn't cry, but the tears gathered.

"Is there anything the matter, *gaspadin?*" the stewardess asked, addressing me as a citizen of the West.

I started to reply *nyet,* but the word would not come out. My whole body suddenly began to shake; an indescribable weight had been lifted from my shoulders. In only a few minutes, I would be free. Free to live my life. I attempted a smile; there wasn't one in me.

She touched my shoulder, then retreated, saying, "Soon we will be in Copenhagen. It is a fine city."

I moved over next to the window. The sun was breaking through the clouds, ushering in a new day, affirming that change was about to happen—change, the only absolute constant in life. The plane creaked, groaned, shuddered, and then slowly began to move away from the terminal. It was really happening. This was not one of those dreams. I had made it.

I sat watching the runway disappear as the plane lifted into an azure sky, heading west. When it touched down again, I would be free.

~ CUSTOMS IN Copenhagen took only a perfunctory interest in me. One valise. One American passport. I breezed through. I walked casually out of the airport building, and two vehicles quickly caught my eye—one with a flag of the stars and stripes, the other with the hammer and sickle. I walked quickly to the one with the American flag, and as I approached, the driver got out.

"Can you help me," I asked. "Can you tell me where the U.S. Embassy is?"

"You're not Mooradian, are you?"

"Yes, I am." I was surprised that he knew my name.

"We have someone in there looking for you. Wait here, and I'll be right back."

The man disappeared, and a few minutes later reappeared with a second man, who introduced himself as a consulate official. Without asking me for my passport or questioning me, he said, "I was told you'd be arriving on this plane, but I was looking for a much older person. Jump in."

Once we were comfortably seated in the vehicle, he asked, "How was your flight?"

"Uneventful," I said.

"That's always the best, isn't it?"

"Yes."

"And how do you feel?"

"Great. Like Alice in Wonderland."

He laughed, then said that I was booked on a flight to New York that afternoon. "We're going to the embassy, and you can rest up there until then. Is there anything you need?"

"No, not really. I have everything I ever wanted—now."

He smiled.

~ I DID NOT follow protocol. I did not communicate my arrival to the Soviet Embassy. I never wanted to see another Soviet again.

"How long have you been in the Soviet Union?" the consulate official asked, in an attempt to put me at ease.

"About thirteen years," I said without hesitation.

"Thirteen years. Incredible. Thirteen years in the Soviet Union? You're lucky they let you out."

"Luckier than you can ever imagine. I have lived for this day."

That afternoon, I left Copenhagen for New York City. When I finally boarded the flight to Detroit, I was exhausted, drained. I could not remember the last time I had had something to eat. I didn't care. I was on American soil at last. And nobody was staring at me or even looking my way. I was one of a crowd.

~ AT ABOUT three in the morning on August 3, three days after my thirty-second birthday, we landed in Detroit. I was the last to get off the plane. Except for a few men and women cleaning the concourse, the terminal was empty. I looked around for a telephone booth to call home, but I decided not to call because of the hour. I didn't want to disturb my parents. I sat on one of the benches and waited for dawn to break. I fell asleep.

I was awakened by someone gently touching my shoulders, urging me to wake up.

"Tommy, it's me, George."

The voice was my brother's. I was afraid I was dreaming.

Slowly, I opened my eyes, and George came into focus. He laughed quietly and said I had been sleeping with my eyes open. He explained that the embassy had called to let them know my flight and arrival time.

"So, you finally made it."

"I told you I wouldn't come home in a box."

He stared at me as if I weren't for real. "I don't remember you saying anything like that. Come on, let's go to my place, and we'll call the folks later." He picked up my valise, asking if that was all of my luggage.

"That's all they'd allow me to take out of the country. Plus a hundred bucks."

"So you have the hundred?"

"No. Somehow the money disappeared from my wallet," I said, not wanting to admit to my stupidity.

As he had done a thousand times before when we played basketball, he patted me on my butt. "There are a lot of guys who want to talk to you. Your friends have heard that you were coming home."

"That's good," I said, as I took off his high school ring and handed it back to him.

He looked at it, puzzled. "Where did you get this? I have been looking for it for years."

"Don't you remember—when I boarded the *Rossia?*"

He paused for a moment to think. "Yeah, that's right. Now I remember. I gave it to you for good luck. Nice to have my little brother back." And he patted me on my butt again.

"Don't do that!"

"Do what?" he asked.

"Pat me on my butt."

"And why not?"

I stared at him and broke into a smile. I wanted to explain, wanted to tell him, but decided that it wasn't the time.

"Never mind. It's a long story. Come on, let's go home."

For Further Reading

Applebaum, Anne. *Gulag: A History of the Soviet Camps*. New York: Random House, 2003.

Belli, M. Melvin, and Jones R. Danny. *Belli Looks at Life and Law in Russia*. Indianapolis: Bobbs-Merrill, 1963.

Leder, M. Mary. *My Life in Stalinist Russia*. Bloomington: Indiana University Press, 2001.

Levine, R. Irving. *Main Street, U.S.S.R.* Garden City, N.Y.: Doubleday, 1959.

Luttwak, N. Edward. *The Grand Strategy of the Soviet Union*. London: George Weidenfeld and Nicolson, 1983.

McMillan, Priscilla J. *Marina and Lee*. New York: Harper & Row, 1977.

Pares, Bernard. *A History of Russia*. New York: Alfred A. Knopf, 1944.

Ramsdell, Mike. *A Train to Potevka*. Layton, Utah: Zhivago Press, 2006.

Rounds, Frank, Jr. *A Window on Red Square*. Boston: Riverside Press, 1952.

Salisbury, E. Harrison. *American in Russia*. New York: Harper & Brothers, 1955.

Salisbury, Y. Charlotte. *Russian Diary*. New York: Walker & Co., 1974.

Strong, Anna Louise. *The Stalin Era*. New York: Mainstream, 1956.

Taubman, William. *Khrushchev: The Man and His Era*. New York: W.W. Norton, 2004.